Mortgage Valuation Models

FINANCIAL MANAGEMENT ASSOCIATION

Survey and Synthesis Series

Mortgage Valuation Models

Embedded Options, Risk,
and Uncertainty

ANDREW DAVIDSON

AND

ALEXANDER LEVIN

OXFORD
UNIVERSITY PRESS

Oxford University Press is a department of the University of Oxford.
It furthers the University's objective of excellence in research, scholarship,
and education by publishing worldwide.

Oxford   New York

Auckland   Cape Town   Dar es Salaam   Hong Kong   Karachi
Kuala Lumpur   Madrid   Melbourne   Mexico City   Nairobi
New Delhi   Shanghai   Taipei   Toronto

With offices in

Argentina   Austria   Brazil   Chile   Czech Republic   France   Greece
Guatemala   Hungary   Italy   Japan   Poland   Portugal   Singapore
South Korea   Switzerland   Thailand   Turkey   Ukraine   Vietnam

Oxford is a registered trademark of Oxford University Press
in the UK and certain other countries.

Published in the United States of America by
Oxford University Press
198 Madison Avenue, New York, NY 10016

Library of Congress Cataloging-in-Publication Data
Davidson, Andrew S.
Mortgage valuation models : embedded options, risk, and uncertainty / Andrew Davidson, Alex Levin.
pages cm.—(Financial Management Association survey and synthesis series)
Includes bibliographical references and index.
ISBN 978–0–19–999816–6 (alk. paper)
1. Mortgage-backed securities.   2. Mortgage-backed securities—Valuation—United States.   I. Title.
HG4655.D383 2014
332.63′23—dc23
2013034515

1 3 5 7 9 8 6 4 2
Printed in the United States of America
on acid-free paper

CONTENTS

PART FOUR Analysis of the 2008–2009 Financial Crisis

PART FIVE Building a Healthy Housing Finance System

INTRODUCTION

Mortgage-backed securities (MBS) are among the most important and arguably the most complex fixed-income investment vehicles in the United States. Their advent allowed millions of Americans to own homes as they effectively connected the needs of investors and borrowers. MBS models should account for multiple economic factors and an uncertainty of borrower behavior. With two options in hand—a call on the loan and a put on the property—each borrower makes individual decisions that cannot be accurately predicted by MBS investors. Given this, it is amazing how many "accessible" books have been written about this market. We should credit Frank Fabozzi for educating several generations of MBS practitioners, but the industry is still awaiting a book focused on financial engineering for MBS, and we have tried to fill that need with this book.

If we could give our book a motto, it would be "OAS and far beyond." We do explore various recipes for implementing the popular option-adjusted spread (OAS) method, including closed form, backward induction, and Monte Carlo methods of valuation. However, we firmly view the OAS method as a necessary engine, not yet a car you can drive. We believe that MBS requires blending empirical analysis of borrower behavior with mathematical modeling of interest rates, home prices, and... again, borrower behavior. This book is a detailed description of the sophisticated theories and advanced methods that we employ in the analysis of mortgage-backed securities. Issues such as complexity, uncertainty, and model risk play a central role in our approach to MBS.

Often new ideas draw on a good, and maybe forgotten, past. We found our inspiration in the capital asset pricing model (CAPM) and the arbitrage pricing theory (APT). Not that these fundamental financial theories have been forgotten by any means—they are simply rarely used to explain structure of investment return for MBS. Using these theories, we explain why OAS levels differ among agency MBS and how these differences can be associated with bearing prepayment model risk. Similarly, we show how the credit risk—that is, risk of principal losses—should be accounted for in the non-agency MBS. In all the practical cases, we discuss how "risk-neutral" models should be designed well beyond the widely used no-arbitrage interest-rate processes. Risk-neutralization of MBS valuation models, in both economic risk and model risk dimensions, is the central theme of our book.

Among other known ideas that found many entries to our book is the Vasicek loan loss model, which explains the existence of an empirical S-curve in prepayments, defaults, and other transitions of loans from one status to another. We refer to this theory not simply to prove that an S-curve is not an optical illusion, but also to extend and explore. We demonstrate that a "3-Part Vasicek" extension, with some loans that never default, some that always default, and others that follow the standard Vasicek distribution, leads to a more adequate view of losses arising in mortgage pools. This extension provides an ability to create comprehensive credit risk reports and even to replace Monte Carlo in many cases.

In terms of coverage, this book spans the range of mortgage products from TBA (to-be-announced) agency pass-through to subordinate tranches of subprime-mortgage securitizations. In terms of complexity and prerequisites, the book is not a primer on or an introduction to MBS but is intended for educated MBS investment professionals—traders, portfolio managers, risk managers, and, of course, modelers. Although it s not a textbook by design, its parts can help students majoring in financial engineering, mathematical finance, or similar professions. For those who are looking for background material, *Securitization, Structuring and Investment Analysis,* by Davidson, Sanders, Wolff, and Ching, has several chapters on analytical methods that would be useful and a variety of exercises (and a CD-ROM) that cover the basics of mortgage calculations. The *Mortgage-Backed Securities Workbook,* by Davidson and Herskovitz might also be valuable. Interested readers might also want to consult a standard book on option pricing models such as John Hull's *Options, Futures and Other Derivatives.*

The book is designed as follows. Part 1 describes approaches to modeling and valuation used throughout the book; we do not recommend skipping it. It is in this part that we recognize the role of uncertainty in modeling; introduce the Vasicek distribution, CAPM, and APT; and discuss the need for risk neutrality in each dimension of risk, not only interest rates. We introduce a partial differential equation for valuing MBS and the OAS method in formal terms. We also show how to value assets in the absence of reliable benchmarks by using a so-called "capital charge" method. Effectively we emulate an investment position with expected losses and unexpected losses. Part 1 contains chapters on interest-rate modeling and modeling of home prices in the presence of a forward or a futures market.

Modeling methods for agency and non-agency MBS are quickly converging, and we acknowledge this trend. Nevertheless, for the reader's convenience, we decided to keep these two themes separate. Part 2 introduces methods of modeling agency MBS. The most important viewpoint we employ there is pool-level modeling. We describe factors of prepayments, prepayment model structure, and the method of active-passive decomposition (APD) that splits a path-dependent pool into two path-independent subpools. This method allows us to simulate the burnout effect arising due to an unobserved heterogeneity of loans. Using this modeling approach we can value simple MBS pools via backward induction on interest-rate trees or grids or even closed-form solutions. The Monte Carlo method, a must for more complex MBS, is explained in chapter 9. Chapter 10 discusses applications of the OAS method and results we can expect it to generate. Chapter 11 introduces the first important extension of the OAS method, the so-called prOAS (prepay-risk-and-option-adjusted spread) approach, where the OAS engine is used in conjunction with a risk-neutralized prepayment model. This method levels the playing field for return expectation among agency MBS otherwise differing in their exposure to prepayment speeds.

Part 3 focuses on modeling credit risk and losses by using a loan-level viewpoint. We start with describing our loss-forecasting model, the loan dynamics model (LDM), in chapter 12. We then proceed to developing the "Credit OAS" methodology in the space of random interest rates and home prices (chapter 13). Chapter 14 is dedicated to stochastic home-price modeling, which is a necessary ingredient of the credit OAS process. Finally, chapter 15 demonstrates theoretical shortcuts in credit analysis on a scenario grid using the 3-Part Vasicek approximation we mentioned.

Part 4 draws on the recent financial crisis. It explains the housing drama by a detailed, factual, analysis of affordability, explains why the collateralized debt obligation (CDO) "diversification" was doomed and why MBS prices fell as deeply as they did. In particular, we show how one can separate credit losses from technical distress and use the limited market information for solid accounting.

Part 5 is a look into the future. Using the information provided in the book, we describe sound methods of risk measurement and capital assignment, dynamic deal rating, and a risk-based new-loan pricing. We try to predict how housing finance in the United States would look in the future and which topics of MBS modeling should get attention.

Creative efforts and the dedication of many current and past AD&Co employees contributed to analytical products and the knowledge base utilized in this book. We thank Anne Ching, Sanjeeban Chatterjee, Daniel Swanson, Dan Szakallas, Hikmet Senay, Herb Ray, Nadya Derrick, John Ferrante, Stefano Risa, Kyle Lundstedt, and Mark Williams, all of whom contributed to developing prepayment and default models widely used in the MBS industry and described in chapters 7 and 12. The MBS valuation system we developed and used is a product of several generations of AD&Co's engineers. Among them are Eknath Belbase, Nathan Salwen, Valentine Zavgorodnev, George De Laura, Will Scarle,

Atul Shrivastava, Steve Heller, and Jay DeLong. Chapter 15 uses Will Searle's work comparing the grid-based theoretical approximation to Monte Carlo simulations. When writing chapter 19, we included Ming Zheng's analysis of historical breakpoint ratios versus the traditional credit rating. Levy He contributed the material on Sobol quasi-random sequences for chapter 9 and checked formulas in some other chapters. We extend our special gratitude to Nancy Davidson, who served as the internal editor of the manuscript and shielded us from many production burdens. We acknowledge the help of Shariff Harris, who designed the graphical illustrations and the diligent efforts of Cathryn Vaulman of Oxford University Press and Saranya Prabuthass of Newgen in ensuring the production quality.

Over years, many clients and other MBS professionals outside AD&Co have provided us with valuable thoughts, which we used in shaping this book. In particular, we appreciate Kevin Atteson and Peter Carr's feedback on chapters 4 and 6 and Anthony Sander's suggestions for shaping the book.

Despite its advances of the past 25 years, MBS modeling is an ever-evolving field. No amount of knowledge and experience leads to an ultimate truth or a point of no further revision. We hope that this book will serve as a foundation for the future development of models for mortgage-backed securities.

PART ONE

Fundamentals of Mortgage-Backed Securities Risk and Valuation

Dimensions of Uncertainty

Analyzing mortgage-backed securities (MBS) is an exercise in quantifying uncertainty. Uncertainty arises in multiple dimensions; each must be assessed and addressed within an appropriate framework. We shall explore some of the sources of uncertainty in this chapter.

When a household (a family, a couple, an individual) decides to buy a home, often the cost of the home that they can buy is determined by the mortgage market. The market limits borrowers in two ways. First, many mortgages require a minimum down payment. A typical down payment is 20%, but many first time home buyers take advantage of programs that allow them to put down 10%, 5%, or in some cases even less. The loan amount (100% minus the down payment) when stated as a percentage of property value is called loan-to-value, or LTV. For a 20% down payment, the LTV is 80. For a 5% down payment the LTV is 95.

The second limitation is the size of mortgage payments relative to borrowers' incomes. Normally debt service, that is, the principal and interest payments on the loan, should not exceed 30 to 40% of the borrowers' income. This is called debt to income or DTI. Borrowers who have a prior record of poor payment history on mortgage loans or other debt often face stricter requirements in terms of lower allowable LTVs and DTIs. Typical DTI ratios vary from 25% to 45%.

The amount of debt service is determined by the interest rate on the mortgage loan and the structure of the loan. In the United States, the predominant form of mortgage is the thirty-year, fixed-rate, level-pay, fully pre-payable mortgage. Thirty years is the maturity of the loan. Fixed rate describes the coupon or interest rate on the loan. Level pay means that the monthly payment on the loan is constant for 360 months, and it incorporates interest and principle in changing proportions. Fully prepayable means the borrower can pay off the loan, in full or in part, at any time, without penalty. In addition, if the borrower cannot or will not make the required payments, the borrower would likely lose the home to foreclosure.

For a thirty-year, fixed-rate, level-pay mortgage, the amount of the monthly mortgage payment is given by

$$f = \frac{Payment}{Loan\,Amt} = \frac{P}{L} = \frac{(c/12)(1+c/12)^n}{(1+c/12)^n - 1} \tag{1.1}$$

where c is the annual coupon rate and n is the number of periods in months of the term of the loan.

The balance outstanding of the loan at the beginning of any period k is

$$\frac{Balance_k}{Balance_0} = \frac{(1+c/12)^n - (1+c/12)^k}{(1+c/12)^n - 1} \tag{1.2}$$

Each monthly payment consists of both interest and principal payments. The interest payment in period k is $(c/12)* Balance_k$ and the principal payment is

$$Balance_k \frac{c/12}{(1+c/12)^{n-k} - 1}$$

For a coupon rate of 6%, the annual payment is $0.072 per $1.00 of loan amount. If the DTI requirement is 35%, the maximum amount of the loan would be about five times the income of the borrower, since DTI = Payment/Income and f = Payment/Loan Amount, then Loan Amount = (DTI/f) * Income.

EMBEDDED OPTIONS

Financially speaking, the mortgage has two embedded options: a call option on the loan, and a put option on the house. How borrowers exercise these options and how they affect investors in the mortgages and mortgage-backed securities is the subject of this book. But before we get too far into the investor's viewpoint, let's get back to the borrower.

Every month a payment is due on the mortgage. The borrower receives a monthly statement showing the balance remaining on the loan and the required monthly payment. The borrower can choose to pay the required monthly payment, or pay more than required (perhaps the full balance) or something less than the required monthly payment (perhaps nothing).

For most borrowers in most months, borrowers make the monthly required payments. Probably there is little thought put into this choice, as borrowers have incorporated their monthly mortgage payment into their ongoing budget and financial plans. A portion of their monthly income is directed to pay their mortgage, as well as other living expenses such as food and utilities. The original mortgage represents an equilibrium reflecting the borrowers' desire to own (and occupy the house), the borrowers' income relative to the mortgage payments, and economic factors such as current interest rates and home prices. When one or more of these change, the equilibrium is upset and there could be some change in the borrowers' choices for mortgage payment.

When borrowers choose to make more than their required payment it is generally because they have chosen to move, and therefore must repay the mortgage, or they have chosen to refinance their mortgage. These events are called *prepayments*. A small percentage of borrowers make partial pre-payments that are sometimes called *curtailments*.

When borrowers chose not to make their payments, it is generally because they are unable or unwilling to do so. When a borrower misses payments, they are technically in *default* of the mortgage loan. The industry however calls such borrowers and their mortgages *delinquent*. Delinquency brings penalties and more aggressive contact from the lender. Loans that remain delinquent for long periods of time are subject to *foreclosure*, where the lender seeks to gain possession of the mortgaged property.

A borrower's decision to exercise the options embedded in the mortgage contract reflect a complex interaction of financial and personal motivations. If borrowers were pure financial players we would see virtually no prepayments when interest rates rose and 100% prepayments as interest rates fall. Instead we see that some borrowers prepay even when interest rates rise, and not all borrowers prepay when interest rates fall. Each borrower faces a unique set of circumstances: changes in family, job status, personal preferences all affect the borrower's decision because the mortgage is not just a financial instrument, but is also closely linked to the borrower's life.

SOME MORTGAGE CALCULATIONS (COMPUTING TERMINATION RATES)

Let's take a look at the payment history on a few individual loans. Ps represent the monthly payments by the borrowers.

Loan 1: PPPPPPPPPPPPPPPPPPPPPPPPPPPPPPPPPPPPP…
Loan 2: PPPPPPPPPPPPPPPPPPPP**B**
Loan 3: PPPPPPPPPPPPPPPPPPPPPPPPPPPPPPPPPPPPPP…
Loan 4: PPPPPPPPPPPPPPPPPPPPPPPPP
Loan 5: PPPPPPPPPPPPPPPPPPPPPPPPPPPPPPPPPPPPPPP.…

Loan 2 prepaid in month 20, as reflected by the **B**, representing payment of the full balance. Loan 4 stopped paying in month 25. In some data sets Loan 4 would be shown as

Loan 4: CCCCCCCCCCCCCCCCCCCCCCCCCC369FFFFR

where C means current, 3 means 30 days late, 6 means 60 days late, 9 means 90 days late, F means in foreclosure, R means Real Estate Owned.

At the level of the individual borrower, we can look at the amount of time, T, until the borrower takes a certain action such as prepaying the mortgage which terminates the loan. In statistics we could think of this as survival analysis and we could analyze the function:

$$S(t) = prob\ (T > t), \quad \text{where } T \text{ is a random variable.} \tag{1.3}$$

The flip side of survival analysis is the hazard rate, λ, which represents the percentage of the remaining loans which terminate during a given time period.

$$\lambda \text{ is given by } -S'(t)/S(t) \quad \text{where } S'(t) = dS(t)/dt \tag{1.4}$$

If the mortgages did not have a maturity date and the hazard rate λ was constant, then the expected time to termination $E(T)$ would equal $1/\lambda$. For most mortgage analysis, we focus on hazard functions.

The decisions of each individual borrower are multiplied by the tens of millions of households in the United States that have mortgages. The collective action of these tens of millions of borrowers determines the performance of the mortgage market. Individual decisions resolve into patterns and affect the economy.

To better understand these patterns, mortgage analysts gather data on mortgage loans and produce statistical measure of performance. In moving from individual loans to large numbers of loans, we lose the connection to the motivations of the individual borrowers—how the household's hopes and dreams are linked to their home—rather we see how broad economic factors such as interest rates and home prices affect the collective action of borrowers.

When we look at aggregated data we tend to look at the amount of principal that prepays or defaults during the measurement period. For example the standard method for reporting prepayments is to compute the amount of unscheduled principle payments divided by the total scheduled principal balance. In order to do these calculations we need to clarify the dates of balances and payments. Generally, we assume that balances are as of specific dates, typically the beginning of each month and payments occur during the month.

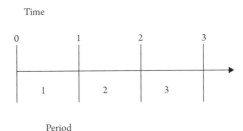

The scheduled principal balance is given by

$$B_k^{sched} = B_{k-1} - p_k \qquad\qquad (1.5a)$$

And the prepayment rate (or termination rate) is given by

$$\lambda_k = [B_k^{sched} - B_k] / B_k^{sched} \qquad\qquad (1.5b)$$

where B_k = actual balance at time k, B_k^{sched} = scheduled balance at time k, p_k = scheduled principal payment for period k, based on B_{k-1}. *Note:* period k occurs between time $k-1$ and time k.

Monthly prepayments, λ_k, are often called single monthly mortalities (*SMM*) and are converted to annual conditional prepayment rates (CPR) using the formula

$$CPR = 1 - (1 - SMM)^{12} \qquad\qquad (1.6)$$

The annual rates are reported to investors and reflect the aggregate behavior of the borrowers in a certain cohort or group of loans. Terminations of mortgages, which lead to lower balances, can be voluntary or involuntary. *Voluntary* terminations are generally called prepayments or repayments, *involuntary* prepayments are generally called defaults. Both terms are confusing as prepayments sometimes refer to all terminations, voluntary and involuntary, and default is a vague term. As discussed earlier, any time the borrower stops making payments is technically a default. The termination of the loan typically occurs through foreclosure and the subsequent sale of the home by the lender. These topics will be discussed in more detail in chapter 12, which discusses credit modeling.

Figure 1.1 is an example of prepayment rates during the beginning of the century for a cohort of mortgages originated prior to 2000. The chart shows actual prepayment speeds, in CPR, and model results. As the chart shows, prepayments can be quite volatile, varying from single digits to over 60% annual termination rates. Prepayment models will be discussed in more detail in chapter 7. The remainder of this chapter will focus on some principles for better understanding the sources of uncertainty for prepayments and other mortgage terminations.

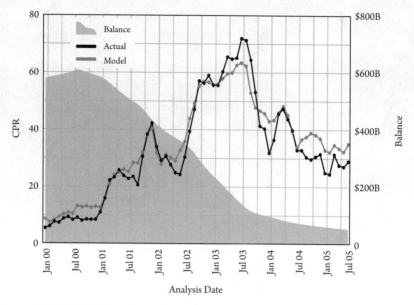

Figure 1.1 Historical Prepayment Rates

Prepayments rates can be viewed from two perspectives. From the point of view of a pool of loans, the prepayment rate represents the percentage of borrowers who terminate their loans. On the other hand, from the point of view of an individual loan, it represents a probability of termination, or the hazard function.

Keeping both of these perspectives in mind can help in better understanding the analysis of mortgages and MBS. To facilitate calculations on MBS, which are concerned about dollars and not borrowers, mortgage prepayment calculations are generally performed on balances, not on the number of loans. This introduces a subtle change in the two interpretations described above. From the point of view of the pool it is the percentage of scheduled balance that terminates or prepays during the period, and from the point of view of individual loans it is balance-weighted probability of termination. That is, higher balance loans contribute more to the computation of the probability than low balance loans.

The prepayment rate can be viewed as balance-weighted probability that a borrower will prepay, in other words, prepayments in a pool can be expressed as

$$\frac{\sum_{i=1}^{N} \lambda(i) * B^{sched}(i)}{\sum_{i=1}^{N} B^{sched}(i)} \tag{1.7}$$

where $\lambda(i)$ is the prepayment rate and $B^{sched}(i)$ is the amortized balance of borrower (i).

The weighting by scheduled balance arises from the definition of prepayment in equation (1.5a).

The use of the scheduled balance weighted approach is beneficial for calculations, but it may disguise the underlying probabilistic cause of prepayments. This leads many analysts to view prepayments as deterministic aggregate behavior of the cohort, rather than as the aggregated statistical behavior of individual borrowers.

MODELING UNCERTAINTY

To better understand the underlying statistical nature of borrower behavior, a diversion into the world of baseball may be useful.

Randomness of Individual Outcomes

At the start of the baseball season in 2011, Derek Jeter, the long-time captain of the New York Yankees, needed 74 hits to become the twenty-eighth player to reach the 3000 hit milestone. A cottage industry grew up around forecasting the date they he would reach the goal. Studying these forecasts provides some insight into several dimensions of uncertainty.

Over Derek Jeter's career, he had about 1.27 hits per game. On that basis it could be expected that he would reach 3000 after 59 games. But even a consistent hitter like Jeter doesn't get a hit every day. Joe DiMaggio's record streak in 1941 was 56 games. Clearly there is some uncertainty about when Jeter would reach 3000 hits.

Instead of looking at hits per game we can look at hits per plate appearance. Jeter averaged about 4.6 plate appearances per game through 2010 and got hits 27.7% of the time. Plate appearances include walks, hit by pitch, and sacrifices, as well as hits. His batting average was .313 and he averaged 4.06 at-bats per game.

With this approach we can construct the probability of reaching 74 hits by a certain number of games. The fastest one could achieve the goal would be in 16 games, by getting a hit at every plate appearance. The odds of such an event are astronomically small. At the other end of the spectrum, with a sustained batting slump, it would be possible not to get 74 hits all season, but this would also be an extremely unlikely outcome for a 300 hitter.

More probable would be a range from about 40 days to 80 days with a 50% chance of completing the task in 54 to 62 days. If instead we focused on Jeter's 2010 record, the 50% chance range would be from 60 to 70 days.

The two lines in Figure 1.2 show two different kinds of uncertainty. Each bell shape reflects the uncertainty as to the timing of hits, even while maintaining a

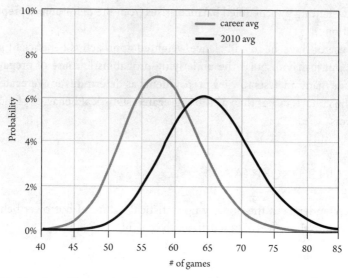

Figure 1.2 Number of Days to Reach 3000 Hits

given average. The difference between the two bell curves represents the uncertainty as to the underlying parameters. Which Jeter would show up: the Jeter of 2010 or the Jeter of the preceding 15 seasons?

Suppose you were asked to make a forecast of which date Jeter would reach 3000 hits:

What would you forecast?

What would you forecast if you would receive a reward of $10 dollars if you were right, but the fee would be reduced by $1 dollar for each day that you missed by? That would probably get you to focus more on the problem but probably would not change your forecast.

What if you would receive a fee of $10 dollars if you were right, but it decreased by $1 dollar for every day that you were early but only 50 cents for every day that you were late? Would this change your forecast? By how many days?

As it turned out, Derek Jeter reached 3000 hits on July 9, 2011, 87 games into the season (three games were rained out)—well outside the range of both forecasts. The failure of both forecasts was a result of another type of uncertainty. Derek Jeter was injured and missed 18 games. The probability of injury and the likely duration were not included in the forecasting method described earlier.

This third type of uncertainty was certainly conceivable, but it was probably difficult to forecast with any degree of precision.

As Joe DeLessio, the forecaster in *New York Magazine*, put it:

Once a week until Derek Jeter gets his 3,000th hit, we'll take a quick and dirty look at which game we anticipate he'll get it in, based on his 2011 numbers to that point. Obviously, buy tickets (or fly to some random city) at your own risk, especially since a lot can change in the coming weeks: Jeter could get hotter or colder, games could be rained out, he could get more frequent days off, or be dropped in the batting order, or get hurt, or whatever.

The fourth type of uncertainty is DeLessio's "whatever." In any forecast there are things that weren't even conceived of as risks.

Now imagine that instead of one Derek Jeter there were hundreds of Jeters, each starting the year with 2924 hits and vying to reach 3000 hits first. Instead of asking when would Jeter reach the target date, we could ask: What percentage of the Jeters would reach 3000 by each date? Instead of looking at the marginal probabilities of Figure 1.2, we now would look at cumulative probabilities in Figure 1.3. They look very much like the curves that we will see for prepayment and default functions.

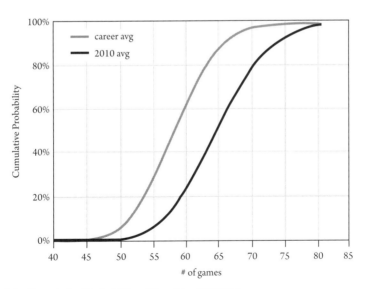

Figure 1.3 Cumulative Probability of Reaching 3000 Hits

In this book we will address the four forms of uncertainty just described. Each poses unique challenges:

- The fundamental uncertainty of random processes
- The uncertainty about parameter values
- The uncertainty as to what factors to include in the forecast
- The uncertainty due to unanticipated events.

Common Factors

While each borrower is unique and has individual motivations for exercising their mortgage options, all borrowers are affected by common economic forces such as home prices and interest rates. Oldrich Vasicek developed a framework for looking at portfolio of loans with a common driving factor. His analysis was developed for corporate bond default analysis, but it can be applied to mortgage defaults and even to voluntary mortgage prepayments.

The Standard Vasicek Model

The set up for Vasicek's approach is that there are a large number of borrowers who will each default if the value of their asset (home) falls below the value of their loan (mortgage). This is the Merton Model of how corporations default on their liabilities and is a special case of option pricing theory. In the Vasicek approach, the values of the assets are driven by a common economic factor and by asset-specific factors. Each borrower has the same probability of default at the start of the analysis, and each will have a unique default behavior based upon the realization of the common economic factor and the asset-specific factors.

We demonstrate here a short derivation of the standard Vasicek model. Let us assume that a borrower defaults when his asset (A) falls below liability (L). Asset values are normally distributed and correlated to each other. Consider the following random variables:

$$A_i = x\sqrt{\rho} + \varepsilon_i\sqrt{1-\rho}, \quad i=1,2,\ldots \qquad (1.8)$$

where x is a common risk factor, and ε_i is a loan-specific factors. Assuming that these two sources of risk are taken from the standard normal distribution and are independent, it is easily verified that all As will be standard normal variables and $corr(A_i, A_j) = \rho$ for any $i \neq j$.

We further assume that each loan has the same probability of default that is denoted as π: $\pi = P(A_i < L) = N(L)$ where N stands for the cumulative standard normal distribution. Note that, given x, probability of default for a single loan is equal to the default rate (d) for an infinite-size pool. This is the consequence of the Law of Large Numbers, i.e. complete diversification of loan-specific randomness. Hence,

Default Rate

$$d = P\left(A_i < L|x\right) = P\left(x\sqrt{\rho} + \varepsilon_i \sqrt{1-\rho} < L|x\right) = P\left(\varepsilon_i < \frac{L - x\sqrt{\rho}}{\sqrt{1-\rho}}\bigg|x\right)$$

To complete derivation, we replace unobservable liability L level with $N^{-1}(\pi)$ and account for the fact that ε_i is taken from the standard normal distribution:

$$\text{Default Rate} = d = N\left[\frac{N^{-1}(\pi) - x\sqrt{\rho}}{\sqrt{1-\rho}}\right] \tag{1.9}$$

This is the standard Vasicek formula. It is often rewritten via distribution-generating uniform variable $w = N(x)$. The cumulative probability function is obtained via resolving (1.9) for w:

$$1 - \text{CDF} = w = N\left[\frac{N^{-1}(\pi) - \sqrt{1-\rho}N^{-1}(d)}{\sqrt{\rho}}\right] \tag{1.9--inv}$$

Formula (1.9) lets us generate Vasicek random default rate d by varying w uniformly in $[0, 1]$.

Sometimes, instead of knowing expected default rate π, we possess a median default rate, π_{med}. Vasicek probability formulas can be maintained by replacing $N^{-1}(\pi)$ with $\sqrt{1-\rho}N^{-1}(\pi_{med})$. This can be seen by setting $x = 0$ in equation (1.9) and solving for $N^{-1}(\pi)$ because the relationship between d and x is monotonic and $x = 0$ is the median of common risk factor.

In formula (1.9) we show that the probability of default as a function of the driver variable x is a cumulative normal distribution, N. If, however, the idiosyncratic terms ε_i are not normally distributed but instead are drawn from some distribution M, then we would get that the default rate is

$$\text{Default Rate} = d = M\left[\frac{N^{-1}(\pi) - x\sqrt{\rho}}{\sqrt{1-\rho}}\right] \tag{1.9-M}$$

In other words, the function M is the distribution of the idiosyncratic terms that define the default curve, not the distribution of the driver x. If there are many borrowers and many independent sources of idiosyncratic behavior, then the total will likely approximate the normal distribution based upon the Central Limit Theorem.

Applying Vasicek

We can apply this approach to an analysis of mortgage defaults. Suppose there is a 1% chance of default and that there is a 30% correlation between the values of the underlying homes. When the underlying economic driver is unchanged, $(x = 0)$, the default rate d is 1%. As it falls by one or more standard deviations $(x = -1, x = -2,$ etc.) the default rate rises as shown in Figure 1.4.

As the probability of x achieving various values is determined by the normal distribution, it is possible to show the cumulative probability of being below various default levels. This is shown in Figure 1.5. Given the low base case probability and the low correlation of the underlying asset values, very high default rates are unlikely.

When we turn to voluntary prepayments we can get a different picture. For voluntary prepayments the base case driving factor is interest rates, and borrowers experience very similar interest rate effects. Figure 1.6 shows the Vasicek results assuming a correlation of 95% and a base case (or median) prepayment rate of 10%. The higher correlation produces a more rapid change in termination rates.

The Vasicek formulation will lead to close to 100% terminations if the options are sufficiently in the money. In practice, we do not observe such extreme values for either defaults or prepayments. Such results are likely because the borrowers do not all have the same characteristics as required by the Vasicek theory.

Given the ability of borrowers to prepay their mortgages when refinancing becomes economic, interest rates are a major driver of borrower behavior.

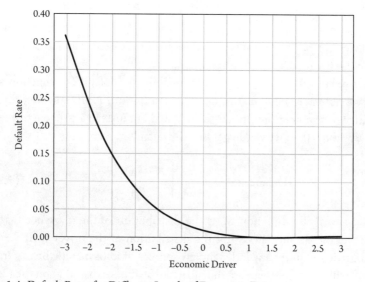

Figure 1.4 Default Rates for Different Levels of Economic Driver

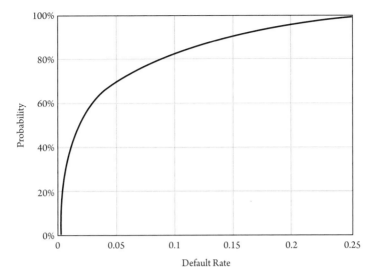

Figure 1.5 Cumulative Default Probability

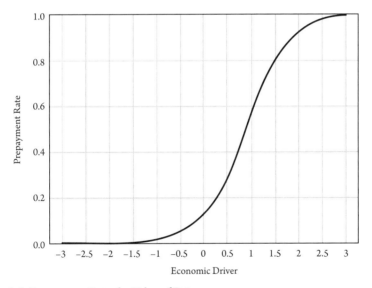

Figure 1.6 Prepayment Rates by Value of Driver

Figures 1.7a and 1.7b show this effect. Actual mortgage data shows the patterns of the Vasicek theory. Figure 1.7a shows the default rate on Prime mortgages originated prior to 2007, over the period of 2007 to 2010. As home prices fell, the default rate increased. Figure 1.7b shows the same data as a scatter plot with the home-price index on the x-axis and the default rate on the y-axis. Notice the

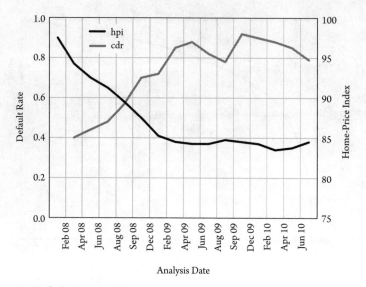

Figure 1.7a Default Rates and Home Prices by Date

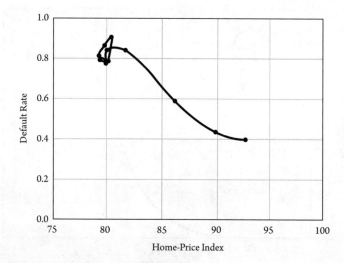

Figure 1.7b Default Rates versus Home Prices

similarity to Figure 1.4. A more complete description of default modeling will be provided in chapter 12.

Figure 1.8a shows a time series of prepayment rates and the mortgage rate during 2000 to early 2004. As mortgage rates fell, prepayment rates rose. Figure 1.8b shows the same data as a scatter plot with the mortgage rate on the x-axis and the

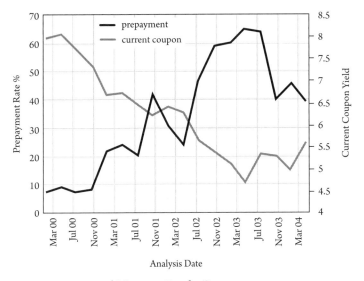

Figure 1.8a Prepayments and Mortgage Rate by Date

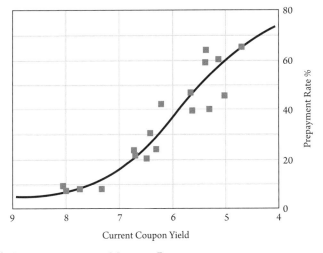

Figure 1.8b Prepayments versus Mortgage Rate

prepayment rate on the y-axis. We have reversed the order of the interest rates in Figure 1.8b, as is traditional in mortgage analysis, to be consistent with graphs such as Figure 1.6 (notice the similarity). A more complete description of prepayment modeling will be provided in chapter 7.

HETEROGENEITY: OBSERVED AND UNOBSERVED

The framework for uncertainty we have developed so far shows that even with borrowers who are homogeneous, uncertainty and probability plays a role in predicting borrower behavior. But just as there is only one Derek Jeter, each borrower is unique. Heterogeneity adds another layer of complexity to the analysis of borrower behavior.

In Figure 1.9 we see that during the period of January to June of 2003, prepayments on Fannie Mae 30-year mortgages originated before 2000 were almost constant. However, it would be a mistake to assign the same prepayment rate to all of these loans. Figure 1.10 makes it clear that if we segmented these loans by coupon, they would have very different prepayment rates. Borrowers with higher mortgage rates have greater incentive to refinance. Splitting borrowers by an observed characteristic that is linked to prepayments reflects "observed heterogeneity."

Generally we find that mortgages can differ along three dimensions: the note/loan, the borrower, and the collateral. The coupon is an example of a loan characteristic. Borrower characteristics could include items such as income and credit score. Collateral characteristics include measures such as the location and value of the home.

While there are a wide range of characteristics that could affect borrower actions, some characteristics such as borrower age, marital status, height, weight, and other items we might know about Derek Jeter, and other characteristics

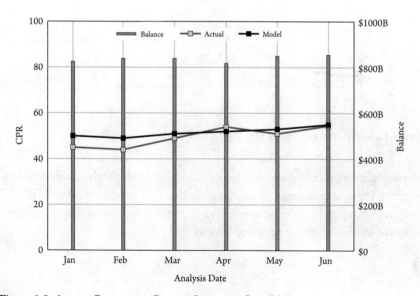

Figure 1.9 Average Prepayment Rates in January to June 2003

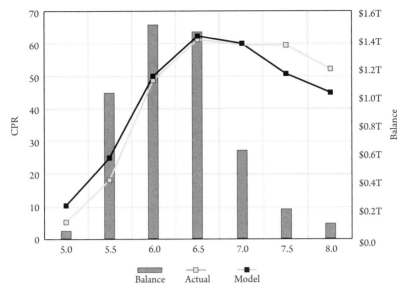

Figure 1.10 Prepayment Rates by Mortgage Coupon in January to June 2003

(such as borrower income and assets) that might be even more important to mortgage performance will probably not be available when analyzing motgage prepayments and defaults. Yet borrowers' propensity to prepay or default might be linked to these characteristics. This "unobserved heterogeneity" may also have a significant impact on prepayments.

By definition, if heterogeneity is not observed, we cannot determine which borrowers are likely to be fast prepayers and which ones are likely to be slow prepayers. However, over time, the fast prepayers will leave the pool more rapidly than the slow prepayers. This will lead to a decline in the average prepayment speed of the pool.

Consider the following formulation for the total termination rate of the pool consisting of borrowers of type a and type b:

$$\lambda(k) = \psi_a(k)\lambda_a(k) + \psi_b(k)\lambda_b(k)$$

$$\psi_a(k) + \psi_b(k) = 1 \tag{1.10}$$

and

$$\psi_a(k+1) = \psi_a(k)\frac{1-\lambda_a(k)}{1-\lambda(k)} \tag{1.11}$$

where $\psi_x(k)$ is the proportion of type x-borrowers, $\lambda_x(k)$ is the termination rate for each set of borrowers, a and b.

For the specific case of fixed termination rates with fast prepayers represented by f and slow prepayers represented by s, the termination rate at time k is given by

$$\lambda(k) = \frac{\psi_0 \left(1-\lambda_f\right)^k \lambda_f + (1-\psi_0)\left(1-\lambda_s\right)^k \lambda_s}{\psi_0 \left(1-\lambda_f\right)^k + (1-\psi_0)\left(1-\lambda_s\right)^k} \qquad (1.12)$$

where ψ_0 is the initial proportion of fast prepayers, λ_f is their constant termination rate, and λ_s is the constant termination rate of the slower prepayers. We call this *active-passive decomposition*.

An example of this calculation is shown in Figure 1.11a, which shows a pool of loans where 80% of the loans are fast pre-payers, paying at 9% per month, while the remaining 20% are slow prepayers paying at 1% per month. Even through the termination rate of each category of borrowers is constant, the weighted average rate of the pool vdeclines over time.

Figure 1.11b shows actual prepayments that match the pattern of Figure 1.11a. The chart shows prepayment speeds during the period from 2003 to 2005 for a Fannie Mae 7 mortgage that originated in 2002. When we observe a pattern like this, where terminations decline over time given constant economic conditions and no observable characteristic that explains the results, we generally assume that there is unobserved heterogeneity. This declining pattern of prepayments is also called *burnout*.

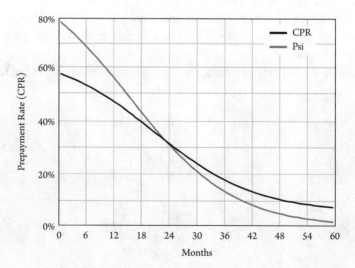

Figure 1.11a Active-Passive Prepayment Rates (Active Speed 9% *SMM*, Passive Speed 1% *SMM*)

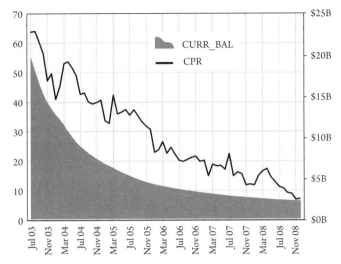

Figure 1.11b Burnout of FNMA 7s in 2003 to 2008

CONCLUSION

Uncertainty is at the core of mortgages and MBS; it arises because of the fundamental statistical nature of the actions of individuals. The uncertainty of drivers of economic behavior such as interest rates and home prices further contributes to the variability of outcomes. In some cases we can identify characteristics of mortgages and borrowers that will lead to different expected behavior, at other times we need to infer heterogeneity. At all times we need to understand and address uncertainty in our models and valuation approaches. Uncertainties can and should be modeled via the dynamics of risk factors, model risk parameters, and pool decomposition. These themes will be explored throughout this book.

2

Fundamentals of Securitization

For the mortgagee (the lender), a mortgage and the associated mortgage note represent a complex bundle of legal, operational, and financial risks, with reward primarily in the form of interest earned on the money lent to the mortgagor.

When the mortgage (and the note) is held by the same bank that created the loan, it can manage its relationship with the borrower to minimize the risks and maximize the returns. Well-developed financial theory (Coase, 1937) argues that at times it makes sense for various functions to be performed by separate entities. In the case of mortgages, that may mean splitting the operational roles of origination, servicing, and investing. *Origination* is the process of underwriting and funding loans. *Servicing* is the process of collecting payments and foreclosing on defaulted borrowers if necessary. *Investing* is the process of funding the mortgage loans and bearing or managing the investment risks. As functions are split between various parties, it is necessary to establish contractual relationships to ensure proper performance for the mutual benefit of all parties. This is referred to as Agency Theory (see Jensen and Meckling, 1976). While this book focuses on investment analysis, it is important to remember that the agency risks are always lurking in the background. Poor underwriting, incorrectly executed documents, and haphazard servicing can all contribute to investment risks that are not easily controlled or analyzed by the investor.

The separation of the investment function from origination and servicing is usually accomplished through securitization, that is, by transforming individual mortgage loans into more easily transferable securities backed by pools of loans. In the United States, there are three mainly utilized forms of securitization: government, agency, and private. (At the time of publication in 2014, the mortgage-backed securities market has not yet fully recovered from the massive disruptions of 2007 and 2008. It is likely that an outcome of the crisis will be significant changes in the structure of the securitization markets for mortgages in the United States, and perhaps in the rest of the world. It is instructive to understand the structure of the market pre-crisis, recognizing that, hopefully, when you read this, there will be new and improved institutional frameworks in place.)

Each of these three forms of securitization differs in how the fundamental risks of the mortgage loans are distributed among various parties. In addition to the origination risks and servicing risks, there are also a variety of investment risks that are apportioned by these securitization methods.

INVESTMENT RISKS

There are five basic types of investment risks, each adding to the uncertainty of mortgage investing. The five categories of risk are closely linked, so any particular decomposition is somewhat arbitrary. Nevertheless categorization can lead to insight. The five categories[1] are

- Funding
- Interest rate
- Prepayment
- Credit
- Liquidity

More than anything else, mortgages represent the **funding** of home purchases. The ten trillion of mortgages outstanding in 2012 represents funding for the residential real estate of the country. The mortgage market is vast system of financial plumbing that takes cash provided by investors throughout the world and makes it available for individual borrowers to make a cash payment to the seller of a home. The system then lets the payments made by the borrower flow back through to the investors. This system functions so well that borrowers and investors seldom stop to contemplate the enormity of the operation.

In addition to managing the flow of cash the system must also track the loan documents and recorded mortgages. With the tremendous stress on the mortgage finance system since the financial crisis of 2007, the system of tracking loan documents and foreclosing on defaulting borrowers has faced serious challenges. This has added a greater degree of risk and uncertainty to investors for a process that was previously considered to have minimal risk.

The government plays a very large role in the funding of mortgages. A variety of government programs and government chartered institutions facilitate this process. For example, the bank holders of mortgages rely on deposit insurance and

---

[1] Over the course of the book, we will introduce a model-based view of these risks. See, for example, chapter 19 for a complete discussion.

also have access to the Federal Home Loan Bank system to provide "advances," which are primarily a short-term funding mechanism for mortgages. Fannie Mae and Freddie Mac hold mortgages on their balance sheet and rely on the implied guarantee of the government (and now a funding agreement from Treasury) to fund their loans. Mortgage-backed securities issued by Fannie Mae and Freddie Mac also have the implied guarantee of the US government. Finally Ginnie Mae MBS have the full faith and credit guarantee of the US government.

Interest-rate risk arises due to the fixed coupon on mortgages. As prevailing interest rates change, the value of an instrument with a fixed coupon fluctuates. For adjustable-rate mortgages interest-rate risk arises from the caps, floors, and other coupon limitations present in residential mortgage products. Interest-rate risk is compounded by prepayment risk.

Interest-rate risk can be explored by considering successively more complex instruments. The least complex instrument is a very short (say, one day to one month) discount note from an extremely high credit quality counterparty, like the US government. This instrument bears little risk to the investor either in terms of income uncertainty or price uncertainty. The return on such an investment is typically called the risk-free rate. Note, however, if the investor has a longer investment horizon, the investor faces the risk that when the investment matures, the prevailing interest rates could be lower, thereby creating income uncertainty.

The next level of complexity would be to extend the maturity of such an instrument. Let's say its maturity is extended to five years. In this case, there is little risk if your investment horizon is exactly five years. However, if you have a shorter investment horizon, or otherwise need to liquidate the position prior to maturity, then the value of the security may have fallen if prevailing interest rates have risen.

A further level of complexity occurs if the bond has embedded-option features such as being callable. Typically, if interest rates fall, the issuer of the callable bond has the right to repay the principal on the bond. In this case, when interest rates fall, the investor will receive back the principal and need to invest at a lower interest rate. If interest rates rise the investor bears the cost of earning lower than prevailing market rates. In most cases, investors receive incremental compensation for bearing the risk of optionality.

Because borrowers generally have the right to prepay their loans, most US mortgages and MBS have features similar to callable bonds. The valuation and risk management techniques that will be discussed in this book were developed in part to deal with these features. Interest-rate risk models are the subject of chapters 5 and 6.

Prepayment risk reflects both a systematic component that arises from the option to refinance (creating the option features of MBS) and the additional uncertainty created by the difficulty in accurately forecasting the behavior of borrowers. As one of the major causes of prepayments is borrower refinancing to obtain lower interest rates, prepayment risk and interest-rate risk are very closely linked. Often it is more convenient to include the expected prepayments (including the changes in prepayment rates associated with interest-rate changes) into an interest-rate risk analysis and to put the unexpected changes in prepayments (what one might call model error) into the prepayment risk category. The reason for this is that the changes in prepayment rates associated with interest rates can be managed via interest rate related instruments such as swaps, swaptions, and callable debt, while the unexpected changes in prepayment rates cannot be hedged with these instruments and therefore require a different type of analysis and a different approach to hedging.

Much of the analytical toolbox that is developed in this book addresses this type of uncertainty. Recognizing the limitations of models and of our ability to fully predict the behavior of individuals is an important component of our analytical methods. This uncertainty teaches mortgage analysts to be humble and to recognize the limitations of analytical methods. Even our methods that attempt to capture uncertainty are subject to some of the same potential weaknesses. Prepayment models and model uncertainty are the subjects of chapters 7 and 11.

Credit risk represents the possibility that borrowers will be unable or unwilling to make their contractual payments. Credit risk reflects the borrower's financial situation, the terms of the loan, and the value of the home. Credit risk has systematic components related to the performance of the economy, idiosyncratic risks related to individual borrowers, and operational risks related to underwriting and monitoring.

Most credit analysts refer to a borrower's ability and willingness to make payments in assessing credit risk. For mortgages, ability is mostly related to income; thus it is closely tied to job loss and to family dynamics such as divorce and medical expenses. Ability to pay can also be a factor if the original underwriting of the loans was improper due to fraud or if it paid insufficient attention to borrower income and expense.

Willingness to pay is primarily related to borrowers' desire to maintain their credit rating, moral stance on debt payment, and equity in the home. With positive equity in the home, borrowers are motivated to find alternative means of making loan payments or selling the home to in order to avoid foreclosure and lose the equity value. In some cases, borrowers are also subject to "recourse" where the lender could seek payment from other assets if a borrower defaults on a mortgage and the proceeds from a foreclosure sale are not sufficient to cover the amount of the loan.

While individual borrowers may be unable or unwilling to pay for a variety of reasons, large changes in the overall rate of delinquency and foreclosure are largely related to two macroeconomic factors: home prices and unemployment. Both of these factors are somewhat difficult to forecast and to hedge. Credit modeling is discussed in Part 3 of the book.

A significant potential source of credit risk is related to the choice of who to lend to and how much to lend. Underwriting standards are established to limit credit risk. Underwriters are charged with the duty of assessing borrowers to determine that the borrowers have sufficient financial resources to meet the obligation of the loans and that the information they provide to lenders is accurate. The failure of the securitization industry in 2006–2008, is due at least in part to a failure of the securitization system, or the failure of the "originate to distribute" model to maintain underwriting discipline.

The basic mechanism used to ensure that the originators maintain discipline in the underwriting process is called *Representations and Warranties.* These contractual obligations, which are also known as "Reps and Warrants," are designed to limit the risk of investors for poorly underwritten loans.

Usually the originator, or other seller of a loan, states that the loans were originated according to certain standards and that certain facts have been verified. These may include the borrower's income, credit score, appraisal values, and that the title for the home has been appropriately transferred to the mortgage holder. As a rule, if one or more of these representations is found to be false, the seller has the obligation to repurchase the loan at its par (or face value) from the buyer. It turned out during the home-price bubble of the mid 2000s, that this mechanism was insufficient to prevent a decline in underwriting standards, as some sellers did not survive to fulfill their obligations and private-label securitizations did not have adequate mechanisms to enforce the Reps and Warrants.

Liquidity represents the ability to transfer the funding obligation and/or the risks of the mortgages. As described above, an individual mortgage is a bundle of legal, operational, and financial risks that are not easily separated or transferred to others. One goal of securitization is to make it easier to separate and transfer these risks. Liquidity can be thought of as the cost or time it takes to transfer the mortgage or its component risks from one investor to another.

For example, transferring a set of loans (often called whole loans) from the originator to another investor could take weeks or months, with the involvement of numerous lawyers, accountants, servicing professionals, and others, while selling the risk associated with Fannie Mae guaranteed MBS can be done at a cost of less than 1/32 of 1% and transactions in the hundreds of millions of dollars can be done in a few minutes if not seconds in the TBA (to-be-announced) market.

THE STRUCTURE OF THE MARKET

About one-half of mortgages outstanding are held by financial institutions as loans. The primary investors in loans are banks and the government-sponsored enterprises (GSEs) Fannie Mae (FNMA) and Freddie Mac (FHLMC). These institutions bear all of the risk of the mortgages they hold. They may reduce those risks through hedging activities. As noted above, the US government plays an important role in the funding of those loans. Banks can raise insured deposits. This provides them with a stable source of funding. They also have access to the Federal Home Loan Bank System, which allows them access to low-cost funding for mortgages and mortgage-backed securities. Banks may issue longer term liabilities or utilize interest-rate swaps to reduce the interest-rate risk of their mortgage holdings.

The GSEs Fannie Mae and Freddie Mac issue debt to fund their holdings of mortgages and also issue longer term bonds and callable bonds; they also utilize interest-rate derivatives to hedge the interest-rate risk of their mortgage holdings. Usually, they bear the prepayment uncertainty and credit risk of the mortgages they hold.

There are many investors who are unable or unwilling to hold mortgages in the form of loans. Securitization developed to expand the investor base for mortgages. There are basically three forms of securitization: government, GSE, and private.

The structure of the mortgage market is currently undergoing significant changes. Where it will end up is still uncertain at this point. In order to understand where the market will end up, it may be useful to look at the market on the eve of the crisis. Figure 2.1 shows the composition of the mortgage market by type of securitization at the end of 2006.

At that time, there were about $10 trillion of mortgages outstanding. About one half of those held as loans were held in some form of securitization structure.

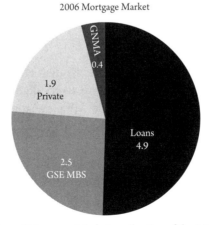

Figure 2.1 Composition of Mortgage Market on the Eve of the Meltdown

The other half remained as loans, held primarily on the balance sheets of banks and the GSEs. About $1.5 trillion of the $4.9 trillion of mortgage loans were held by the GSEs. The banks and the GSEs were responsible for all of the financial risks of the underlying mortgages.

In the case of the GSEs they would have had mortgage insurance on loans with LTVs greater than 80%. They would also use their access to the capital markets to fund the mortgages they held and to hedge the interest-rate risk of the loans. The banks would typically hold adjustable-rate mortgages and hybrid mortgages with less interest-rate risk. Funding for the banks would come from deposits, Home Loan Bank advances and other forms of borrowing.

Mortgage-backed securities (MBS) exist in three forms that provide different levels of government involvement. Sometimes RMBS is used to distinguish residential MBS from commercial MBS (CMBS); in this book we focus only on residential MBS. GNMA securities are backed by Federal Housing Administration (FHA) and Veterans Affairs (VA) loans. For these securities, the US government provides a full faith and credit guarantee to the investors in the MBS. That is, credit risk is completely removed from the investor equation. The elimination of credit risk also serves to facilitate the liquidity and funding of these loans.

MBS issued by Fannie Mae and Freddie Mac did not carry a full faith and credit guarantee of the US government, but instead carried an "implicit" guarantee. In September 2008, that implicit guarantee moved closer to explicit as Treasury agreed to cover any shortfall in GSE equity, thus essentially providing a government guarantee for these securities. Prior to the government guarantee in September 2008, the credit risk of the GSE loans was theoretically borne by the shareholders of Fannie Mae and Freddie Mac. The GSEs capital requirement for bearing credit risk was 0.45% of outstanding balances, while banks would have had about nine times the requirement, with a 4% minimum capital requirement for mortgage loans. The capital requirement for these companies was so low that it is not surprising that their capital was insufficient to cover losses in a significant home-price decline.

Nevertheless, despite the low capital requirement and the lack of an explicit government guarantee, GSE MBS traded in a very liquid market with little or no investor focus on credit risk. Instead the MBS investors provided funding for the mortgage market and bore the interest-rate risk and prepayment risk of the underlying loans.

In 2006, private-label securitization, without any guarantee from the government, was booming. For these loans, all of the financial risks were borne by investors. The essential ingredient that made this market work was the role of the credit rating agencies. These securities were structured in such a way to split the credit risk and funding of the underlying loans. Structuring will be discussed in more detail in the next few pages. Senior, triple-A rated bonds were thought to have little or no credit risk and thus provided the funding for the market. Junior bonds with lower credit ratings were sold to investors to bear credit risk. Unfortunately this market collapsed under its own weight as the incentive structures built into the securitization process failed to limit the provision of credit appropriately.

Private-label mortgages are generally split between prime, alt-A, and sub-prime. *Prime* loans generally mean fully documented loans to high credit quality borrowers. *Alt-A loans* generally mean less than full documented loans for high credit quality borrowers, and *subprime* means below high quality borrowers. Subprime securities are also sometimes referred to as HELs (home equity loans), or ABS (asset-backed securities). During the build-up to the housing crisis in 2003 through 2007, these definitions—prime, alt-A, and subprime— became blurred as low documentation loans were made to borrowers across the credit quality spectrum and deal labels did not always reflect the risk characteristics of the underlying loans.

Table 2.1 shows the different forms of mortgage investment and identifies which risks are born by the investors. It also shows the primary investors for each form of investment and the primary loan types. (Hybrids are mortgages that have a fixed coupon for a few years and then revert to floating.) Private-label MBS investors bear some liquidity risk, but usually not as much as loan investors. GSE issuance is split into GSE MBS and GSE debt. GSE debt was used by the GSEs to shed funding and interest-rate risk, while the GSEs retained the other risks of the loans they held on balance sheet. Figure 2.2 shows the distribution of investors in the mortgage market, and Figure 2.3 shows the allocation of each of the investor types to the mortgage market structures.

Table 2.1 RISK OF MORTGAGE SECURITIES

	Loans	Private MBS	GSE & Govt MBS	GSE Debt
Funding	•	•	•	•
Interest	•	•	•	•
Prepay	•	•	•	
Credit				
Systematic	•	•		
Origination	•	R&W*		
Liquidity	•	□		
Investors	Banks	Funds	Funds	Banks
	GSEs	Insurance	Insurance	Foreign
Primary Product	Hybrid	Hybrid	Fixed	Fixed

*Reps and Warrants

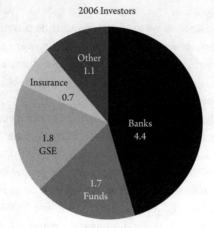

Figure 2.2 Investors in the Mortgage Market

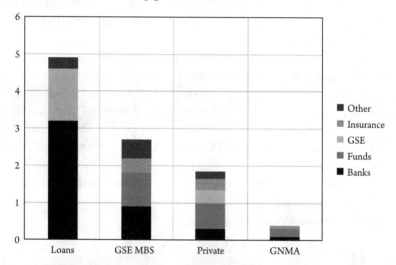

Figure 2.3 Investors in Mortgages by Form of Investment

STRUCTURING

In addition to securitization, structuring has been an important financial tool for the mortgage market. Structuring involves splitting the cash flows of mortgages (often called collateral in this context) into several different securities. The goal is to create value by creating securities with different risk characteristics.

Basic algebra would argue that structuring does not add value. Suppose that $p_{i,t}$ is the price of a rudimentary instrument that pays a dollar under economic scenario i at time t and nothing otherwise. This is called an Arrow-Debreu price. Suppose that the projected cash flows of a mortgage are $c_{i,t}$.

The value of the mortgage would then be

$$Price(c) = \sum_{i,t} c_{i,t} * p_{i,t} \qquad (2.1)$$

Suppose that c is structured into two bonds a and b, and a and b have the feature that $a_{i,t} + b_{i,t} = c_{i,t}$, that is the sum of the cash flows of bonds a and b equals the cash flow of the collateral.

The prices of bonds a and b are given by

$$Price(a) = \sum_{i,t} a_{i,t} * p_{i,t}$$

$$Price(b) = \sum_{i,t} b_{i,t} * p_{i,t}$$

It's not hard to see that

$$Price(a) + Price(b) = Price(c).$$

Keeping in mind that there are costs involved in structuring securities, it would seem that structuring would never be possible. Nevertheless, we do observe a substantial amount of structuring in the market. Structuring, therefore, is only economic if the Arrow-Debreu prices do not exist. That is, the prices $p_{i,t}$ must depend on the characteristics of bonds a and b, not just on scenario i and time t. Although the Arrow-Debreu prices do not exist, much of the analysis we perform is under the assumption that such a methodology is at least approximately correct. Constructing $p_{i,t}$ based on observable market prices represents one of the fundamentals of MBS analysis.

There are two main forms of structuring in the mortgage market: collateralized mortgage obligations (CMOs) and senior/subordinated. CMO structuring is primarily used for agency mortgages and senior/sub structuring is the basis for much of the non-agency mortgage market. CMOs represent the structuring of the timing of principal cash flows and the amount of interest paid on outstanding balances. Senior/subs represent the allocation of cash flows to protect senior bonds from credit risk. In both cases the goal of structuring is to create bonds that have greater value than the collateral. In order to do this, it is usually necessary to create some bonds that have substantially less risk than the collateral, in one or more of the risk dimensions described earlier, and find investors who are willing to pay higher prices for cash flows in that form than they would have for cash flows with the full complement of risks. Unfortunately, structuring has also been used to hide risks, so that investors unwittingly take on incremental risk without appropriate compensation.

CMO Structuring

CMO structuring for the most part establishes rules for the payment of principal and interest from the underlying collateral. We will assume for the moment that the collateral is guaranteed so that there is little or no credit risk in the structure.

The most common principal cash flow rules are sequential, pro rata, or priority.

Sequential allocation of principal means that principal cash flows are first allocated to one bond until it is fully paid down and then is allocated to the next bond.

Pro rata allocation of principal means that principal cash flows are split proportionally between two or more bonds. The main reason for pro rata allocation is to create bonds with different coupons, as will be discussed later.

Priority allocation of principal means that cash flows are allocated to one bond to maintain a schedule of payments close to a target redemption schedule with another bond absorbing the remaining principal cash flows. One typical type of priority bond is a PAC (planned amortization class) with its companion bond called a support bond.

Whether the structuring is sequential, pro rata, or priority, the cash flows must obey certain rules: As the total amount of principal cash flow remains fixed, the weighted average life of the bonds must remain equal to the weighted average life of the collateral. For pro rata allocations, the weighted average life of the pro rata bonds will always be the same. For sequential bonds, the average life of the bond with the first principal payment will always remain less than the average life of the other sequential bonds.

Second, for priority allocation, a bond cannot have shorter or longer average lives than the average life of the first or last principal payments received by the collateral which represent the same proportion of the collateral balance as the bond.

Figure 2.4 demonstrates these two rules. This chart shows the average life of the bonds and the collateral under several interest-rate scenarios. The PAC represents approximately 80% of the principal amount of the collateral. It is fairly clear that the weighted average of the average lives of the PAC and support bond are equal to the average life of the collateral. Note how the average life variability of the support bond is substantially greater than the average life variability of the PAC bond which receives cash flows on a priority basis. The PAC bond serves to reduce two kinds of risk for the investor: First, it reduces the optionality of the investment by limiting the variability of average life from changes in interest rates; second, it reduces the risks associated with prepayment model error, as the cash flows of the PAC bond tend to be fixed within a range of actual prepayment outcomes. Due to these benefits, PAC bonds may expand the investor base for MBS and may create incremental value for those mortgage cash flows.

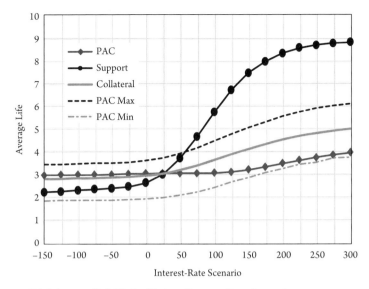

Figure 2.4 PAC Average Life Under Various Interest-Rate Scenarios

The dashed lines represent the average life of the first 80% of the collateral cash flows and the average life of the last 80% of the collateral cash flows. As the collateral average life increases in the rising interest-rate scenarios, the PAC bond is not able to keep its average life of about three years as the amount of short-term principal cash flows are insufficient.

Pro rata principal allocations allow for the creation of two bonds with the same principal cash flows, but different coupons. The primary constraint is that the sum of the interest cash flows on the pro rata bonds equals the interest cash flows on the combined bond.

Suppose for example that a support bond with a coupon C is split into two pro rata bonds. Also suppose that bond 1 represents w% of the support bond principal.

Coupons on bonds 1 and 2 can be set such that

$$w * C_1 + (1-w) * C_2 = C, \text{ provided } C_1 \text{ and } C_2 \geq 0 \qquad (2.2)$$

For example, if $C = 5\%$ and $w = 66.66\%$, C_1 and C_2 could have the following values:

C_1	0	0.5%	1.0%	1.5%	2.0%	2.5%	3.0%	3.5%	4.0%	4.5%	5.0%	5.5%	6.0%	6.5%	7.0%	7.5%
C_2	15%	14%	13%	12%	11%	10%	9%	8%	7%	6%	5%	4%	3%	2%	1%	0%

CMO structurers may seek to create some bonds with lower coupons and some bonds with higher coupons in order to find bond investors with different views of bond risk. In particular, bonds with higher coupons and bonds with lower coupons have very different performance as prepayment expectations change.

An extreme form of this structuring is to create one bond that has all of the principal and no interest and another bond that has all of the interest and no principal. These are called *principal only* (PO) and *interest only* (IO) bonds. The IO bond carries a coupon based upon a notional principal balance. A notional principal balance can be thought of as the principal balance of a reference pool or bond.

It is also possible to create bonds where the coupons on the bonds are not fixed, as long as the combined bonds continue to satisfy formula (2.2). Suppose Bond 1 has coupon with formula, $L + m$, where L is LIBOR (London interbank offered rate) and m is a fixed margin. These are called *floating-rate* bonds or *floaters*. Bond 2 would then have a coupon of

$$C_2 = max\left[0, \left(\frac{C}{1-w}\right) - \left(\frac{w}{1-w}\right)(L+m) \right] \tag{2.3}$$

To find the maximum coupon of Bond 1, set $C_2 = 0$ and solve for $L + m$.

$$Max\, C_1 = \left[\frac{C}{w}\right]$$

Bond 1 is then a capped LIBOR floater with margin m and cap C / w.

Inverse floaters can also be created without any principal balance, much like an IO security. These are called *inverse IOs* (IIOs). In this case the coupon on the IO relative to its notional balance is simply:

$$C_2 = max\left[0, C - (L+m) \right]$$

C_2 looks much like the formula for an interest-rate swap with fixed coupon $C - m$ and an interest-rate cap at $LIBOR = C - m$.

Figure 2.5 shows the price profile of a floater, inverse floater and the underlying bond that was split to make the floater/inverse combination. In this case, the inverse is an IIO; it does not receive principal payments and has the same notional principal amount as the actual principal of the associated floater. The floater coupon is 1Mo LIBOR + 0.70% with a cap of 8% and a floor of 0.7%. The inverse floater coupon is 7.3% – 1 Mo LIBOR with a floor of zero.

The graphs show that within some range of interest rates, the floater value remains near constant (at around par). Thus the IIO price sensitivity looks very much like the underlying bond. The IIO can be viewed as an interest-rate swap or a very leveraged position in the underlying bond. As

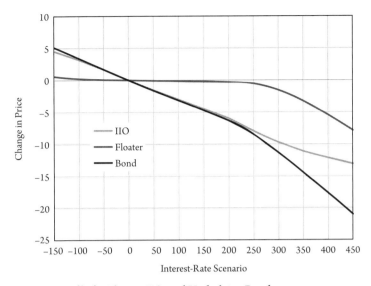

Figure 2.5 Price Profile for Floater, IIO, and Underlying Bond

the floater nears its interest-rate cap of 8%, its value begins to decline. The IIO is near its corresponding floor so its value declines less rapidly than the underlying bond.

Accrual is a structuring rule that combines interest payments and principal payments. This rule transforms interest into principal and creates a bond with no interest payments for some period of time. Suppose the collateral is split into two sequential bonds. Both bonds earn interest on a current basis at the same coupon rate. The interest on the longer of the two sequential bonds is paid as principal on the shorter bond. At the same time, the same amount of principal on the shorter bond is transferred to the longer bond. During the accrual period, the principal amount of the accrual bond (also called a Z-bond) is increasing, while the first sequential bond is retired sooner. Once the first sequential bond is fully retired, the Z bond begins to receive both principal and interest payments. The two bonds continue to satisfy the rules that the sum of the principal payments of the two bonds is equal to the principal payments of the collateral. (A similar approach of transferring rights to principal payments is used in structuring bonds for credit risk.)

[Question for readers: How should one compute the average life of the Z-bond? Keep in mind that the average life of the collateral needs to be equal to the average life of the bonds.]

A general theme of CMO structuring is the creation of one bond that has a more stable investment profile and a corresponding bond that absorbs the remaining risk of the mortgages. In almost every case we find that the stable investment bond retains some of the risk of the collateral, especially in extreme economic environments. Analytical methods such as those described later in this book can help investors determine the amount of risk they bear, as well as whether they are being adequately compensated for these risks. Simple measures based upon yield or average life profiles may not be sufficient to evaluate these complex securities.

Senior/Subordinated and Credit Structuring

Just as the PAC/support reduces the prepayment risk for some investors while concentrating and leveraging risk for others, it is possible to segment the credit risk of mortgages. A common structure is the senior/subordinated shifting interest structure. The goal of this structure is to protect some investors from the credit risk of the mortgages.

For many high quality mortgage products, credit losses, even in extreme economic environments, are not likely to exceed 3 to 5% of the loan balance of a well-diversified pool. This may seem surprising given recent experience, but many of the loans that have experienced high losses were made at high LTVs and to borrowers with poor credit histories. These losses were compounded by concentrated run ups and declines in home prices.

Given the small amount of losses, it is possible to create a structured security that is protected from losses over a wide range of economic environments. This is done by issuing one or more bonds that have different claims on the mortgage assets. For a simple example, assume that there are $100 million of mortgages. A senior bond has a claim on 90% of the cash flow of those mortgages and the junior or subordinate bond has a claim on 10% of the cash flow. The two bonds can be structured so that if there are losses, say 2% of the principal balance, the principal amount of the 10% subordinate bond is decreased from $10 million to $8 million, while the other bond remains at $90 million. The bonds now have a 91.84% and a 8.16% claim on the remaining cash flows.

In addition, to ensure that the subordinate bond is still outstanding, even if losses take place after some time, or after there have been significant prepayments, the subordinate bond is usually locked out from receiving prepayments for some period, much like a PAC bond with a long average life. For example if there is a 5% prepayment on the remaining $98 million balance of collateral, $4.9 million of principal will go to the senior bond, increasing the allocation of the subordinate bond up to 8.59%. These deals often have triggers tied to subordination amounts, delinquency levels, and cumulative losses that determine when principal prepayments can be paid to the subordinate bond.

The Vasicek model described in chapter 1 provides a good framework for assessing the probability of loss at different levels of economic stress. This and other modeling approaches will be discussed in Part 3 of the book.

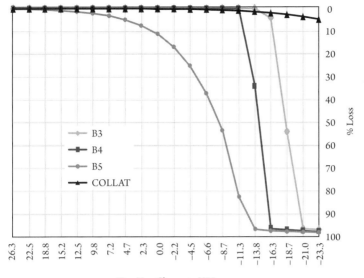

Two Year Change in HPI

Figure 2.6 Senior/Subordinated Loss Allocations

Figure 2.6 shows the allocation of losses across bonds in the senior/sub structure. This chart shows the losses for bonds of SEMT 2011-2, one of the few deals issued in the post crisis period. Losses are allocated first to the B5 tranche and then to the B4 and B3 tranches. The chart shows the expected amounts of loss based upon our models as a function of home-price changes. The A1 tranche, not shown, did not have any losses for the first 4.7% of losses of the collateral.

Collateralized Debt Obligations

A final type of structuring that was important to the mortgage market was the collateralized debt obligation (CDO). CDOs played an important role in the financial crisis and are discussed in more depth in chapter 17.

The basic idea of a CDO is that a portfolio of bonds allows for diversification so that it supports debt with less credit risk than the underlying bonds that are the collateral for the CDO. This is very similar to the idea of diversification of credit risk that is used to create the senior subordinated structures. While each bond may have a 5% chance of default in a stress scenario, 95% of the bonds would not default in that scenario. Thus it should be possible to segment the risk and create a bond with a lower probability of default.

The essential assumption of the CDO is that the there is a low correlation between the losses of the underlying bonds. If all of the bonds default at the same time, then there is no cash flow that can be used to create the lower risk bonds. The massive failure of this market is an indication that rating agencies, dealers, and investors applied incorrect and inappropriate correlation assumptions in developing this market.

The mortgage market offers investors a wide range of investment vehicles that provide for a complex allocation of the risks of the underlying mortgages. This book covers methods to analyze these risks.

3

Investors in Mortgage-Backed Securities

There are four basic types of investors in the market. They differ in terms of their investment time frames, their regulatory framework and their ownership structures. All four are linked by common principles of *income, risk,* and *capital* as summarized in Table 3.1. This chapter will look at each of these types of investors as they relate to income, risk, and capital.

Table 3.1 BASIC TYPES OF INVESTORS

	Income	Risk	Capital
Depository	Net interest margin	Income volatility	Regulatory
Trading	P & L	Max loss	Leverage limit
Total Return	Value + cash flow	Tracking error	Implied
Absolute Return	Change in NAV	Draw down	Investment

INCOME

All investors would like profits on their investments. **Income** can take the form of cash flow or changes in market value.

Depository institutions represent a classic form of investing. Banks or other depository institutions raise funds from depositors. They promise to pay these funds back with interest. Depositories then invest in instruments that they expect to produce income in excess of their liability to the depositors. Banks earn the difference between the income on their assets and the expense on their liabilities. These institutions are less focused on the changes in the market value of their investments. Table 3.2 and Figure 3.1 show the balance sheet of a bank or depository investing in mortgages funded with debt. In this example, we start

Table 3.2 Depository Balance Sheet

		Start	1	2	3	4	5
Mortgage	5.00%	100.0	95.0	85.1	76.2	68.2	61.1
L1	4.50%	40.0	40.0	40.0	40.0	40.0	40.0
L2	3.50%	20.0	20.0	20.0			
Cash	2.00%	36.0	31.2	21.7	33.1	25.5	18.6
Capital		4.0	3.8	3.4	3.0	2.7	2.4

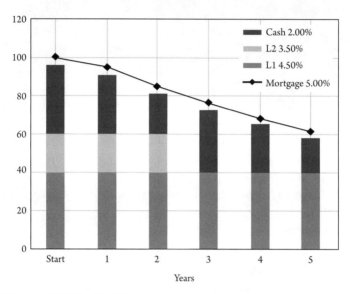

Figure 3.1 Asset/Liability Matching

with $100 million of mortgages with a 5% interest rate. The firm is required to maintain capital of 4% of the amount of mortgages. The firm funds the mortgages with a combination of five-year debt, paying 4.5%, two-year debt, paying 3.5%, and short-term borrowing at 2%. In this example, we assume that the mortgages pay down at a rate of 10% per year. The amount of cash is computed so that assets equal liabilities plus capital. Dollar amounts for each year represent the average balance during the year.

The portfolio of mortgages and debt generates income for the firm, as shown in Table 3.3. The net interest income represents the difference between the income on the assets and the expenses on the debt. The income of the firm is further reduced by credit losses and general and administrative expenses. Credit losses are assumed to be realized on a delayed basis. The firm is evaluated based upon the return on equity, which is the net income divided by the amount of capital.

The return can also be evaluated as the net present value (NPV) of the cash flows to equity (Tables 3.3 and 3.4). To do this, the change in capital is added to the net

Table 3.3 DEPOSITORY INCOME STATEMENT

YEAR	1	2	3	4	5
Interest Income	**4.75**	**4.25**	**3.81**	**3.41**	**3.05**
Liability1	1.80	1.80	1.80	1.80	1.80
Liability2	0.70	0.70	0.00	0.00	0.00
Cash	0.62	0.43	0.66	0.51	0.37
Interest Expense	**3.12**	**2.93**	**2.46**	**2.31**	**2.17**
NII	**1.63**	**1.32**	**1.35**	**1.10**	**0.88**
credit loss		0.48	0.43	0.38	0.34
G&A	0.48	0.43	0.38	0.34	0.31
Net Income	**1.15**	**0.42**	**0.54**	**0.38**	**0.24**
ROE	30%	12%	18%	14%	10%

Table 3.4 NPV OF EQUITY

	Beginning	1	2	3	4	5	Ending
Δ Capital	−4.00	0.20	0.40	0.36	0.32	0.29	2.44
cash flow	−4.00	1.35	0.82	0.90	0.70	0.52	2.44
NPV@15%	0.47						

Table 3.5 TRADING BLOTTER

Day	B/S	Face		Bond	Price	Price Spread
Monday	Buy	100	mm	MBS 5	102.5	
	Sell	100	mm	MBS 4.5	100.5	2
Tuesday	Buy	50	mm	MBS 5	102.1	
	Sell	50	mm	MBS 4.5	100.1	1.9
Wednesday	Sell	150	mm	MBS 5	101.7	
	Buy	150	mm	MBS 4.5	99.2	2.1

income and the present value is computed. In this case, the strategy has a slight positive NPV at a 15% discount rate. Capital will be discussed in more detail at the end of this chapter.

Trading accounts seek to profit from the bid/ask spread. They buy bonds from clients and resell those bonds to other clients. Trading accounts, however, may keep an inventory of bonds that they have purchased and not yet sold. They are much like absolute-return investors (described later) except that leverage is typically higher, time horizons are shorter, and the primary source of revenue is profit on order flow. The primary measure of income for traders is daily profit and loss or P&L.

The next example shows how the P&L is computed. The blotter shows the trading activity (Table 3.5). The trader purchases $100 million face amount of a 5% coupon MBS on Monday for a price 102.5, or 102.5% of $100 million dollars for a total cost of $102.5 million. Assuming that these MBS are for forward settlement, no cash changes hands. Later in the week, the trader will sell those MBS, for a price of 102.5. The trader loses $0.8 million on that block of MBS. Similar computations can be done for the other trades. While it would be possible to wait until all trades were settled, it is desirable to know how well the trader is doing each day.

In order to do so, the position is marked to market each day and the daily P&L is computed based upon that mark (Table 3.6).

The Daily P&L shows the change in value each day. The trader made $0.3 million entering into the trade on Monday. On Tuesday, the trader lost $0.45 million and was in a losing position. That loss was more than recouped on Wednesday with a gain of $1.2 million. The trader produced a net profit on both a cost and mark to market basis of $0.75 million by the end of trading on Wednesday when the open positions were fully offset.

For **total-return** investors, income consists of coupon income and change in value of the portfolio. Total-return investors are generally unleveraged and unhedged. The total return of a portfolio can be computed two ways. The simple way is to compare the value of the portfolio at the end of the measurement period, usually one month or one quarter, with the value of the portfolio at the beginning of the period and then account for any inflows or outflows during the period. Without any additions or redemptions the computation is as seen in Table 3.7a.

Alternatively, the return can be computed for each instrument individually and split by component of return (Table 3.7b). Each component represents the change in value associated with that component divided by the value of the asset (Face * Price) at the start of the period.

Returns for the fund are computed for each period. Figure 3.2 shows the quarterly returns of a hypothetical portfolio over a five year period.

Table 3.6 DAILY MARK-TO-MARKET

Day	Face	Bond	Mark	Daily mark	Daily change in cost	Cumulative cost	Mark - cost	Daily P&L	Mark Price Spread
Monday	100	MBS 5	102.7						
	−100	MBS 4.5	100.4	2.3	2	2			2.3
							0.3	0.3	
Tuesday	150	MBS 5	102.2						
	−150	MBS 4.5	100.3	2.85	1	3			1.9
							−0.15	−0.45	
Wed	0	MBS 5	101.5						
	0	MBS 4.5	99.2	0	−3.75	−0.75			2.3
							0.75	1.2	
						Total P&L		0.75	

Table 3.7a COMPUTATION OF TOTAL RETURN

Coupon 5%	**Beginning**	**Ending**
Face Amount	$100 million	$99 million
Price	98.5	99.25
Cash	0	$2.25 million (from $1 million pay-down and $1.25 quarterly interest payment)
Period NAV	$98.5 million	$100.5075 million
Quarterly Return	EOP NAV/BOP NAV -1 = 2.04%	

Table 3.7b RETURN BY COMPONENT

	Quarterly Return	
	$millions	**Return**
Coupon	1.25	1.27%
Paydown	0.015	0.02%
Price	0.7425	0.75%
TOTAL	2.0075	2.04%

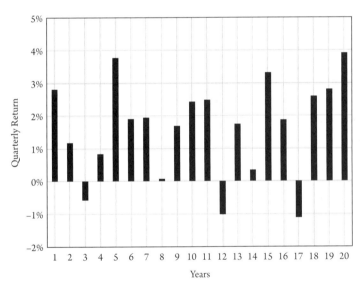

Figure 3.2 Quarterly Total Returns

The periodic returns can also be combined together using the formula

$$1+R_{1,2} = (1+R_1) \times (1+R_2)$$

These are time weighted returns and generally ignore how the amount invested in the fund changes over time. Time weighted returns reflect the amount that a theoretical investor would have earned if she invested in the portfolio at the start of the measurement period and did not make any additional contributions or withdrawals during the investment period and if all profits were reinvested in the fund.

Figure 3.3 reflects the cumulative total return of the fund based on the periodic returns just shown.

Absolute-return investors seek to earn a positive return in all economic environments. Many absolute-return investors are hedge funds. In contrast with total return investors, hedge funds are leveraged and hedged. In contrast to depository institutions, funding is generally short term, via repurchase agreements (repo) or margin rather than through long-term debt or deposits.

For example, a hedge fund with $20 million of investable capital might purchase $100 million of mortgage-backed securities and take a short position in other mortgage-backed securities or interest-rate swaps.

Asset:	$100 million 5% MBS
Borrowing:	$80 million repurchase
Hedge:	$50 million 4.5% MBS
	$40 million 4% 4-year swap

Analytically, we can represent the hedge and swap as a short position in the fixed-rate asset and a long position in cash. Thus, the hedge fund balance sheet from an analytical perspective is as shown in Table 3.8.

Absolute-return investments are evaluated on a monthly or quarterly basis using the same computation as total-return investments.

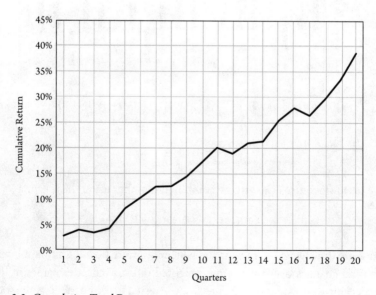

Figure 3.3 Cumulative Total Return

Table 3.8 HEDGE FUND NET ASSET VALUE

FACE	Asset	Coupon	
100	MBS	5%	
−50	MBS	4.5%	
−40	Swap	4%	
−80	Cash	LIBOR+.25%	repo
50	Cash	LIBOR	MBS short
40	Cash	LIBOR	Swap
20	**NAV**		

RISK

Risk represents the uncertainty of the amount or timing of income. It arises from the varying performance of the assets and liabilities, long and short positions, and the fundamental uncertainties of the financial instruments. In chapter 2 we described the uncertainties created by changes in interest rates, prepayment rates, credit quality, liquidity, and the supply of funding. Changes to each of these can be reflected in either changes to the cash flows of the MBS or in changes to the traded price of the MBS.

For **depository institutions** risk is ultimately reflected in changes in the net interest margin. There are two main sources of risk for a spread investor. First there is the credit risk associated with the assets owned by the institution. If the borrowers fail to make their payments, then the amount of cash flow received by the bank will be reduced. Consider the example in Table 3.3.

The other form of risk is a mismatch between interest-rate characteristics of the assets and liabilities. Suppose a bank funds its investment in fixed-rate mortgages using floating rate debt or other liabilities whose rate can fluctuate. If interest rates rise, the interest income on the assets is fixed, but the cost of the liabilities can increase. For this reason, banks attempt to match the maturity of their assets and liabilities.

Figure 3.1 (earlier in the chapter) shows a typical funding strategy for an amortizing asset like a mortgage. The asset is funded in part by fixed rate liabilities of different maturities and part by cash. Such a strategy would remove much of the interest-rate risk from the bank.

Unfortunately, when investing in mortgages or mortgage-backed securities the problem becomes more complicated. If interest rates fall the mortgage borrowers are more likely to refinance their mortgages in order to take advantage of more attractive rates. Their prepayments will reduce the amount of mortgages held by the bank. If the amount of reduction is sufficiently large, the bank may be forced to reinvest the proceeds of the refinancing at the lower prevailing interest rates.

Figure 3.4 shows how the balance of the mortgages could be less than the fixed-rate debt. The negative cash liability reflects the additional investment in cash that the bank needs to enter into.

The net income of the bank becomes negative as the earnings from the assets are not sufficient to cover the cost of the liabilities, as shown in Table 3.9. (The money-market rate is assumed to have fallen to zero.) Table 3.10 summarizes these results for a variety of scenarios. For falling interest-rate scenarios prepayment rates increase and asset earnings are insufficient to cover net interest income.

Because of this profile, spread investors in mortgages and mortgage-backed securities need to use dynamic hedging strategies and utilize options such as callable debt or swaptions to control the risk of their portfolios.

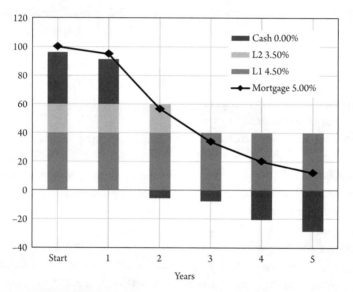

Figure 3.4 Asset-Liability Mismatch

Table 3.9 INCOME STATEMENT WITH FALLING RATES

	1	2	3	4	5
Income	4.75	2.84	1.69	1.01	0.60
Liability1	1.80	1.80	1.80	1.80	1.80
Liability2	0.70	0.70	0.00	0.00	0.00
Cash	0.00	0.00	0.00	0.00	0.00
Interest Expense	2.50	2.50	1.80	1.80	1.80
NII	2.25	0.34	−0.11	−0.79	−1.20
Credit Loss		0.48	0.28	0.17	0.10
G&A	0.48	0.28	0.17	0.10	0.06
Net Income	1.78	−0.42	−0.56	−1.06	−1.36
ROE	47%	−19%	−41%	−131%	−281%

Table 3.10 SCENARIO ANALYSIS OF NET INCOME

	Short-Term Interest Rate	Prepay Rate	NI_1	NI_2	NI_3	NI_4	NI_5	NPV
Up 2	4.00%	7%	0.53	0.01	−0.10	−0.11	−0.12	−1.45
Up 1	3.00%	8%	0.84	0.23	0.25	0.18	0.12	−0.40
Base	2.00%	10%	1.15	0.42	0.54	0.38	0.24	0.47
Dn 1	1.00%	20%	1.46	0.30	0.35	0.00	−0.29	−0.22
Dn 2	0.00%	40%	1.78	−0.42	−0.56	−1.06	−1.36	−1.63

Table 3.11 PRICE RISK OF MBS

		DV01	Modified Duration	Spread Risk Correlation
Risk	MBS 5	3.8	4.3	0.8
	MBS 4.5	4.7	5.3	
	10-yr Treasury	8.6		

Due to the uncertainty of the exact relationship between interest rates and prepayments and due to the uncertainty of credit losses, some amount of risk is likely to remain in any such investment strategy. One way of limiting risk would be to use a very large number of options in the funding strategy. In our example, the bank could have fully funded with five-year callable debt. In that way, the bank could be fully protected for both rising and falling interest rates. Unfortunately, such debt is usually costly. For example, if the interest rate on that debt was 5.25%, and the bank exactly matched the amount of debt to the outstanding balance of mortgages, the bank would be fully hedged, but it would be losing money in every month in every scenario. This dynamic will lead to trade-offs between the amount of risk that an institution can and will bear and its potential profitability. That is the role of capital, which is discussed in the next section.

For the depository institution, the price of the assets and liabilities did not enter directly into the evaluation of the strategy. However, for **trading accounts**, the primary risk is associated with mark to market, rather than with funding or cash flows. Traders often enter into offsetting hedge positions to limit the volatility of their holdings so that the profits they make from order flow are not overwhelmed by the volatility of the market. For fixed-income securities, including MBS, many traders will compute an equivalent position in a benchmark security, such as the 10-year treasury, to measure the amount of exposure they have to the general level of interest rates. This can be seen in Tables 3.11 and 3.12. Table 3.11 shows the risk of each bond in terms of dollar value of a basis point (or DV01).

Table 3.12 MBS POSITION IN 10-YEAR EQUIVALENTS

	Face ($mm)		DV01	10-yr Equiv
Monday	100	MBS 5	3.8	44.2
	−100	MBS 4.5	−4.7	−54.7
		Net TSY	−0.9	−10.5

Table 3.13 DAILY PRICE RISK ESTIMATE

	10-yr	Spread	
Yield daily std dev	10	3	
	Rate risk	Spread risk	Total
Position daily std dev ($mm)	0.090	0.095	0.131

This is the amount that the price of the instrument would change for a one basis point change in rates. (Later we discuss how to compute these measures.)

Even though the net exposure to mortgages seems to be zero with the $100 million long offset by $100 million short, this position will likely perform like a $10.5 million short position in the 10-year treasury.

In addition to the net exposure to interest rates, the position is also subject to the incremental volatility of each position. This is often called spread risk, as it results from changes in the difference (or spread) between the yield of the position and the yield of the benchmark. Assets with from similar asset classes may have highly correlated spread risk. Table 3.13 shows the expected daily volatility of the trader's position based upon a decomposition of the risk into treasury equivalents and spread risk, based upon assumed standard deviation of risk for each component.

Trading desks may measure the amount of spread risk they bear as well as the amount of market risk. They may measure the amount of residual risk. Using techniques of combining the statistical distributions they can compute the amount of loss they might expect over different time periods and different levels of probability: This approach is commonly called value at risk (VaR). Note that the amount of risk from spreads is about the same as the amount of interest-rate risk. Even if the portfolio were hedged with an additional $10.5 million of treasuries or treasury equivalents, the spread risk would remain.

As an alternative to the parametric approach to VaR based on risk exposures, some firms calculate what the P&L of the current position would be if it were held over historical market moves. (We don't recommend this approach.) The VaR approach will be discussed in chapter 19.

For **total return funds**, the fluctuation in both the value of the assets, as reflected by market price, and the asset cash flows are components of risk. Figure 3.2 showed the quarterly returns for the fund. It may seem that the changes in the returns would be a good measure of risk. They would be a good measure of risk if the objective of the fund was to have a stable value. However, most funds are established with investment benchmarks that reflect the performance of a benchmark portfolio. Given the objective of outperformance of benchmark, risk is best measured relative to the benchmark.

Figure 3.5 shows the performance of the fund relative to its benchmark. This chart shows that the volatility of the fund is largely explained by the index. A good measure of risk is the difference between the performance of the fund and the index. This is called tracking error and is shown in Figure 3.6.

Note how the standard deviation of the tracking error which is about 0.45% is much less than the standard deviation of the fund's returns of 1.49%. On average, the fund is producing a return of 0.13% higher than the index. Over time the standard deviation will grow at approximately the square root of time, while the excess return will grow linearly with time. Therefore on an annual basis, standard deviation of the tracking error is. 90% while the expected return is 0.52%.

Over the five-year period shown in the graphs, the standard deviation of returns is 2.02% while the excess return is 2.57%. Assuming a normal distribution, the probability of the fund outperforming the index over a quarter is about 60%, but this probability increases to about 90% over the five years.

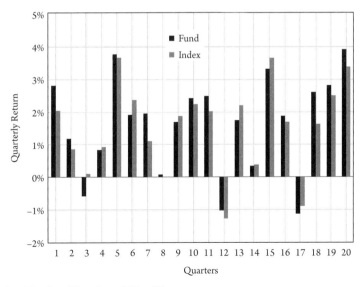

Figure 3.5 Fund and Benchmark Total Return

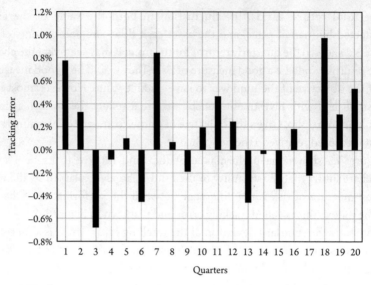

Figure 3.6 Tracking Error

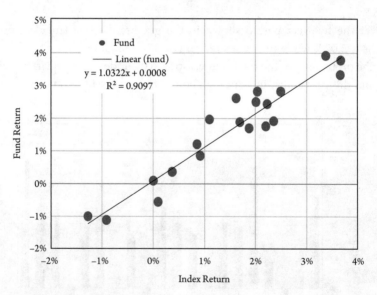

Figure 3.7 Fund Beta to Index

Investors in this fund may also be interested in whether or not the fund has the desired exposure to the underlying index. This can be measured using regression analysis. The regression is shown in Figure 3.7. In this case, the regression has a beta of near 1. This demonstrates that the fund has nearly the same exposure to the market as the index. If that beta was not near 1, it would indicate that the fund might not have the appropriate risk exposure to the market.

As **absolute-return** accounts represent a blend of total return and trading their risk measures are usually similar to both. For absolute-return investors, the goal is to produce excess returns, without taking on significant exposure to major market indexes or economic factors. Investors therefore frequently would like to validate that the absolute-return funds have low correlations with market indexes. Absolute- return investors also like to look at the number of months that a fund has negative returns over a given period, although this measure has little or no economic significance.

CAPITAL

Capital represents the money required to enter into the investment or trading strategy. Capital is often supplemented by leverage to increase the amount of assets. Leverage may be in the form of short-term borrowing, long-term borrowing, or it can be imbedded directly in financial instruments. The amount of leverage utilized is the result of a compromise between two opposing forces. Increasing leverage increases returns.

$$ROE = (R_A - D * R_L)/E$$

where E is % Equity, D is Debt = 1 – E, R_A is Return on Assets, R_L is Return on Liabilities.

Using algebra one can show that this is equivalent to

$$ROE = (R_A - R_L)L + R_L$$

where L is Leverage: $L = 1/(1-D) = 1/E$

Thus increasing the amount of leverage, L, increases the Return on Equity, provided that the return on assets, R_A is greater than the return on liabilities, R_L. We know however that R_A is uncertain. Thus increasing L also increases the risk of loss of equity and thereby increases the risk of default.

Assuming for a moment that the cost of liabilities is deterministic,

$$\text{Std dev}(ROE) = L * \text{Std dev}(R_A)$$

Leverage increases both risk and return. Thus capital and the related leverage is the arbiter between income and risk.

While financial theory allows a wide range of possibilities for leverage, in practice, for financial institutions, equity holders generally require a minimum level of expected return of 10 to 20% in excess of the risk-free rate. On the other hand, lenders to financial institutions generally would like to have investment-grade or high-quality debt. Investment-grade debt generally would have a lower than 2.5% chance of default over a ten-year period. This would require equity to cover about two standard deviations of risk. In practice, many large financial institutions seek to issue debt with lower probability of default than the minimum investment grade requirements, so that equity likely covers five or six standard deviations of risk. A numerical example can show how this works (Table 3.14).

In practice, unless the entity can issue government guaranteed debt (such as a GSE like Fannie Mae or Freddie Mac) or through deposit insurance, the expected return (or cost) of liabilities would rise as the loss coverage ratio fell. It is unlikely that that a private institution could have 20 to 50 times leverage without facing significantly higher borrowing costs.

For **depository institutions** with a government guarantee on their deposits, capital requirements are set by a regulator. We can see from the preceding analysis that if not, the institution would seek ever greater levels of leverage, thus increasing the expected return to equity holders while passing on the risk of default to the government.

There are also other spread investors in the market. In particular, real estate investment trusts (REITs) act much like depository institutions, but they do not have access to deposit insurance. For REITs, leverage is generally limited by their access to leverage. A typical source of leverage for a REIT is repo, or repurchase agreements, whereby they pledge their assets in exchange for debt financing. Lenders establish "haircuts" or limits on how much debt they will provide for particular assets and for individual firms.

Table 3.14 LEVERAGE, RISK AND RETURN

R_A	6%	6%	6%	6%	6%	6%
R_L	5%	5%	5%	5%	5%	5%
Std dev (R-sub-A)	1.50%	1.50%	1.50%	1.50%	1.50%	1.50%
A/L	100/0	100/50	100/80	100/90	100/95	100/99
E	100%	50%	20%	10%	5%	1%
L	1	2	5	10	20	100
Income	6.00%	3.50%	2.00%	1.50%	1.25%	1.05%
ROE	**6%**	**7%**	**10%**	**15%**	**25%**	**105%**
Std dev (ROE)	**2%**	**3%**	**8%**	**15%**	**30%**	**150%**
Loss coverage	66.7	33.3	13.3	6.7	3.3	0.7
Prob default	0.00%	0.00%	0.00%	0.00%	0.04%	25.25%

Trading desks typically have capital assigned to them from their parent company. The amount of capital is often linked to the size of the position held by the trading desk as well as the volatility of the P&L as measured historically (e.g. using VaR).

For **total return** accounts, investments are typically unlevered. However, many total return investors have liabilities that they seek to cover with the total return investments. Measures of risk, such as tracking error and beta, serve as proxies for the amount of capital that are exposed in the strategies.

Absolute-return accounts generally achieve leverage through repo, margin, and leverage built into the assets they purchase. Some investors require specific limits on leverage; others track the volatility of the funds. Many investors in absolute-return strategies focus primarily on downside risks, that is, historical losses, and fail to fully understand the sources of risk and return.

CONCLUSION

The approaches we use for valuation utilize the concepts of income, risk, and capital described in this chapter. The total-return approach is used to construct partial differential expressions that are the kernel of many valuation measures. Throughout this work, we discuss risk; we focus on capital in chapter 19. We also discuss many different approaches to valuation, but ultimately the choice of analytical method depends upon the goals and objectives of each firm.

4

Valuation with Risk Factors and Risk Neutrality

Valuation is a process of predicting the market value of an instrument, be it a bond, a stock, or a commodity. In this chapter, we focus on how MBS prices can be derived and how this process accounts for risks borne by investors. An MBS price is not just the present value of predicted cash flows. If this were the case, market participants would never agree on a price, as they typically have divergent views on expected cash flows, rates, and risk aversion. We also introduce our central theme in valuation: risk-neutral modeling. This is a transformation of a model built for economic factors or modeling uncertainties that endogenously accounts for the associated price of risk. We explain how this concept can be established and used. The price of mortgage-backed securities follows a partial differential equation (PDE) that serves as a root of the popular OAS method and its extensions. This chapter requires some knowledge of stochastic calculus and partial differential equations.

VALUATION RELATIVE TO THE MONEY-MARKET ACCOUNT

In the modern theory of valuation of financial instruments, there are two key terms: *numeraire* and *martingale*. While practitioners may find these notions to be foreign and irrelevant to them, they play an important role in the derivation of formulas for MBS pricing. Numeraire is the term for a financial instrument used as a benchmark for valuation. Money-market accounts, zero-coupon bonds, and annuities are often used for this purpose. Martingale is a random process $X(t)$, the mathematical expectation of which is equal to its starting value, $E[X(t)] = X(t_0)$, given the information at time $t_0 \leq t$.

The main valuation assumption is that, for a given asset or asset class, there exists a numeraire, so that the ratio of the asset's value to the value of that numeraire is a martingale. In practical terms, this statement means that an investor's return expectation for the asset is the same as for the benchmark. To illustrate how this can be used in practice, let us use a money-market account in the role of numeraire. The value $M(t)$ of this account grows randomly at the risk-free market rate r:

$$dM = rMdt \quad \text{with the solution being} \quad M(t) = M(0)exp\left[\int_0^t r(\tau)\,d\tau\right] \quad (4.1)$$

Let the total value of asset $A(t)$ be growing at a random rate (with dividends reinvested, if any), but promising the same return (at any point of time) as money-market account $M(t)$. This is equivalent to saying that the ratio of $A(t)$ to $M(t)$ is a martingale:

$$E\frac{A(t)}{M(t)} = \frac{A(0)}{M(0)}$$

Assuming we deposited $M(0) = 1$ dollar at time zero,

$$A(0) = E\frac{A(t)}{M(t)} = E\left\{A(t)exp\left[-\int_0^t r(\tau)\,d\tau\right]\right\} \quad (4.2)$$

For example, an asset paying \$1 with certainty at time t should be valued at

$$E\left\{exp\left[-\int_0^t r(\tau)\,d\tau\right]\right\}.$$

This fact is utilized by MBS valuation systems, which simulate the risk-free rate r, generate the asset's cash flows, and employ formula (4.2) for each dollar received by the asset.

Money-market account is a common, but not the only possible, selection of a valuation's numeriare. Another frequently used choice is a zero-coupon bond maturing at time T. In contrast to the money-market account, a zero-coupon bond has a certain *final* value paid at maturity T. The price of this bond is equal to the observed *discount factor* $P(t,T)$, which, in turn, can be computed using the entire short rate forward curve $f(t)$ integrated from t to T:

$P(t,T) = exp\left[-\int_t^T f(\tau)\,d\tau\right]$. Using the martingale assumption for the $A(t)$ to $P(t,T)$ ratio, we can obtain the following formula:

$$\frac{A(0)}{P(0,T)} = E\frac{A(t)}{P(t,T)} = \left|\text{ for } t = T\right| = E\frac{A(T)}{P(T,T)} = E[A(T)]$$

because $P(T,T) = 1$ at maturity. Hence,

$$A(0) = P(0,T)E[A(T)] = exp\left[-\int_0^T f(t)\,dt\right]E[A(T)] \qquad (4.3)$$

There is a significant difference between valuation formulas (4.2) and (4.3). In (4.2), the discount factor is random and depends on the integral of risk-free rate $r(t)$. In (4.3) the discount factor is deterministic. Formulas (4.2) and (4.3) would be identical if the asset was independent of interest rates. Of course, this is not the case with MBS. Hence, formulas (4.2) and (4.3) can generally yield the same asset value only if the expectation operator E works with respect to two differing *probability measures*. The *money-market measure* will force all risk factors to develop so that assets remain martingales with respect to the money-market account $M(t)$. We could denote the expectation in (4.2) as E^M to manifest this important detail. We could denote expectation in formula (4.3) as E^{P_T} to stress that it is computed with respect to the *T-maturity zero-coupon bond measure*. In order to use valuation formula (4.3), we should assume a different distribution of interest rates than when using formula (4.2); under this distribution, assets will remain martingales with respect to $P(t,T)$.

We now choose the money market measure for the remainder of this section and show how MBS price can be derived. First, we should note that an MBS is not a risk-free instrument and it does not generally pay a certain cash flow. At this point, we simply assume that there exists some applicable expected rate of return R that may be different from the risk-free rate r. Second, an MBS has many cash flows of both principal and interest. The MBS price will then be the sum of prices for each, generally random, payments. To make formulas more tractable and illustrative, we continue using the continuous-finance set-up where rates and cash flows are functions of continuous time t rather than monthly vectors.

For an MBS paying interest at a $c(t)$ rate computed on a $B(t)$ balance, which retires to zero at a $\lambda(t)$ speed, and paying principal, the price $P(0)$ should integrate all components generated by formula (4.2) from 0 to some horizon T:

$$P(0) = E\int_0^T B(t)\left[c(t) + \lambda(t)\right]exp\left[-\int_0^t R(\tau)\,d\tau\right]dt + E\left\{P(T)B(T)exp\left[-\int_0^T R(\tau)\,d\tau\right]\right\}$$

Now, balance $B(t)$ follows an ordinary differential equation: $dB = -\lambda B dt$, which, assuming the starting balance of $B(0) = \$1$, is solved like an amortizing money-market account: $B(t) = exp\left[-\int_0^t \lambda(\tau)d\tau \right]$. Therefore,

$$P(0) = E\int_0^T [c(t) + \lambda(t)]e^{y(t)}dt + E[P(T)e^{y(T)}] \qquad (4.4)$$

where $y(t)$ denotes the natural logarithm of an artificial discount factor arising in our formulas

$$dy = -(R + \lambda)dt$$

Integrating by parts, we can establish the following useful identity

$$\int_0^T [R(t) + \lambda(t)]e^{y(t)}dt \equiv 1 - e^{y(T)}$$

Therefore, price discount $p \equiv P - 1$ will be presented as

$$p(0) = E\int_0^T [c(t) - R(t)]e^{y(t)}dt + E[p(T)e^{y(T)}] \qquad (4.4p)$$

The obtained result states that the premium (discount) of an MBS consists of two components. The first one sums up the differentials between the paid rate and the expected rate of return (the discount rate). These differentials are discounted at an artificial rate, which is equal to the sum of the actual discount rate R and the rate of balance amortization λ. The second component is the expected terminal premium value (if any) also discounted at the abovementioned artificial rate. If we transform the economy, having shifted all interest rates (c and R) by a time-varying, generally random rate of amortization $\lambda(t)$, formula (4.4) will be reduced to a constant-balance, bullet-bond, asset-pricing formula.

A choice of the time horizon T is determined by the nature of the asset and the desired computational set-up. For normally maturing assets, T can be the MBS maturity, thereby eliminating the terminal value. On the other hand, for a balloon MBS, one may prefer to keep the terminal value in order to avoid using infinite $\lambda(T)$ when balance "pops."

In one special case, when $c(t) = R(t)$, the instrument will be valued at par, regardless of its amortization. Such an instrument is called a *perfect floater*. Formula (4.4) can be easily extended to more general cases we find important in the mortgage industry. If MBS is not paying its full principal—whether by design (interest-only strip or IO introduced in chapter 2) or because of a principal loss—one can adjust the derivations to prove that

$$p(0)=E\int_0^T[c(t)-d(t)-R(t)]e^{y(t)}dt+E[p(T)e^{y(T)}]\qquad(4.4d)$$

where $d(t)$ denotes the principal loss (or non-payment) rate. For example, a bond will still be valued at par, regardless of the interest rates and amortization, if it pays a floater, $c=R+m$, indexed to the selected discount rate R with the margin $m(t)$ exactly equal to the expected loss rate $d(t)$. This was the case with most ABS deals at origination.

Another special case is an agency IO. It pays interest, but not principal:

$$P(0)=E\int_0^T c(t)e^{y(t)}dt+E[P(T)e^{y(T)}]\qquad(4.4io)$$

PARTIAL DIFFERENTIAL EQUATION FOR MBS PRICE

The family of formulas (4.4) expresses the price of an MBS via mathematical expectation. There is an important dual representation involving a partial differential equation (PDE). We illustrate this concept assuming that the MBS market is disturbed by a single risk factor $x(t)$. We treat it as a continuous random process (*diffusion*) having a (generally, variable) *drift rate* μ and *volatility* σ, and being disturbed by a standard Brownian motion $z(t)$, that is,

$$dx=\mu dt+\sigma dz\qquad(4.5)$$

The MBS price P is viewed now as a function of time and factor, i.e. $P(t,x)$. The Ito's Lemma claims that $P(t,x)$ follows a stochastic differential equation

$$dP=\left(\frac{\partial P}{\partial t}+\mu\frac{\partial P}{\partial x}+\frac{1}{2}\sigma^2\frac{\partial^2 P}{\partial x^2}\right)dt+\sigma\frac{\partial P}{\partial x}dz\qquad(4.6)$$

Let us collect mathematically all the terms contributing to MBS's expected return over an infinitesimal horizon. We continue using notations from the previous section, B for balance, λ for amortization, c for coupon rate. The total value of MBS is $V=PB$. Note that, unlike price P, balance B does not immediately depend on factor x. The expectation over time of the differential of value V is

$$E(dV) = E\left[d(BP)\right] = E\left[BdP + PdB\right] = B\left(\frac{\partial P}{\partial t} + \mu\frac{\partial P}{\partial x} + \frac{1}{2}\sigma^2\frac{\partial^2 P}{\partial x^2}\right)dt - P\lambda Bdt$$

$$(4.7)$$

Note that when deriving (4.7), we substituted the expression (4.6) for dP and dropped the last term as $E(dz) = 0$. The investment will also accrue interest cash flow $(cBdt)$ and principal cash flow (λBdt)—assuming the latter is paid. Adding these two terms to $E(dV)$ defined in (4.7) and dividing by the investment value $V = PB$ and the infinitesimal time increment dt, we obtain the total expected annualized return:

$$Expected\ Rate\ of\ Return = \frac{1}{P}\left(\frac{\partial P}{\partial t} + \mu\frac{\partial P}{\partial x} + \frac{1}{2}\sigma^2\frac{\partial^2 P}{\partial x^2} + c + \lambda\right) - \lambda$$

On the other hand, this should be equal to R, the appropriate rate-of-return expectation target for MBS, yet to be determined. This gives us the following linear partial differential equation followed by the unknown price function $P(t, x)$ in the space of two variables, time t and the market factor x:

$$\frac{\partial P}{\partial t} + \mu\frac{\partial P}{\partial x} + \frac{1}{2}\sigma^2\frac{\partial^2 P}{\partial x^2} + c + \lambda - \lambda P = RP \qquad (4.8)$$

An alternative derivation of this PDE that cites the Feynman-Kac theorem can be found in Levin (1998), but the PDE itself goes back, at least, to Fabozzi and Fong (1994). A notable feature of the above written PDE is that it does not contain the balance variable, B. The entire effect of possibly random prepayments is represented by the amortization rate function, $\lambda(t, x)$. Although the total cash flow observed for each accrual period does depend on the beginning-period balance, solving the PDE will require knowledge of $\lambda(t, x)$, not the balance. This observation agrees with a trivial practical rule stating that the trade price is generally independent of the face value of the investment.

For a principal-loss case or an IO, PDE (4.8) should be modified accordingly to exclude part or full principal payment rate (λ), but not the balance amortization rate:

$$\frac{\partial P}{\partial t} + \mu\frac{\partial P}{\partial x} + \frac{1}{2}\sigma^2\frac{\partial^2 P}{\partial x^2} + c - d + \lambda - \lambda P = RP \qquad (4.8d)$$

$$\frac{\partial P}{\partial t} + \mu\frac{\partial P}{\partial x} + \frac{1}{2}\sigma^2\frac{\partial^2 P}{\partial x^2} + c - \lambda P = RP \qquad (4.8io)$$

where, as before, d denotes the loss rate.

Any PDE has to be complemented by a suitable set of terminal and boundary conditions. For example, if we know that the terminal balance, if any, will be paid at maturity, then $P(T,*)=1$. For an IO, $P(T,*)=0$ will be the appropriate terminal condition. As for the boundary conditions for PDE (4.8), they cannot be established easily from the definition of mortgage instruments. Most likely, an MBS will have a "saturated" reaction to a very high or a very low level of factor x. We will discuss these conditions further in chapter 8.

Much like in the previous section, it is apparent that the total amortization rate λ enters valuation PDE (4.8) as an add-on to other rates, the coupon rate c and the return rate's expectation R. The amortization rate λ may depend on factor x, time t, and even price P itself. The latter case is particularly interesting and unusual and will be discussed in chapter 8. Expressing prepayment speed as an S-like function of a pool's value may present a universal and robust prepayment model. If c, R, d and λ depend on information available at time t, the problem is termed *path-independent*. One can find and apply available algorithms to solve the PDE working backwards, starting from maturity T.

Often, rate $\lambda(t)$ depends on the entire history of factor $x(\tau)$, $\tau \leq t$. This is a *path-dependent* case that makes PDE (4.8) difficult to solve. Normally, a path-dependent problem can be translated into a path-independent one by increasing the number of factors or *state variables*. The APD form of the prepayment model introduced in chapter 1 (and discussed in more detail in chapter 7) offers a more elegant, structural way to cope with path-dependence. Instead of attempting to increase the dimensionality of the MBS valuation problem, we postulate that an MBS pool consists of two path-independent groups. Hence, we simply need to solve PDE (4.8) for each of the two groups and add up the prices computed at $t=0$.

PDE (4.8) can be modified and generalized for the cases when factor $x(t)$ is neither a diffusion nor a scalar. For example, if $x(t)$ is a vector of continuous random factors, the underlying dynamics will be described by a system of stochastic differential equations that can be written in a compact vector-matrix form:

$$dx = \mu dt + Bdz \qquad (4.5v)$$

where x, μ, z are now vectors, and B is a matrix. The vector of Browning motions' increments dz is assumed to have the variance-covariance matrix Qdt. Then, PDE (4.8) is modified as

$$\frac{\partial P}{\partial t} + \frac{\partial P}{\partial x}\mu + \frac{1}{2}tr\left[BQB^T \frac{\partial^2 P}{\partial x^2}\right] + c + \lambda - \lambda P = RP \qquad (4.8v)$$

where the *trace* operator (tr) is the sum of matrix's diagonal elements.

Note that the MBS-specific terms defined by coupon rate c and amortization rate λ remain unaffected. What changed is the so-called *PDE operator* that combines the derivatives of the price taken with respect to time and factor.

INTRODUCTION TO THE OPTION-ADJUSTED SPREAD (OAS) METHOD

While there are more rigorous methods of determining the MBS return expectation R, it has become particularly popular to view R as the sum of the risk-free rate r and so-called *option-adjusted spread* (OAS): $R = r + OAS$. The OAS can be viewed as an additional return compensating for risks not fully reflected by the dynamics of modeled risk factor or factors.

The popularity of this view stems from several useful facts. First, the method is simple to implement and the result is easy to interpret. If MBS's market price $P[0, x(0)]$ is known today, we can solve for OAS using either PDE (4.8)

$$\frac{\partial P}{\partial t} + \mu \frac{\partial P}{\partial x} + \frac{1}{2}\sigma^2 \frac{\partial^2 P}{\partial x^2} + c + \lambda - \lambda P = (r + OAS)P \qquad (4.8\text{oas})$$

or the integral (4.4). If the OAS is known, we can find price.

Second, there are always pricing factors that are difficult to include accurately (e.g. liquidity). Hence, allowing an OAS term to be added to the otherwise well-known risk-free rate becomes a practical necessity. Third, the MBS market is not a perfect market and may misprice instruments. Traders would be very interested to know which of two available instruments is "cheaper." Because the instruments may differ in type and design rules, the direct price comparison is rarely useful. Finding each asset's OAS is the critical step allowing to compare two expected returns; a larger ("wider") OAS would point to a cheaper asset.

Finally, the OAS method is frequently employed to measure sensitivity to various pricing factors ranging from interest rates to prepay (or default) modeling parameters. The questionable assumption behind this common practice is that the OAS, being a compensation for un-modeled risk or mispriced risk, will not change if the market conditions get stressed.

The OAS method has a danger of masking risky returns. A wide spread "promised" by an instrument may arise due to anticipated cash flow losses not included by the model. Or can they arise from an exposure to uncertainties (like housing turnover and/or refinancing abilities) that the analyst fails to assess. For example, a large OAS of 1,000 bps for a non-agency MBS computed without a loss model is not very convincing evidence of cheapness and should not be used for investment decision. Similarly, the fact that agency interest-only strips (IOs) are priced wider than principal-only strips (POs) suggests that there may be a systematic risk not included in the OAS model. Parts 2 and 3 of the book focus on these types of risks and their models.

Within portfolios, a weighted OAS can be computed, but this exposes another potential issue with the method. Let us have two MBS priced at differing OAS levels and each subjected to PDEs (4.8oas) and create a portfolio combining w_1 shares of MBS_1 and w_2 shares of MBS_2, $P = w_1 P_1 + w_2 P_2$, assuming $w_1 + w_2 = 1$. One can combine PDEs (4.8oas) to see that the portfolio's value satisfies PDE (4.8oas) with weighted characteristics:

$$c = w_1 c_1 + w_2 c_2, \quad \lambda = \frac{w_1 \lambda_1 (1 - P_1) + w_2 \lambda_2 (1 - P_2)}{1 - P}, \quad OAS = \frac{w_1 OAS_1 P_1 + w_2 OAS_2 P_2}{P}$$

From the last formula, we see that if both MBS were priced at an identical *OAS*, the portfolio's *OAS* would be the same and would not depend on prices. For the $OAS_1 \neq OAS_2$ case, portfolio's *OAS* depends on the market share of each of two positions, which follows $P_1(t,x)$ and $P_2(t,x)$ changing in time and space. Although this is a trivial observation, it reveals some troubles in using the OAS method for portfolios, synthetic MBS, or for sensitivity analysis. For example, if the market conditions change (e.g., interest-rates move), positions' prices, hence shares, move too. This may also happen with a simple passage of time. Therefore, if the assumption of OAS constancy holds for MBS_1 and MBS_2, it will generally not hold for their portfolio. In some cases, "portfolio" can be just another MBS. For example, an MBS pool can be synthetically stripped into an interest-only strip (IO) and a principal-only strip (PO). Using differing OAS levels for the three instruments may lead to troubles many practitioners do not anticipate. We illustrate this in an example at the end of chapter 10.

EXPECTED RETURN WHEN BEARING RISK

The capital asset pricing model (CAPM) and the arbitrage pricing theory (APT) provide fundamental statements about the structure of expected investment return for risky assets. Let us start with the simplest, but important, case when there is one common risk factor in the economy. We will show that the expected return for all assets exposed to that risk factor is equal to the sum of the risk-free rate and *risky return*, which is proportional to the asset's volatility (arising due to the factor); the coefficient of this proportionality is called *price of risk*.

We will provide and analyze two proofs of this proposition. The first one called *the arbitrage argument* requires a short position (hedge) to exist. The second one is free of this restriction.

THE ARBITRAGE ARGUMENT (ASSET AND HEDGE)

Let us assume that there exist two non-dividend paying assets, random values of which (A_1, A_2) depend on the evolution of a common risk factor associated with a Brownian motion $z(t)$:

$$dA_1 = \mu_1 A_1 dt + \sigma_1 A_1 dz$$

$$dA_2 = \mu_2 A_2 dt + \sigma_2 A_2 dz$$

(4.9)

In this system, Mus are expected returns (drifts) of the assets, Sigmas are their relative volatilities. Let us further assume that we are free to combine these assets with any weights, including negative ones, that is, a short (hedge) position is permissible. Let us combine w_1 shares of the first asset and w_2 shares of the second. Portfolio's value $P = w_1 A_1 + w_2 A_2$ is subject to the following stochastic differential equation:

$$dP = w_1 \mu_1 dA_1 + w_2 \mu_2 dA_2 = (w_1 \mu_1 A_1 + w_2 \mu_2 A_2)dt + (w_1 \sigma_1 A_1 + w_2 \sigma_2 A_2)dz$$

(4.10)

Let us choose w_1 and w_2 so that $w_2 = -w_1 \sigma_1 A_1 / \sigma_2 A_2$ thereby eliminating the diffusion term in (4.10). Since values and volatility coefficients are positive, this assumes a long position in one asset and a short position in the other. Portfolio's value will now become $P = w_1 A_1 (1 - \sigma_1 / \sigma_2)$ and differential equation (4.10) will become

$$dP = w_1 A_1 \left(\mu_1 - \mu_2 \frac{\sigma_1}{\sigma_2} \right) dt = \frac{\mu_1 \sigma_2 - \mu_2 \sigma_1}{\sigma_2 - \sigma_1} Pdt$$

Now we see that the portfolio is riskless (over an infinitesimal horizon), hence, its expected return (drift rate) must be equal to the risk-free rate r: $(\mu_1 \sigma_2 - \mu_2 \sigma_1)/(\sigma_2 - \sigma_1) = r$. Re-arranging, we get

$$\frac{\mu_1 - r}{\sigma_1} = \frac{\mu_2 - r}{\sigma_2} \equiv \pi$$

(4.11)

Therefore, the expected excess return over the risk-free rate computed per unit of volatility must be identical for both (and all other) assets that are exposed to the common risk factor. This measure is denoted π and called *price of risk*; for any asset, $\mu = r + \pi\sigma$.

THE ALTERNATIVE INVESTMENT ARGUMENT

Let us consider a money-market account M and a risky asset A exposed to a risk factor $z(t)$:

$$dA = \mu A dt + \sigma A dz$$

$$dM = rM dt$$

Let us combine w shares of the asset and one share of cash to create portfolio $P = wA + M$ and compute its differential:

$$dP = wdA + dM = (w\mu A + rM)dt + w\sigma A dz \equiv \mu_p P dt + \sigma_p P dz$$

where portfolio's expected return and volatility are

$$\mu_p = (w\mu A + rM)/(wA + M)$$

$$\sigma_p = w\sigma A/(wA + M)$$

Excluding M we can link μ_p and σ_p as

$$\mu_p = \frac{w\mu A + rwA\sigma/\sigma_p - wrA}{wA\sigma/\sigma_p} = r + \frac{\mu - r}{\sigma}\sigma_p \equiv r + \pi\sigma_p$$

Note that the price of risk $\pi = (\mu - r)/\sigma$ depends only on parameters μ and σ of asset A and not on a portfolio's composition. We have proven that any combination of the risky asset and money-market account results in another risky asset, the expected return of which exceeds the risk-free rate by $\pi\sigma_p$. We did not have to use a short position.

The two proofs given in this section represent two financial points of views. The arbitrage argument requires a hedge instrument to exist. Speaking practically, if some asset was mispriced so that it was expected to return more than what the theory requires, we would combine this asset with its hedge to create a risk-free portfolio surely yielding more that the risk-free rate. If an asset was expected to return less than it should, we would use this asset as the hedge. The alternative investment argument shows that the existence of a hedge is not required for the expected return to be in the form the theory states, or for taking advantage of an asset mispricing. If an asset promises a higher return per unit of risk than other assets, investors will favor it. If it promises a lower return, investors will ignore it and instead combine a higher yielding asset with a money-market account, thereby achieving same level of risk σ_p, but a higher return expectation μ_p. Such an investor's behavior will increase or decrease the demand for the mispriced asset and likely cause a price correction.

GENERALIZATIONS

In the preceding discussion we provided the theoretical result assuming that assets pay no dividends and are exposed to a single common risk factor. If assets are paying dividends, the derivations remain valid, but we should simply subtract the known dividend rate from the risk-free rate. This is a very useful fact because MBS pay both principal and interest. The MBS dividend rate is not merely the coupon paid, but also the premium or discount that amortizes due to the principal pay-down.

Let us now assume that, in addition to the common factor, each asset depends on an idiosyncratic factor, i.e. a factor that influences only that i-th asset:

$$dA_i = \mu A_i dt + \sigma A_i dz + \sigma_i A_i dz_i \qquad (4.9\text{i})$$

where Brownian motion z_i is independent of the common driver z and all $z_k, k \neq i$. Without a loss of generality, let us assume that there are many assets that follow equation (4.9i) with common μ and σ and their values are scaled to identical level so that $A_1 = A_2 = \cdots = A_N \equiv A$ right now. In essence, A can be interpreted as a value of equally weighted portfolio of assets, $A = \dfrac{1}{N}\sum A_i$ that follows differential equation similar to (4.9i):

$$dA = \mu A dt + \sigma A dz + \frac{1}{N}\sum \sigma_i A_i dz_i \equiv \mu A dt + \sigma A dz + \tilde{\sigma} A d\tilde{z} \qquad (4.9\text{p})$$

where $\tilde{\sigma}^2 = \sum \sigma_i^2 / N^2$ and $\tilde{z}$ is just another Brownian motion. This large portfolio equation (4.9p) is nearly identical to the single asset version (4.9i) except the last term has volatility vanishing at a $O(1/\sqrt{N})$ rate. Therefore, combining a large number of similar assets we reduce ("diversify") idiosyncratic risk. It needs not be priced by the market nor taken by investors. In fact, we arrived at the famous CAPM result.

Our derivations can be extended to the case of multiple *systematic* risks, each having its own price; this result constitutes the essence of APT.

A RISK-NEUTRAL TRANSFORMATION OF THE VALUATION PROBLEM

By now, we have learned what the expected rate of return R should be. In the presence of risk factor x that follows stochastic equation (4.5), the relative volatility of price caused by that factor is going to be equal to the product of volatility σ of x and the partial logarithmic derivative of $P(t,x)$ taken with respect to x. Therefore, $R = r + \pi\sigma(\partial P / \partial x)/P$ and, substituting this expression into PDE (4.8), we will have

$$\frac{\partial P}{\partial t} + (\mu - \pi\sigma)\frac{\partial P}{\partial x} + \frac{1}{2}\sigma^2\frac{\partial^2 P}{\partial x^2} + c + \lambda - \lambda P = rP \tag{4.12}$$

This equation is visually similar to (4.8) except for the drift rate now being $\mu - \pi\sigma$ instead of μ and the expected return R becoming the risk-free rate r. Let us alter the underlying process (4.5):

$$dx = \mu' dt + \sigma dz \quad \text{where} \quad \mu' = \mu - \pi\sigma \tag{4.5rn}$$

If we use (4.5rn) instead of (4.5), the PDE (4.8) derived for the risky asset (an MBS) becomes identical to PDE (4.12) where the expected rate of return is set to be the risk-free rate r:

$$\frac{\partial P}{\partial t} + \mu'\frac{\partial P}{\partial x} + \frac{1}{2}\sigma^2\frac{\partial^2 P}{\partial x^2} + c + \lambda - \lambda P = rP \tag{4.8rn}$$

We have proven a very important fact: If we transform the dynamics of our risk factor $x(t)$ by shifting its drift term by $-\pi\sigma$, this transformation will produce the risky return required by the CAPM. Using the altered process for $x(t)$ results in a pricing PDE, in which the expected rate of return is set to the risk-free rate. This PDE will not carry a price of risk anymore—the entire role of risk and its valuation implication is reflected in the transformation of the dynamics of $x(t)$ called a *risk-neutral transformation*.

In order to illustrate risk-neutral modeling in simple practical terms, let us assume that $\pi > 0$ and $\partial P / \partial x > 0$ so that investors will lose value if factor x goes down. Naturally, they want to be compensated for bearing that risk. The risk-neutral transformation $\mu' = \mu - \pi\sigma$ will move the risk factor x toward the adverse direction (down). Only after this adjustment is made will the investors be seeking to earn the risk-free rate. The price of risk π is defined relatively to factor x. It depends on the "feared direction" of market moves and can be positive or negative. For example, if we change the sign of our risk factor x, we effectively change the sign of π. Different risk factors can have different prices of risk—even if they cause same volatility of asset's price.

An explicit separation of the drift term into μ and $\pi\sigma$ may not always be practical and necessary. Often, we are given the information that is necessary and sufficient to derive the risk-neutral drift μ', but not each component separately. For example, the knowledge of a forward curve is critical to obtaining the resultant risk-neutral drift in an interest-rate model (chapters 5 and 6). On the other hand, an empirically robust prepayment model may be valuable in both its subjective form (chapter 7) and a risk-neutralized form (linked to market prices); see further in chapter 11.

VALUATION WITH A RISKY PARAMETER

Instead of treating risk factors as continuously changing variables ("processes"), we can conceive of them as uncertain parameters. This means that our risk factor x will not change over time—it is an unknown constant drawn once from some distribution. In fact, we find this interpretation of risk factors to be rather common when dealing with model risk, that is, with situations when some modeling parameters (scales, slides, etc.) are determined from historical experience and not surely known even at time $t=0$.

Let us assume that volatility σ is time-dependent and not constant, namely, its square is proportional to the Dirac function, $\sigma^2(t) \propto \delta(0)$. This means that volatility is zero for any $t>0$ and infinite when $t=0$. The integral of $\int_0^t \sigma^2(\tau)d\tau$ over any internal $(0,t)$ is finite, constant, and equal to the variance of random parameter x; Let us denote it σ^2, without parenthesis.

A continuous random process, with a Dirac-like variance $\sigma^2(t)=\sigma^2\delta(0)$ and without a drift is equivalent to a random parameter drawn from a normal distribution of a zero mean and a σ^2 variance. In order to build a clean mathematical bridge between continuous risk and parameter risk, let us consider a family of processes (defined by parameter a that we are going to push to infinity),

$$dx = \sigma_a^2(t)dz \quad \text{where} \quad \sigma_a^2(t) = ae^{-at}\sigma^2 \tag{4.13}$$

The Dirac function can be viewed a limiting case of ae^{-at}. Indeed, for any $t>0$ and $a \to \infty$:

a. This function approaches zero.
b. The integral of ae^{-at} taken over internal $(0,t)$ is equal to $1-e^{-at} \to 1$.

The stochastic differential equation (4.13) is a special case of diffusion (4.5), but its solution converges to a random constant when $a \to \infty$. Let us apply the risk-neutral transformation to "process" (4.13) and use a price of risk in the form dependent on parameter: $\pi_a = \frac{1}{2}\pi\sqrt{a}$. The risk-neutral version of (4.13) will then become

$$dx = -\pi_a \sigma_a(t)dt + \sigma_a^2(t)dz \qquad (4.13\text{rn})$$

The solution to this equation is

$$x = -\frac{1}{2}\pi\sqrt{a}\int_0^t \sigma\sqrt{ae^{-a\tau}}\,d\tau + \int_0^t \sigma_a^2(\tau)\,dz(\tau) = -\pi\sigma\left(1 - e^{-0.5at}\right) + \int_0^t \sigma_a^2(\tau)\,dz(\tau)$$

$$(4.14)$$

When $a \to \infty$, the first term converges to $-\pi\sigma$ for any $t > 0$. The second term is the source of randomness with the same zero mean and the same σ^2 constant variance as for the solution of the initial equation (4.13). Therefore, when dealing with a risky, normally distributed parameter, the risk-neutral transformation is a simple shift of expected value.

As a comment to our line of proof, the seemingly frivolous selection of the functional dependence of the price of risk on parameters a ($\pi_a \propto \sqrt{a}$) is the only feasible choice. Any other would lead to either zero or an infinite risk-neutral term as $a \to \infty$; none of them would make financial sense. Also, the assumption of normality for x is not a severe constraint. In most cases, risk factors are either normally distributed themselves or functions of normally distributed variables. Hence, if $x = f(y)$ where y is normally distributed parameter, we can first view y as the risky factor, apply our result, and conclude that the risk-neutral transformation of x is dictated by the shift in the mean value of y. To the extent of function $f(y)$ being nonlinear, this shift may change both expectation and variance of x.

Having learnt how to deal with both risky parameters and risky continuous processes, we can find a risk-neutral transformation for the hybrid case when a process $x(t)$ is a source of continuous financial risk with an uncertain initial condition x_0. In this case, the risk-neutral transformation implies shifts both in the initial condition and in the drift term.

THE CAPITAL CHARGE METHOD

A unique risk-neutral transformation may exist if there is a market that lets us gauge the price of risk. One can imagine a different case when neither hedging nor alternative investment is accessible. Consider, for example, a mortgage insurance (MI) company or a GSE that guarantees residential loans. Both are chartered with providing protection against possible losses. One can derive an idea how credit risk is priced in non-agency MBS structures, as we demonstrate later in the book (Part 3). However, even if taking a long position in MBS credit were more profitable, an MI company or a GSE would not be able to change its charter. In addition, the amount of credit risk these giant organizations carry can be well beyond the size of existing credit derivatives market. The loan insurance business represents an example (not uncommon) of an inability to apply arguments we utilized to derive the expectation of return, as neither hedge nor alternative investment may be feasible. In such a case, we may consider the following *capital charge* argument. It leads to a well-defined, possibly excessive, risk adjustment.

A Single-Period Model

In order to quantify the risk-adjusted pricing and link it to financial rationale, let us review a position of loan insurer (limited insurance coverage) or GSE (unlimited insurance). In either case, a business would need to charge a premium (p) to make it profitable. Without doubt, the insurer must charge more than the expectation of losses (μ) in the real world. By definition, insurance provides protection against worse-than-average loss l_{max}, so capital (c) must be maintained to back the obligation. This capital must stand ready; we assume it earns the risk-free rate[1] (r), which is normally much lower than a return on capital target (R). Let us assume that the capital is allocated and the premium is collected at the beginning of the insurance's term whereas claims are paid at its end.

The expected total return will reflect ($+$) risk-free return on capital, ($+$) guarantee fee and risk-free return on it, and ($-$) expected claim μ

$$1+R=\frac{(c+p)(1+r)-\mu}{c}=1+r+\frac{p(1+r)-\mu}{c} \tag{4.15}$$

under the constraint that the capital plus the premium account is large enough to cover maximal loss

$$(c+p)(1+r)\geq l_{max} \tag{4.16}$$

From (4.15), the insurer is interested in achieving the highest return R by charging $p \geq \mu/(1+r)$ and minimizing the capital c. From (4.16), the minimal

---

[1] We assume that our model is risk-neutral with respect all factors other than credit risk. If not, rate r may include prices of other risks.

level of required capital is $c_{min} = l_{max} / (1+r) - p$. Substituting this minimal capital into (4.15) we find p:

$$p(1+r) = \mu + (l_{max} - \mu)\frac{R-r}{1+R} \equiv \mu + c_{min}(R-r) \qquad (4.17)$$

with

$$c_{min} = \frac{l_{max} - \mu}{1+R} \qquad (4.18)$$

(if $l_{max} = \mu$, no capital is required; if $R = r$, capital is required, but costs nothing).

Formula (4.17) gives us the insurance premium that minimizes insurer's capital given risk-free rate r, return target R, insurance limit l_{max}, and the expected loss μ. The result is stated in the form of "expected loss plus capital charge." The annualized p is known as "guarantee fee," "insurance premium," or "CDS rate."

Example of input values: $\mu = 5$ bps/yr, $l_{max} = 30$ bps/yr, $R = 25\%$, $r = 5\%$.

Outputs: $c = 24$ bps/yr, and the premium $p = 9$ bps/yr, 4 bps/yr of which is the capital charge.

Some observations follow immediately:

A. Capital is proportional to $l_{max} - \mu$, the insurance coverage, and independent of r. Insurance premium p is linear in $l_{max} - \mu$.
B. If the desired return rate R grows, capital is initially affected marginally. The insurance premium p is almost linear in R. However, when R goes to infinity, required capital vanishes and insurance fee converges to $l_{max} / (1+r)$, i.e. completely covers worst losses (discounted at the risk-free rate) by itself.
C. If we present the unexpected loss as a scale of loss' volatility, i.e. $l_{max} - \mu \equiv k\sigma$, then the price of a unit of risk will be $\pi = k(R-r)/(1+R)(1+r)$. Price of risk depends on the risk-free rate, return target, and insurance confidence. The latter may differentiate various insurance policies.

Formulas of this method require knowledge of market participants' views of expected loss. These formulas may be necessary to find economic value of unique financial instruments when it is hard to find an established benchmark market that would allow one to rely on the arbitrage argument or the alternative investment argument.

How does this economic reasoning relate to risk-adjusted pricing? A mortgage insurance business assesses the premium it offers by plugging required assumptions into formula (4.17). This represents a risk-adjusted *subjective* expectation of losses, in present dollars. Eventually, market players taking long position (insurance company) and short position (borrowers) agree on some premium p. This forms the *objective* risk-adjusted expectation of losses. The losses on loans guaranteed by insurance companies can be viewed as an "underlying" instrument, which can be used, in principle, to value other credit-sensitive instruments ("derivatives").

The concept of capital charge can be extended to a general purpose MBS investor that has no specific liability limit. It can define l_{max} as the worst loss given some probabilistic confidence $1-\alpha$ (e.g. 95% with $\alpha = 5\%$). In such case, the minimal capital will insure solvency with a $1-\alpha$ confidence. One can also consider outcomes in the worst α-percent cases and average them out. This measure is known as *Expected Shortfall*: $l_{ES} = (1/\alpha) \int_{1-\alpha}^{1} loss(F) * dF$ where F stands for cumulative probability. Then the one-period price of credit loss ("premium") and the minimal capital will be computed as

$$p(1+r) = \mu + (l_{ES} - \mu)\frac{R-r}{1+R}$$

$$c_{min} = \frac{l_{ES} - \mu}{1+R}$$

Note that $l_{ES} \geq l_{max}$ always so both p and c_{min} are larger when using l_{ES} than l_{max}. The Expected Shortfall measure allows for a practically useful financial interpretation. As in all cases, the expected return on equity is set equal to R; the expected return on equity *conditional on being in the worst scenarios* is negative 100%, i.e. a full loss of capital, but not more.

A Multi-Period Model

In the previous section, we demonstrated a single-period financial rationale for finding a risk-adjusted insurance premium and, more generally, a subjective risk-adjusted loss expectation. An extension of this logic to the multi-period case is not trivial but results can be produced using simplifying assumptions. The main challenge is an unknown per-period loss allowance l_{max} (or l_{ES}) that enters the formulas. Most insurance contracts do not state periodic coverage limits, but rather limit lifetime loss or shortfall. Adequate capital needs to be raised at the inception of the business. Although this problem generally requires complex simulations of economic scenarios, a key simplifying assumption introduced further in the section will allow us to extend the single-period model and obtain closed-end solution for the premium rate and the capital.

To facilitate derivations, let us introduce the following convenient notations Let $PO(R)=E\int_0^T \lambda e^{y(t,R)}\,dt$ denote the expected present value of a principal-only strip discounted at the rate R that enters the cumulative deflation factor y introduced at the beginning of this chapter. As before, amortization rate λ includes both voluntary and involuntary terminations. Let $IOM(R)=E\int_0^T e^{y(t,R)}\,dt$ denote "IO Multiple," that is the value of 1% interest-only strip, $IOF(x,R)=E\int_0^T x(t)e^{y(t,R)}\,dt$ be the value of an interest-only floater paying at the rate of $x(t)$, and $L(R)=E\int_0^T l(t)e^{y(t,R)}\,dt$ be the expected present value of losses (where $l(t)$ is an instantaneous loss rate), all discounted at the rate of R.

Let us start with a single-payer insurance assuming that the lone payment P is made at time zero. We will put it into an "account" A that earns the risk-free rate. We will release $(\lambda + r)A$ continuously from this account (with λ being the pool's amortization rate):

$$dA = -\lambda A dt$$

Hence,

$$A(t)=P*exp\left\{-\int_0^t \lambda(\tau)d\tau\right\}$$

with cash flow stream being $[r(t)+\lambda(t)]A(t)$. Now that cash flow stream discounted at the (generally, time-dependent) equity rate $R(t)$ has an expected present value of

$$PV(R)=E\int_0^\infty [r(t)+\lambda(t)]A(t)exp\left\{-\int_0^t R(\tau)d\tau\right\}dt$$
$$= PE\int_0^\infty [r(t)+\lambda(t)]exp\left\{\int_0^t-[R(\tau)+\lambda(\tau)]d\tau\right\}dt$$
$$\equiv P[IOF(r,R)+PO(R)]$$
$$= P[IOF(r,R)+1-IOF(R,R)]=P[1-IOF(R-r,R)]$$

Assuming that the risky ROE rate, $R-r\equiv\tilde{R}$, is a constant, $IOF(R-r,R)\equiv\tilde{R}*IOM(R)$.

Similarly, we assume that the capital will be invested in the risk-free account and released at the same rate $\lambda(t)$. All three components of the cash flow, the capital release, the premium release and losses L, make up the net return to capital. Discounted at the equity rate, their sum should be equal to the amount of capital:

$$c=(c+P)[1-\tilde{R}*IOM(R)]+L(R) \qquad (4.19)$$

Let us now establish the minimal capital condition. Let us demand that the expected shortfall L_{ES} (discounted at short rate) be equal to c plus P. Indeed the PV of cash flow stream generated by account A and discounted at the risk-free rate r is equal to $PV(r) = P$. Hence,

$$c = L_{ES}(r) - P \qquad (4.20)$$

Excluding capital c from (4.19) and (4.20) we solve for P:

$$P = L_{ES}(r)\tilde{R} * IOM(R) + L(R) \qquad (4.21)$$

In these derivations, the account release rate was assumed to be equal to the pool amortization rate λ. This is the most important simplifying assumption that allows us to derive a closed-form solution. A more accurate, but much more complex, approach would be to first compute $L_{ES}(r)$ as a function of time and market factors, then match this function with the insurer's account. It is feasible with a low-dimensional factor space, but a typical credit analysis involves home prices, interest rates, and loan statuses as multiple state factors. The assumption about how insurer or guarantor will release the c-plus-P account evades the numerical challenge and leads to a statement that the account stays proportional to pool's balance. We will quantify the role of this assumption further in this section.

We now switch to the periodically collected payments case and claim that an equivalent annual premium rate should be equal to $p = P/IOM(r)$ because we can always trade an IO priced at P. This choice will make the initial value of protection position equal to zero. In general, to value a legacy position that collects periodic premium p, we need to replace P with $P + p * IOM(r)$ in formulas (4.19) through (4.21). Any part of the single payment P can be viewed as a value of an IO plus the market value of position.

If losses are deterministic, one cannot earn $R > r$ in a competitive market and the IOF factor becomes zero. Given the certainty of losses, the protection seller should be able to borrow at a risk-free rate r against the mismatching streams of incomes and losses and avoid holding capital. This argument helps us interpret formulas (4.19) to (4.21) in special cases and split insurance premium into loss expectation and capital charge. The loss expectation term is simply $P_0 = L(r)$. This is how much insurance premium would be with a complete certainty of losses. Then, the capital-charge component would be the difference between the full premium and P_0:

$$\text{Capital charge} = P - P_0 = L_{ES}(r)\tilde{R} * IOM(R) + L(R) - L(r)$$

Given all else even, each unit of loss uncertainty reflected in the expected shortfall term adds $\tilde{R} * IOM(R)$ units to capital charge, hence, premium. This makes clearer the role of our key simplifying assumption concerning the release of the insurer account $A(t)$. If it has to be released at a rate that differs from pool's amortization speed λ, this will simply alter the IOM value entering all the formulas. For example, if the account $A(t)$ has a slower amortization rate, that is a longer average life, the IOM value will rise, making the single-premium payment larger and capital required lower. Since this capital decrease will not alter return on equity R (a fixed input to the model), the insurance product will become more expensive and less competitive. The opposite happens if the loss structure and its timing permits a quicker release of account $A(t)$; this is in the interest of both protection sellers and buyers.

The Paradox of the Capital-Charge Method

The main paradox arising in a review of valuation via cost-of-capital is that the price of an instrument is independent of a holding period, whereas required capital should be commensurate with it. In the application of the method's formulas, a smaller capital is required for a short-term holding (e.g. trading account) than for holding until maturity (e.g. insurance contact), yet, according to CAPM and APT, the market value of an instrument should not depend who invests and for how long. The difference is particularly clear from the single-period model analysis when we consider holding period t a vanishing parameter. The risk, hence capital, will vanish at a $\sqrt{t}$ rate, thereby making the capital charge *rate* infinitesimal. In contrast, CAPM and APT lead to a finite risky *rate* of return, no matter the investment horizon.

Understanding the differences in assumptions between these two approaches can provide insight. CAPM/APT assumes that the asset can be traded continuously and its price is discovered by a market. In the presence of active and liquid credit markets, losses in loans and securities can be priced more explicitly and objectively using the concept of risk-neutrality (see further in chapters 13 and 15) than by a direct application of the capital charge method with subjective views of losses. However, with an incomplete or illiquid market, the CAPM/APT assumption of continuous trading does not hold. It does not mean that a competitive market cannot exist—insurance companies do compete for clients. However, in pricing illiquid insurance claims, a prevailing risk-holding period—typical for the industry—and a competitive equity rate R must both be considered. Formulas (4.20) and (4.21) can apply assuming any holding period, with all values entering these formulas adjusted accordingly. Both the expected loss and the capital charge terms will likely be smaller as the horizon shrinks, although the loss terms $L(R)$ and $L_{ES}(r)$ have to include the end-period expectations for loss and shortfall, correspondingly. When an asset must be held to maturity, capital, hence capital charge, is greatest. Therefore, the capital charge method can be used to value illiquidity as well as economic risks.

The risk-neutral pricing method and the capital charge method do not contradict each other, in spite of how it may seem. The CAPM is based upon the capital requirement of the marginal investor, rather than the capital requirement of an individual firm. The capital requirement of the marginal investor is also likely to be related to the aggregate amount of capital available to bear investment risks. As one firm seeks to off-load risk to a liquidity provider, that liquidity provider needs to have the capital to bear the risk or the ability to identify an investor who has that ability. Therefore, a firm that has a lower capital requirement than the marginal investor may be able to hold even tradable assets more cheaply, while a firm with a higher capital requirement will find it more profitable to sell the asset or to hedge the risk with market instruments.

One interesting example backing our conclusions is a comparison of CDS and GSE guaranty. One could think that, given everything, a more-liquid CDS should trade with a lower price of risk than a much less-liquid loan insurance or GSE guaranty—despite the apparent similarity in the underlying economic risks. In historical reality, this theoretically sound conclusion did not quite hold true when CDS writers operated under higher capital requirements than GSE did.

The method revolving around the concept of capital charge is a subjective approximation reflecting investor economics and simplified loss assumptions, given a prevailing holding period. We show some examples of capital computation in chapter 19.

HISTORICAL REMARKS

The price of risk analysis used as a pivot point in our derivations has a long history. CAPM was introduced and developed by a number of economists, most notably, J. Lintner and W. Sharpe. In 1976 S. Ross extended CAPM to APT. The concept of risk-neutrality is described in every book on valuation; J. Hull [2005] gives an accessible description.

Despite its rich history, the theory of valuation has been slowly adapted by MBS practitioners and most books do not cover the link between MBS valuation and pricing of risks beyond interest rates. For quite a long time, mortgages were valued on a yield or a Z-Spread basis until OAS models gained popularity in the second half of 1980s—in recognition of essential optionalities that MBS bear. A pricing PDE for MBS was considered in Schwartz and Torous (1989), one of the first and few academic works on MBS. However, in its form presented in our book, this PDE goes back to Fabozzi and Fong (1994) and Levin (1998); it is also used in the works of Goncharov (2005). The concept of risk-neutrality for MBS beyond interest-rate risk is conveyed in Levin and Davidson (2005) for prepayment-model risk and in Levin and Davidson (2008) for credit risk; we cover these topics in chapters 11 and 13.

5

Short-Rate Term-Structure Modeling

Prevailing interest rates strongly affect refinancing decisions by homeowners. Typically, a drop in funding rate allows mortgage bankers to offer a lower rate to borrowers while maintaining profitability. Likewise, an increase of the funding rate would force bankers to increase the loan rates offered to homebuyers or refinancers. Historically, the rates of mortgage products have been closely related to the rates of both Treasury bonds and LIBOR swaps. At times, the three markets may experience dislocation. It has become more common to use swap rates to model mortgage rates as the prevailing funding methods— direct borrowings (Federal Home Loan Bank advances) and repurchase agreements—are closely related to LIBOR rates. Hence, an MBS valuation model has to generally start with the modeling of LIBOR rates and/or some other important reference rates.

This chapter describes some interest-rate modeling principles widely employed by market participants. The goal of these models is the creation of a mathematical formulation of economic randomness that is consistent with observed prices of traded bonds or swaps and interest-rate options. Computer models can use such a formulation to value MBS relatively to other interest-rate dependent instruments. As we saw in chapter 4, there is some type of "risk-neutral" stochastic modeling that describes the mathematical behavior of prices for investment assets. An asset can be a bond or a swap, thereby making interest rates a derived random factor. A rate modeling process is often called "term-structure modeling" because one can value an any-maturity bond and thereby reconstruct the entire yield curve using only the dynamics of one-period rate; see, for example, Davidson et al. (2003, chapter 12), Fabozzi (1994, chapter 6). Interest-rate models operating with the short (one-period) rate $r(t)$ as its main object are commonly referred to as "short-rate models." They are different by construction from so-called "forward-rate models," such as the Heath-Jarrow-Morton (HJM) model (1992) described in the next chapter of this book. Both types of interest-rate modeling are designed to solve the same problems, and they are widely used for the valuation of fixed-income options and embedded-option bonds but operate with different mathematical objects. Unlike the short-rate modeling family, forward-rate models employ and randomly evolve the entire forward curve of the short rate, $f(t,T)$, in which t is time and T is the forward time, to which the short rate applies.

We restrict our attention in this chapter to short-rate modeling. This restriction does not assume that any short-rate term-structure model has only one random factor or depends only on the short rate.

CONSTRUCTING AND USING A SINGLE-FACTOR PRICING TREE

Before we embark on a journey of mathematical derivations, let us start with illustrating how term-structure models can be implemented on discrete binomial trees. They can be used for the valuation of American or Bermudan options, and even MBS (see chapter 8). Each node represents a state of economy, that is, the entire set of the yield-curve points. The "zero node" is called *the root*; it contains today's rates. At each attained stage, the tree shows two possible ways the economy can evolve to, the up ("U") step, and the down ("D") step. The tree is said *to recombine* in the sense that the result of an up step followed by a down step is the same as the result of a down step followed by an up step. Hence, the "UD" node is the same as the "DU" node. There will be n nodes at the n-th time step, and $n(n+1)/2$ nodes in an entire n-step binomial recombining tree. The rate evolution on the tree attempts to mirror that of a continuous stochastic model, just in a discrete fashion. The displacement between the up moves and the down moves agrees with the selected model's volatility. The valuation rule (4.2) introduced in chapter 4 is required for working on a tree: $A(0) = E\{A(t)exp[-\int_0^t r(\tau)d\tau]\}$. The prices are found backwards (*backward induction*), starting from the instrument's maturity when the value is surely known.

Let us illustrate this approach assuming a lognormal model for the one-period rate $r(t) = R(t)exp[x(t)]$ where $x(t)$ is a normal deviate and $R(t)$ is called a calibrating function. We will assume that $r(t)$ is compounded periodically rather than continuously and a one-period discount factor is $1/(1+r)$ rather than $exp(-r)$. For simplicity, assume that $dx = \sigma dz$, with volatility σ being 20% per period, zero initial value, $x(0) = 0$, and a zero drift. We can implement this process on the binomial tree setting each move to be either 0.2 up or 0.2 down with

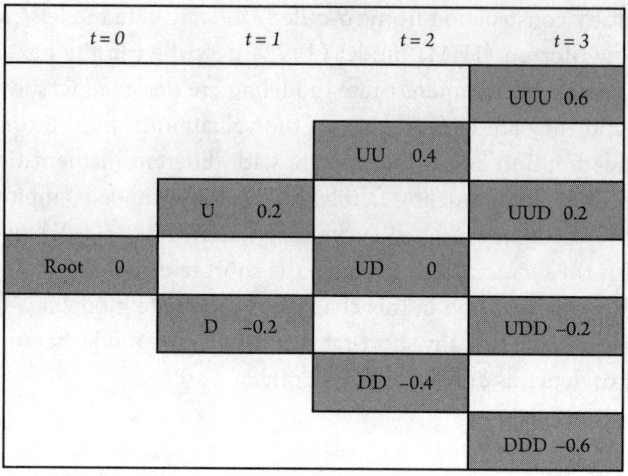

$t = 0$	$t = 1$	$t = 2$	$t = 3$
			UUU 0.6
		UU 0.4	
	U 0.2		UUD 0.2
Root 0		UD 0	
	D −0.2		UDD −0.2
		DD −0.4	
			DDD −0.6

Figure 5.1 Binomial Tree for the Auxiliary Variable $x(t)$

50/50 probability (Figure 5.1). This set up indeed results in a zero drift and a 20% deviation for each one-period horizon. The distribution of $x(t)$ is not going to be normal: a discrete set of outcomes is not identical to the continuous normal process. However, for a small time step, this binomial scheme may be considered a reasonable approximation. After implementing three time steps, we will have the tree for $x(t)$ shown in Figure 5.1.

If we knew the calibrating function $R(t)$, we could easily compute the discount rates for every node of the tree. We can, therefore, employ the fair value formula (4.2) and proceed to calculating values when stepping backward. Suppose that the interest-rate market is given by the coupon rates of 4% (one period), 6% (two periods), and 7% (three periods). Hence, $R(0) = r(0) = 4\%$ since the current one-period rate is not random. Considering the two-period coupon bond priced at par ($100) we know that it pays $100 + \$6 = \$106$ at time $t = 2$, and $6 at time $t = 1$. Hence, the value at node "U" is $P_U = 106 / [1.0 + R(1)e^{0.2}]$ and the value at node "D" is $P_D = 106 / [1.0 + R(1)e^{-0.2}]$. Continuing our backward transition we have at Root $P = [\frac{1}{2}(P_U + P_D) + 6] / (1.04) = 100$, which is satisfied if $R(1) = 8.026\%$ (see Figure 5.2a). We now know that the one-period rate should be equal to $R(1)e^{0.2} = 9.803\%$ at node "U" and $R(1)e^{-0.2} = 6.571\%$ at node "D"; those rates are shown below the nodes' prices. Note that we did not need to know the rates in period three.

We will have to extend the calibration process to fit the par price for a given 7% three-period bond. Having already calibrated for the first two

(a)

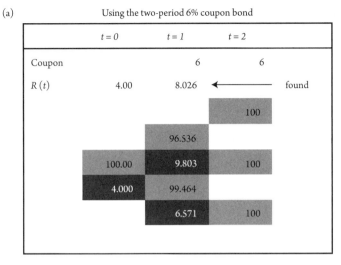

Using the two-period 6% coupon bond

(b)

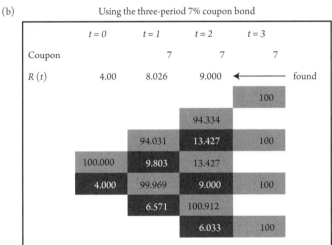

Using the three-period 7% coupon bond

Figure 5.2 Sequential Calibration of $R(t)$

periods we now iterate to obtain $R(2) = 9.000\%$ (see Figure 5.2b). This process reveals one-period rates at nodes "UU" (13.427%), "UD" (9.000%), and "DD" (6.033%).

We now can use the tree to price other financial instruments and to obtain useful information. These and other examples can be found in detail in Davidson et al. (2003, chapter 12).

Example 1. Finding Long Rates on Each Node

Many interest-rate sensitive instruments including MBS require explicit know-ledge of multi-period rates at each node. Finding a long zero-coupon rate for future nodes calls for a backward pricing of the matching-maturity zero-coupon bond (let us denote it Z). Finding a long coupon-bond rate requires computing values for two instruments: the zero-coupon bond and the same-term annuity paying \$1 per period (denote it A). Since a coupon bond is the zero-coupon bond plus the annuity paying the bond's coupon rate c (rather than \$1), then this unknown rate is recovered as $c = (100 - Z) / A$.

For example, if we were interested in computing the two-period coupon rate at node "U", we would find $Z = 81.922, A = 1.730$, hence, $c = 10.450$. If we need to know the two-period zero-coupon rate at node "U", it is equal to $100 * [(100 / Z)^{1/2} - 1] = 10.484$.

Example 2. Pricing Options and Embedded-Option Bonds

The backward valuation on a binomial tree can be generalized to include any explicit call or put (or even call *and* put) provision. For example, such an option may have American or Bermudan exercise that cannot be valued by the Black-Scholes model. Suppose that the three-period 7% coupon bond shown in Figure 5.2 is actually callable at par, at any moment. Therefore, the value of this instrument cannot exceed 100 at any node. Hence, the theoretical value 100.912 found in node "DD" would have no financial significance for the investor as long as he knows the issuer can call the bond at \$100. Only a minor change in the backward induction algorithm accommodates for embedded options: Capping all computed prices by the call strikes if the call can be exercised at that time. Once this is done, we proceed backward as before. Since the value found at node "DD" affects values at preceding nodes ("D" and "Root"), reducing it from 100.912 to 100 affects the entire valuation process. In particular, the bond's price will be reduced from 100 to 99.794, a 0.206 reduction attributed to the value of embedded call.

Similarly, if the bond is putable, the investor can sell it at the strike. This sets a floor on potential price drops. For example, a bond putable at 97 cannot be cheaper than 97 at any node. An adjustment will be necessary at node "UU" and will propagate to preceding nodes ("U" and "Root"). Had we applied this adjust-ment, the bond's price would rise from 100 to 101.427; this difference is the put option value.

We learned from these simple examples that probability trees contain-ing possible braches of economic scenarios can be utilized to value complex fixed-income instruments. For valuation of mortgage pools using the backward induction method, read chapter 8 of this book.

ARBITRAGE-FREE CONDITIONS AND INTER-RATE RELATIONSHIPS

The tree example showed that one can calibrate the random future to market prices of option-free bonds and derive any-maturity rate at any node. Let us show how these tasks can be expressed in general mathematical terms. Assume that we have a stochastic process, possibly multifactor, describing the short-rate dynamics $r(t)$. Let us denote $P_T(t)$ to be the market price observed at time t of a T-maturity zero-coupon bond, that is, a bond paying \$1 at $t+T$. This price is exponential in the yield to maturity ("rate") $r_T(t)$ of this bond: $P(t,t+T) \equiv P_T(t) = exp[-r_T(t)T]$. On the other hand, we can use the risk-neutral argument explained in Chapter 4 and claim that, once the instruments' prices reflect rate expectations and risks, the ratio of a bond's value to the value of a money-market account (accrued at the short rate) should be a martingale. This will remove any preference in investing in either of the two. Applying the relationship (4.2) to the bond, that is, setting $A(t) = P(t,T)$, and knowing that $P(T,T) = 1$, we get $P_T(0) = E_0\left\{exp[-\int_0^T r(\tau)d\tau]\right\}$, or, more generally, $P_T(t) = E_t\left\{exp[-\int_t^{t+T} r(\tau)d\tau]\right\}$ for any t, where E_t denotes the time-t risk-neutral expectation. Hence,

$$r_T(t) = -\frac{1}{T}LnE_t\left\{exp[-\int_t^{t+T} r(\tau)d\tau]\right\} \tag{5.1}$$

Formula (5.1) allows us to compute any-maturity zero-coupon rates via some expectation involving random behavior of the short rate. Of course, once we establish the entire zero-coupon curve, we can restore the yield for any other bond including a coupon-paying one. To compute the expectation in (5.1), we must know two things: stochastic equation (or equations) for $r(t)$ and initial (time t) conditions. The latter represents public information about the market at time t and includes every factor affecting the short rate. Therefore, it would be correct to state that *any-maturity rate can be recovered using only factors that determine the evolution of the short rate.* In particular, if only one Brownian motion drives the short-rate dynamics, it will define the entire yield curve as well.

Consistency with the Initial Yield Curve

Let us apply the inter-rate relationship (5.1) to the initial point of time, $t = 0$:

$$r_T(0) = -\frac{1}{T} LnE_0 \left\{ exp\left[-\int_0^T r(\tau)\, d\tau \right] \right\} \tag{5.2}$$

The left-hand side of this formula is known from today's term structure of interest rates. Hence, the short-rate dynamics $r(t)$ must be such as to ensure (5.2) holds. In practical terms, adjusting a rate process to fit the initial yield curve is part of a more general task often termed "calibration." Without this necessary step, an interest-rate model cannot be used to value even simple, option-free, bonds. Computation of expectation in formulas (5.1) and (5.2) can be done numerically or, in some models, analytically.

Consistency with European Option Values

If a term-structure model is built to value complex derivative instruments, it must value, at minimum, simple European options. Suppose we have an option that is exercised at a future point of time t and generates a cash flow ("payoff") that we denote $g[r(t)]$, that is, some nonlinear function of the short rate observed at t. Note that actual option's exercise may be triggered by a long, rather than the short, rate; nevertheless, it will depend either on $r(t)$ (single-factor models) or all market factors (multi-factor models) known at t. The value of the option is going to be

$$option = E_0 \left\{ g[r(t)] exp\left[-\int_0^t r(\tau)\, d\tau \right] \right\} \tag{5.3}$$

where E_0 denotes the same risk-neutral expectation taken at time 0, as before. We may now demand the short-rate process $r(t)$ produces options values (5.3) that match market prices. Most commonly, term-structure models are calibrated to LIBOR caps, or European options on swaps (swaptions), or both. These are standard, widely traded European options.

For example, a call option on a T-maturity swap will generate cash flow equal to $g[r(t)] = A_T(t)[K - c_T(t)]^+$ where A denotes annuity, c denotes the swap rate, both measured at t, and superscript '+' indicates that only a positive value is taken. A LIBOR cap made of caplets, that is, European calls on some relatively short rate, is another example. A T-maturity LIBOR caplet ($T = 3$ months for standard caps) expiring at t pays $[r_T(t) - K]^+$ at $t + T$. To recognize the time difference T between caplet's expiry and the actual pay, we can "move" the pay-off from $t + T$ to t and express it as $g[r(t)] = [r_T(t) - K]^+ / (1 + Tr_T(t))$. We then have to make sure that formula (5.3) yields correct values for the caplets. Note that the cap market does not usually quote caplets directly; however, their values can be assessed by bootstrapping.

In the next section, we describe several single-factor models, which employ the short rate as the only factor. We also give some evidence on the relative performance of the models. For each of the models, we emphasize three key aspects, the model's formulation, its arbitrage-free calibration, and the inter-rate relationship that recovers the entire term-structure contingent on the dynamics of the short rate.

A REVIEW OF SINGLE-FACTOR SHORT-RATE MODELS

The Hull-White (1990) Model

The Hull-White (HW) model describes the dynamics of the short rate $r(t)$ in the form:

$$dr = a(t)[\theta(t) - r]dr + \sigma(t)dz \qquad (5.4)$$

Once again, $\sigma(t)$ stands for volatility, $a(t)$ denotes mean reversion; both can be time-dependent. The short-rate process is disturbed by a Brownian motion $z(t)$. Function $\theta(t)$ is sometimes referred to as "arbitrage-free" drift. This terminology reflects the fact that by selecting proper $\theta(t)$ we can match any observed yield curve. The short rate is normally distributed in this model, so the volatility represents absolute, rather than relative, changes. The HW model was preceded by the Vasicek (1977) model having $\theta(t) = const$.

Differential equation (5.4) is a linear equation disturbed by the Brownian motion (a normally distributed variable); the short rate is normally distributed as well. Therefore, its integral is normally distributed too, and the expectation found in the right-hand side of formulas (5.1), (5.2), and, in some cases, (5.3) can be computed in a closed form. Without going through the math, we provide here the analytical calibration results to the observed short forward curve $f(t)$ for the case of constant a and σ:

$$\theta(t) = f(t) + \frac{1}{a}\frac{df(t)}{dt} + \frac{\sigma^2}{2a^2}(1 - e^{-2at}) \qquad (5.5)$$

The short rate's expectation is found as

$$E_0[r(t)] = f(t) + \frac{\sigma^2}{2a^2}(1 - e^{-at})^2 \qquad (5.6)$$

The last term in (5.6) is called *the convexity adjustment*, that is, the difference between mathematically expected short rates in the future and the forward short rates. This adjustment is proportional to volatility squared; for zero mean reversion, it is simply equal to $\frac{1}{2}\sigma^2 t^2$. It is therefore up to financial engineers to make sure the convexity adjustment is properly implemented in a pricing system; it is very volatility-sensitive.

The expected value for any long, T-maturity, zero-coupon rate is proven to be in the same form: forward rate + convexity adjustment:

$$E_0\left[r_T(t)\right] = f_T(t) + \frac{\sigma^2}{4a^3T}\left(1-e^{-aT}\right)\left[2(1-e^{-at})^2 + \left(1-e^{-2at}\right)\left(1-e^{-aT}\right)\right] \quad (5.7)$$

Figure 5.3 illustrates the size of convexity adjustment for different tenors using a zero mean reversion $(a=0)$. The adjustment grows with maturity and forward time. Note that, at $t=0$, the slope is proportional to T and becomes zero for the short rate.

Any long zero-coupon rate is normally distributed, too, and known to be linear in the short rate; deviations from their respective mean levels are related as

$$\frac{\Delta r_T}{\Delta r} \equiv \frac{r_T(t) - E_0\left[r_T(t)\right]}{r_T(t) - E_0\left[r(t)\right]} = \frac{1-e^{-aT}}{aT} \equiv B_T \quad (5.8)$$

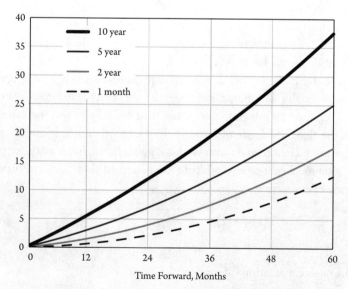

Figure 5.3 The HW Convexity Adjustment (in bp) for Various Tenors of Zero-Coupon Rates

The function B_T of maturity T plays an important role in the HW model. It helps, for example, to link the short-rate volatility to the long-rate one and explicitly calibrate it to the market. If $a = 0$, this function becomes identical to 1, regardless the maturity T (Figure 5.4). This important special case, called the Ho-Lee model, allows for a pure parallel change in the entire curve (every point moves by the same amount) and can be suitable for standardized risk measurement tests.

The HW model provides a very tractable arbitrage-free model, which allows for the use of analytical solutions as well as Monte Carlo simulation. The volatility σ and mean reversion a can be analytically calibrated to European options on zero-coupon bonds. Most commonly, the HW model is calibrated to either a set of short-rate options (LIBOR caps) or swaptions. In the latter case, very good volatility approximations can be constructed; see Levin (2001), Musiela and Rutkowski (2000). The model's chief drawback is that it produces negative interest rates. However, with mean reversion, the effect of negative rates is reduced. This formulation was appropriate for use during most of the 1990s and 2000s, as we show later in this chapter.

Figure 5.5 depicts 200 short-rate paths sampled over a pentagonal lattice by the HW model with a constant volatility, along with the forward curve (bold solid line) and the average-rate curve (bold dotted line). The lattice's design, more granular for the near-term nodes and sparse in the distant future, reduces computational time without the deterioration of accuracy in valuing embedded

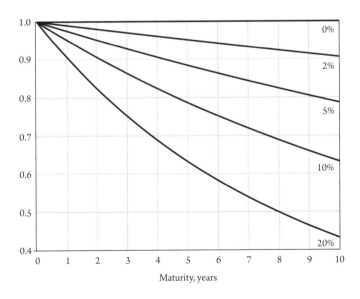

Figure 5.4 The HW Function B_T for Different Levels of Mean Reversion

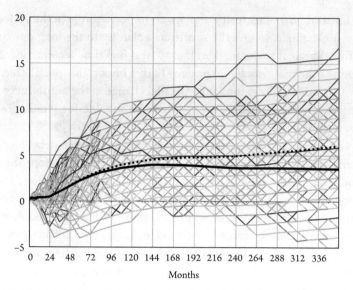

Figure 5.5 Hull-White Model's 200 Short-Rate Paths Sampled over a Lattice

options. Due to a near-zero starting value of 0.19% (as of May 10, 2013), the short-rate can become negative with a reasonably high probability. However, due to the steep forward curve, a deep plunge into the negative territory is unlikely. The visual "center mass" of rates (bold dots) slowly drifts up and away from the forward curve—proving the convexity adjustment.

The Cox-Ingersoll-Ross (1985) Model

The Cox-Ingersoll-Ross (CIR) model is a unique example of a model supported by econometric arguments. The authors argued that the fixed-income investment opportunities should not be dominated by either expected return (the rate) or risk. The latter was associated with the return variance, thus suggesting that volatility-squared should be of the same magnitude as the rate:

$$dr = a(t)[\theta(t) - r]dr + \sigma(t)\sqrt{r}dz \qquad (5.9)$$

Equation (5.9) is actually a no-arbitrage extension to the "original CIR" that allows fitting the initial rate and volatility curves. Since the volatility term is proportional to the square root of the short rate, the latter is meant to remain positive. The extended CIR model is analytically tractable, but to a lesser extent than the HW model. Perhaps the most important result of CIR is that the long zero-coupon rates are also proven linear in the short rate—much like the HW model. However, the slope function has now a quite different form; it depends on both maturity T and time t and found as $B_T(t)=-b(t,t+T)/T$. Function $b(t,T)$, used in this expression, solves a Ricatti-type differential equation, considered for any fixed maturity T:

$$\frac{db(t,T)}{dt}=a(t)b(t,T)-\frac{1}{2}\sigma^2(t)b^2(t,T)+1 \qquad (5.10)$$

subject to terminal condition $b(T,T)=0$.

If the mean reversion a and "CIR volatility" σ are constant (the "original CIR"), equation (5.10) allows for an explicit solution. In this case, $b(t,T)$ is a function of $T-t$ only, and B_T is appeared to be time-independent:

$$B_T=\frac{2(e^{\gamma T}-1)}{T\left[(\gamma+a)(e^{\gamma T}-1)+2\gamma\right]} \quad \text{where } \gamma=\sqrt{a^2+2\sigma^2} \qquad (5.11)$$

Without a mean reversion, this formula reduces to a more concise $B_T=\tanh(\gamma T/2)/(\gamma T/2)$. Note that this ratio is always less than 1. This means that the long rates are less volatile than the short one, even without a mean reversion. This is in contrast to the HW model where, with $a=0$, the yield curve would experience a strictly parallel reaction to a short-rate shock. Figure 5.6 depicts the B_T function family for different values of σ and a. With $\sigma=0$, B_T would be identical to that of the Hull-White model (Figure 5.4). As volatility grows, B_T declines and becomes less dependent on mean reversion.

Generally speaking, calibration to the currently observed short forward curve $f(T)$ cannot be done as elegantly and explicitly as in the HW model. Once the $b(t,T)$ function is found, the calibrating function $\theta(t)$ satisfies an integral equation:

$$-f(T)=\int_0^T \frac{db(t,T)}{dT}\theta(t)a(t)dt+\frac{db(0,T)}{dT}r_0 \qquad (5.12)$$

Numerical methods, well developed for integral equations, should be employed.

It is established that all zero-coupon rates, under the CIR model, have non-central χ-squared distributions and remain positive. Economic rationale, non-negative rates, and analytical tractability have made the CIR model deservedly popular; it is one of the most attractive and useful interest-rate models. It is also consistent with the Japanese market and some periods of the US rate history when rates were very low (e.g. 2003, 2012).

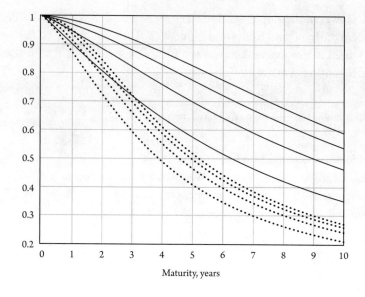

Maturity, years

Figure 5.6 The CIR Function B_T for Different Levels of Volatility and Mean Reversion Solid lines: $\sigma = 0.2$; dotted lines: $\sigma = 0.5$. For each group, $a = 0$ (top line), 5%, 10% and 20% (lower line)

The Squared Gaussian Model (Also Known as Quadratic Model)

The CIR model is not the only model having a square-root volatility specification. Let us define an auxiliary normal variable $x(t)$ using linear differential equation similar to Hull-White's (5.4); we then define the short rate in the form of its square:

$$dx = -a(t)x\,dt + \sigma(t)\,dz$$

$$r(t) = [R(t) + x(t)]^2 \tag{5.13}$$

For convenience, we removed previously used arbitrage-free function $\theta(t)$ from the first equation and introduced a deterministic calibrating function $R(t)$ to the second equation serving the same purpose.[1] The Ito Lemma allows us to convert model (5.13) to a single stochastic differential equation for the short rate:

$$dr = [2R_t'\sqrt{r} - 2a(r - R\sqrt{r}) + \sigma^2]dt + 2\sigma\sqrt{r}\,dz \tag{5.14}$$

[1] We could define the HW model as $r(t) = R(t) + x(t)$.

where R'_t stands for dR/dt. The Squared Gaussian (SqG) model has an apparent similarity to the CIR model in that its volatility term is proportional to the square root of the short rate, too. However, comparing stochastic equations (5.14) and (5.9) we see that they have different drift terms. The SqG model's drift has terms proportional to $\sqrt{r}$ that cannot be eliminated without a loss of the yield-curve calibration power. Therefore, the SqG model and the CIR model cannot be reduced to one another, despite their identical volatility specifications.

The SqG model has been studied by Beaglehole and Tenney (1991), Jamshidian (1996), and Pelsser (1997), among others. The most notable fact established for the SqG model is that any zero-coupon rate $r_T(t)$ is quadratic in $x(t)$, that is, linear in the short rate $r(t)$ and its square-root $\sqrt{r(t)}$:

$$(T-t)r_T(t)= A(t,T)- B(t,T)\sqrt{r(t)}-C(t,T)r(t) \qquad (5.15)$$

Functions A, B, and C satisfy a system of ordinary differential equations:

$$A'_t = BR'_t +\sigma^2\left(\frac{1}{2}B^2 +C\right)+aRB \text{ with } A(T,T)=0 \qquad (5.16a)$$

$$B'_t = aB-2CR'_t -2aCR -2\sigma^2 BC \text{ with } B(T,T)=0 \qquad (5.16b)$$

$$C'_t =1+2aC -2\sigma^2 C^2 \text{ with } C(T,T)=0 \qquad (5.16c)$$

where, for brevity, A'_t, B'_t, C'_t denote derivatives with respect to time t and the dependence of all functions on t and T is omitted. Note that all the terminal conditions are set to zero. Indeed, once t is equal to T, both sides of relationship (5.15) must become zero for any value of r; this is possible if and only if functions A, B, and C turn to zero. Much like in the CIR model, equation (5.16c) for the linear term's slope, this time denoted via C, is of a Ricatti type and can be solved in a closed-end form. In fact, it is identical to already solved equation (5.10) of the CIR case except it operates with a doubled mean reversion and a doubled volatility. Other equations in (5.16) and calibration to the initial yield curve can be solved numerically.

The short rate has a non-central χ-squared distribution with one degree of freedom. Long rates are mixtures of normal and χ-squared deviates. Like the CIR model, the SqG model ensures positive rates; the square-root specification of volatility is suitable for many options. Due to some analytical tractability and known form for long rates, the volatility function and mean reversion can be quite accurately calibrated to traded options.

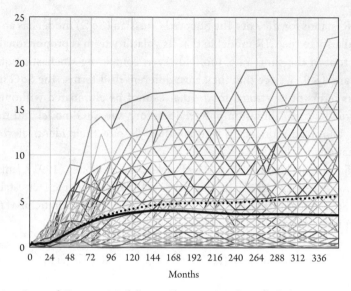

Figure 5.7 Squared Gaussian Model's 200 Short-Rate Paths Sampled over a Lattice

Figure 5.7 depicts 200 random paths sampled by the SqG model over a lattice constructed similarly to the HW case. Volatility and mean reversion are assumed to be constant, best calibrated to the swaption volatility surface. Unlike in Figure 5.5, we do not see negative rates (as is expected), and the distribution is apparently asymmetric as volatility rises with rate.

The difference between average and forward rates is comparable to that of Figure 5.5. Convexity adjustment arises due to a positive convexity of the discounting operation and depends much more on the size of volatility and much less on a rate model selection. When various rate models are calibrated to the same market conditions, convexity adjustments should end up being comparable in size.

The Black-Karasinski Model (1991)

Once a popular model, the Black-Karasinski (BK) model expresses the short rate as $r(t) = R(t)exp[x(t)]$, where, as in the previous case, random process $x(t)$ is normally distributed. The short rate is, therefore, lognormally distributed. Assuming the same process for $x(t)$ we can write the stochastic differential equation for the short rate as

$$dr = r\left(\frac{R'_t}{R} + \frac{1}{2}\sigma^2 - aln\frac{r}{R}\right)dt + r\sigma dz \qquad (5.17)$$

The rate's absolute volatility is therefore proportional to the rate's level. Although the entire short-rate distribution is known (including the mean and variance), no closed-form pricing solution is available. This is because the cumulative discount rate, the integral of r, has an unknown distribution.

Traditionally, the BK model is implemented on a tree. Calibration to the yield curve and volatility curve can be done using purely numeric procedures. For example, one could iterate to find $R(t)$ period-by-period until all the coupon bonds or zero-coupon bonds (used as input) are priced exactly. We demonstrated this process using a binomial tree approximation in the beginning of the chapter. Alternatively, one could find approximate formulas and build a faster, but approximate scheme.

Despite its past popularity, the BK model's main assumption, the rate's lognormality, is not supported by recent rate history. The volatility parameter σ entering the BK model is not the same as the Black volatility typically quoted for swaptions or LIBOR caps. For example, selecting $\sigma=0.15, a=0$ does not ensure 15% Black volatility, even for European options on short rates (caplets). Hence, calibrating the model to volatilities found in the option market is not an easy task.

The Flesaker-Hughston Model

The interesting Flesaker-Hughston model is different from all previously described ones in that it allows for computing the coupon rates analytically. The model starts with defining a random process $M(t)$, which is any martingale starting from 1, and two deterministic positive functions $A(t)$ and $B(t)$, decreasing with time t. Then, at any point of time t, a zero-coupon bond maturing at T has its price in a rational-functional form of $M(t)$:

$$P(t,T)=-\frac{A(T)+B(T)M(t)}{A(t)+B(t)M(t)} \qquad (5.18)$$

Taking the natural logarithm of this expression, changing the sign, and dividing it by $T-t$ gives us the zero-coupon rate. In order to derive a coupon rate $c(t,T)$, let us recall that a coupon-bearing bond generates periodic payments at a rate of c and returns the principal amount ($\$1$) at maturity. Let us denote the time-t value of this bond as $P^C(t,T)$:

$$P^C(t,T)=\sum_{i=1}^{n}cP(t,t_i)+P(t,T)$$

where t_i are the timings of coupon payments, with $t_n = T$. To express the par coupon rate c, let us equate this $P^C(t,T)$ to 1 and substitute the postulated expression (5.18) for all discount factors:

$$c(t,T) = \frac{A(t) - A(T) + [B(t) - B(T)]M(t)}{\sum_{i=1}^{n}[A(t_i) + B(t_i)M(t)]}$$

$$r(t) = -\frac{A'_t(t) + B'_t(t)M(t)}{A(t) + B(t)M(t)}$$

(5.19)

Hence, all coupon rates and zero-coupon rates are also rational functions of $M(t)$. If we select a positive martingale process $M(t)$, for example, a lognormal one, $dM = \sigma M dz$, then all rates will stay positive. Functions $A(t)$ and $B(t)$ can fit the initial term structure of rates and volatilities. See Flesaker and Hughston (1996) or James and Webber (2000) for additional details.

Other Single-Factor Models

There are a fair amount of other "named" models. They differ in specifications of drift and volatility functions. We will briefly list some of them.

The already mentioned *Ho-Lee model (HL)*, predecessor to the HW model, was offered as a discrete-time, arbitrage-free, model. Its continuous version is equivalent to the HW model with zero-mean reversion. Hence, all analytical statements made for the HW model are valid for the HL model. An earlier constant-coefficient version belongs to Merton.

The *Black-Derman-Toy (BDT) model* is a lognormal short-rate model with endogenously defined mean-reversion term equal to $\sigma'_t(t)/\sigma(t)$. This specification means that a constant volatility leads to a zero-mean reversion; a growing short-rate volatility function $\sigma(t)$ causes a negative mean reversion thereby destabilizing the process. Once popular in financial industry, BDT was replaced by the BK model; both of these models are now considered to be outdated.

The *Kalotay-Williams-Fabozzi (KWF) model* is a special case of the BK model with zero-mean reversion. Models operating without a positive-mean reversion are not asymptotically stable as they allow process' variance to increase with no bounds.

The *Brennan-Schwartz model* is a proportional volatility, mean-reverting, short-rate model. Introduced in 1979 as an equilibrium model, it has some similarity in its volatility specification to lognormal models; however, rates are not lognormally distributed.

Calibration Issues

The Vasicek model and the original Cox-Ingersoll-Ross model laid the foundation of term-structure modeling. Despite their unquestionable historical importance, traders almost never employ them today. The reason is fairly simple: Built with constant "equilibrium" parameters, these models can't be calibrated to the market accurately. The extensions, known as the Hull-While ("extended Vasicek") model and the extended CIR model, allows for selecting time-dependent functions $a(t), \sigma(t)$ and $\theta(t)$ so that the model produces exact or very close prices for a large set of widely traded fixed-income instruments, ranging from option-free bonds (or swaps) to European ("vanilla") options on them and more. In particular, function $\theta(t)$ [or $R(t)$] is usually selected to fit the entire option-free yield curve, as formula (5.5) demonstrates. In contrast, functions $a(t), \sigma(t)$ are typically found to match the prices of European options. For example, using just a pair of constants (a, σ) one can match exactly the prices of two options, for example, a 1-year option on the 2-year swap and 10-year swap. Clearly, we can match many more expiration points if we make $a(t), \sigma(t)$ time-dependent. In some systems, volatility function is allowed to be time-dependent, but mean reversion remains a positive constant. This way, one can fit the expiration curve of the options only on average, but the model remains stable and robust. Note that a negative mean reversion may destabilize a dynamic process.

As we pointed out, single-factor models possess various degrees of analytical tractability. When using the HW model, a large portion of calibration work can be done analytically—starting from formula (5.5). The CIR model and the SqG model are somewhat analytical, but, practically speaking, require numerical solutions to ordinary differential equations. The BK model has no known solution at all. A lack of analytical tractability does not preclude using numerical methods or efficient analytical approximations that are beyond the scope of this book.

Single-factor models cannot be calibrated to all market instruments. For example, each of the models we have considered thus far creates a certain dependence of the European option's implied volatility on the option's strike, known as the volatility skew. Once a model is selected, luckily or not (read the next section), the skew implied by it can't be changed by the model's parameters. Another problem is that all rates are perfectly correlated in any single-factor model. Hence, none of them can replicate values of "spread options" or "curve options", that is special derivatives that get exercised when the yield curve flattens or steepens. The solution may lie in using multi-factor models as discussed further in this chapter.

WHICH MODEL IS BETTER?

Choosing one model over another may be less a matter of taste and more of a conscientious decision. There are objective criteria for selecting the most suitable model that are described in this section. The HW model, the CIR model, the SqG model, and the BK model are special cases of a more general class of "CEV models" introduced in the 1980s:

$$dr = (Drift)dt + \sigma r^\gamma dz \tag{5.20}$$

Parameter γ is called Constant Elasticity of Variance (CEV). For $\gamma = 0$, we may have the HW model, for $\gamma = 0.5$—the CIR model or the SqG model, for $\gamma = 1$—the BK model. There are no specific economic arguments supporting the r^γ functional form for volatility. Commonly, the CEV constant lies between 0 and 1, but not necessarily.

Measuring Volatility Skew

Blyth and Uglum (1999) linked the CEV constant to the observed volatility skew, that is dependence of the Black volatility (also called implied volatility) on option's strike, found in the swaption market. They argue that market participants should track the Black volatility according to the following simple formula:

$$\frac{\sigma_K}{\sigma_F} = \left(\frac{F}{K}\right)^{\frac{1-\gamma}{2}} \tag{5.21}$$

where σ_K is the Black volatility for the option struck at K, σ_F is the Black volatility for the "at-the-money" option struck at today's forward rate, F. Importantly, one can recover the best CEV constant to use in the model by simply measuring the observed skew.

The skew measured for the 5-year option on the 10-year swap quoted for the period of 1998–2004 suggests $\gamma = 0.14$ being optimal, on average, see A. Levin (2004). This means that the most suitable model lies between the HW model and the CIR/SqG model (Figure 5.8). We also see that low-struck options are traded with a close-to-normal volatility, while high-struck options are traded with a square-root volatility profile. This fact may be a combination of "smile" effect, discussed toward the end of this chapter, and the broker-commission demand. As shown a little further, the square-root volatility specification becomes very suitable in a low-rate environment.

A similar analysis conducted in 2012 indicated a considerable drift of the CEV constant towards the 0.5 level (Levin [ADQP 2012]). This showed that the very

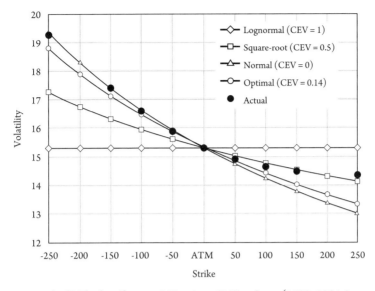

Figure 5.8 Implied Volatility Skew on 5-Year-into-10-Year Swap (1998–2004 Averages)
Source of actual volatility: Bank of America; volatility for 200 bps ITM/OTM was not quoted

low rate environment makes the CIR/SqG modeling necessary: Under the HW model, the probability of getting negative LIBOR rates is exaggerated.

Using Volatility Index

To compare rate models, it is useful to design a market volatility index—a single number reflecting the overall level of option volatility deemed relevant to the interest-rate market. Levin (2004) describes a method of constructing such an index by first designating a family of at-the-money (ATM) swaptions ("surface"), that is options on swaps struck exactly at the current forward rate. Then, assuming zero mean reversion, one can optimize for the single short-rate volatility constant σ (volatility index) best matching the swaptions' volatility surface, on average. This measure is model-specific; unlike some other volatility indices, it is not a simple average of swaption volatilities. The internal analytics of each model, exact or approximate, is used to translate the short-rate volatility constant into swaption volatilities used for calibration. Note that this constant-volatility, zero-mean reversion setup is employed only to define the index; it is not a recommended setup for pricing complex instruments.

Figure 5.9 depicts the history of three volatility indices (Sigmas) computed from the beginning of 2000 for the Hull-While model, the Black-Karasinski model, and the squared Gaussian model. Each index is calibrated to the same

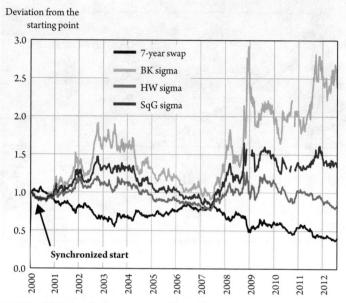

Figure 5.9 What Volatility Index is Most Stable?

family of equally weighted ATM swaptions on the 2-year swap and the 10-year swap with expirations ranging from six months to ten years. For comparison, we have added a line for the seven-year rate level, and scale all four lines relative to their respective January 2000 values so that they start from 1.0.

Figure 5.9 strongly confirms that the volatility index constructed for the HW model have been the most stable one for a long time, except when interest rates are very low. For example, the swap rate plunged a good 60% between January 2000 and June 2003, but the HW volatility index barely changed. The two other models produced volatility indexes that looked mirror-reflective of the rate level (the lognormal model does by far the worst job). A similar observation is valid for the 2007–2011 period. However, as rates were dragged close to zero in 2012, the SqG index became the most stable.

Note that neither the rate history of the past 20 years, nor the available swaption volatility skew data support lognormality, although earlier rate history did appear to support $\gamma > 1$, see Chan et al (1992). In the next section, we show how to extend the short-rate modeling framework to multi-factor models, which are often constructed in so-called "affine" analytical form.

Adding a Second Factor to Short-Rate Models

Let us consider a fixed-income instrument that pays floating coupon indexed to some short rate (such as 3-month LIBOR). The payer does not want to pay too much in case the curve inverts, so a cap is established equal to the level of some long, say 10-year, rate. How much is this cap worth? Practically speaking, the inversion of a curve is not so rare a phenomenon in the fixed-income market. However, if the initial curve is steep, we will greatly undervalue the cap using any of the single-factor models described above. This example highlights the limitation of single-factor modeling; all rates change in unison. Instruments that contain "curve options", that is, asymmetric response to a curve's twist or butterfly moves, cannot be valued using single-factor term structures. Much more complex examples requiring multi-factor modeling include American or Bermudan options, certain collateralized mortgage obligations (CMO) as discussed in chapter 10.

Mathematically, a two-factor normal model can be constructed in a fairly simple way. Suppose that, instead of having one auxiliary Gaussian variable $x(t)$, we have two, $x_1(t)$ and $x_2(t)$, that follow linear stochastic differential equations:

$$dx_1 = -a_1(t)x_1 dt + \sigma_1(t)dz_1$$
$$(5.22)$$
$$dx_2 = -a_2(t)x_2 dt + \sigma_2(t)dz_2$$

Brownian motions $z_1(t)$ and $z_2(t)$ have correlated increments: $corr[dz_1, dz_2] = \rho$. Let us assume that ρ is equal to neither $+1$ nor -1, and mean reversions $a_1(t)$ and $a_2(t)$ are positive and not identical to one another. These conditions ensure that the system (5.22) is stable and cannot be reduced to single-factor diffusion.

We now define the short rate simply as $r(t) = R(t) + x_1(t) + x_2(t)$ where deterministic function $R(t)$ is chosen to fit the initial yield curve. The short rate will be normally distributed; it can be shown that such a model possesses analytical tractability similar to the Hull-White single-factor model, see Levin (1998). In particular, for the constant-parameter case, the calibrating function $R(t)$ can be computed analytically given the forward curve $f(t)$ and the initial conditions $x_1(0)$, $x_2(0)$:

$$R(t) = f(t) + \frac{1}{2}\sum_{i=1}^{2}\frac{\sigma_i^2}{a_i^2}(1 - e^{-a_i t})^2$$
$$(5.23)$$
$$+ \rho\frac{\sigma_1\sigma_2}{a_1 a_2}(1 - e^{-a_1 t})(1 - e^{-a_2 t}) - x_1(0)e^{-a_1 t} - x_2(0)e^{-a_2 t}$$

The long zero-coupon rates are now linear in $x_1(t)$ and $x_2(t)$,

$$r_T(t) = A(t,T) + B_{1T}(t,T)x_1(t) + B_{2T}(t,T)x_2(t) \qquad (5.24)$$

Functions B depend on time t only if the mean reversions a do. If a are constant, then functions B depend only on maturity T and have a familiar HW form: $B_{iT} = (1 - e^{-a_i T}) / a_i T$, $i = 1$ or 2.

The normal deviates, $x_1(t)$ and $x_2(t)$ bear no financial meaning. However, we can transform the model by complementing the short rate with an independent "slope" variable, $v = x_1 + \beta x_2$ with $\beta = -\sigma_1(\sigma_1 + \rho\sigma_2) / \sigma_2(\sigma_2 + \rho\sigma_1) \neq 1$. The new variable has increments dv mathematically uncorrelated to dr; it therefore can be interpreted as the driver of long rates independent of the short rate. Levin (1998) developed a three-point calibration method that analytically computes parameters of the two-factor model using volatility of and correlation between the short rate and two long rates. The method allows for constructing term-structure models with inter-rate correlations selected by user and maintained steadily over time. The later property can be achieved by constructing a model with constant mean reversion parameters a_1 and a_2, and a constant $\sigma_1(t) / \sigma_2(t)$ ratio.

Interestingly enough, all stable two-factor normal models having two real eigen-values can be presented in the above-written form. Hull and White (1994) introduced a two-factor model that was designed in the form of a single-factor HW model for the short rate (factor 1) with a random long-term equilibrium rate (factor 2). Their approach draws on Brennan and Schwartz (1979). It is now clear that such an appeal to the financial meaning was unnecessary, and the general mathematical approach is as good or even better.

Let us view the (r, v) pair as model's two independent drivers so we can construct *principal components* of the term structure associated with each of them. These are changes in long rates, as functions of maturity T, induced by a shock in either r or v, scaled to volatility; let us denote them B_{rT} and B_{vT}. Given the definition of r and v, the principle components for zero-coupon long rates will be linear combinations of already defined B_{1T} and B_{2T}:

$$B_{rT} = (B_{1T} - \beta B_{2T}) / (1 - \beta), \; B_{vT} = (B_{2T} - B_{1T}) / (1 - \beta)$$

Figure 5.10 depicts the principal components for both zeros and coupons. As expected, factor v does not affect r_0 and drives the change in long rates that are independent of the short rate. On the other hand, the change induced by the short rate is not exactly a parallel one.

Levin (2001) proposed using another "practical" transformation of the model, which has the 7-year rate as the primary factor; the second (independent) factor is the twist around the 7-year pivot point. He showed that that transformation was stable over historical periods and that it resembles the way practitioners think of the interest-rate risk composition; an almost-parallel risk (consistent with the single-factor view) plus a twist. Principal components of that model are also depicted in Figure 5.10 with the twist factor naturally crossing the x-axis at the seven-year point (the model's parameters are taken from Levin's paper).

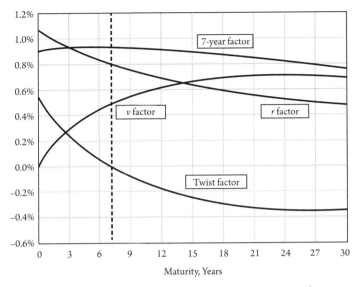

Figure 5.10 Principal Components of the Two-Factor Gaussian Model (Scaled to Average Volatility)

Understanding the term-structure model's principal components is necessary to understand the main sources of interest-rate risk. A pair of factors replicates yield curve's dynamics better that a single factor does and usually well enough for risk reporting and hedging purposes.

If we transform $x_1(t)$ and $x_2(t)$ nonlinearly, we can get multi-factor versions of other previously considered single-factor models. For example, we could define the short rate as $r(t) = R(t)exp[x_1(t) + x_2(t)]$, thereby creating a two-factor lognormal model. As one would expect, such models inherit the main properties of their single-factor parents, but add a greater freedom in changing the curve's shape and calibrating to volatility and correlation structures.

The Concept of Affine Modeling

"Affine" modeling is a method introduced by Duffy and Kan (1996). It is a class of term-structure models, often multi-factor, where all zero-coupon rates are linear functions of factors. Therefore, the zero-coupon bond pricing has an exponential-linear form. Let us generalize the starting equation for the short rate:

$$dr = \mu(t,x)dt + \sigma(t,x)dz$$

Duffy and Kan showed that the model will be affine if the drift term and the square-of-volatility term are both linear in rate r, or, more generally, in all market factors x. In order to illustrate the main idea, let us assume for the sake of simplicity that $r \equiv x$, the lone market factor.

Consider a T-maturity zero-coupon bond; it is a special case of MBS having $c=\lambda=0$. Hence, its price $P(t,x)$ satisfies a reduced-form differential equation (4.8) from chapter 4, as follows:

$$\frac{\partial P}{\partial t}+\mu(t,x)\frac{\partial P}{\partial x}+\frac{1}{2}\sigma^2(t,x)\frac{\partial^2 P}{\partial x^2}=xP \tag{5.25}$$

subject to the terminal condition, $P(T,x)=1$ (bond pays sure \$1 at maturity regardless of the market conditions). Suppose now that functions $\mu(t,x)$ and $\sigma^2(t,x)$ are linear in x:

$$\mu(t,x)=\alpha_1(t)+\alpha_2(t)x, \quad \sigma^2(t,x)=\beta_1(t)+\beta_2(t)x$$

It turns out that the solution to equation (5.25) will have an exponential-linear form:

$$P(t,x)=exp[a(t,T)+b(t,T)x] \tag{5.26}$$

To prove this conjecture, we place the preceding expressions into equation (5.25), take all derivatives, and observe that all the terms are either independent of x or linear in x. Collecting them, we get two ordinary differential equation defining unknown functions $a(t,T)$ and $b(t,T)$:

$$b'_t(t,T)=-\alpha_2(t)b(t,T)-\frac{1}{2}\beta_2(t)b^2(t,T)+1 \tag{5.27}$$

$$a'_t(t,T)=-\alpha_1(t)b(t,T)-\frac{1}{2}\beta_1(t)b^2(t,T) \tag{5.28}$$

The terminal conditions, $a(T,T)=b(T,T)=0$, are dictated by the terminal condition for the price function, $P(T,x)=1$ for any x. Note that equation (5.27) contains one unknown function $b(t,T)$. Once it is solved, we can solve (5.28) for $a(t,T)$.

It is clear that the HW model and the CIR model we considered earlier in the chapter were affine. Indeed, in the HW model, β_2 is zero, α_2 is $-a$, β_1 is σ^2 and (5.27) becomes a linear differential equation. In the CIR model, β_1 is zero, α_2 is again $-a$, and β_2 is σ^2; (5.27) becomes the Ricatti equation (5.10). In fact, these two models cover most important specifications of the affine modeling, for the single-factor case. The concept of affine modeling lets us build multi-factor models systematically. The two-factor Gaussian model we introduced earlier was affine. Much more complex three-factor affine models were analyzed by Balduzzi et al. (1996) and by Dai and Singleton (2000). Among early works, we should mention the model of Longstaff and Schwartz (1992). In their model, both the short rate and its volatility are affine in two factors that follow CIR-like processes.

THE JUMP-DIFFUSION CASE

All term-structure models considered thus far are based on "diffusion"—a continuous random disturbance known as Brownian motion (Wiener process), $z(t)$. As shown in Figure 5.11, long rates are chiefly continuous whereas shorter rates are somewhat "sticky" and "jumpy" and may require an addition of the Poisson process for modeling.

The jump-diffusion extension to the affine modeling concept has been considered by many authors, see Duffie and Kan (1996), Das et al. (1996), and Das (2000). The key point is that, under certain conditions, addition of jumps does not change the complexity of the problem; long rates remain affine in factors and even equation (5.27) for $b(t,T)$ remains unaffected.

Under the presence of jumps, the main stochastic differential equation for the short rate (or other market factors) gets an additional term:

$$dr = \mu(t,x)dt + \sigma(t,x)dz + \sigma_j(t)dJ$$

where J is the Poisson-Merton jump variable having an intensity of $\gamma(t,x)$. When a jump occurs, dJ is drawn from the standard normal distribution $N_{[0,1]}$; it stays 0 otherwise. Note that we allow the jump's intensity $\gamma(t,x)$, but not the size $\sigma_j(t)$, to be factor-dependent.

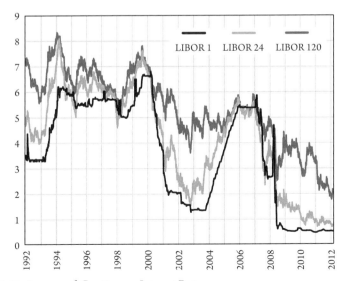

Figure 5.11 Jumpy and Continuous Interest Rates

With jumps, the partial-differential equation (5.25) will get one additional term to its right-hand side. If a jump of size δ occurs, the price of a zero-coupon bond, $P(t,x)$ before the jump, will become $P(t,x+\delta)$. The probabilistically weighted change of price can be written as

$$\int_{-\infty}^{\infty} [P(t,x+\delta)-P(t,x)]n_{[0,\sigma_j]}(\delta)d\delta$$

where, as usual, n denotes a normal density function. This expression captures the randomness of jump's size, not the randomness of jump's occurrence. Multiplying it by the probability of a jump to occur between t and $t+dt$ (i.e., γdt) we get the cumulative expected effect of price change. Finally, dividing by dt we get the annualized return component caused by the jumps. Therefore, the partial-differential equation (5.25) will now become a partial-integral-differential equation:

$$\frac{\partial P}{\partial t}+\mu\frac{\partial P}{\partial x}+\frac{1}{2}\sigma^2\frac{\partial^2 P}{\partial x^2}+\gamma\int_{-\infty}^{\infty}[P(t,x+\delta)-P(t,x)]n_{[0,\sigma_j]}(\delta)d\delta=xP \qquad (5.29)$$

For the diffusion case, we required functions $\mu(t,x)$ and $\sigma^2(t,x)$ to be linear in x. Let us extend this condition to jump's intensity: $\gamma(t,x)=\gamma_1(t)+\gamma_2(t)x$. It turns out that the exponential-linear form (5.26) still fits the equation. Again, collecting terms, we get two ordinary differential equation defining unknown functions $a(t,T)$ and $b(t,T)$:

$$b_t'(t,T)=-\alpha_2(t)b(t,T)-\frac{1}{2}\beta_2(t)b^2(t,T)-\gamma_2(t)\left\{exp\left[\frac{1}{2}b^2(t,T)\sigma_j^2(t)\right]-1\right\}+1$$
$$(5.30)$$

$$a_t'(t,T)=-\alpha_1(t)b(t,T)-\frac{1}{2}\beta_1(t)b^2(t,T)-\gamma_1(t)\left\{exp\left[\frac{1}{2}b^2(t,T)\sigma_j^2(t)\right]-1\right\}$$
$$(5.31)$$

with the same terminal conditions, $a(T,T)=b(T,T)=0$ as before. Notably, if $\gamma_2=0$, equation (5.30) for function $b(t,T)$ will coincide with the previously introduced equation (5.27). If we have a single-factor model, the linear relationship between long rates and the short rate will have a slope of $b(t,t+T)/T$. This slope, found for an affine diffusive model, will not change if we add jumps of factor-independent intensity and size. Hence, in such affine models, jumps and diffusions are equally propagated from the short rate to long rates. Knowing that the actually observed long rates are mostly diffusive and the short rate is notably jumpy, one can conclude that the jump-diffusion setting makes more practical sense within the scope of multi-factor modeling.

Using jump-diffusion models may be required when valuing options struck away from the current forward rate (i.e., the ATM point). Aside from the volatility skew, option pricing features a volatility "smile," or simply an excessive convexity in strike. Revisiting Figure 5.8, we can notice that the actual dependence of volatility on strike is more convex than even the optimal CEV model predicts. This is the smile effect, albeit fairly modest for options on long rates. Smiles for options on shorter rates are very apparent, especially for short expirations. Figure 5.12 depicts swaption volatility measured in basis points per day, as a function of strike.

In this normalized scale, all panels of Figure 5.12 exhibit similar volatility skews, the ones close to normal ($CEV = 0$). However, the smile effect looks very different in panels (a), (b), and (c); it clearly fades with maturity of the underlying rate and option's expiry. The presence of jumps fattens the distribution tails and inflates out-of-the money or in-the money option values relatively to the ATM values. Therefore, jump modeling can capture the smile effect and explains its dependence on the swap's maturity and option's expiry: Jumps allowed to occur over a longer time horizon look more like diffusion.

The jumpy nature of the short LIBOR rates suppresses the values of their ATM options and inflates OTM/ITM options—relative to the same-variance diffusion process. This can cause problems when using LIBOR caps for calibration of purely diffusive models—like those typically utilized for MBS pricing. For example, if a single-factor model is calibrated to caps, the prepayment option embedded into MBS is likely to be undervalued.

CONCLUSION

In this chapter, we described the concept of short-rate modeling, which serves as a foundation of the fixed-income derivatives market and valuation models for MBS. Short-rate models can themselves be single- or multi-factor, but their central object is a theoretical risk-free rate. Models employed in the financial markets have to be calibrated to the initial yield curve and simple options; some models let us solve this task analytically. We described a number of single-factor models, their main properties, distribution of rates, inter-rate relationships, and ability to fit the swaption market. The Hull-White (normal) model fits the observed volatility skew the best; its volatility index had been the most stable over last decade until the rates became very low. In a low-rate environment, the use of the Squared Gaussian model or the Cox-Ingersoll-Ross model should be favored.

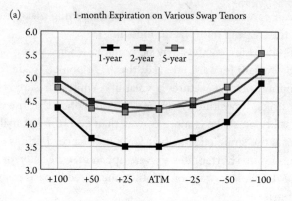

(a)   1-month Expiration on Various Swap Tenors

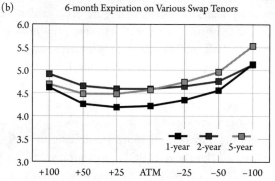

(b)   6-month Expiration on Various Swap Tenors

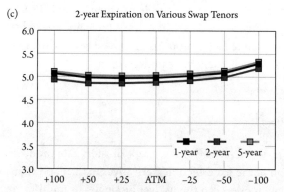

(c)   2-year Expiration on Various Swap Tenors

Figure 5.12 Daily Normalized Volatility Smile for Traded Swaptions (bp/day)
Data courtesy of Bear Stearns, January 2007

We then showed how to construct a two-factor normal model borrowing the recipes of so-called "affine" modeling. Such a model can be used to price complex derivatives that are asymmetrically exposed to changes in the yield curve's shape. We explained the affine modeling method in more detail including its theoretical roots and a jump-diffusion extension. With jumps included, models can be employed to capture volatility "smile," that is, value options struck far out-of or in-the-money. However, calibration of diffusive rate models to at-the-money caps may results in a spurious suppression of volatility and undervaluing embedded prepayment option.

6

Risk-Neutral Modeling Using Forward and Futures Prices

This chapter presents an alternative approach to risk-neutral modeling, which can also apply to the modeling of home-price indices (HPI) and many commodities. It works for some assumed set of assets ("basis"), along with permissible trading strategies. If an asset can be traded both long and short continuously in a spot market (i.e., can be *stored*), its risk-neutral return is expected to be equal to the risk-free rate. Furthermore, if the same asset is also traded in a forward or futures market, a well-known relationship between its spot price and its forward price will exist based on interest rates and cost of carry that precludes arbitrage. Both results do not hold when a spot market does not exist, is not continuous, or when the asset cannot be stored.

From the MBS modeling standpoint, an important example of an asset that cannot be stored is a home-price index. Although an HPI can be thought of as an average home price backed by actual purchases, its replication via a large number of individual trades is impractical. During the decline of the housing market in the United States in 2008, quotes on forward or futures contracts were found noticeably below published spot HPI values, with no way to exploit this "arbitrage." Given these limitations, where can the risk-neutral conditions come from? As we show below, if $S(t)$ is the spot value of an HPI, its risk-neutral evolution has to be tied to the forward or futures price process $F(t,T)$. The method we demonstrate in this section is akin to that of the Heath-Jarrow-Morton (HJM) (1992). In this special case, in which assets are bonds, we will have a specification for the HJM interest-rate model, also explained in this chapter.

DERIVATION OF A RISK-NEUTRAL SPOT HOME-PRICE INDEX PROCESS

Let us assume that an HPI is continuously traded forward and that the HPI forward price $F(t,T)$ observed at time t for exercise at $T \geq t$ is a single-factor diffusion:

$$\frac{dF(t,T)}{F(t,T)} = \mu(t,T)dt + \sigma(t,T)dz(t) \tag{6.1}$$

Denote $f(t,T) \equiv lnF(t,T)$, then, by Ito's Lemma,

$$df(t,T) = \left[\mu(t,T) - \frac{1}{2}\sigma^2(t,T)\right]dt + \sigma(t,T)dz(t), \quad f(0,T) = lnF(0,T) \tag{6.2}$$

and its solution

$$f(t,T) = lnF(0,T) + \int_0^t [\mu(\tau,T) - \frac{1}{2}\sigma^2(\tau,T)]d\tau + \int_0^t \sigma(\tau,T)dz(\tau) \tag{6.3}$$

Therefore,

$$F(t,T) = F(0,T)exp\left\{\int_0^t [\mu(\tau,T) - \frac{1}{2}\sigma^2(\tau,T)]d\tau + \int_0^t \sigma(\tau,T)dz(\tau)\right\}$$

This expresses the forward price as a function of time and the history of $z(\tau), 0 \leq \tau \leq t$. We can relate this to the spot price since, by definition, $S(t) \equiv F(t,t)$:

$$S(t) = F(0,t)exp\left\{\int_0^t [\mu(\tau,t) - \frac{1}{2}\sigma^2(\tau,t)]d\tau + \int_0^t \sigma(\tau,t)dz(\tau)\right\} \equiv exp[f(t,t)]$$

Let us write down the stochastic differential equation (SDE) for the spot-value return rate $f(t,t)$. Note that it will differ from (6.2) not only by notation (t instead of T), but also by the fact that this second argument t is a variable. Hence, $df(t,t)$ will include all the terms from (6.2) plus the differential of the right-hand side of (6.3) taken with respect to the second argument T and evaluated at $T = t$:

$$df(t,t) = \left[\mu(t,t) - \frac{1}{2}\sigma^2(t,t)\right]dt + \sigma(t,t)dz(t)$$

$$+ \left\{\frac{F_t'(0,t)}{F(0,t)} + \int_0^t [\mu_t'(\tau,t) - \sigma(\tau,t)\sigma_t'(\tau,t)]d\tau + \int_0^t \sigma_t'(\tau,t)dz(\tau)\right\}dt$$

Now, $S(t) = F(t,t) = exp[f(t,t)]$, via Ito's Lemma we obtain the SDE for the spot value:

$$\frac{dS(t)}{S(t)} = M(t)dt + \Sigma(t)dz(t) \tag{6.4}$$

where volatility function $\Sigma(t)$ and the drift $M(t)$ are equal to

$$\Sigma(t) = \sigma(t,t) \tag{6.5}$$

$$M(t) = \frac{F_t'(0,t)}{F(0,t)} + \mu(t,t) + \int_0^t [\mu_t'(\tau,t) - \sigma(\tau,t)\sigma_t'(\tau,t)]d\tau + \int_0^t \sigma_t'(\tau,t)dz(\tau) \tag{6.6}$$

Formula (6.5) shows us that the volatility of the spot-value process is that of the forward price computed at $T = t$. In general, the drift of the spot-value process is random and non-Markov even if the forward-price volatility function $\sigma(t,T)$ is a deterministic function of t and T. It depends on the entire history of $z(\tau), 0 \leq \tau \leq t$, via the last term in (6.6). Note that the risk-neutral drift only depends on random factors that enter the forward-price process.

To clarify the importance of this remark, let us consider the case when $F(t,T)$ represents the HPI futures price and the futures contracts can be traded continuously. It is known that $F(t,T)$ will be a zero-drift martingale, i.e. $\mu(t,T) = 0$. Let us further assume that our volatility function $\sigma(t,T)$ depends only on t, and not on T. This assumption means that the entire family of futures prices $F(t,T)$ moves at the same rate independent of T. Then we will have a dramatic simplification of (6.6):

$$M(t) = F_t'(0,t) / F(0,t)$$

meaning that the risk-neutral HPI value $S(t)$ must drift deterministically along the initial forward curve.

A MEAN-REVERTING MARKOV CASE

In the absence of traded options, the critical forward volatility function $\sigma(t,T)$ can be estimated using historical quotes for $F(t,T)$. For example, having reviewed the daily trading forward quotes of the RPX-25 index for the second half of 2008, we estimate the annualized volatility at 6.6% for the 2008-end settlement, 11.9% (2009-end), 12.7% (2010-end), 12.0% (2011-end), and 12.5%

(2012-end). Other historical periods exhibit different levels, but a similar pattern: the nearest contract is the least volatile one and the long-term volatility structure almost saturates for the second-year contract. These observations suggest a mean-reverting pattern in T so that $\sigma(t,T)$ starts from $\sigma_0(t)$ when $T=t$ (i.e. the spot-volatility level) and converges to $\sigma_\infty(t)$ with $T \to \infty$; both levels can be random or deterministic in t. Let us assume that $\sigma(t,T)$ follows a simple linear ordinary differential equation in T,

$$\sigma'_T(t,T) = a[\sigma_\infty(t) - \sigma(t,T)], \text{ initialized at } \sigma(t,t) = \sigma_0(t),$$

so that, with changing T, $\sigma(t,T)$ indeed changes exponentially between $\sigma_0(t)$ and $\sigma_\infty(t)$. Now, the last term in (6.6) becomes a state variable $N(t) \equiv \int_0^t \sigma'_t(\tau,t)dz(\tau)$ subject to an SDE:

$$dN(t) = -aN(t)dt + a[\sigma_\infty(t) - \sigma_0(t)]dz(t), \ N(0) = 0 \qquad (6.7)$$

and with the zero-drift of the futures price, the risk-neutral drift for spot HPI becomes

$$M(t) = \frac{F'_t(0,t)}{F(0,t)} - \int_0^t \sigma(\tau,t)\sigma'_t(\tau,t)d\tau + N(t)$$

This result can be further simplified when $\sigma_0(t)$ and $\sigma_\infty(t)$ are constants. In this case, function $\sigma(t,T) = (\sigma_0 - \sigma_\infty)exp[-a(T-t)] + \sigma_\infty$ will be stationary, i.e. depends only on $\tau = T - t$. We will denote it σ_τ, in a way consistent with the already introduced notations σ_0 and σ_∞. Since $\sigma'_t(\tau,t) = -\sigma'_\tau(\tau,t)$, we can explicitly integrate

$$M(t) = \frac{F'_t(0,t)}{F(0,t)} - \int_0^t \sigma(\tau,t)\sigma'_t(\tau,t)d\tau + N(t) = \frac{F'_t(0,t)}{F(0,t)} + \frac{\sigma_0^2}{2} - \frac{\sigma_t^2}{2} + N(t)$$

$$(6.8)$$

Recall that $M(t)$ is the drift rate of our spot-HPI process, $S(t)$. The home-price appreciation (HPA) rate is defined as $x(t) \equiv dX(t)/dt \equiv dlnS(t)/dt$, hence, its continuous part will be equal to $M(t) - \frac{1}{2}\Sigma^2(t)$, that is, the drift of HPI reduced by Ito's convexity of logarithm. According to (6.5), $\Sigma(t) = \sigma(t,t) = \sigma_0$, therefore, the total risk-neutral HPA rate will be equal to

$$HPA(t) = \frac{F'_t(0,t)}{F(0,t)} - \frac{\sigma_t^2}{2} + N(t) + \sigma_0 w(t) \qquad (6.9)$$

Interestingly, this risk-neutral HPA is not continuous and appears in the form "white noise plus mean-reverting diffusion" because the first two terms in (6.9) are deterministic and $N(t)$ reverts to zero in the absence of random forces; the diffusion $N(t)$ is disturbed by the same noise $w(t)$.

EMPIRICAL EVIDENCE FROM THE RPX FORWARD MARKET

RPX denotes an HPI developed and published by Radar Logic. In 2008–2009, forward contracts on RPX were actively offered by dealers. A contract would pay the difference between HPI published on contract's settlement dates and the contract's strike price. Settlement dates were set at the end of each year, that is, December 31. The market was offering contracts for the 28-day average on 25-MSA Composite index (RPX25), as well as on four geographical indices: Los Angeles, Miami, New York, and Phoenix. Despite the modest size of the RPX market, one could obtain valuable information about the perceived relationships between the forward and the spot quotes by market makers. Figure 6.1 shows the dynamics of the quotes during 2009.

The published spot index was first falling, then stayed steady, then started to rise. The dataset shows that forward quotes were, in fact, below spot prices; that is, the dealers expected HPI to fall, with no way of taking an arbitrage opportunity. Furthermore, for every move of the spot index, the forward quotes responded

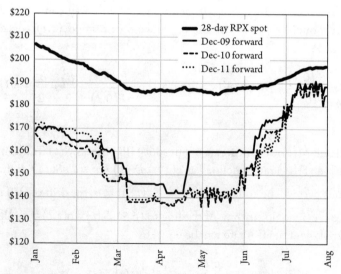

Figure 6.1 RPX25 Spot and Forward Prices in 2009
Source: Radar Logic

with two- to four-fold enlarged volatility. The forward quotes were not in exact synch with spot HPIs, but the trend was obvious.

If an HPI were a spot-traded index (like bonds or stocks that traders could store), the $F < S$ situation would assume high dividends or otherwise allow an immediate arbitrage. Also, a shift in the index should have caused a *smaller, not larger*, shift in the forward prices. The phenomena and paradoxes of the HPI forward market can be clearly explained by the fact that an HPI cannot be stored and there is no arbitrage to exploit. In summary, real estate indices are not expected to return a risk-free rate, their forward volatility is likely to exceed spot volatility, the HPA process is not continuous and can be modeled as a combination of white noise and a mean-reverting diffusion. We use these valuable properties to construct an empirical HPI model in chapter 14.

THE HEATH-JARROW-MORTON MODEL OF INTEREST RATES

We now show how no-arbitrage interest-rate models can be designed using an observed forward curve and forward volatility function. In fact, the HJM rate model can be viewed as a special case of derivations shown in the previous section. Let us assume that $F(t,T) = P(t,T)$, the value of a zero-coupon bond maturing at T and measured at t. The bond's value is equal to par at maturity, $S(t) = P(t,t) \equiv 1$ for any t, hence, $M(t) \equiv 0$. On the other hand, a bond can be continuously traded, therefore, its price is expected to drift at the risk-free rate, $\mu(t,T) \equiv r(t)$, hence, $\mu'_T(t,T) = 0$. Furthermore, at any point of time, a bond's price can be re-expressed via the instantaneous forward curve $f(t,T) = -dLnP(t,T)/dT$. Let us substitute these values into expression (6.6) and rearrange

$$r(t) = f(0,t) + \int_0^t \sigma(\tau,t)\sigma'_t(\tau,t)d\tau - \int_0^t \sigma'_t(\tau,t)dz(\tau) \tag{6.10}$$

This is a representation of the risk-free rate process in the HJM model. The last integral in the right-hand side is the source of randomness, be it Markov or not. The second term is the convexity adjustment, that is, the difference between a risk-neutral expectation of $r(t)$ and the forward curve's level. Due to the relationship between forward rates and prices, $\sigma'_T(\tau,T)$ is exactly equal to the volatility of $f(t,T)$. The differential equation for $f(t,T)$ can be obtained by using (6.2), changing its sign and differentiating with respect to T:

$$df(t,T) = \sigma(t,T)\sigma'_T(t,T)dt - \sigma'_T(t,T)dz(t)$$

or

$$f(t,T)=f(0,T)+\int_0^t \sigma(\tau,T)\sigma_T'(\tau,T)d\tau - \int_0^t \sigma_T'(\tau,T)dz(\tau) \qquad (6.11)$$

Note that despite the apparent similarity between (6.10) and (6.11), these are different equations. Whereas integration runs from 0 to t in either case, in (6.10), the second parameter is t, not T.

An HJM model usage usually starts with observing (or postulating) the entire volatility function $\sigma(t,T)$ and its derivative, $\sigma_T'(t,T)$. Then, short rate $r(t)$ as well as the entire forward curve $f(t,T)$ can be simulated using random processes (6.10) and (6.11), correspondingly.

Markovian specifications of $\sigma(t,T)$ often convert HJM models into known short-rate models. For example, let us introduce again a constant-maturity variable $\tau = T-t$ and assume that volatility function of forward rate $f(t,T)$ is a deterministic function of τ that declines exponentially, $\sigma_T'(t,T)=\sigma e^{-a\tau}$, so that the volatility function of the zero-coupon bond $P(t,T)$ is $\sigma(t,T) \equiv \sigma_\tau = \sigma(1-e^{-a\tau})/a$, or in terms of the notations used in the previous section, $\sigma_0 = 0, \sigma_\infty = \sigma/a$. Substituting these expressions into solutions (6.10), (6.11) we will get

$$r(t)=f(0,t)+\frac{\sigma_t^2}{2}-N(t) \qquad (6.10\text{-HW})$$

$$f(t,T)=f(0,T)+\frac{\sigma_T^2-\sigma_{T-t}^2}{2}-e^{-a(T-t)}N(t) \qquad (6.11\text{-HW})$$

where, as before, $N(t)$ is an Ornstein-Ulenbeck diffusion that follows the ordinary differential equation (6.7). Representations (6.10-HW), (6.11-HW) are equivalent to the single-factor Hull-White model, in which the first two terms account for the expected rate and the last one is a normal deviate. The relationship between forward-rate volatility and the short-rate volatility $\sigma_f(t,T)=\sigma e^{-a\tau}$ (with $\tau = T-t$) holds true even when σ changes over time.

Note that the expectation of $r(t)$ in (6.10) always exceeds today's forward rate $f(0,t)$ [the bond's volatility $\sigma(\tau,t)$ is positive as is the forward rate's volatility $\sigma_t'(\tau,t)$]. In contrast, the expectation of HPA is always below the forward HPA rate implied by the forward prices, i.e. $F_t'(0,t)/F(0,t)$ in (6.9). This difference arises due to the nonlinearity of exponentiation. Forward HPI integrates and exponentiates HPA rates and is, therefore, positively convex. The bond's price does the same with interest rates, but using the opposite sign. This changes the sign of convexity adjustment.

The constant-coefficient CIR short-rate model can be produced from the HJM framework using $\sigma(t,T)=\sigma\sqrt{r(t)}(T-t)B_{T-t}$ where the term structure function B_T is defined by formula (5.11) from chapter 5. In contrast to the Hull-White model, this form of the bond's volatility does not depend solely on $T-t$, but also includes the explicit dependence on $r(t)$. Now $\sigma'_T(t,T)\neq-\sigma'_t(t,T)$, which is a formal barrier to simplifying (6.10) and (6.11).

The CIR specification for $\sigma(t,T)$ belongs to a more general class of volatility function that separates the dependence on $r(t)$ from a deterministic dependence on t and T. This form is described in Cheyette (1992, 2002), Ritchken and Sankarasubramanian (1995): $\sigma_f(t,T)=v(r,t)exp\left[-\int_t^T k(u)du\right]$ where $k(u)$ is a deterministic "mean reversion." Substituting this specification into (6.10) does not let us integrate in a closed-end form, but lets us express the model in terms of two state variables r and V

$$d\tilde{r}(t)=\left[V(t)-k(t)\tilde{r}(t)\right]dt+v\left[r(t),t\right]dz(t), \quad \tilde{r}(0)=0$$

$$(6.12)$$

$$dV(t)=\left\{v^2\left[r(t),t\right]-2k(t)V(t)\right\}dt, \quad V(0)=0$$

where $\tilde{r}(t)=r(t)-f(0,t)$ denotes the deviation of short rate from its initial forward curve. The apparent convenience of differential equations (6.12) is that they generate a no-arbitrage short-rate process, step-by-step, starting from $t=0$, without using a closed-end form for calibration function. The system (6.12) includes the short rate itself and a "convexity adjustment account" $V(t)$. Once the two state variables, $r(t)$ and $V(t)$, become known at time t, the entire forward curve (hence, long rates) can be reconstructed as their linear combination:

$$f(t,T)=f(0,T)+exp\left(-\int_t^T k(u)du\right)\left[\tilde{r}(t)+V(t)\int_t^T exp\left(-\int_t^s k(u)du\right)ds\right]$$

James and Webber (2000) provide details and conditions on other variations of Markovian HJM models.

HPI MODEL REVISITED: FORWARDS VERSUS FUTURES

Let us revisit the HJM-based home-price modeling framework. We made a comment that a futures' price is a zero-drift martingale. Similarly, process $F(t,T)$ will have a zero drift if it is quoted by forward contracts (rather than futures) but is independent of random interest rates. Otherwise, $F(t,T)$ will drift at a non-zero rate derived in this section.

We can view a forward contract as a non-dividend traded asset, the value of which $V(t,T)$ has to drift at a risk-free rate $r(t)$ in the risk-neutral model. On the other hand, it is equal to the product of a discount bond's price $P(t,T)$ and $F(t,T)$: $V(t,T) = P(t,T)F(t,T)$. Combining the SDE (6.1) for the forward HPI $F(t,T)$ with a similarly written SDE for $P(t,T)$ disturbed by forward rate's increments $\sigma_f(t,T)dz_f(t)$ and drifting at the risk-free rate, we can derive the SDE for $V(t,T)$. Skipping these derivations, we present the result as

$$\frac{dV(t,T)}{V(t,T)} = \left(r(t) + \mu(t,T) - \rho\sigma(t,T)\int_0^T \sigma_f(t,\tau)d\tau \right)dt$$

$$+ \sigma(t,T)dz(t) - \left(\int_t^T \sigma_f(t,\tau)d\tau \right)dz_f(t)$$

where ρ denotes a correlation between $dz_f(t)$ and $dz(t)$. Equating the drift term to the risk-free rate $r(t)$, we obtain the required drift for the forward-price process:

$$\mu(t,T) = \rho\sigma(t,T)\int_0^T \sigma_f(t,\tau)d\tau \qquad (6.13)$$

Hence, if forward price $F(t,T)$ is independent of interest rates ($\rho=0$), it will be a zero-drift martingale. With a positive (negative) correlation to interest rates, it must drift upward (downward). Naturally, the drift of forward price must offset the drift of discount bond's value, that is, compensate for convexity of the product of two. For this reason, the forward-price drift is sometimes also called the convexity adjustment. At expiration of the forward and futures contract, $S(T) = F(T,T)$, that is, spot, forward, and futures prices are identical. Since the forwards and futures have differing drifts, we conclude that their values must differ prior to expiration. Convexity adjustment is a known difference between forwards and futures when the underlying depends on interest rates. One example is Treasury bond futures; the forward price must be above its futures price when $t < T$ because the bond's value negatively correlates to the forward rate.

In the presence of both a liquid futures market and a forward market on the same home-price index, one could infer the HPI dependence on interest rate from the futures/forward bias. This would deliver important information for HPI modeling. Unfortunately, at the time of writing, neither the futures nor the forward markets were sufficiently liquid to take these measurements.

For reference, we conclude this chapter with an overview of the existing HPI derivative markets.

AN OVERVIEW OF HOME-PRICE DERIVATIVES

Home prices are measured by indices, some of which are "traded," that is, used to define the payoff of certain financial contracts. The five major families of US home-price indices (HPI) are those compiled and published by Federal Housing Finance Agency (FHFA), S&P/Case-Shiller (CS), Radar Logic (RPX), Core Logic, and the National Association of Realtors (NAR).[1] The FHFA indices, the Core Logic indices, and the NAR indices are widely cited, but they do not trigger any market transactions, unlike the CS indices and the RPX indices.

The CME Case-Shiller Futures

The Chicago Mercantile Exchange (CME) market started trading Case-Shiller futures in May 2006. It engages the same exchange mechanics as all other futures markets and removes the counter-party risk, i.e. the risk that a party facing an adverse market development will stop honoring its liability. Futures' expirations are set in February, May, August, and November; contracts are reset daily and therefore have zero value at any point in time.

Each participant has an account that is continuously credited or debited as the futures price moves. As in other futures markets, a futures price is a martingale. At maturity of the contract, the futures last value is set to be equal to the published underlying Case-Shiller home-price index. Note that HPI futures are priced by publication date, not the measurement reference date. A November contract expires on the last Tuesday when the Case-Shiller index is published (this publication refers to the September measurement).

The Case-Shiller futures are traded in 10 geographical segments (Boston, Chicago, Denver, Las Vegas, Los Angeles, Miami, New York City, San Diego, San Francisco, and Washington, D.C.), in addition to the composite index containing all 10 cities. The offered product line includes up to a five-year expiration, but only a few indices actually trade that far. In addition to futures, CME offers options on futures, but most actually traded option contracts, calls, and puts have been so far limited to a one-year expiration. CME also offers over-the-counter custom-tailored contracts. The market is brokered by major Wall Street dealers as

---

[1] Appendix to chapter 14 contains descriptions of these indices, including methodology and geographical coverage.

well as facilitated by inter-broker traded platforms, for example, TFS. The CME CS market is described in detail on the CME website, www.cme.com.

The RPX Forwards and Futures

Another market utilizing the 28-day version of the RPX index family started trading in September of 2007. At the inception, it offered two types of over-the-counter contracts, a total return swap (TRS), and a simple forward agreement. TRS involved periodic cash flow exchange, with the floating leg receiver getting paid market return on the index. Since September 2008, the market has been quoted solely in terms of forward contracts.

The RPX forwards are settled at each year-end based on the Radar Logic index published for five preceding consecutive business days. Much like in the case of the CME CS market, it is the publication date that matters, not the period of measured real-estate transactions. The RPX market does not currently offer options; it has just few geographical segments traded (New York, Los Angeles, Miami, and Phoenix), along with the 25-MSA Composite. The Composite index is traded up to five years forward, whereas forward contracts for geographical indices do not extend beyond three years. The market is brokered by major Wall Street dealers as well as facilitated by inter-broker traded platforms, for example, ICAP.

In February 2012, a futures market utilizing the RPX family of indices was inaugurated at CBOE Futures Exchange (CFE). Settlement dates are set at the end of March, June, September, and December, with the proposed set of reference indices including the Composite (initially), and four geographical regions (Midwest, Northeast, West, and South) compiled from the same 25 major MSAs.

The HPI derivatives markets are currently small in both trading volume and instrument selection. For example, the total quarterly RPX trading volume peaked in the last quarter of 2008 at $835 million with the bid-ask spread reaching two or more percentage points. By the end of 2012, the entire size of RPX futures market had only 160 open contracts or a tiny $0.3 million. Therefore, government agencies or large loan insurers cannot hedge out their credit exposure simply due to lack of market size. However, some MBS investors or home builders can hedge their risk. The market can be also used by speculators who are willing to take directional bets. The HPI derivatives markets are currently dominated by credit protection buyers and include a large risk premium. Hence, forward prices inferred from the CS futures or the RPX forwards or futures are likely to be lower than real-world ("physical") expectations.

Although forward and futures prices cannot be used in lieu of real-world expectations, they "predicted" the 2008 home-price decline. For example, the CMI CS futures pointed to home-prices depreciating at a time when real-estate fever was still strong and even many Street analysts expected a "soft landing" rather than a decline.

PART TWO

Modeling and Valuation of Agency Mortgage-Backed Securities

Agency Pool Prepayment Models

Prepayments are the essential feature of mortgage-backed securities. They reflect the collective action of millions of individual borrowers and create the unique investment features of mortgage-backed securities. There is a tremendous amount of prepayment data spanning millions of mortgages over several decades, which has been studied extensively by academic and Wall Street researchers. Despite this deep database and tremendous amount of study, prepayments at least to some extent remain uncertain and resistant to efforts to model.

As described in chapter 1, the fundamental uncertainty of prepayments, which derives from the complexity of borrower decisions and situations, is the motivation for the development of many of the techniques described in this book. Before we spend too much time on uncertainty and what we do not know, it is perhaps best to focus first on what we do know about prepayments and prepayment models.

The goal of prepayment models is to estimate the probability of loan termination, primarily due to borrower actions, using information about the loan, the borrower, the collateral, and economic conditions. The model should produce measures that will be useful for valuation and risk assessment of mortgage and mortgage-backed securities portfolios. The focus of this chapter will be pool level models of *total terminations* for agency loans.

AGENCY POOLS

Agency loans represent loans in securities issued by Fannie Mae, Freddie Mac, and Ginnie Mae. These programs were described in chapter 2. Agency securities carry guarantees from the issuers so that investors are not subject to the

risk of non-payment of principal or the receipt of interest on the full outstanding balance. Investors are only subject to the risks associated with the timing of
cash flows.

Agency loans are pooled for securitization. Each issuer has rules that define
which loans can be combined into a single pool. These rules generally limit the
range of maturity, coupon, loan size, and underwriting requirements allowed in
a single pool. From a practical standpoint, most loans in a pool also represent a
common origination period. The analysis of prepayments in this chapter is conducted at the pool level. That is, the prepayment rate represents the percent of the
pool that prepays during a given period. Such models generally depend on the
average characteristics of loans in a pool.

For each pool, each month, there is a published *pool factor*. The pool factor
represents the fraction of the original pool balance still outstanding expressed as
a decimal with eight digits, for example, 0.87654321. As prepayments represent
only the pay down of the mortgages beyond the anticipated amortization, the
average coupon and maturity of the loans in the pool must be used to estimate
the amortization before computing the prepayment rate.

As in chapter 1, prepayments are computed by comparing prepaid principal
to the amortized outstanding balance. Amortization is given by formula (1.2b).

$$smm = (factor(k) - factor(k+1) - amort(k)) / (factor(k) - amort(k))$$
$$amort(k) = factor(k) \frac{c/12}{(1+c/12)^{n-k} - 1} \tag{7.1}$$

The pool factor does not distinguish the source or reason for the decline in pool
balance. It could be because the borrower has prepaid the loan, or because the
borrower has become delinquent on the loan and the loan has been removed
from the pool by the issuer or servicer. In chapter 12, we will look at loan level
modeling with separate treatment of prepayments and defaults.

MODELING PREPAYMENTS

At one extreme, modeling of prepayments could be viewed as a statistical exercise. With millions of loans and years of data, it should be possible to fit a statistical model using any one of a variety of techniques. At the other extreme,
modeling of prepayments could be viewed as a financial engineering problem,
and prepayment rates could be constructed from economic fundamentals. In
practice we find that neither of these extremes produces reliable results. Instead

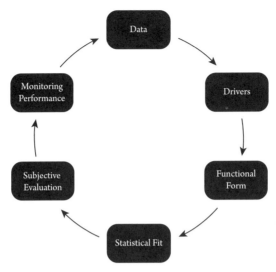

Figure 7.1 Flow of Prepayment Modeling

it is necessary to combine both statistics and financial engineering in developing models of borrower behavior.

As such we find that the following paradigm, shown in Figure 7.1 is a good framework for model development. While there is a general flow from one step to another, it is probably best to view these as concurrent activities.

DATA

Due to securitization, especially for pass-through mortgage structures, there is a tremendous amount of data on mortgage prepayments. As the cash flows to investors are related directly to the cash flows of the underlying mortgages, it is necessary for issuers to provide data to investors. Some of the data is required just for the investors to know what cash flows they will receive. Coupon rates and pool factors are examples of this type of data. Other data is made available to investors so that they can better assess the likelihood of prepayments. For agency pools the basic variables are pool factor, loan program, weighted average coupon (WAC), and weighted average loan age (WALA). Other variables are also available over time and are discussed at the end of this chapter.

Figure 7.2 shows prepayment data for 30 year-fixed rate mortgages, from 1994 to 2012. Average prepayment speeds vary from a conditional prepayment rate (CPR) of a few percent to almost 60% CPR. Clearly this range of prepayments could make a significant difference in the performance of mortgage investments,

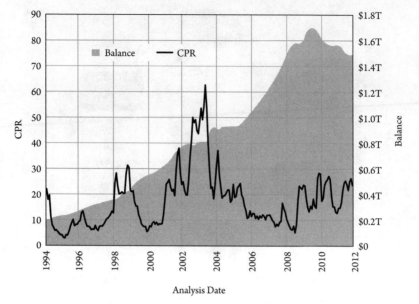

Figure 7.2 Prepayment Rates for 30 Year Fannie Mae MBS

as the underlying average life of the investments could vary from 1.1 years to 10.5 years. Also note the extremely large balance of loans, with about $1.8 trillion dollars of mortgages represented by Fannie Mae 30-year fixed rate loans, the largest mortgage program.

Figure 7.3 shows prepayments on 15-year fixed-rate mortgages. Each line represents the prepayment speeds for loans originated during one-year time periods.

There is a range of mortgage products that may have similar prepayment patterns but need to be differentiated in the modeling process. Figure 7.4 shows a comparison of prepayment speeds for 7-year balloon loans and 30-year loans. Note that the prepayment behavior is very similar up until 2008. The 7-year loan program is much smaller, with peak outstanding volume of under $20 billion, and it has diminished substantially in the wake of the financial and housing crisis.

The complex patterns in Figures 7.2 and 7.4 can be better understood if we segment the data by the basic variables coupon and age. Figure 7.5 shows prepayments by coupon for 30-year fixed rate loans during two different time periods. It is clear that mortgages with higher coupons have higher prepayment speeds, but the slope of the prepayment curve can vary significantly depending on the period.

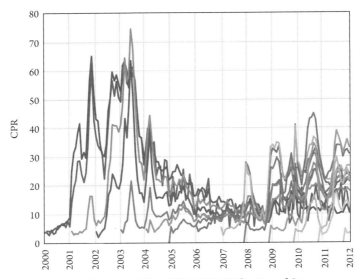

Figure 7.3 Prepayment Rates on 15-Year FHLMC MBS by Year of Origination

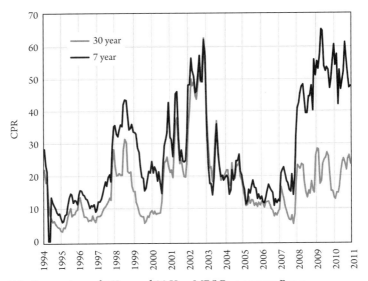

Figure 7.4 Comparison of 7-Year and 30-Year MBS Prepayment Rates

Figure 7.6 shows prepayments rates by age. Here it is clear that the aging patterns of loans with low coupons (so-called discount mortgages, because the mortgage-backed securities based on these loans would trade at a price below par) is much different than the aging pattern of the premium (above par) loans.

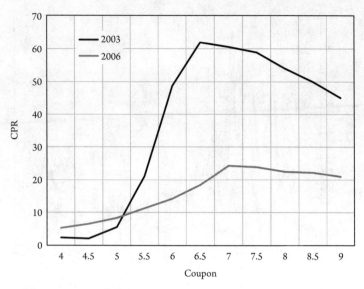

Figure 7.5 Prepayment Rates for 30-Year MBS by Coupon

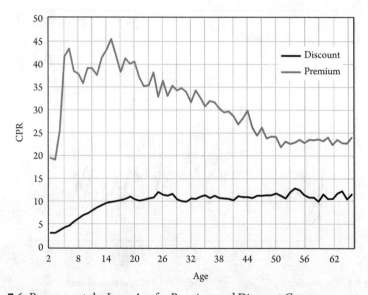

Figure 7.6 Prepayments by Loan Age for Premium and Discount Coupons

DRIVERS OF PREPAYMENTS

While the figures above show prepayment behavior, they do not provide an explanation. A statistical approach to develop a model would be to identify variables
that had high correlations with prepayment behavior and use those to develop a

regression equation. A typical approach would be to recognize that prepayment rates must be between 0 and 100%. A logit model is then used in a regression, so that the result always falls between zero and 100%.

$$Ln[smm/(1-smm)] = \alpha + sum\sum \beta_i x_i + \varepsilon \qquad (7.2)$$

While this approach may lead to a reasonable fit to historical prepayments, it is not the approach we recommend or utilize. Instead we believe that the first step should be to understand the process that is being modeled and then use statistics to better fit the model to the data.

Prepayments generally arise from four major sources. First, borrowers moving and prepaying their mortgages when they sell their houses. This is often called *turnover*. Second, borrowers *refinancing* their existing mortgage while remaining in the house. Borrowers generally refinance either to lower their mortgage payments or to receive additional cash using their home as collateral. In the wake of the financial crisis, some borrowers have refinanced to pay off their debt faster. Third, in the case of agency MBS, loans from borrowers who are delinquent on their loans are bought out of the pools and appear to investors as prepayments. Fourth, partial prepayments: Some borrowers also make additional principal payments beyond the required amount. These are sometimes called *curtailments*, because once a borrower makes a partial prepayment, they are still required to make the same monthly payment. The net effect is to shorten the maturity of the mortgage, thus the life is "curtailed."

While these are known to be the significant contributors to prepayments, the split between them is not provided in the mortgage data. Instead, all prepayments from these, as well as any other potential sources, merely show up as a reduction in the pool balance. Nevertheless, with these motivations in mind, it is possible to theorize on what variables might be drivers of prepayments. Notice the difference in terminology from the statistical approach. In the statistical approach, the focus is on finding correlated variables; in the financial approach, the emphasis is on finding drivers.

Freddie Mac provides two reports on refinancing transactions that they call "Refinance Activities Reports" that can help provide insight into refinancing behavior. One report shows the product choice of refinancing borrowers, the other provides information on cash-out refinancing. While these reports provide insight, it is difficult to use them in modeling as they are not tied to specific loans or specific pools.[1]

As turnover and refinancing have different drivers, turnover will be easiest to observe in discount mortgages, where the impact of refinancing is reduced.

---

[1] For access to these reports see: http://www.freddiemac.com/news/finance/refi_archives.htm.

Premium mortgages are likely to exhibit the combined impact of refinancing and turnover. A quick look at the relative speeds of discount versus premium mortgages gives a good idea of the relative magnitude of the two effects. Discount mortgages generally have prepayment speeds under 10% CPR, while premium mortgages can exhibit prepayments speeds well above 50% CPR. Clearly for premium mortgages the refinancing effects can dominate turnover.

Turnover

The drivers of turnover are likely to be those features of the loans and economy that affect when people move. Turnover then would be closely related to home sales. While it might make sense to model turnover as a function of home sales, this would not provide much insight, as home sales and turnover are basically two manifestations of the same economic activity. When examining the data it becomes clear that a major factor in both home sales and prepayments is seasonality or the month of the year. Prepayments are higher in the summer months and slower in the winter months. Also, as shown in Figure 7.4, there seems to be a strong relationship between loan age and prepayments, at least for discount mortgages.

It is probably possible to relate turnover to GDP as well, but this would mean that mortgage models would require a GDP model. Turnover is also likely tied to

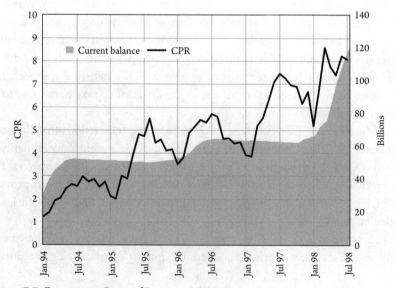

Figure 7.7 Prepayment Rates of Discount Mortgages

changes in home prices as rising home prices may be related to greater economic activity and the ability of homeowners to trade up.

Refinancing

For refinancing, the primary driver is interest rates. The greater the differential between the borrowers mortgage rate and prevailing interest rates, the greater the incentive to refinance. Figure 7.8 shows the relative incentives under four different approaches to modeling the interest-rate incentive. Each approach is shown in two different economic environments. The first is for 10% mortgages in an environment where mortgages fall to 6.5%. The second is for 7% mortgages, perhaps representing refinanced 10% mortgages, in an environment where rates

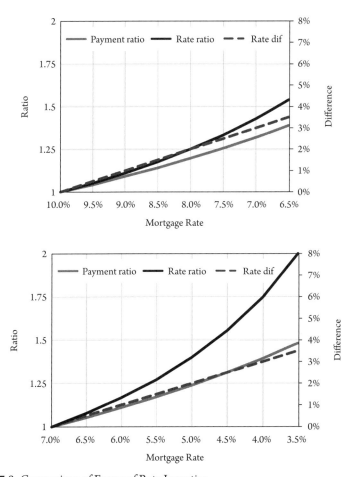

Figure 7.8 Comparison of Forms of Rate Incentive

fall further. While the methods have similar sensitivities in the first environment, they produce very different results in the second.

Understanding the borrower's perspective might be helpful in formulating an approach. We believe that borrowers are mostly motivated by the ability to lower their mortgage payments. Moreover, we believe that it is best to view the reduction relative to the current payment the borrower faces. A borrower with a $1000 a month payment will view a $100 reduction more favorably than a borrower with a $3000 per month payment.

While this is our opinion, it is an empirical question as to which of the interest-rate incentives provides the best fit to prepayment data. On the other hand, the empirical data often is limited by the range of prior experience. A good model will need to function outside of the range of historical data. Therefore even formulations which provide a good fit in sample should be rejected if their out of sample extrapolation produces results that are economically unreasonable.

Another important decision in the modeling process is the choice of interest rate available to borrowers. Borrower decisions are most likely driven by the rates that are available to them. The mortgage rate is often called the primary rate as opposed to the secondary rate, which reflects the pricing of traded MBS. Unfortunately it is difficult to view the primary rate directly. One source of primary rates is the Freddie Mac Weekly Primary Mortgage Market Survey® (PMMS®). Other sources include a firm called HSH and bankrate.com.

Traders cannot rely on historical surveyed rates; they need to compute the value of their positions based on current, live market rates. Therefore, secondary mortgage rates are often preferred for mortgage valuation. Even these have limitations, as most valuation models need to be linked to the treasury yield curve or the LIBOR yield curve.

Cash Out Refinancing

As some borrowers refinance their loans to take cash out of their homes, it is clear that home prices could have a significant impact on refinancing as well as turnover. Rising home prices might lead to greater cash out refinancing, while falling home prices could limit the ability of borrowers to refinance. [Government policies during 2009 to 2012 and beyond, generally under the name HARP were aimed at overcoming some of the obstacles for "underwater" borrowers to refinance their loans.]

Just as home-price appreciation could affect borrowers' ability to refinance, so might other aspects of borrower creditworthiness affect prepayments. In the absence of detailed credit data on borrowers, proxies of borrower creditworthiness might be useful measures of these effects. In particular, the interest rate paid by borrowers relative to other borrowers taking out loans at the same time turns out to be a good proxy. This proxy is called SATO, or spread at origination. Borrowers who pay higher mortgage rates are generally believed to have impaired credit and may therefore exhibit less ability to prepay.

HETEROGENEITY AND BURNOUT

In chapter 1, we discussed the role of heterogeneity. Given that the agency data represents pools of mortgages, we would expect there to be differences among the mortgages in the pool. Figure 7.9 demonstrates this. The dotted line shows the interest rate on new current coupon mortgages. The solid line shows the prepayment rate on 8% net rate mortgages originated during 2000. As mortgage rates fell below 7%, the prepayment speed on the loans rose rapidly. However, not all the loans prepaid. After 2004, although interest rates remained below 6%, the prepayment rates fell, so for the same incentive the prepayment rate was lower. This is called *burnout* and reflects the differential in responsiveness to prepayments of borrowers within a pool. Burnout also creates path dependency in mortgage prepayment rates. That is, the prepayment rate in this period depends on the interest rates experienced by the pool in prior periods. Path dependency limits the use of certain backward induction based valuation methods, as discussed in chapter 8.

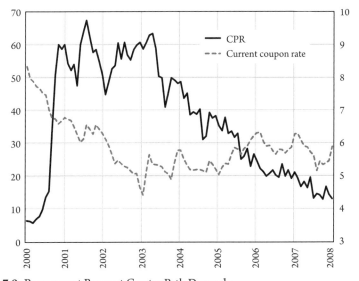

Figure 7.9 Prepayment Burnout Creates Path Dependence

The use of multi-population models can replicate burnout and restore path independence to mortgage valuation. In one of the earliest modeling attempts, Davidson (1987) and Davidson et al. (1988) proposed the Refinancing Threshold model in which collateral is split into three or more American option bonds having differing strikes. A conceptually similar approach proposed by Kalotay and Yang (2002) divides collateral into bonds differing by their exercise timing. Such structures naturally call for the backward induction pricing, but they fall short in replicating actually observed, probabilistically smoothed prepayment behavior—even if many constituent bonds are used. On the other hand, analytical systems used by Wall Street firms have employed multi-population mortgage models (see Hayre, 1994, 2000) but do not seek any computational benefits, as they rely heavily on Monte-Carlo pricing anyway. The method we use here was introduced by Levin (2001).

Based on the drivers described earlier it might be possible to build a prepayment model using loan program, WAC, WALA, interest rates, and home prices. A simple model using these factors is the subject of the next section.

FUNCTIONAL FORM OF A PREPAYMENT MODEL

In chapter 1, we discussed several basic principles in understanding the behavior of borrowers.

- The randomness of individual outcomes
- Common factors
- Heterogeneity: observed and unobserved

These principles need to be honored in developing a functional form for the prepayment model. In addition, the insights from studying the data and identifying key drivers need to be incorporated into the model. Based on these factors the model should include

- Components for refinancing and turnover
- Vasicek like S-curves for behaviors driven by common factors
- Role for unobserved heterogeneity since this is a pool model

A simple candidate model therefore is

$$\lambda(t) = \psi(t)\lambda_a(t) + [1 - \psi(t)]\lambda_p(t)$$

and

$$\psi(t+1) = \psi(t)\frac{1-\lambda_a(t)}{1-\lambda(t)}$$

(7.3)

$$\lambda_a(t) = ActiveSMM = TurnoverSMM + RefiSMM$$

$$\lambda_p(t) = PassiveSMM = TurnoverSMM + \beta * RefiSMM$$

$$TurnoverSMM = f(age, rate, hpa) * Seasonality\ (month)$$

$$RefiSMM = g(credit, hpa) * N(h(rate\ incentive, hpa, credit))$$

where $\psi(t)$ is the proportion of active borrowers, $\lambda_x(t)$ is the termination rate for each set of borrowers, a and p, $\beta < 1$, $N(z)$ is the cumulative normal density function, f, g, are functions on $[0,1]$, h is a continuous function on $(-\infty,\infty)$.

The model uses active/passive decomposition to model burnout (unobserved heterogeneity) as we described in chapter 1. For the active and passive segments the model splits prepayments into *turnover* and *refinancing*. Both segments have the same turnover, but the refinancing portion of the passive segment is lower. Prepayments from defaults and curtailments are not specifically modeled but will be incorporated into the model fit by finding model parameters that match total terminations including these other factors.

Turnover is a function of loan age and month, as well as smaller effects from interest rates and home prices. Refinancing is modeled as cumulative normal distribution, representing the impact of common factors on a population, but unlike the Vasicek model, the total prepayment rate in any one period is capped at an amount that will be determined empirically by the function g. (We know that prepayment rates for large cohorts of pools rarely exceed 15% in any one month.)

The refinancing incentive has been modeled in a variety of ways. As discussed in chapter 1 and shown in formula (1.9-M), there are many possible functions that could be used for the refinancing incentive that reflect the idiosyncratic nature of individual borrower motivations for refinancing. Some common forms for the refinancing S-curve are the arctangent curve, piecewise linear functions, and the cumulative normal distribution, used here. In all cases, the functional forms need to be scaled and transformed so as to match actual prepayment data. Figure 7.10 shows these three functions. Each of these functions is shown with payment ratio as the driver of refinancing. Borrowers with the greatest percentage savings in payment have the greatest motivation to prepay. All three functions have been scaled to produce a maximum monthly prepayment rate of 0.1 (10%).

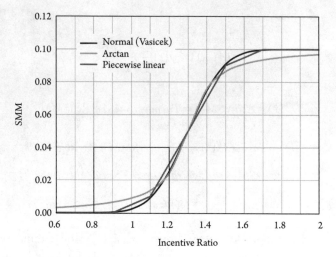

Figure 7.10a Refinancing Functions

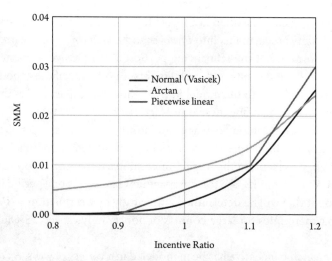

Figure 7.10b Detail of Refinancing Function

The arctangent function was one of the first functions used for prepayment models because it had the appropriate S-like shape. However, it does not have any economic meaning, as borrowers are unlikely to base their personal financial decisions on trigonometric functions.

The piecewise linear approach allows the fine tuning of prepayment functions to data, but can create discontinuous sensitivity measures such as duration.

The normal distribution is consistent with the logic of the Vasicek formula which assumes that borrower decisions are driven by a common economic factor and by normally distributed idiosyncratic factors. The Vasicek formula matches the normal distribution shown in Figure 7.10a, assuming a standard deviation of interest rates of 85bp/year (which translates into a 0.1 change in payment ratio) and a correlation of prepayment incentive of 30%, indicating the dispersion of borrower behavior. Higher loan value correlations would lead to a steeper refinancing curve, as more borrowers would refinance with the same incentive.

Figure 7.10b is a detail of Figure 7.10a and makes it easier to see the difference between the arctangent, piecewise linear, and normal functions. The piecewise and normal function parameters have been set to bring the two in line with each other.

Credit variables such as SATO and home prices can accentuate or diminish the rate incentive. An example of how credit variables can interact with refinancing incentive using the preceding functional form is shown in chapter 12.

FITTING THE MODEL TO THE DATA

Model fitting is the process of finding parameters for the desired functional form that provides a good fit of model results to actual data. The model fit process is also a time to reassess the choice of functional form or to choose between competing approaches.

While the amount of model data is vast, the economic environments covered by the data may be limited. Figure 7.11a shows the Fannie Mae current-coupon rate (the secondary rate) and the FHFA HPI over the period from January 1994 through mid-2012. All mortgages outstanding during this period experienced only these economic environments; thus while there may be tens of millions of mortgage loans, there are about a dozen economic scenarios represented in the data.

For example, prior to 2007 there were no periods of declining home prices on a national level. Also during the full-time period there were no sustained periods of rising interest rates. Figure 7.11b shows this data in another way. It is a scatterplot of the one year changes in mortgage rate and home-price index during this time period. As shown in the chart most of the data represents changes in interest rates of less than 200 basis points and there are only two periods where interest rates rose more than 100 basis points. Any model results outside of the range of these changes will represent an extrapolation of the model fit. The limits on the extent of the data are one reason why the choice of functional form is so important.

As we have placed choice of functional form above ease of calculation, we face a significant obstacle in statistical analysis. For the most part, we find that we need to use non-linear optimization methods. These methods are generally

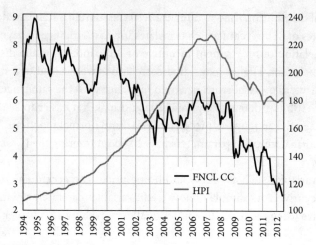

Figure 7.11a Home Prices and Mortgage Rates

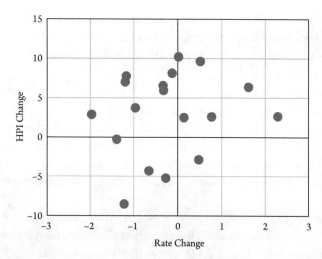

Figure 7.11b Home-Price Change and Interest-Rate Change Environments

search algorithms that look for global and local minimums for likelihood estima-
tors. These searches are frequently unstable and left to their own devices might
find fits that are economically unreasonable. Therefore the process of optimization is often iterative and requires a substantial amount of judgment on the part
of the modeler.

Another side effect of our choice of functional form over ease of calculation
is that the statistical properties of the errors of the model and the errors in parameter estimates are essentially unknown. Even measures such as R-squared are
not always reliable measures of model fit.

Some modelers choose to underweight or overweight segments of data to ensure model "focus" on important portions. For example, pools can be equally weighted regardless of the number of loans or outstanding balance, or they can be weighted by balance. It is difficult to provide any strict guidelines as to which of these approaches is preferred.

Subjective Evaluation

In the end, model fit is a reflection of how well the model fits the data, the reasonableness of model forecasts, and the usefulness of the analytical results produced using the model. Figure 7.12 shows the forecasts of the model under a variety of scenarios. The modeler needs to look at forecasts such as these and determine if they seem reasonable. Often it is easier to develop a model that provides a good fit to historical data than to produce a model that provides reasonable forecasts.

Monitoring

As with any model, actual experience will deviate from forecast. It is extremely important to monitor the performance of the model to determine if there have been significant deviations of model from actual. For prepayment models,

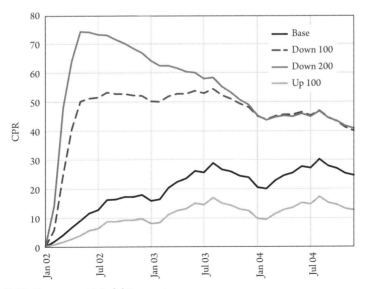

Figure 7.12 Prepayment Model Forecasts

forecasts are conditional on the level of the economic variables, in this case interest rates and home prices. Monitoring should therefore focus on the performance of the model conditional on the economic data.

Figure 7.13 shows the actual performance of Freddie Mac 30-year 6% mortgages originated during 2003 versus the Andrew Davidson & Co., Inc. prepayment model for dates from 2004 through 2012. Several features of the figure are worth noting.

We consider this to be a good fit of model to actual. The model was developed using data through October 2006. Out of sample, the model generally captures the changes in prepayment rates, at least through mid-2009. It is important to note that even during in-sample periods and periods of good fit there will be differences between actual and model. Some of those differences persist for extended periods.

During the period post mid-2009, there was a significant drop in actual prepayments; this was most likely due to economic factors related to the financial meltdown that are not features of the model. One approach to periods such as this, which are likely to be transitory, is model tuning. Tuning allows the user of a model to make adjustments to the model for particular uses. An example of tuning would be to reduce the refinancing component of the model by 25% during a period of economic distress. Another possible tuning would be to alter the refinancing incentive by having the model act as though the borrowers face higher mortgage rates than the primary or secondary rates would indicate.

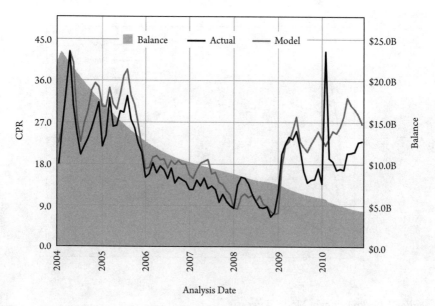

Figure 7.13 Prepayment Performance Monitoring

The figure also shows a spike in prepayments in February 2010. This spike is so large that it looks like a data error. In fact, this spike is from a change in policy (a single-month buyout) at Freddie Mac related to the treatment of delinquent mortgages. Such an event would have been unthinkable, let alone unforecastable, when the loans were originated in 2003.

An important component of model monitoring is to assess the likelihood that a change in prepayment behavior is transitory or permanent. Thus, divergence of model from actual is usually a call for more analysis rather than a clear signal that the model should be updated.

As important as the need to monitor and update models is the need to incorporate the fact that there will be model error in the analysis of mortgage-backed securities. Mortgage investment should not be based on the idea that the model captures all risk and uncertainty. Rather, mortgage modeling should be based upon the idea that there is considerable uncertainty about what actual prepayments will be, even given a high quality forecast based upon a well thought out and well implemented model.

MODEL ADAPTATION TO NEW DATA

Traditionally, prepayment modelers attempt to find variables that explain prepayment and use historical relationships for projecting prepayments in the future. As new prepayment data becomes available, a decision is made to either keep the model (if the model performs well) or re-design it (if it performs poorly).

An attractive and intriguing alternative is to adapt a model to new prepayment data continuously using the Bayesian estimation approach. It combines new data on a more dynamic basis with a previously existing model (called *prior*). In order to demonstrate the use of adaptive modeling concept, let us assume that prepayment model follows our general refinancing-turnover design [compare with specification (7.3)] with uncertain scales:

$$\tilde{\lambda} = \rho R + \tau T$$

where R and T are refinancing and turnover models, correspondingly, and ρ and τ are normally distributed uncertainties with known standard deviations σ_ρ and σ_τ. For each time step, the expectations of those uncertainties are equal to prior-period values and, at time 0, $\rho = \tau = 1$.

At each point of time t, we observe actual prepayments $\lambda_{k,t}$ of a number of pools indexed by k. It is important to realize that each-pool prepayment observation may be random due to not only economic factors or a model uncertainty, but also because of a limited number of loans. Namely, a single-loan prepayment conditional on unbiased expectation $\tilde{\lambda}$ is distributed binomially with the mean of $\tilde{\lambda}$ and the standard deviation of $\sigma_t = \sqrt{\tilde{\lambda}(1-\tilde{\lambda})}$. Hence, for k-th pool of N_k loans, the standard deviation of observations given economic factors and pool data will be equal to $\sigma_{k,t} = \sigma_t / \sqrt{N_k}$. Let us assume for simplicity that, for a typically large N_k, the distribution of $\lambda_{k,t}$ is close to normal.

At each point of time t, independent Bayesian innovations ρ_t and τ_t can be chosen to maximize the quadratic log-likelihood function

$$L(\rho_t, \tau_t) \equiv -\frac{(\rho_t - \rho_{t-1})^2}{2\sigma_\rho^2} - \frac{(\tau_t - \tau_{t-1})^2}{2\sigma_\tau^2} - \sum_k \frac{[\lambda_{k,t} - \rho_t R_{k,t} - \tau_t T_{k,t}]^2}{2\sigma_{k,t}^2} \qquad (7.4)$$

Maximization is achieved in a closed form, in which optimal corrections are linear combinations of the model's errors:

$$\rho_t - \rho_{t-1} = \sum_k F_{k,t}(\lambda_{k,t} - \tilde{\lambda}_{k,t})$$

$$\tau_t - \tau_{t-1} = \sum_k G_{k,t}(\lambda_{k,t} - \tilde{\lambda}_{k,t})$$

$$(7.5)$$

with coefficients F and G being functions of the sigmas, R and T and turning zero when $\sigma_\rho = 0$ and $\sigma_\tau = 0$, correspondingly. The solution finds the best compromise between deviations of the model from the prior and observed prepayments from the model.

Naturally, the adaptive scales will not change if the model perfectly predicts the outcome, i.e. $\lambda_{k,t} = \tilde{\lambda}_{k,t}$ for all k. The same holds true if we are certain that the model is accurate ($\sigma_\rho = \sigma_\tau = 0$). In the other extreme case, when the sizes of pools with observed prepayments are very large and $\sigma_{k,t}$ are close to zero, the last term of the log-likelihood function $L(\rho_t, \tau_t)$ dominates. Note that this term does not contain the prior values ρ_{t-1}, τ_{t-1} so the adaptation will not depend on them either.

The adaptive modeling approach has many applications and extensions. It can be used for parameters and factors other than prepayment scales and for uncertainties other than normal; it can be used assuming that Bayesian innovations ρ_t and τ_t are correlated. Instead of a large number of loan pools or cohorts, one can consider adaptation of a particular pool (see the next section).

When we apply the adaptive algorithm (7.5) to the pre-2007 model and start with $\rho_0 = \tau_0 = 1$ in 2007, the abnormally slow actual prepayment experience gradually moves ρ_t, τ_t down. This action is similar to the model tuning process we would apply using the results of straight monitoring. However, a modeler would not alter the model every month—unlike the adaptive algorithm (7.5).

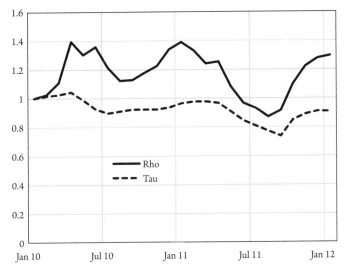

Figure 7.14 The Rho-Tau Adaptation of the Post-2007 Model

For example, its application to the 2010–2011 two-year period reveals deviations in physical prepayment speeds from model values (Figure 7.14).

Adaptive modeling will likely produce a more accurate short-term forecast. However, it uses a recent experience that may be short-lived, transitional, or indeed serve as a signal of permanent shift. For example, the decline in prepayment speeds during the 2007–2009 crisis was evidence of a long-term and severe friction in mortgage origination. In contrast, the February 2010 spike we earlier observed in Figure 7.13 was a one-month event that needs to be ignored for model adaptation purposes. In order for monthly prepayment data to be used for a long-term model's adaptation, an additional filter must be employed. For example, one can apply innovations (7.5) using an additional "modeling" uncertainty imposed on top of the uncertainty of prepayments created by limited pool size. This way, each observation point will contribute to adaptation, but it will take a number of months before an established new trend is accounted for in the long-term model. The variation in Rho and Tau shown here will be reflected in the risk-neutral modeling discussed in chapter 11.

ENHANCED VARIABLES

Prepayment modelers understood that borrower credit had an impact on prepayment behavior and sought ways to infer the credit characteristics of the borrowers. SATO, spread at origination, described earlier, was one such method.

Beginning in 2003, Freddie Mac began releasing additional data about the mortgage pools. This gave modelers and investors the ability to more specifically integrate credit information and other characteristics into prepayment forecasts. The enhanced data was provided at the pool level on a weighted average and quartile basis:

- Loan size at origination
- Credit score at origination
- LTV at origination
- Loan purpose
- Property type
- Occupancy
- Geographical distribution (by state)

While it might be better to look at this data at the loan level, the availability of even pool level data can enhance prepayment forecasts. Figure 7.15 shows the prepayment behavior of actual pools during 2006. Each line represents a pool with different mortgage net coupons. Note that there is a strong significant effect of LTV on prepayments, even at the pool level. The impact of LTV is different for the higher coupons than for the lower coupons. This indicates that the LTV would have a differing impact for the turnover and refinancing components of prepayments.

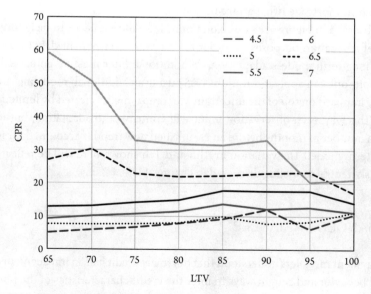

Figure 7.15 Prepayment Speeds by Pool Loan-to-Value

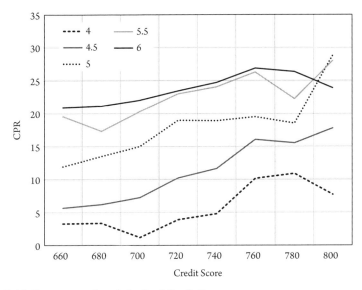

Figure 7.16 Prepayment Speeds by Pool Credit Score

Figure 7.16 shows a similar analysis for credit score. This chart is for 2011, during the financial crisis when borrower credit had a significant impact on credit access. Here we see that higher credit scores produced higher prepayment speeds across the coupon spectrum. Credit score appears to have the greatest impact on the lower coupons, as the high credit score/low coupon borrowers most likely had the ability to refinance into even lower coupon mortgages while the low credit score borrowers would not have that opportunity.

These variables can be incorporated into prepayment models by scaling the turnover and refinancing functions as shown in (7.6).

$$\lambda_a(t) = ActiveSMM = M_T * TurnoverSMM + M_R * RefiSMM$$

$$(7.6)$$

$$\lambda_p(t) = PassiveSMM = M_T * TurnoverSMM + \beta * M_R * RefiSMM$$

where M_T and M_R are scalars based on the enhanced variables.

M_T and M_R can be computed based on variables such credit score, LTV, and loan size. They can be computed using simple tables or more complex functions that look at the interaction of the enhanced variables. This approach is discussed in Szakallas, Davidson, and Levin (2006).

The enhanced pool level disclosure does not allow for the full analysis that would be possible with loan level data. For example, suppose there are two pools with two loans each. Both pools have weighted average credit score of 700

Table 7.1 Pool Composition Example

Pool A	Credit Score	LTV
Loan A1	800	70
Loan A2	600	90
Average	*700*	*80*

Pool B	Credit Score	LTV
Loan B1	800	90
Loan B2	600	70
Average	*700*	*80*

and weighted average LTV of 80. Both pools also have the identical distributions of each variable, since these pools are constructed by switching the combination of LTVs and credit scores (see Table 7.1).

Borrower A1 with a high credit score and a low LTV has much more financial flexibility and ability to prepay than Borrower A2 with a lower credit score and a higher LTV. In the second pool the credit characteristics of each borrower are mixed. These pools could have very different prepayment characteristics, despite the same average features because the response to these variables can be non-linear and depends on iterations. For example, if interest rates fall, the low credit score, high LTV borrower (A2) will be much less able to take advantage of the opportunity to refinance than all of the other borrowers, and therefore Pool A might have lower prepayments than pool B. Pool A also has a higher probability of default for moderate declines in home prices.

The adaptive (Bayesian) modeling approach we discussed in the previous section can be used to tune specified-pool scalars M_T and M_R. Say we use the new data to adapt the overall model for all Fannie Mae fixed-rate 30-year mortgages first. We then define M_T and M_R from specified-pool enhanced dataset (loans size, credit score, etc.) as the prior model used at origination. As actual prepayments of the pool become known, we alter parameters using the Bayesian technique. A single pool may not have enough data experience to separate changes in both M_T and M_R accurately; we can consider adapting the overall scale instead.

In chapter 12 we discuss loan level modeling of prepayment and default. Loan data provides a much more reliable way to incorporate loan features and transform some unobserved heterogeneity into observed heterogeneity.

8

Engineering of Valuation Models without Simulations

Chapter 4 introduced and explained the two most important financial principles of valuing risky assets such as MBS. First, we showed that every asset is expected to return the risk-free rate plus a compensation for bearing risk, often called "risky return." Second, we proved that a risky return can be formed automatically by shifting the underlying risk process. This shift is called risk-neutral and can apply to both economic variables (interest rates, home prices) and a model's own uncertainties such as a systematic bias in a model's specification or the risk that such a bias can arise in the future. Chapters 5 and 6 of this book deal with risk-neutral models of economic factors whereas chapters 11 and 13 will describe how one can design risk-neutral models of borrower behavior, that is, a prepayment model or a loss model.

This line of thought has led us to the ultimate practical recipe of valuation modeling: price $P(t,x)$ of an MBS solves a partial differential equation (PDE) or, equivalently, it can be computed as a mathematical expectation over a risk-neutral evolution of risk factors. For the reader's convenience, we rewrite these key mathematical facts as follows:

$$\mathcal{D}p \equiv \frac{\partial p}{\partial t} + \mu \frac{\partial p}{\partial x} + \frac{1}{2}\sigma^2 \frac{\partial^2 p}{\partial x^2} - (r + OAS + \lambda)p = -c + r + OAS, \quad p(T,x) = 0$$

$$(8.1)$$

$$p(0) = E \int_0^T [c(t) - r(t) - OAS]e^{y(t)}dt$$

$$(8.2)$$

$$dy = -(r + \lambda + OAS)dt$$

where $p = P - 1$ is price premium (or discount) and OAS is a discount spread. The three rates, the risk-free rate r, coupon rate c, and principal pay-off rate λ, can be functions of time t and the risk factor x that has volatility of σ and risk-neutral drift of μ. Usually, the terminal time T is set to maturity or balloon so that $p(T,x) = 0$ is surely known. The OAS term in (8.1) and (8.2) stands in recognition that, practically speaking, not all risk factors can be reflected in the dynamics of $x(t)$, be it a scalar or a vector of many factors. Some risk factors may be difficult to quantify accurately (e.g., liquidity) and, at times, MBS can be simply mispriced. Most commonly used agency MBS valuation engines ("OAS models") are designed either to solve PDE (8.1) or (much more often) to compute expectation (8.2).

This chapter demonstrates how to achieve these goals without Monte Carlo simulations. The challenges arise largely due to the complexity of the prepayment models described in the prior chapter. In our valuation equations, prepayments enter into the rate λ, which is the total balance amortization rate. Unlike standard options, prepayments are an inefficiently exercised American option. Prepayments are often modeled as a function of rate, rather than price, and are path-dependent.

EXPLORING CLOSED-FORM SOLUTIONS

Generally, financial engineers would like to obtain closed form solutions to value financial instruments as such solutions can be fast and accurate. However, production models that closely resemble borrower behavior and complex MBS cash flows will not allow closed form valuation solutions to exist. Therefore, the questions we plan to address in this section are

A. When can a closed-form solution be obtained?
B. What is that solution?
C. Once obtained, how can it be practically utilized?

Gaussian Models

Let us start with the Gaussian case studied by Levin (1998) and continue using the continuous-time formulation. Assuming that all the rates (r, c, λ) are normally distributed, mathematical expectation in (8.2) can be found analytically and expressed in the form of a deterministic integral computed from 0 to T. This statement utilizes the following fact: for two normally distributed variables, vector s and scalar y

$$E\left[g(s)e^y\right] \equiv E\left[g(u)\right]E(e^y) \tag{8.3}$$

where $u = s + Cov(s,y)$ and $g(s)$ is an arbitrary function.

If all the rates are Gaussian, the same can be said about y, and the analytical form for $E(y)$, $Var(y)$ and $Cov(s,y)$ must exist. In (8.2), y is defined as an integral of $-(r+\lambda+OAS)$, $s = c - r - OAS$, a scalar, and $g(s) = s$. Note that $E(e^{y(t)})$ has the meaning of the present value (measured at time 0) of the time-t asset's balance.

For example, assume a constant-parameter Hull-White model for the short-rate process $r(t)$ with expectation given by formula (5.6) of chapter 5:

$$E\left[r(t)\right] = f(t) + \frac{\sigma^2}{2a^2}(1 - e^{-at})^2$$

Denote $dy' = rdt$ with the additional statistics we now need

$$E[y'(t)] = \int_0^t f(\tau)d\tau + \frac{\sigma^2}{2a^2}\left(t - 2\frac{1-e^{-at}}{a} + \frac{1-e^{-2at}}{2a}\right)$$

$$\frac{1}{2}Var[y'(t)] = E[y'(t)] - \int_0^t f(\tau)d\tau = \frac{\sigma^2}{2a^2}\left(t - 2\frac{1-e^{-at}}{a} + \frac{1-e^{-2at}}{2a}\right)$$

$$Cov(r(t), y'(t)) = E[r(t)] - f(t) \equiv \frac{\sigma^2}{2a^2}(1 - e^{-at})^2$$

Now set $\lambda = \lambda_0(t) + \lambda_1 r$, $c = c_0(t) + c_1(t)r$ with coefficients possibly changing in time in a deterministic way (except for λ_1). Then, applying the (8.3) expectation transformation rule, we get:

$$p(0) = \int_0^T \left\{c_0(t) - OAS + [c_1(t) - 1]\left\{E[r(t)] - (1 + \lambda_1)Cov[r(t), y'(t)]\right\}\right\} *$$

$$exp\left\{-(1+\lambda_1)E[y'(t)] - OAS * t - \int_0^t \lambda_0(\tau)d\tau + \frac{1}{2}(1+\lambda_1)^2 Var[y'(t)]\right\}dt$$

$$\tag{8.4}$$

with all necessary statistics already listed previously.

Therefore, the MBS valuation problem becomes a matter of integrating deterministic functions of time. The main limitation of this approach comes from making the assumption that the total amortization rate λ is linear in r, hence, normally distributed. As we indicated in many places in this book, prepayment modelers think of $\lambda(r)$ as an S-curve, which varies between 0 and 1. A normally distributed variable can take any value, thereby contradicting not only prepay modeling limitations, but even the prepayment speed definition. However, $\lambda(r)$ can be linearized within some limited deviations of interest rates.

An Affine Modeling Solution

The class of models that enable a close-end solution with random amortization is not limited to Gaussian models. Let us show how we can employ the affine modeling approach described in chapter 5. Instead of computing integral (8.2) explicitly, we will try to solve PDE (8.1). We first introduce a homogeneous version of PDE (8.1) by dropping its free terms:

$$\mathcal{D}P \equiv \frac{\partial P}{\partial t} + \mu \frac{\partial P}{\partial x} + \frac{1}{2}\sigma^2 \frac{\partial^2 P}{\partial x^2} - (r + \lambda + OAS)P = 0, \quad P(T,x)=1 \qquad (8.1\text{-h})$$

Assuming the "affine" form for μ and σ^2

$$\mu(t,x) = \alpha_1(t) + \alpha_2(t)x, \quad \sigma^2(t,x) = \beta_1(t) + \beta_2(t)x$$

we can effectively follow the relevant section of chapter 5. Setting $r = x$ and assuming $\lambda = \lambda_0(t) + \lambda_1(t)r$, the solution to (8.1-h) will again be in the form (5.26), $P(t,T,x) = exp[a(t,T) + b(t,T)x]$, with Ricatti equations for unknown deterministic functions $a(t,T)$ and $b(t,T)$, similar to (5.27), (5.28):

$$b_t'(t,T) = -\alpha_2(t)b(t,T) - \frac{1}{2}\beta_2(t)b^2(t,T) + 1 + \lambda_1(t) \qquad (8.5)$$

$$a_t'(t,T) = -\alpha_1(t)b(t,T) - \frac{1}{2}\beta_1(t)b^2(t,T) + OAS + \lambda_0(t) \qquad (8.6)$$

subject to the terminal conditions, $a(T,T) = b(T,T) = 0$.

Function $P(t,T,x)$ solving (8.1-h) is called the *fundamental solution* or the *Green function*. It can be interpreted as factor-x, time-t price of the MBS's terminal balance for time T (i.e. a bond amortizing at the random rate, but paying no principal or interest until T). This Green function pivots the solution to the PDE (8.1) with the free term, $-c + r + OAS$. This solution is

$$p(t,r) = \xi_0(t) + \int_t^T \xi_1(\tau) P(t,\tau,r) d\tau - \xi_0(T) P(t,T,r) \qquad (8.7)$$

where deterministic functions $\xi_0(t)$ and $\xi_1(t)$ are related to model's variable coefficients as

$$\xi_0(t) = \frac{c_1(t)-1}{1+\lambda_1(t)}, \quad \xi_1(t) = \xi_{0t}'(t) - [\lambda_0(t) + OAS]\xi_0(t) + c_0(t) - OAS \qquad (8.8)$$

Solution (8.7) can be verified by the direct substitution into PDE (8.1), using the fact that $\mathcal{D}P = 0$ and separating terms that are linear in r from those free of r. It is evident that the terminal condition $p(T,x) = 0$ is satisfied. In order to interpret the structure of solution (8.7), let us set $c_1 = \lambda_1 = 0$. This is the case when MBS pays interest rate c_0 and is prepaid at rate λ_0 that don't depend on r. From (8.8) we will have $\xi_0(t) = -1, \xi_1(t) = c_0(t) + \lambda_0(t)$ thereby making solution (8.7)

$$p(t,r) = \int_t^T [c_0(\tau) + \lambda_0(\tau)] P(t,\tau,r) d\tau + P(t,T,r) - 1$$

The first term integrates interest and principal payments to be received at $\tau \geq t$ and gives the present value at time t. The second term is the present value of the terminal balance (if any). The last term subtracts par value to obtain the premium or discount. Note that the $c_0(\tau) + \lambda_0(\tau)$ factor is deterministic and known. This clear and simple case is quite different from the general situation when c_1 or λ_1 are non-zeros. In that case, solution (8.7) cannot be reduced to a mere integration of cash flow rate $c + \lambda$ known at t.

Solution (8.7), much like (8.4), expresses the MBS price via a deterministic integral. The randomness of variables entering the valuation problem is addressed either explicitly or implicitly. In comparison to computing mathematical expectation directly, the affine modeling method allows for obtaining closed-end formulas with fewer restrictions on the underlying process for $r(t)$. Yet the assumption that the pay-off speed is linear in market rate remains a severe limitation. For example, the CIR model for $r(t)$ leads to positive rates. Then, setting a negative λ_1, we ensure total amortization rate λ to never exceed λ_0. This will serve a better assumption than the one employed by Gaussian models. However, the floor for λ will not be set, therefore, $\lambda(r)$ cannot be a true S-like function.

The Kolbe-Zagst Approximation

Kolbe and Zagst (2009) proposed to present the S-like prepayment curve in a piece-wise form

$$\lambda(t,r)=max\left[min\left(\lambda_0+\lambda_1 r,\lambda_{max}\right),\lambda_{min}\right]$$

which keeps the linear prepayment function within some maximal and minimal values. They further decompose this S-function into the linear part, a "prepayment cap" and a "prepayment floor":

$$max\left[min\left(\lambda_0+\lambda_1 r,\lambda_{max}\right),\lambda_{min}\right]=\lambda_{linear}+\lambda_{floor}-\lambda_{cap}$$

$$\lambda_{linear}=\lambda_0+\lambda_1 r, \quad \lambda_{floor}=(\lambda_{min}-\lambda_0-\lambda_1 r)^+, \quad \lambda_{cap}=(\lambda_0+\lambda_1 r-\lambda_{max})^+$$

We now return to mathematical expectation (8.2) and rewrite it as

$$p(0)=E\int_0^T\left[c(t)-r(t)-OAS\right]e^{y(t)}dt=E\int_0^T\left[c(t)-r(t)-OAS\right]$$

$$\times exp\left(-\int_0^t(r+OAS+\lambda)(\tau)d\tau\right)dt$$

$$=E\int_0^T\left[c(t)-r(t)-OAS\right]exp\left(-\int_0^t(r+OAS+\lambda_{linear})(\tau)d\tau\right)$$

$$\times exp\left(-\int_0^t(\lambda_{floor}-\lambda_{cap})(\tau)d\tau\right)dt$$

The Kolbe and Zagst approximation involves a key assumption that the floor and cap terms are not large and rarely reached so that $exp\left(-\int_0^t(\lambda_{floor}-\lambda_{cap})(\tau)d\tau\right)\approx 1-\int_0^t\lambda_{floor}(\tau)d\tau+\int_0^t\lambda_{cap}(\tau)d\tau$. This transforms the formula for price premium into

$$p(0)=p_{linear}(0)-p_{floor}(0)+p_{cap}(0) \qquad (8.9)$$

where

$$p_{linear}(0)=E\int_0^T\left[c(t)-r(t)-OAS\right]exp\left(-\int_0^t(r+OAS+\lambda_{linear})(\tau)d\tau\right)dt$$

$$p_{cap}(0)=E\int_0^T\left[c(t)-r(t)-OAS\right]exp\left(-\int_0^t(r+OAS+\lambda_{linear})(\tau)d\tau\right)\int_0^t\lambda_{cap}(\tau)d\tau dt$$

$$p_{floor}(0) = E \int_{0}^{T} [c(t) - r(t) - OAS] exp\left(-\int_{0}^{t} (r + OAS + \lambda_{linear})(\tau) d\tau \right) \int_{0}^{t} \lambda_{floor}(\tau) d\tau dt$$

Let us explain the meaning of these three terms and how they can be evaluated in closed form. The first term, $p_{linear}(0)$ is the MBS price premium that assumes prepayment rate is linear in market rate. We have already shown that this case enables analytical solutions when the market rate is Gaussian, or more generally, affine. The two other terms represents MBS premium arising from values of prepayment cap and floor, respectively, in an economy discounted at an affine short rate with a balance amortizing according to an affine prepayment rate that is linear in market rate. Kolbe and Zagst provide closed-end formulas for a constant-coefficient CIR short-rate process. They find that the approximation is computationally efficient and "proves to be able to explain major market price movements successfully."

Gorovoy and Linetsky (2006) also considered a piece-wise linear form for prepayment function, $\lambda(t,r) = \lambda_0(t) + \gamma(k-r)^+$ when $r(t)$ follows the CIR diffusion. This form implicitly results in an S-like curve with a forced floor of $\lambda_0(t)$ and a natural cap of $\lambda_0(t) + \gamma k$ because $r > 0$. They present a solution in terms of a functional series. Its complexity is rather high and the required mathematical apparatus is beyond the scope of this book.

Finding a closed-form solution to the MBS valuation problem is challenging and difficult. For example, the assumption that the S-curve depends linearly on r within some boundaries, while attractive and intuitive, may result in getting bad Greeks. For realistic specifications of prepayment function or CMO payment rules, a closed-form solution is unlikely to exist or to be necessary. Surrogates can be derived; some were described in this section. They can be used for some purposes, for example, as *control variates* that complement numerical methods and improve their accuracy. We will describe these options in the next chapter.

VALUATION ON A PROBABILITY TREE USING THE ACTIVE-PASSIVE DECOMPOSITION POOL MODEL

The APD model we described in the previous chapter simulates prepayment burnout, but it also opens a door for MBS valuation via backward induction. With the migration between the two groups prohibited, the method decomposes a path-dependent pool into two path-independent parts, the active and the passive.

The Method

We start with the pool's maturity T when the price function is surely known and can be set to 1 (0 for price premium or value of an IO). Working backward, we derive prices at age $t-1$ from prices already found at age t. In doing so, we replace derivatives in PDE (8.1) with finite difference approximations, or weigh branches of the lattice by explicitly computed probabilities. If the market is multi-factor, then x should be considered a vector; the lattice will require more dimensions. Generally, the efficiency of finite-difference methods deteriorates quickly on high-dimensional grids because the number of nodes and cash flows grows geometrically; probability trees may maintain their speed, but at the cost of accuracy, if the same number of emanating nodes is used to capture multi-factor dynamics.

In this section, we illustrate the method operating on a probability tree. For every branch

$$P_{t-1} = \frac{c_t + P_t + \lambda_t(1-P_t)}{1+r_t+OAS} \tag{8.10}$$

where P_{t-1} is the previous-node value deduced from the next-node value P_t. Of course, probability weighting of thus obtained values applies to all emanating branches. Consider, for example, the binomial tree constructed and calibrated in chapter 5. We now complement Figure 5.2b with a tree of prepayment speeds $\lambda(t,r)$; that tree is shown in Figure 8.1, beneath the price/rate tree.

We selected a three-period pool, paying a 7% coupon and amortizing at a random speed dictated by the short rate only. The $\lambda(r)$ relationship is chosen to be $\lambda_t = 0.06 + 0.44N[40(7-r_{t-1})]$ where N stands for the standard cumulative normal distribution. Therefore, our prepayment curve is centered on a 7% rate and varies between 6% and 50%. Figure 8.1 demonstrates the use of iterative rule (8.10) for each branch of the tree with $OAS=0$. For example, price 101.438 at the root of the tree is found as

$$\frac{94.433+7+0.4494*(100-94.433)}{1+0.04}*0.5$$
$$+\frac{100.103+7+0.4494*(100-100.103)}{1+0.04}*0.5$$

Note that we linked the pay-off speed to the prior-period interest rate. This normally reflects how borrowers exercise their prepayment option. Our pricing

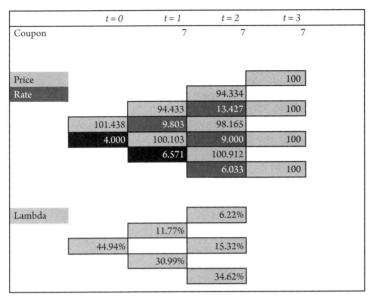

Figure 8.1 Pricing a Randomly Amortizing Three-Period 7-Percent Pool

method will work fine as long as we can obtain all the ingredients of formula (8.10) at every pricing node.

Let us consider a more realistic case when the pool is heterogeneous, but can be split into active and passive parts. If we decide to employ the APD model for backward valuation, we do not need to innovate path-dependent variables, ψ and total λ, or keep track of their dynamics. Here are few simple steps to perform:

Step 1: Recover today's value of the population variable, $\psi(t_0)$.

Step 2 Active: Generate rates c and λ on each node of a pricing grid (tree) for the active part only and value it using a backward inducting scheme that follows pricing rule (8.10).

Step 2 Passive: Do the same for the passive part.

Step 3: Combine thus obtained values as

$$P(0,x) = \psi(t_0)P_{active}(0,x) + [1 - \psi(t_0)]P_{passive}(0,x) \qquad (8.11)$$

Next we discuss several possibilities of exploring and extending the tree-based APD pricing framework. We complete the section by disclosing its expected accuracy and limitations.

Computing Interest-Rate Sensitivities Directly Off a Pricing Tree

Let us illustrate how interest-rate exposures can be efficiently computed using prices produced on a pricing tree. The idea is to augment the tree with "ghost nodes" as shown in Figure 8.2.[1]

The tree grows from its root and includes nodes (market conditions) that can be attained as shown by solid lines and circles. We augment that actual tree with nodes marked by "Up" and "Down." Those nodes cannot be reached from the root, but they can be perceived theoretically as results of immediate market shocks. We can add as many nodes at time $t = 0$ as we would like. These nodes and the emanating transitions are marked by dashed lines. If we assign transitional probabilities according to the law of our interest-rate model and carry out the backward valuation process (8.10), we will end up with vectors of Active, Passive, and Total prices at time $t = 0$. We can now measure duration and convexity using these prices and even compile a risk report covering a substantial range on interest-rate moves. These calculations will require carrying out the backward induction algorithm on a somewhat expanded tree, but otherwise, no extra computing efforts. We apply formula (8.11) for any node at $t = 0$, but we cannot use it for future nodes because we know only $\psi(t_0)$—today's value of ψ.

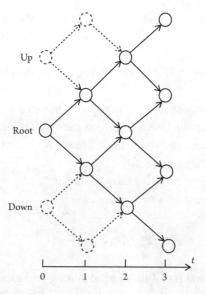

Figure 8.2 Extended Pricing Tree

[1]When using finite difference grids for solving the pricing PDE, the ghost nodes are part of the grid.

The extended tree can be viewed as a rectangular grid, from the data-storage and algorithmic points of view. Most MBS systems operate with paths (scenarios) rather than nodes. The easiest way to visit every node and collect information necessary for using formula (8.10) is to run "horizontal" rate scenarios. Each scenario will keep the level of the risk factor $x(t)$ constant. We can assume that $x = 0$ for the central path that starts from the root; $x = h$ corresponds to the path that starts from the Up node, $x = kh$ denotes the k-th level above the Root, $x = -h$ starts from the Down node, etc. If the tree carries N levels, we would need to run N deterministic scenarios of the active component of the pool and the same scenarios for the passive one. Therefore, this preparatory step will require generating $2N$ cash flow vectors and storing $r(t,x), c(t,x)$ and $\lambda(t,x)$ arrays. Once this is accomplished, the backward induction process starts from maturity utilizing the rule (8.10) for each branch and weighing results by probability. This design can be naturally extended to trinomial and multinomial trees.

One practical question a reader may have is whether interest-rate shocks that are reflected in the Up, the Down, and other nodes are, in fact, parallel moves. In most cases, they will be not. Each node of the valuation tree represents the full set of market conditions altered by a single factor (e.g. the short rate). At each node, the entire yield curve becomes known via the relevant law of the term-structure model. For example, long rates move less than the short rate if the single-factor model is mean reverting; the rate's move may be comparable on a relative, not absolute, basis if the model is lognormal, etc. These examples illustrate non-parallel moves in the yield curve. In these cases, it would be practically advisable to measure the Greeks with respect to the "most important" rate, such as the MBS current-coupon rate, or the 10-year reference rate.

Among a vast family of known short-rate models described in chapter 5, there exists one special model whose internal law is consistent with the notion of parallel shocks. This is the Hull-While model with a zero-mean reversion, also known as the Ho-Lee model[2] (see, for example, Hull, 2005). When the short rate moves by x basis point, every zero-coupon rate will move by the same amount, regardless of its maturity. If the Ho-Lee model is not employed, and the sensitivity to parallel shocks of interest rates is necessary, the tree-based valuation will have to be repeated using user-defined parallel moves of the yield curve. Whereas some advantages of the backward induction's superior speed will be forfeited, the method will still stand as a viable alternative to Monte Carlo.

---

[2]Historical calibration of the Hull-White model to the swaption volatility surface often reveals small-to-zero level of the mean reversion constant.

Residual Sources of Path-Dependence

The APD model takes care of the major source of path-dependence for fixed-rate mortgages, the burnout effect. After the decomposition is done, we need to review residual sources of path-dependence and arrange the numerical valuation procedure such as to reduce or eliminate potential pricing errors.

Prepayment lag, a look-back option feature, is such a source. Applications to obtain a new mortgage replacing an old one enter the origination pipeline 30 to 90 days before the loan is actually closed and the existing debt is paid off. If the prepayment model features a lag, but the backward valuation scheme is unaware of its existence, the pricing results can be somewhat inaccurate. This ignorance of the lag by the backward induction scheme usually causes small errors for pass-through securities. However, mortgage strip derivatives are highly prepay-sensitive, and the lag may change their values in a sizable way.

It is generally known that look-backs with short lag periods can be accounted for in the course of a backward induction process (see Hull, 2005). Let us assume, for example, that, on a binomial monthly tree, speed λ_t actually depends on market rates lagging one month. Hence, the MBS value will also depend on both the current market and one-month lagged market. This is to say that each valuation node of the tree should be "sliced" into two sub-nodes keeping track of prices matching two possible historical nodes, one month back. Of course, this costs computational time; efficiency may deteriorate quickly for deeper lags and more complex trees.

Approximate alternatives do exist and it is feasible to reduce pricing errors without much of a trouble. For example, AD&Co employs a progressively sparse recombining pentagonal tree, which does not branch off every month. Branches of the tree are made from two to 12 months long so that the lagged market rates are explicitly known for most monthly steps. The look-back correction can also be adapted for "fractional" prepayment lags that usually exist due to the net payment delay between the accrued-month-end and the actual cash flow date. In such a case, λ_t could be interpolated between the current-month and the previous-month values. Thus, the total lag processing should account for both prepay look-back and payment delay.

Another example of path-dependence not cured by pool decomposition is the *coupon reset* for adjustable-rate mortgages (ARMs). Both reset caps and nonlinear relationship between prepayments and coupon make it difficult for a backward induction scheme to fully account for this feature. One possible solution is to extend the state space and create an additional dimension that would keep track of the coupon rate for an ARM (Dorigan et al., 2001). This state-space extension will come at a cost of both computational efficiency and memory consumption. Levin (2002) suggests that the reset provisions found in typical ARMs allow for backward valuation with a practically acceptable accuracy, without any special measures of curing this path-dependence. However, the accuracy deteriorates for rarely used reset structures (such as "5/5")–especially if the valuation date is near to the next reset.

Tree-based valuation can produce fast and quite accurate results. We showed how valuation of MBS can take advantage of the grid's ability to provide needed rates for multiple points on the yield curve and gauge interest-rate sensitivities with little additional computation time.

BACKWARD INDUCTION USING FINITE DIFFERENCE GRIDS

Assuming again the APD pool model, we consider another way of solving PDE (8.1). Let us create a rectangular grid of time (step τ) and factor (step h) and denote price premium at time t, node k as $p_{t,k}$. Finite-difference methods solve PDEs or ODEs by approximating the derivatives with finite differences

$$\frac{\partial p}{\partial t} \approx \frac{p_{t,k} - p_{t-1,k}}{\tau}, \quad \frac{\partial p}{\partial x} \approx \frac{p_{t,k+1} - p_{t,k-1}}{2h}, \quad \frac{\partial^2 p}{\partial x^2} \approx \frac{p_{t,k+1} - 2p_{t,k} + p_{t,k-1}}{h^2}, \quad p = p_{t-1,k}$$

$$(8.12\text{-ex})$$

where we purposely assign the p-proportional term of PDE to be taken from the next step (in the course of backward induction), $t-1$. This choice reflects the fact that we would like to treat the effective price return expectation $(r + OAS - c)$ as a rate applied to the starting-period price. Using the approximations (8.12-ex) in lieu of actual terms, we can replace PDE (8.1) with a system of linear algebraic expressions:

$$[1 + \tau(r + \lambda + OAS)]p_{t-1,k} = p_{t,k} + \tau\mu \frac{p_{t,k+1} - p_{t,k-1}}{2h}$$

$$+ \frac{1}{2}\tau\sigma^2 \frac{p_{t,k+1} - 2p_{t,k} + p_{t,k-1}}{h^2} - \tau(r - c + OAS)$$

$$(8.13\text{-ex})$$

Starting from maturity, $t = T$, we deduce the entire price vector at time $t-1$ from the one already computed at t. One does not need to solve any multi-dimensional systems of equations when using (8.13-ex), which forms the *explicit finite difference method*. The method is only $O(\tau)$ accurate and stable if $\tau\sigma^2 < h^2$, i.e. the time step τ has to be commensurate with volatility σ and the spatial step h. These are two limitations of the otherwise very simple and fast approach. Using an explicit method is akin working on a trinomial probability tree, in which, at each pricing node, $p_{t-1,k}$ is expressed (before discounting) as a weighted average of $p_{t,k-1}, p_{t,k}$, and $p_{t,k+1}$. The weights in (8.13-ex) are $\tau A_{k,k-1}, 1 + \tau A_{k,k}$ and $\tau A_{k,k+1}$, correspondingly, where

$$A_{k,k-1} = -\frac{\mu}{2h} + \frac{\sigma^2}{2h^2}, \quad A_{k,k} = -\frac{\sigma^2}{h^2}, \quad \text{and} \quad A_{k,k+1} = \frac{\mu}{2h} + \frac{\sigma^2}{2h^2} \quad (8.14)$$

The weights add up to 1, but, unlike probabilities, they can be negative. Let us introduce a differential operator $\mathcal{A}p \equiv \mu(\partial p / \partial x) + (1/2)\sigma^2(\partial^2 p / \partial x^2)$. It is easy to check that, with the derivatives replaced by finite differences, the vector of values observed for operator $\mathcal{A}p$ will be precisely $\mathbf{A}p$ where the non-zero elements of matrix $\mathbf{A}$ are stated above in (8.14).

Variables r, c, λ, μ and σ generally depend on time t and factor x. We did not specify which values to use in (8.13-ex), the ones known at time t or at $t - 1$. Since either of them is known on grid, the choice belongs to the financial engineer. Practically speaking, MBS pay interest and principal monthly, so c and λ known at $t - 1$ should be used to compute cash flows received at time t. Likewise, a system operating with a 1-period rate $r_{t-1,k}$ that discounts from t to $t - 1$, should use $r_{t-1,k}$ as r in (8.13-ex). We keep these rules in mind when introducing other finite-difference schemes.

The limitations of the explicit method can be overcome by the *implicit finite difference method* or the *Crank-Nicholson* method. The implicit method approximates partial derivatives at $t - 1$ rather than t:

$$
\begin{aligned}
&\frac{\partial p}{\partial t} \approx \frac{p_{t,k} - p_{t-1,k}}{\tau}, \frac{\partial p}{\partial x} \approx \frac{p_{t-1,k+1} - p_{t-1,k-1}}{2h}, \\
&\frac{\partial^2 p}{\partial x^2} \approx \frac{p_{t-1,k+1} - 2p_{t-1,k} + p_{t-1,k-1}}{h^2}, p = p_{t-1,k}
\end{aligned} \quad (8.12\text{-im})
$$

Now, each step on the grid requires solving a system of linear algebraic equations that can be written in a compact vector-matrix form

$$\mathbf{T}_{t-1}\mathbf{p}_{t-1} = \mathbf{I}\mathbf{p}_t + \tau\left(\mathbf{c}_{t-1} - \mathbf{r}_{t-1} - OAS * \mathbf{1}\right) \quad (8.13\text{-im})$$

where $\mathbf{T} = \mathbf{I} + \tau\mathbf{R} - \tau\mathbf{A}$, $\mathbf{I}$ is the identity matrix, $\mathbf{R} = diag(r_k + \lambda_k + OAS)$, $\mathbf{c}$ and $\mathbf{r}$ are vectors of values on the spatial grid, all known at $t - 1$; $\mathbf{p}$ is the vector of price premium, and $\mathbf{1}$ is a vector of 1s.

Matrix T is a tri-diagonal *step matrix* so the system (8.13-im) can be solved using standard, computationally efficient methods. The most well-known of them is the so-called LU-decomposition explained in most books on numerical algebra. The number of operations required by this method is of the order of matrix's size, i.e., $O(N)$. However, a reduced Gauss elimination method will run at the same speed; this method eliminates the non-zero sub-diagonal elements, but skips the zeros. In contrast, the full Gauss elimination would require $O(N^3)$ operations.

The implicit method is still only $O(\tau)$ accurate, but stable assuming $(r_k + \lambda_k + OAS) > 0$. This condition ensures the norm of matrix T is above 1 and, ignoring the free terms, its inversion reduces the norm of p_{t-1} relatively to the norm of p_t. Usually this is not a binding constraint, as the period-to-period discount factor (including amortization) is positive. The time step τ does not have to be small. However, the implicit method is usually more time consuming than the explicit method because of the linear system of equations arising in its implementation.

The Crank-Nicholson method approximates partial derivatives by averaging (8.12-ex) and (8.12-im), that is, using $\frac{1}{2}(p_{t-1} + p_t)$ rather than p_t or p_{t-1}. The method can be viewed as an explicit/implicit combo: a transition from t to $t-1$ is split into two semi-steps, first explicit from t to $t-\frac{1}{2}$, then implicit from $t-\frac{1}{2}$ to $t-1$. The resultant algorithmic step can be expressed as

$$\left(I + \frac{\tau}{2}R_{t-1} - \frac{\tau}{2}A_{t-1}\right)p_{t-1} = \left(I - \frac{\tau}{2}R_{t-1} + \frac{\tau}{2}A_{t-1}\right)p_t + \tau\left(c_{t-1} - r_{t-1} - OAS*1\right)$$

$$(8.13\text{-cn})$$

where, as before, we attribute variable coefficients to the values known at time $t-1$.

The Crank-Nicholson method is the most commonly used numerical method in solving PDEs. It is as stable as the implicit method, requires roughly similar computational time that is mostly due to the implicit step, but is $O(\tau^2)$ accurate. Therefore, the method is more accurate than the implicit method or the explicit method—even if variable coefficients are kept constant between $t-1$ and t. It can be extended to multi-factor grids, as we show further.

Boundary Conditions

PDE (8.1) with the terminal condition $p(T,x) = 0$ represents an *initial value problem* called the *Cauchy problem*. There are no boundary conditions for the spatial variable x as the PDE reflects some financial law for any value of this economic factor. In its actual implementation, a finite difference grid must be bounded. When constructing the grid, a question arises as to how we can limit the propagation of partial derivatives. Indeed, a formal use of approximations (8.12) for $\partial p / \partial x$ and $\partial^2 p / \partial x^2$ at the grid-point (t,k) requires the knowledge of p above and below that point, possibly beyond the borders.

Unlike some other valuation problems, MBS pricing does not have boundary conditions that could be naturally established based on the problem at hand. Levin (2000) offers a way of handling this issue by postulating that an MBS should be viewed as a "static" financial instrument if the interest-rate factor is very high or very low. This means that variability of embedded options (such as the prepayment option) is saturated for both deep in-the-money cases and out-of-the-money cases. An example of a smooth boundary condition is a third-order equation

$$\frac{\partial}{\partial x}\left(\frac{1}{P}\frac{\partial^2 P}{\partial x^2} \right)=0 \tag{8.15}$$

Condition (8.15) states that the MBS convexity remains constant and factor-independent, across each boundary. This assumption is surely correct for a T-maturity zero-coupon bond having the constant convexity of T^2. For an MBS, if the rates are very high (or very low and deeply negative), the nearest (the farthest) cash flow dominates, so that the MBS approaches the zero-coupon limit. If we use a positive-rate model, then function $r(x)$ will weaken its dependence on x as $r \rightarrow 0$, and (8.15) holds.

Assumption (8.15) works well in practice. It requires some pre-processing of the T matrix, which temporarily loses the computationally valuable tri-diagonal property. Consider the use of (8.12-im) at the top node of the grid, $k=0$. It involves the use of p_{k-1} which becomes p_{-1}, i.e. a "ghost" point above the border. To exclude p_{-1}, we approximate (8.15) by last available differences as

$$\frac{p_{t-1,1}-2p_{t-1,0}+p_{t-1,-1}}{1+p_{t,0}} = \frac{p_{t-1,2}-2p_{t-1,1}+p_{t-1,0}}{1+p_{t,1}} \tag{8.16}$$

Note that we treat the denominator in the explicit way, i.e. using prices already obtained at time t rather than $t-1$. This allows us to retain the linearity with respect to unknown prices at time $t-1$. We can now exclude $p_{t-1,-1}$ from (8.16) by expressing it via $p_{t-1,0}$, $p_{t-1,1}$ and $p_{t-1,2}$ and use that expression when approximating partial derivatives. This substitution will change elements of the first and the last row of matrix T and make it a non-tri-diagonal structure as elements $T_{1,3}$ and $T_{n-2,n}$ become non-zeros. This seemingly serious obstacle is easy to overcome. Assuming that element $T_{2,3}$ is not a zero, one can multiply the second row by $T_{1,3} / T_{2,3}$ (along with all free terms) and subtract it from the first row thereby eliminating $T_{1,3}$ while keeping all the zero elements unchanged. Similarly, we eliminate $T_{n-2,n}$ by combining the last two rows. After this quick preprocessing, the system of equations arising in the implicit scheme or the Crank-Nicholson scheme will be tri-diagonal again.

The Two-Factor Case

Let us consider the valuation of MBS under the two-factor Gaussian rate model introduced in chapter 5. The model can be expressed via two independent factors, the short rate r and the slope factors v, having drifts μ_r and μ_v and volatilities σ_r and σ_v, correspondingly. Their actually expressions can be found using the model's analytical relationships and are not important for our purposes. The PDE (8.1) in the space of two independent factors will become

$$Dp \equiv \frac{\partial p}{\partial t} + \mu_r \frac{\partial p}{\partial r} + \frac{1}{2}\sigma_r^2 \frac{\partial^2 p}{\partial r^2} + \mu_v \frac{\partial p}{\partial v} + \frac{1}{2}\sigma_v^2 \frac{\partial^2 p}{\partial v^2} - (r+OAS+\lambda)p = -c+r+OAS$$

(8.1-rv)

$$p(T,r,v)=0$$

We assume that a three-dimensional grid (t,r,v) is created with the step of the grid being τ, h_r, h_v, respectively. At each node, numbered (t,i,j), partial derivatives are replaced with finite differences. The two-dimensional explicit method is again quite simple:

$$\left[1+\tau(r+\lambda+OAS)\right]p_{t-1,i,j}$$
$$= p_{t,i,j} + \tau\mu_r \frac{p_{t,i+1,j}-p_{t,i-1,j}}{2h_r} + \frac{1}{2}\tau\sigma_r^2 \frac{p_{t,i+1,j}-2p_{t,i,j}+p_{t,i-1,j}}{h_r^2}$$
$$+ \tau\mu_v \frac{p_{t,i,j+1}-p_{t,i,j-1}}{2h_v} + \frac{1}{2}\tau\sigma_v^2 \frac{p_{t,i,j+1}-2p_{t,i,j}+p_{t,i,j-1}}{h_v^2} - \tau(r-c+OAS)$$

(8.17-ex)

As in the single-factor case, the entire right-hand side is known at t, so that the backward induction process is straight-forward, fast and requires no equations to solve, but is only conditionally stable.

For using the implicit method or the Crank-Nicholson method, special schemes have been developed for two-dimensional problems. They make it unnecessary to deal with the Cartesian product of two dimensions and to solve equations with very high-dimensional matrices. The two strongest known methods are the *alternating-direction implicit method* (ADI) and the *Crank-Nicholson split method* introduced next.

In order to describe those methods, we first introduce differential operators $\mathcal{A}_r p \equiv \mu_r \dfrac{\partial p}{\partial r} + \dfrac{1}{2}\sigma_r^2 \dfrac{\partial^2 p}{\partial r^2}$ and $\mathcal{A}_v p \equiv \mu_v \dfrac{\partial p}{\partial v} + \dfrac{1}{2}\sigma_v^2 \dfrac{\partial^2 p}{\partial v^2}$. For example, notation $\mathcal{A}_r p_t$ means that the differential operator $\mathcal{A}_r$ applies to all $n_r n_v$ nodes of the pricing grid at time t. With these notations, PDE (8.1-rv) can be written as

$$\frac{\partial p}{\partial t} - (r + OAS + \lambda)p + \mathcal{A}_r p + \mathcal{A}_v p = -c + r + OAS$$

Each of the three methods symbolically shown below requires solving only one-dimensional problem at time.

IMPLICIT SPLIT METHOD

This is a two-step method, which uses only part of the full operator at each step:

$$\frac{p_t - p_{t-\frac{1}{2}}}{\tau} + \mathcal{A}_r p_{t-\frac{1}{2}} - \frac{1}{2}(r + OAS + \lambda)p_{t-\frac{1}{2}} = -c + r + OAS \qquad (8.18\text{-r})$$

$$\frac{p_{t-\frac{1}{2}} - p_{t-1}}{\tau} + \mathcal{A}_v p_{t-1} - \frac{1}{2}(r + OAS + \lambda)p_{t-1} = 0 \qquad (8.18\text{-v})$$

First we solve (8.18-r) for $p_{t-\frac{1}{2}}$, then (8.18-v) for p_{t-1} with each step being of size τ and implicit in one dimension, so our previous-section recommendations apply.

ALTERNATING-DIRECTION IMPLICIT (ADI) METHOD

This method, unlike the prior one, uses the entire operator at each step, which is half-sized ($\tau/2$):

$$\frac{p_t - p_{t-\frac{1}{2}}}{\tau/2} + \mathcal{A}_r p_{t-\frac{1}{2}} + \mathcal{A}_v p_t - (r + OAS + \lambda)p_{t-\frac{1}{2}} = 2(-c + r + OAS) \qquad (8.19\text{-r})$$

$$\frac{p_{t-\frac{1}{2}} - p_{t-1}}{\tau/2} + A_v p_{t-1} + A_r p_{t-\frac{1}{2}} - (r + OAS + \lambda) p_{t-1} = 0 \qquad (8.19\text{-v})$$

CRANK-NICHOLSON SPLIT METHOD

Like in the implicit split method, we use only part of the full operator each time, but now that operator is half-implicit and half-explicit:

$$\frac{p_t - p_{t-\frac{1}{2}}}{\tau} + \frac{1}{2} A_r (p_t + p_{t-\frac{1}{2}}) - \frac{1}{4}(r + OAS + \lambda)(p_t + p_{t-\frac{1}{2}}) = -c + r + OAS$$

$$(8.20\text{-r})$$

$$\frac{p_{t-\frac{1}{2}} - p_{t-1}}{\tau} + \frac{1}{2} A_v (p_{t-\frac{1}{2}} + p_{t-1}) - \frac{1}{4}(r + OAS + \lambda)(p_{t-\frac{1}{2}} + p_{t-1}) = 0 \qquad (8.20\text{-v})$$

Induction (8.20) is of the $O(\tau^2)$ accuracy if operators A_r and A_v are commutable (i.e. $A_r A_v = A_v A_r$). Marchuk (1975) proposed using a four-cycle modification, in which one constantly swaps the order of dimensions within two sequential steps. That is, going from $t+1$ to t we solve first for r, then for v; then, going from t to $t-1$ we solve first for v, then for r. This guarantees the $O(\tau^2)$ accuracy for the Crank-Nicholson split method even if operators A_r and A_v are not commutable.

All three methods are stable provided that the total discount factor (including balance amortization) is positive, which, as we mentioned previously, is not a severe constraint. At each step, we deal with solving a large number of simple systems of equations. For example, if we perform the r-step, we have to fix a value for v. We will be solving n_v systems with tri-diagonal matrices of the n_r by n_r size. To feel and compare the size of computational work, let us assume that $n_r = n_v = 20$, that is, we have 20 grid-points in each dimension. Assuming 360 months in the time dimension, the total number of systems to solve is $360 * 20 * 2 = 14,400$ with each system being a 20-by-20 size, requiring the order of 20 rudimentary operations in the LU decomposition (or reduced Gauss elimination). This will total $2.8_{10}5$ operations. If we did not employ one of the methods described above, at each time step, we would have to deal with a 400 by 400 system of equation, which is not tri-diagonal. A brute-force use of the full Gauss elimination would require $360 * (400)^3 = 2.3_{10}10$ operations, i.e. take 80,000 longer to run.

Regardless of the method, solving the pricing PDE in two dimensions involves a three-dimensional cash flow generation. To visit and produce r, c, λ at every node, we need to generate $n_r n_v = 400$ interest-rate scenarios, 360 months each. Using the APD prepayment structure we need to do so twice, separately for the active part and the passive part. Generally, even best numerical methods of solving PDEs in two dimensions run at a speed comparable to that of the Monte-Carlo simulations explained in the next chapter. One important remaining advantage of the PDE solution is that it delivers more than just the root price $p(0,0,0)$ or the OAS; we will end up with the entire vector $p(0,r,v)$ effectively delivering all deltas and gammas in each risk dimension.

OAS-COMPLIANT PREPAYMENT MODELING

For all valuation methods described in this chapter, we assumed the total pay-off rate $\lambda(t,x)$ be known at every node of our pricing grid. The main component of λ is the refinancing rate and, as the previous chapter explains, it must depend on "refinancing incentive." Borrowers know how much they pay; the question arises as to what the borrower's economic incentive for obtaining a new loan is.

As in chapter 7, refinancing incentive is commonly assessed as a distance (absolute or relative) between old and new payments. The incentive can be a simple difference in rates, a payment ratio, or something else. Regardless of its exact definition, prevailing mortgage rates must be available on the (t,x)-grid in order for $\lambda(t,x)$ be computed. The primary mortgage rate might be the best option to use, but that rate is not unambiguously defined. Normally, primary rates are published by as results of mortgage banking surveys; they are not collected daily, and only few main loan types are covered. It has become a common modeling convention to employ the continuously available secondary-market MBS rate instead and correct it for the primary-secondary rate spread as necessary.

The secondary-market MBS rate, known as the *current-coupon rate*, is a number interpolated from the observed TBA prices. Using two TBAs priced close to par, one at premium and another at discount, we can find the interpolated coupon that would make the price equal to par assuming no delay in payments typically existing in MBS.[3] This last condition is used to express the rate on a bond-comparable scale. Depending on the level of interest rates, with payment delays, the actually interpolated TBA price could be in a 99.6–99.8 range. The "interpolated" TBA is commonly called *current-coupon TBA*.

The current-coupon rate is therefore a derivative measure of TBA pricing, widely available on a daily and even intra-daily basis for many MBS types. This

---

[3]Equivalently, yield to maturity for the interpolated coupon is equal to that coupon, with same compounding.

sets up a modeling dilemma. On the one hand, there is no shortage of empirical data covering the history of interest rates including MBS rates. This fact leads to a temptation to simply regress the current-coupon rate against other interest rates. Perrucci (2008) considers it the first-generation modeling approach. On the other hand, the current-coupon rate is also a product of MBS valuation process. To make this issue clear, let us shock a pricing factor, be it a point on the swap curve or the swaption volatility matrix. This disturbance to the market would alter TBA prices, hence, the derived current-coupon. An empirical regression, on the other hand, may or may not be able to predict it.

The MBS current-coupon rate (cc) can be analytically stated right from the key valuation statement (8.2) assuming that the MBS price is the exact par (premium is zero):

$$cc = \frac{E\int_0^T [r(t)+OAS]e^{y(t)}dt}{E\int_0^T e^{y(t)}dt} \equiv \frac{IO\,Floater}{IO\,Multiple} \qquad (8.21)$$

The numerator represents an IO floater paying market rate plus OAS; the denominator is the value of 1% annuity also known as the IO multiple. Both instruments are amortizing at a speed of the current-coupon TBA and discounted without a payment delay. The cumulative amortization-and-discount factor, $e^{y(t)}$, integrates the balance amortization speed λ, which, in turn, is a function of cc. We will classify contemporary modeling approaches to resolving this circularity as follows:

A. Current-coupon models as empirical regressions of various granularities and sophistications.
B. Current-coupon models integrated into OAS systems and produced by them.
C. MBS valuation models that do not use current-coupon rates at all.

Current-Coupon Models as Empirical Regressions

Belbase and Szakallas (2002) describe a rather simple approach to constructing a current-coupon regression using just a couple of points of the Treasury curve or the swap curve. They admit that there are a large number of options in selecting the explanatory tenors with seemingly comparable explanatory statistical levels. They chose to use the 2-year point and the 10-year point. The reason is related to the range of residential loan products: None of them has an average life expectancy greater than 10 years. For example, regression's betas for the

10-year/2-year yield-curve points were found to be approximately 0.9/0.1 for 30-year fully amortizing loans, 0.8/0.2 for 15-year loans, 0.65/0.35 for the 7-year balloons, etc.

The Belbase and Szakallas family of regressions is an apparent oversimplification that works better than it looks. The main explanation is that a regression's intercept (the alpha) is taken from the current market thereby absorbing the model's omissions. For example, the regression has neither volatility terms nor information about the curve's shape beyond the 10-year point, but these factors are implicitly reflected in the alpha term. In addition, rates often change in unison and a quasi-parallel move of the yield curve is its main principal component (see chapter 5). However, key-rate durations (sensitivity to some points of the curve, KRD) and Vega (sensitivity to volatility) produced by an OAS model would not be compliant with the regression's main assumption: The MBS rate depends only on two points of the curve.

Let us assume that the current-coupon MBS rate is regressed against n points of the curve:

$$cc = \alpha + \sum_{i=1}^{n} \beta_i r_i \qquad (8.22)$$

with some constant α and $\sum_{i=1}^{n} \beta_i = 1$. This last condition ensures that MBS rates move together with the yield curve if that curve experiences a parallel shift. Although it is plausible that MBS rates may change by a different amount than the benchmark, such a dislocation can likely be viewed as temporary. Over the long term, the economics of origination should ensure a steady income spread over funding expense.

From the valuation-definitional standpoint, cc depends on TBA prices. Consider the current-coupon TBA valued according to its definition. If we move the benchmark rate r_i by a small Δr_i, that TBA price will move by the product of KRD_i and Δr_i. Therefore, the current-coupon rate must move, too, so that the price's disturbance is offset. We conclude that, for the regression (8.22) to be compliant with TBA pricing, its betas have to be proportional to key-rate durations of the current-coupon TBA. Figure 8.3 presents relative contributions of four theoretical KRDs, derived from a constant-OAS model and interpolated for the current-coupon point of 30-year Fannie Mae TBAs. Scaled to add up to 1.0, they are good candidates for betas.

Figure 8.3 proves that MBS became "longer" since the financial crisis started as evidenced by the increased presence of the 30-year point and the decreased presence of the 2-year point. We also see that the weights have not been constant as the curve's shape, prepayment sentiments and volatility change over time, all

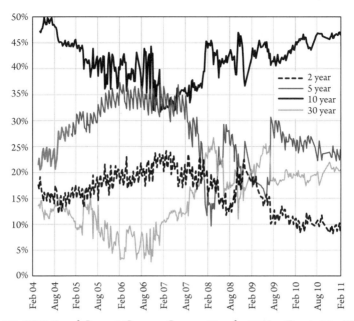

Figure 8.3 KRD-Based Current-Coupon Composition for 30-Year Fannie Mae TBAs

affecting the roles of different points of the curve. Also note that the theoretical KRDs were computed using the constant-OAS concept with a prepayment model operating off the current-coupon regression proposed by Belbase and Szakallas, that is, the one using the 2-year point and the 10-year point only. The fact that we found sizable exposures to the 5-year point and the 30-year point contains an apparent contradiction to the assumption made. Nevertheless, we think that the results shown in Figure 8.3 are valuable and credible. They simply show that the role Belbase and Szakallas attributed to the 10-year point is actually distributed and shared with its neighbors, the 5-year point and the 30-year point. To make the analysis more accurate and to build a better current-coupon model, we should use the computed weights *inside prepayment model*, and then recompute the OAS-based KRDs. We should iterate until there is a match between the computed KRD weights and the ones assumed by the current-coupon model.

Regression-based current-coupon models may fail to expose proper MBS dependence on factors that are not in the regression. One popular example is measuring Vega, i.e. exposure to the rate's volatility. If that volatility is not included into the regression for *cc*, the OAS model will be measuring an incomplete Vega. For example, when volatility is stressed up, the current-coupon rate should widen to swaps thereby slowing prepayment speeds and gaining value for IOs. As a result, most IO strips are expected to have positive Vegas. Without the current-coupon effect, we will likely measure negative Vegas. Levin (ADPN

May 2008) proposes a simple fix to the issue. He shows that, by measuring the "partial" Vega (without volatility presence in the current-coupon regression) and an additional Greek, *current-coupon duration*, one can find a very accurate approximation for a "full" Vega:

$$V_{MB}^{full} = V_{MB}^{part} - D_{MBS}^{s} \frac{V_{CC}^{part}}{D_{CC}^{s} + IOM_{CC}}$$

where D^{s} is duration to the current-coupon rate, IOM is the IO multiple, subscript "MBS" refers to the MBS in question (an IO in our example above), and subscript "CC" refers to the current-coupon TBA pool.

Modeling Current-Coupon within OAS Systems

The issue of making the current-coupon MBS rate compliant with an OAS framework is a circular one. In order to value TBAs, we must know its prepayment model. On the other hand, in order for computing prepayment speeds, we need to know that current rate (cc) at each step. This means TBAs have to be already priced, which brings us to the beginning of a circle. The Monte-Carlo framework explained later in the book would explode if we compound its use, that is, try deriving cc from separate simulations while running "main" simulations. Hence, the main hope to accomplish this goal is to use a backward induction.

Bhattacharjee and Hayre (2006) proposed a current-coupon model operating on a tree (the Citigroup approach), which extends for 60 years and assumes annual branching. They first design a path-independent surrogate of their actual prepayment model. As we explain a bit later, our APD scheme would serve the purpose precisely, without approximation. The 60-year interest-rate tree will let them compute and use conventional current-coupon rates for the first 30 years.

The algorithm starts from year 59 when the current-coupon rate is surely equal to the 1-year benchmark rate plus applicable OAS. Going backward on the tree, the algorithm would know current-coupon rates for all future nodes. The Citigroup approach iterates to find the current-coupon at each node so that the remaining-maturity MBS (not exceeding 30 years and having that coupon) is valued at the required parity level. In other words, each node requires a separate valuation of MBS on the same tree that views this node as the root, that is, a nested backward induction process. One must start with some OAS level and repeat the analysis until the computed current-coupon rate at time 0 matches the market rate. Using current-coupon values stored on the tree, one can now invoke a full-scale path-dependent prepayment model and value any MBS.

One can improve the Citigroup method in a number of ways. First, there is no need to reprice each MBS anew. This requirement takes no advantage of information already available on the tree except for future current-coupon rates. Instead, it is sufficient to value a large number of MBS with all maturities ranging from 1 to 30 years and coupon rates ranging from realistic minimum to realistic maximum. This will require many instruments to be valued on the same tree, but without iterations and repetitions. Valuation of each MBS (say, 30-year TBA 4.5) will utilize prices already found in future nodes for its "tail," that is, 29-year MBS one time step forward, 28-year MBS two steps forward, etc. At each node, the current-coupon rate will be computed from two TBA prices, the cheapest premium and the richest discount. This improvement will collapse two nested backward induction processes into one. If T denotes TBA maturity measured in grid steps (e.g. $T = 30$ for annual grid, $T = 360$ for monthly grid, etc.), the grid has $O(T^2)$ pricing nodes. Then, the original Citigroup method requires $O(T^4)$ operations whereas the enhanced version only $O(T^3)$.

Second, if we were to employ the Citigroup approach, we would not need to approximate a prepayment model as long as it is presented in the APD form. We would carry calculations separately for the active and passive parts of each TBA and combine the computed prices only when a TBA becomes a 30-year instrument or an instrument with postulated TBA remaining term. Since the premium TBA and the discount TBA surrounding the current-coupon one are usually new or recent enough, we can assume that $\psi(t_0) \approx \psi_0$, the model's known parameter. Our implementation would double the number of operations, but without simplification in the prepayment model.

Despite its feasibility, the Citigroup approach seems to be computationally intensive. Although we have no knowledge of how this approach is employed in practice, we assume that the process of computing current-coupon is separated from the real-time analysis. It is unlikely that traders whose interest is often focused on one instrument at a time would have to restore the entire grid of current-coupons for each analysis. OAS levels and most Greeks reported by Bhattacharjee and Hayre are not materially different from those found by a much simpler regression-based model, except for Vega.

Value-Space Prepayment Model Formulation

Although the use of the MBS current-coupon rate in prepayment modeling is very common, there is an alternative, effectively eliminating the needs for current-coupon modeling. Levin (ADQP 2003, ADCP 2006) describes the idea of modeling λ as a function of price premium p itself. Let us consider an agency pass-through and assume that a borrower's decision to refinance is explained by the price of his or her loan. Of course, most borrowers do not know exact market values of their loans; however, their intuitive refinancing incentive is deemed correlated to a loan's value. Trivially, a higher paid rate commonly results in a higher premium value, but the relationship is observed across loan types too. For example, an adjustable-rate loan borrower is less reactive to the same interest-rate incentive than a fixed-rate borrower. When market rates are low, economic benefits of refinancing fade as the reset nears. In contrast, a fixed-rate borrower must pay an unfavorable rate until maturity, thereby creating a stronger incentive to refinance. Typically, for models formulated around the concept of current-coupon rate, such a difference requires the employment of differing modeling specifications for differing loan types. In contrast, a value-based form $\lambda(p)$ can be constructed universally, across loan types.

In order to illustrate this approach, Levin (ADCP 2006) approximately converts the pre-crisis AD&Co's refinancing S-curves from the traditional $\lambda(cc)$ form into $\lambda(P)$. The two-S-curves, separately constructed for the active and the passive parts of the APD model, are shown in Figure 8.4.

The use of backward valuation allows us to co-integrate valuation with prepayment modeling. We solve PDE (8.1) backward and, at each pricing node, compute prepayment speed as a function of price. To streamline the process and keep

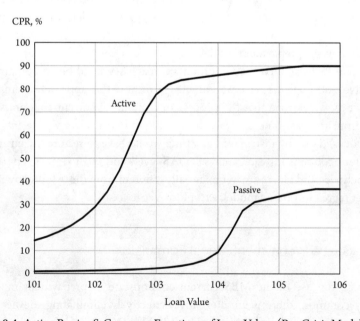

Figure 8.4 Active-Passive S-Curves, as Functions of Loan Values (Pre-Crisis Model)

it linear, we specify $\lambda_t(P_t)$ so that the λ-term is treated explicitly (i.e. known at every node). We can also treat P_t as the price of matching pass-through, rather than loans themselves, as the two are highly correlated with one another. As necessary, λ_t must include scheduled amortization and a housing turnover rate, which are assumed to be P_t-independent. As this is done with the usual APD model, valuation is performed for the active and passive parts separately and the pricing results are added up using the rule (8.11). If we know an OAS input, this completes the process. If we input a price, we will start the backward induction with an initial OAS and iterate until $p(0,0)$ matches the quoted premium.

Regardless of the input, this valuation process allows us to compute active and passive refinancing rates, at each point of the grid—based on the price computed for that node. Figure 8.5 presents results of the process (active part only). Computed CPRs are presented on the (t,x) grid as functions of the rate's shifts level counted off the central level (marked as 0), and the loan's age.

When a loan is new, the S-curves for fixed-rate loans and 5/1 hybrids are close to one another. As a loan ages, the S-curve constructed for hybrid ARMs flattens severely. This can be anticipated; the rate incentive has a shorter life as the reset nears. In essence, this method lets us derive the traditional S-curves for all loan types once it is established for the conventional 30-year fixed rate loans in the

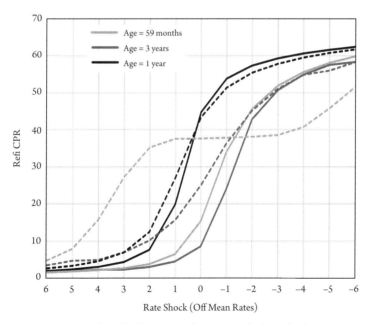

Figure 8.5 Comparison of Implied S-Curves for FRM and 5/1 Hybrid ARM
Solid lines = fixed rate loan, dash lines = hybrid loan

$\lambda_t(P_t)$ form. One can compare different cap structures (5/2/5 versus 2/2/5) or other contributors to the incentive such as prepay penalty, loan size or trans-action cost (see Levin, ADQP 2006). For example, the existence of a prepay penalty provision simply shifts the S-curve to the right. We conducted research studies and verified that this transformation leads to reasonable results in assess-ing penalty's value.

On the other hand, the loan-size effect can be accounted for by changing both scales of the S-curve. Instead of using the collateral price in percentage points, we can consider a more suitable utility function reflecting refinancing decisions made by affluent borrowers as well as corporations. Knowing that an infinite loan-size leads to the optimal call exercise, we can consider a continuous defor-mation of the value-space curve "connecting" the MBS world to the world of callable agency and corporate bonds. Figure 8.6 shows a family of active S-curves obtained by assuming that the utility function is the dollar value of a loan raised to the (2/3) power; the curves were then redrawn against the percentage price.

As seen from Figure 8.6, this approach naturally explains why the refinancing curve stretches up and shifts to the left with rising loan sizes.

The method can be used for CMOs, too, as a prepayment-modeling phase of valuation. We start with CMO collateral and apply the valuation approach described above. At each node, we store separately computed speeds for the

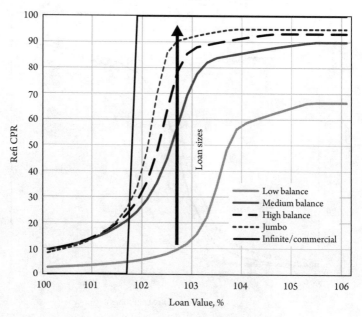

Figure 8.6 Derived Refinancing S-Curve as a Function of Loan Size (Pre-Crisis, Active Part Only)

active part and passive part. The knowledge of the collateral's OAS level or price is necessary for this phase. We then apply Monte-Carlo simulations for the CMO tranche so that rate paths pass through the grid's nodes. At each node, we utilize the previously stored speeds. Note that the first (backward-inducting) phase does not construct the total refinancing speed of the pool; it only keeps track of its active and passive components. The pool's composition variable $\psi(t)$ is not known on the grid until we simulate random rate paths forward.

Kalotay and Yang (2002) considered and implemented a model where the refinancing option is exercised as a call on a bond. They postulate that there are three types of borrowers: those exercising optimally ("financial engineers"), those jumping too early ("leaders") and those reacting too late ("laggers"). The particular valuation scheme that Kalotay and Yang developed allows one to vary the exercise efficiency in implementing the method. Prices are constructed backward, without any postulated S-curves and some other traditional prepayment modeling features, but a price-independent housing turnover rate is permitted. The authors claim to have achieved a good resemblance with pricing profiles normally found in MBS. The Kalotay and Yang model bears some similarity to Davidson's Refinancing Threshold model (1987), which also explains the negative convexity of MBS and their valuation profile. None of them is actually a mortgage-like model and the differences can be seen easily. With rates falling and call exercise conditions triggered, these models cannot explain why there would still be borrowers to prepay, albeit at a decreased speed, in the future. We would have to assume that an idiosyncratic randomness needs to be factored into borrowers' decisions, which would lead to the advent of an S-curve (chapter 1).

9

Monte Carlo Methods

In the previous chapter, we showed the use of non-simulation methods for the valuation of agency MBS. Although we were able to tackle a wide range of interesting problems, a professionally designed MBS valuation system must include simulations. For example, CMOs are complex structured instruments; their path-dependence is well beyond the heterogeneity of a pool, as addressed by the Active-Passive Decomposition (APD) method. If we decided to express the CMO valuation problem in terms of a partial differential equation, the state-space containing all the necessary information at every point in time would be multi-dimensional. For very simple structures (such as sequential tranches), in order to determine the ongoing distribution of principal, it would be enough to keep only information about a pool's factor, thereby adding one state variable. However, the state-space starts growing when we consider more complex structures such as PACs with supports, or structures with priority triggers ("jumps"), etc. The effective dimensionality of valuation problem becomes high enough to yield the right of way to simulation methods commonly called Monte Carlo methods.

EXPECTATION VIA SAMPLING

In order to explain the way these methods work, consider an MBS price in the form of an expectation. We already showed the expressions in chapters 4 and 8 with the use of continuous finance. (See, for example, formula [8.2].) Since MBS cash flows are usually paid monthly, price can be presented as an expectation of the total discounted cash flow

$$P = E \sum_{t=1}^{T} (CF_t)(DF_t) \tag{9.1}$$

where CF_t is the cash flow generated in month t and DF_t is the random discount factor between now and month t. The expectation is taken with respect to risk-neutral interest-rate process and, if necessary, other random factors. The discount factor's form depends on the short-rate definitions. Let us assume that r_t stands for the annualized discount rate applicable to the $[t, t+1]$ monthly step, expressed as the monthly-equivalent yield (MEY). Then,

$$DF_t = \frac{1}{\left(1 + \frac{r_0 + OAS}{12}\right)\left(1 + \frac{r_1 + OAS}{12}\right) \cdots \left(1 + \frac{r_{t-1} + OAS}{12}\right)} \qquad \text{(9.2-me)}$$

The sequence of one-month rates $r_0 - r_1 - \cdots - r_{T-1}$ is random and generated by a no-arbitrage rate model. On the other hand, we can express monthly rates in a continuously compounded form so that the discount factor between t and $t+1$ is $exp[-(r_{t-1} + OAS)/12]$. Then, the discount factor becomes

$$DF_t = exp\left[-\sum_{\tau=0}^{t-1} \frac{r_\tau + OAS}{12}\right] \qquad \text{(9.2-cc)}$$

One-period monthly-equivalent rates utilized in formula (9.1-me) should slightly exceed continuously compounded rates entering (9.2-cc). For example, a 5% monthly equivalent rate is approximately equivalent to a 4.99% continuously compounded rate. Some methods are easier to illustrate using discounting in the form of (9.2-cc) because the rate sequence is additive.

We now return to the valuation problem (9.1) and turn our attention to how simulations can be utilized for computing the expectation. Monte Carlo methods assume that we simulate a fairly large number of scenarios ("paths") for the $r_0 - r_1 - \cdots - r_{T-1}$ rate sequence. We compute the cash flow vectors and the discount factors and then replace expectation with the sample average:

$$P \cong \frac{1}{N}\sum_{k=1}^{N}\sum_{t=1}^{T}(CF_{kt})(DF_{kt}) \qquad \text{(9.3)}$$

where subscript k refers to k-th (out of N) path.

MONTE CARLO VERSUS QUASI MONTE CARLO

The critical issue arising in a practical use of Monte Carlo methods is the issue of convergence. Let us assess the accuracy of a plain Monte Carlo method. Let us assume that we seek mathematical expectation of a random variable V taken from a cumulative distribution $F(v)$:

$$E(V) = \int_0^1 v(F)dF$$

where $v(F)$ is the inverse to $F(v)$. Monte Carlo method simulates a sample of uniformly distributed values F_k of $F \in [0,1]$ and replaces the integral with the sample average: $E(V) \cong \frac{1}{N} \sum_{k=1}^{N} v(F_k)$. Each random term $v(F_k)$ has a variance of σ^2. Assuming that F_k is independent from F_i for $i \neq k$, the variance of the sum is $N\sigma^2$ and the variance of the sample average is σ^2/N. This makes the standard deviation of the sample average equal to $\sigma/\sqrt{N}$. We have proved a well-known fact: The plain Monte Carlo possesses a $N^{-\frac{1}{2}}$ convergence rate; in order to increase its accuracy 10-fold, we need to increase the sample 100-fold. When deriving this result, we only postulated a randomness of V, but did not restrict the source of the randomness to a single-factor risk model. If $V = V(X, Y, ...)$ is a function of multiple random factors and needs to be sampled by sampling a multi-dimensional space $(X, Y, ...)$, the $N^{-\frac{1}{2}}$ convergence still holds true.

Let us now consider a different numerical approach to the integration of $v(F)$, the simple rectangular method. We split the $[0,1]$ interval into N equal steps and select $F_k = k/N$. Now $E(V) \cong \frac{1}{N} \sum_{k=1}^{N} v(F_k)$ replaces the integral with a total area of rectangles and leads to an error of the $O(N^{-1})$ order.

Whereas the rectangular method is considered as primitive as numerical integration can get, it easily beats Monte Carlo in convergence rate. The question arises, why do we need Monte Carlo? Apparently, the value of the MBS depends on the entire path of interest rates, not just one value. Each path branching monthly is driven by a 360-long vector of random increments. Hence, variable V should be treated as a multi-dimensional rather than scalar factor. The number of dimensions will grow further if we increase the number of factors, for example, if we decide to use a two-factor rate model or to incorporate home-price factors. It is not trivial to maintain the ease and quality of rectangular integration. In all these cases, plain Monte Carlo will work without any additional difficulties. The sample average of N randomly and independently chosen values of V will still have a standard deviation of $\sigma/\sqrt{N}$ —no matter how many random factors have been used to generate the sample.

The two ways of numerical integration we introduced illustrate two main alternatives that financial engineers face: Monte Carlo versus quasi Monte Carlo. If the problem is low-dimensional, the use of well-selected deterministic ("quasi-random") points is clearly advantageous and leads to the goal with less effort. This is the quasi Monte Carlo approach. For example, if we chose to test the Black-Scholes formula numerically, we would cover the probability range $[0,1]$ with a uniform deterministic grid, select stock price at expiry for each probability point and apply the rectangular integration formula. As the problem's dimensionality grows, the quasi Monte Carlo approach becomes more convoluted and generally less effective. In contrast, we can still use random simulations that constitute the Monte Carlo method. We can improve its quality using *variance reduction techniques,* described further below.

MONTE CARLO BASICS FOR THE OPTION-ADJUSTED SPREAD FRAMEWORK

Simulating Random Factors

Let us consider how one might run simulations of interest rates. For simplicity, we start with a single-factor model driven by a mean-reverting variate $x(t)$ that follows the Ornstein-Ulenbeck stochastic differential equation:

$$dx = -a(t)xdt + \sigma(t)dz \qquad (9.4)$$

disturbed by Brownian motion $z(t)$. Then, the Hull-White model will have $r(t) = R(t) + x(t)$; for the Squared Gaussian model, $r(t) = [R(t) + x(t)]^2$ and for the Black-Karasinski model, $r(t) = R(t)exp[x(t)]$ where $R(t)$ is a calibrating function selected to match the initial term structure. The goal of the Monte Carlo method is to generate N random trajectories $z_k(t), k = 1, 2, \ldots N$ and solve (9.4) numerically. For example, we can start with a very simple replacement of (9.4) with the equation in differences required by the Euler method's modification:

$$x_{t+1} - x_t = -\tau a(t)x_t - \sqrt{\tau}\sigma(t)w_t \qquad (9.5)$$

where τ is the time step and w_t is a random shock chosen from the standard normal distribution. Mean reversion $a(t)$ and volatility $\sigma(t)$ are assumed to stay constant within each time step, but can change from one step to another. One way to simulate the Brownian motion is to produce serially independent shocks w_t for $t = 0, 1, \ldots 360$ and innovate according to (9.5).

The $\sqrt{\tau}$ scale in (9.5) may look unusual for those unfamiliar with stochastic equations. The usual Euler method computes the right-hand side of an ordinary differential equation at time t, multiplying it by the time step τ and using this value as the unknown's increment. However, in the case of stochastic differential equations, dz / dt is not well defined as it represents a continuous sequence of serially independent shocks of an infinite size. The Brownian motion, $z(t)$ integrates those shocks so that its standard deviation grows in proportion to $\sqrt{t}$. This explains why we scaled the local volatility term in (9.5). We can increase the accuracy in volatility replication if we decide to target the exact theoretical standard deviation of continuous process (9.4) conditional upon the initial condition for each step:

$$stdev[x_{t+1}]|_{x_t} = \sigma(t)\left(\frac{1-e^{-2a\tau}}{2a}\right)^{\frac{1}{2}} \equiv \sigma(t)S$$

Then, we can modify the Euler rule further by scaling volatility more accurately:

$$x_{t+1} - x_t = -\tau a(t)x_t - \sigma(t)Sw_t \qquad (9.5a)$$

Application of formula (9.5a) ensures the exact replication of the theoretical standard deviation at the end of each time step and may be advantageous when time steps are not small.

Simulating Random Shocks

The shocks w's employed for simulating process (9.5) or (9.5a) are sampled from the standard normal distribution. The most commonly used method is the *method of polar coordinates*. It requires generating a pair of random numbers (u_1, u_2) from the uniform $[0,1]$ distribution that get transformed into a pair of normally distributed numbers (w_1, w_2) as

$$w_1 = \sqrt{-2ln(u_1)}cos(2\pi u_2), \quad w_2 = \sqrt{-2ln(u_1)}sin(2\pi u_2)$$

The following well-known algorithm avoids calling trigonometric functions:

1. Generate (u_1, u_2) uniformly from $[0,1]$.
2. Convert them into uniformly distributed $(\tilde{u}_1, \tilde{u}_2)$ from $[-1,+1]$: $\tilde{u}_k = 2u_k - 1, k = 1,2$. These are the polar coordinates.
3. Compute the square of the distance between $(\tilde{u}_1, \tilde{u}_2)$ and the origin: $w = \tilde{u}_1^2 + \tilde{u}_2^2$. If $w < 1$, compute $v = \sqrt{-2ln(w)/w}$; otherwise go to step 1.
4. Produce $w_1 = \tilde{u}_1 v, w_2 = \tilde{u}_2 v$.

When generating uniformly distributed numbers, we prefer to employ determinist sequences like the ones described in Press et al. (1992) over truly random methods that read a computer's registry or a system's time. One serious practical advantage of deterministic methods is the ability to replicate Monte Carlo results, validate and verify them on any computer and operating system.

We will need N sets each having T numbers w_t to solve (9.5) or (9.5a) and generate N paths of interest rates. If we employ more than one economic factor, we will generate more variables for each path, but we will not need more paths. As we pointed out, Monte Carlo accuracy depends on the number of paths, but not on the number of factors. The total number of random numbers that the Monte Carlo method requires is nNT where n is the number of risk factors, N is the number of paths, and T is the number of time steps (e.g. $T = 360$ for the case of monthly steps applied over the 30-yr horizon).

Sampling over Probability Tree

Simulation of the short rate provides us with path-wise discount factors DF_{kt}, but not necessarily prepayment speeds, hence, cash flow arrays CF_{kt}. It may be necessary to know other rates, such as key rates entering an empirical current-coupon rate regression (see the discussion in the previous chapter). If the term-structure model enables a closed-form solution or a very accurate approximation for long rates (e.g. the Hull-White model), we can compute them continuously, as direct functions of random factors we are simulating. For other cases (e.g. the Black-Karasinski model), we may need to construct a probability tree and pre-compute all necessary long rates via the backward induction process. Now we would have to sample random paths over that tree. We will select uniformly distributed random numbers u_t from $[0,1]$ and map emanating branches. For example, assuming a binomial tree with 50/50 probability branching, we would follow the "up" branch if $u_t \geq 0.5$ and the "down" branch otherwise. For multinomial trees, at each node reached at time t, we randomly select the top branch if $u_t > 1 - \pi_1$, the second branch if $1 - \pi_1 \geq u_t > 1 - \pi_2$, etc. where $\pi_1, \pi_2, \ldots$ are probability levels for the branches. A Monte Carlo method using a very large number of paths will be as accurate as the tree-based approximation of valuation problem.

Computing the Option-Adjusted Spread

Computing prices given an OAS and a set of random paths via formula (9.3) is straightforward and requires no further instructions. Assume now that we have market price P and need to compute the OAS. Since the OAS term enters the discount factors and not the cash flows, it is prudent to simulate and store all necessary values in computer memory first. For example, running 500 paths over 360 months, we need to store $500 * 360 = 180,000$ of short rates and the same number of MBS payments (likely doubles) and repeat computations in (9.2), (9.3) iteratively until the price matches the market quote.

One can use a better method requiring us to store only 360 values and do fewer computations. It is easier to demonstrate using the continuously compounding form (9.2cc). Let us combine (9.3) and (9.2cc) to have

$$P \cong \frac{1}{N} \sum_{k=1}^{N} \sum_{t=1}^{T} (CF_{kt}) exp \left[-\sum_{\tau=0}^{t-1} \frac{r_{k\tau} + OAS}{12} \right] \tag{9.6}$$

We can factor out the OAS-dependent terms and change the order of summation:

$$P \cong \frac{1}{N} \sum_{k=1}^{N} \sum_{t=1}^{T} (CF_{kt}) exp \left[-\sum_{\tau=0}^{t-1} \frac{r_{k\tau}}{12} \right] e^{-t*OAS} = \sum_{t=1}^{T} e^{-t*OAS} PV_t \tag{9.7}$$

where

$$PV_t = \frac{1}{N} \sum_{k=1}^{N} (CF_{kt}) exp \left[-\sum_{\tau=0}^{t-1} \frac{r_{k\tau}}{12} \right]$$

Note that PV_t are computed without the knowledge of OAS and stored before we start the iterations for OAS. In fact, PV_t is the present value of time-t cashflow assuming $OAS = 0$ and averaged over N paths.

The method relieves us of the need to store randomly generated interest rates and cash flows. We simply keep collecting 360 sums of path-wise monthly values. Iterations for OAS can be arranged via a highly effective Newton-Raphson method:

$$OAS^{(i+1)} = OAS^{(i)} - (P^{(i)} - P^{market}) / \frac{dP}{d(OAS)}$$

where P^{market} denoted the actual market price we target. It requires having the first derivatives of P taken with respect of OAS, which can be easily produced analytically in the course of PV collection:

$$\frac{dP}{d(OAS)} = -\sum_{t=1}^{T} te^{-t*OAS} PV_t$$

This method can be adapted for the case of monthly compounded short rates when one cannot factor out OAS terms exactly. Instead, we define the array of "equivalent" benchmark rates:

$$\left(1 + \frac{r_t^{eq}}{12} \right)^t = \frac{CF_t}{PV_t} \tag{9.8}$$

where CF_t is the averaged cash flow received in month t, without discounting

$$CF_t = \frac{1}{N} \sum_{k=1}^{N} (CF_{kt})$$

and PV_t is defined above without an OAS entering. We now compute the Monte Carlo price, approximating formula (9.3) with

$$P \cong \sum_{t=1}^{T} CF_t \frac{1}{\left(1 + \dfrac{r_t^{eq} + OAS}{12}\right)^t} \qquad (9.9)$$

Approximation (9.9) requires us to store only sample average vectors, CF_t and PV_t, but otherwise shows no trace of path-wise data. It is surprisingly accurate:

A. For $OAS = 0$, formula (9.9) is, of course, identical to Monte Carlo price due to definition of r_t^{eq}.
B. For a non-zero OAS, the error stemming from this approximation is about 0.01% of the OAS level (e.g. 0.01 bps for 100 bps of OAS). This error is well within the expected practical accuracy of OAS computations in general.

There are numerous techniques for improving the accuracy of Monte Carlo methods for the valuation of MBS and other derivatives. They can be classified as pre-processing and post-processing. Accuracy-improving techniques that require pre-processing are those that specially arrange random shocks or random scenarios before they are actually used. In post-processing techniques, we keep random scenarios that the plain Monte Carlo method randomly generates, but possibly re-weigh or otherwise alter random results. Some methods, such as importance sampling, involve both pre- and post-processing. We will only describe those methods that we have tested and formed opinions about their effectiveness. Some of our conclusions may differ from those published by other authors. An excellent reference for those interested in learning more about Monte Carlo methods and related topics of financial engineering is Glasserman (2004).

VARIANCE REDUCTION TECHNIQUES: PRE-PROCESSING

Before we actually start using random scenarios to generate cash flows and discount factors, we can adjust them to achieve the desired theoretical properties.

Antithetic Reflection

We only generate $N/2$ independent scenarios out of N. The other $N/2$ scenarios will be mirror reflective in terms of the random shocks applied. If $w_{1t}, t=1,\dots,T$ is the array of random shocks to be used for scenario 1, then random shocks for scenario 2 will be $w_{2t}=-w_{1t}$, etc. This is the antithetic reflection method, one of most primitive, but popular, ways to improve Monte Carlo. The method makes shocks symmetrical and unbiased, that is, compliant with some theoretical properties, although it takes half the number of scenarios (i.e. degrees of freedom) to achieve them.

The efficiency of antithetic reflection depends on whether scenarios' symmetry along with a zero bias is important for accurate valuation. Usually they are—although the replication of theoretical volatility is important for valuation of options, too.

Rate Adjustment ("Fudging")

If it is important only to eliminate the bias of scenarios that arise randomly in simulations, we can add a common adjustment vector ε_t to all paths, thereby losing only one degree of freedom rather than $N/2$. Even better, we can find the adjustment vector to ensure certain valuable properties such as having exact discount factors. To illustrate the method, let us apply valuation formula (9.6) to a zero-coupon bond maturing at T, that is, $CF_{kt}=1$ for $t=T$ and zero otherwise. This bond should be valued without an OAS, but the randomly simulated short rates may result in a mismatch with market price $P(0,T)$. Accordingly, we will adjust the short rate using a "fudge" term ε_t, common for all scenarios, so that the market price and the Monte Carlo result match exactly (assuming continuous compounding):

$$P(0,T) = \frac{1}{N}\sum_{k=1}^{N} exp\left[-\sum_{t=0}^{T-1}\frac{r_{kt}+\varepsilon_t}{12}\right] \equiv PV_T exp\left[-\sum_{t=0}^{T-1}\frac{\varepsilon_t}{12}\right] \qquad (9.10)$$

where

$$PV_T = \frac{1}{N}\sum_{k=1}^{N} exp\left[-\sum_{t=0}^{T-1}\frac{r_{kt}}{12}\right]$$

is the computed unadjusted present value, averaged across all scenarios. On the other hand, the market price can be expressed via monthly continuously compounded forward rates:

$$P(0,T) = exp\left[-\sum_{t=0}^{T-1}\frac{f_t}{12}\right] \qquad (9.11)$$

Formulas (9.10) and (9.11) must be correct for any maturity T. Equating their right-hand sides, taking the natural logarithm and differencing, we can now find the entire array of fudge factors easily, month by month:

$$\varepsilon_t = f_t - 12\ln\frac{PV_t}{PV_{t+1}} \qquad (9.12\text{-cc})$$

From (9.12cc), it is apparent that, if the array of averaged PVs follows the forward rates precisely, no correction will be made. The method can be adapted for the case of monthly compounding rates using the OAS search recipe from the previous section. However, since the fudge factors are typically small, a modified application of formula (9.12cc) for monthly compounded rates is expected to be very accurate:

$$\varepsilon_t = f_t - 12\left(\frac{PV_t}{PV_{t+1}} - 1\right) \qquad (9.12\text{-me})$$

One can also correct the long rates. If we know a theoretical mean of, say the 10-year rate, we can simply correct for the difference our sample delivered. Again, the required fudge factors will depend on time, but will be common for all scenarios. The method guarantees theoretically accurate first moments of random paths' distributions, but does not ensure their symmetry.

Second-Moment Matching (Ortho-Normalization of Shocks)

Let us consider matching theoretical standard deviations and the autocorrelation function for $x(t)$. This is often termed *second-moment matching*. If we simulate multiple factors, their cross-correlation functions also fall into this statistical category. Since we simulate scenarios by generating random shocks w_{kt}, we need to ensure these shocks to be (assuming or forcing no bias, $\frac{1}{N}\sum_{k=1}^{N} w_{kt} = 0$ for all t)

(a) scaled to volatility of 1, i.e. $\frac{1}{N}\sum_{k=1}^{N} w_{kt}^2 = 1$, and

(b) serially uncorrelated, i.e. $\frac{1}{N}\sum_{k=1}^{N} w_{kt}w_{k\tau} = 0$ for $t < \tau$

With these two conditions satisfied, the sum of shocks will have its uncertainty growing as $\sqrt{t}$ and there will be no correlations between changes measured over non-overlapping time intervals. Hence, this process will satisfy the axiomatics of random walk.

We start with a plain set of shocks $\tilde{w}_{kt}$ sampled from the standard normal distribution. Applying the Gram-Schmidt transformation method, we convert them into a set of shocks w_{kt} that satisfy conditions (a) and (b). Let $\tilde{w}_t$, w_t be the vector of N random shocks used for month t generated before and after the Gram-Schmidt transformation, correspondingly. We set sequentially

$$w_0 = \tilde{w}_0 \, ; w_1 = \tilde{w}_1 - \frac{\langle w_0, \tilde{w}_1 \rangle}{\langle w_0, w_0 \rangle} w_0 \, ; \quad w_2 = \tilde{w}_2 - \frac{\langle w_0, \tilde{w}_2 \rangle}{\langle w_0, w_0 \rangle} w_0 - \frac{\langle w_1, \tilde{w}_2 \rangle}{\langle w_1, w_1 \rangle} w_1 , \text{etc.}$$

where we use the traditional notation for the product of two vectors: $\langle a, b \rangle = \sum_{k=1}^{N} a_k b_k$.

The only task left is scaling vectors to 1, that is, replacing all w's with $w/\|w\|$. This completes the ortho-normalization process. We can now apply shocks w_{kt} with the confidence that the simulated Brownian motion term $z(t)$ will reproduce the desired theoretical second moments.

There are several issues that users of this method should be aware of. First, an orthogonalization is only possible if $N \geq T$. This fact follows from the basics of linear algebra: having an N dimensional space, one cannot create more than N independent vectors. Therefore, the number of scenarios should be not less than the number of months, or, more generally, branching points of the random process. If the number of paths is too small, it is prudent to consider creating ortho-normal shocks for a shorter (most important) horizon and applying the regular Monte Carlo method thereafter.

Another question is whether the transformed shocks w_{kt} will sample the standard normal distribution like the raw shocks $\tilde{w}_{kt}$. The Gram-Schmidt transformation is almost linear; the only nonlinearity comes from the fact that the coefficients depend themselves on the sample. The distribution may be deformed if vectors $\tilde{w}_t$ happen to be collinear (linearly dependent) or close to be collinear. In addition, it is not recommended to have T to be too close to N even if the condition $N \geq T$ holds. This leaves a too few degrees of freedom in the transformation process. It is advisable to add some control over the selection of raw vectors $\tilde{w}_t$ and the practical horizon T, for which the method is used.

Finally, the Gram-Schmidt process takes additional computing time. It may be negligible when we apply the method to CMOs when most time will be spent on cash flow generation for each scenario.

Measuring and Documenting Accuracy Improvements

In order to assess Monte Carlo accuracy objectively, one needs to repeat the analysis using a different starting point ("seed") for the random number generation. For example, if we are interested in knowing the accuracy achieved by using N random scenarios, we will run the N-path analysis, say, 100 times without re-seeding the random number generator. We will have 100 different results and can compute the root-mean-squared-error (RMSE). This will point to the sampling error. If our Monte Carlo method was designed and implemented with a known bias, we will have to account for it as well. It is common to report Monte Carlo accuracy in a graphical form, with both axes, RMSE and N, being drawn to logarithmic (e.g. base 2) scales. We expect the lines to decline at a $-\frac{1}{2}$ constant slope because, as we showed, $RMSE \sim N^{-\frac{1}{2}}$ for most Monte Carlo methods.

Variance reduction techniques can be combined rather easily. For example, to use the antithetic reflection along with ortho-normalization, we generate independent shocks for $N/2$ scenarios, ortho-normalize them, then create another set of $N/2$ mirror reflections. We can add rate fudging to ensure exact discounting or remove a random bias in other important rates.

To document improvements in accuracy, we consider a number of Fannie Mae 30-year TBA benchmarks (both premiums and discounts) with a pre-2007 prepayment model and market. This will give us a more objective view of possible issues in accurately assessing the value of a prepayment option. TBAs priced at a moderate premium are those located close to the center of a refinancing S-curve; we should expect them to be valued less accurately than TBAs located closer to the saturated (flat) part of the curve and having limited cash flow variability. As we stated in the previous chapter, MBS pass-throughs can be valued rather accurately using a much faster backward induction method. Hence, it is the CMO world that actually mandates the use of Monte Carlo methods, not the pass-through world or its TBA part. Selecting TBAs as the benchmark for our Monte Carlo studies is dictated by the fact that they are standardized and largely represent the world of mortgage-related optionality. Observations regarding a relative power of numerical methods made below will hold for other asset classes although CMO tranches are much richer in special features such as cash flow distribution priority and triggers ("jumps").

Figure 9.1 compares Monte Carlo errors in assessing OAS (averaged across TBA coupons) for various methods, starting from the plain Monte Carlo, which is the least accurate. Since none of them had a bias by design, the reported RMSE serves as an objective statistical error.

The antithetic reflection seems to be the strongest single improvement step (by the scale of almost 4:1), but the rate-fudging and ortho-normalization provides decent improvements in accuracy as well (by the scale of almost 3:1). Combining antithetic reflection or the rate-fudging with ortho-normalization reduces the error further, by an additional factor of 1.7:1 (on average). Therefore, the simple

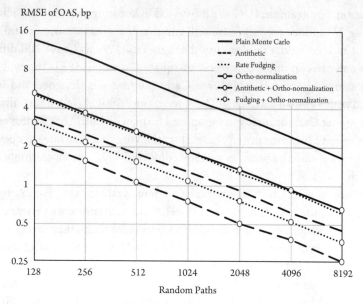

Figure 9.1 Comparative Accuracy of Monte Carlo Methods (Averaged RMSE across TBA Coupons)

pre-processing techniques we described reduce sampling errors by a factor of five to seven. Combining antithetic reflection with rate-fudging (which has a similar purpose) is not an improvement, not recommended and not shown in Figure 9.1.

All lines indeed exhibit a close to the $-\frac{1}{2}$ logarithmic slope. Although antithetic reflection may look like the best first-step method, one can note that fudging the short rate ensures an accurate valuation of static, option-free, instruments. Therefore, when processing a large MBS inventory, one may actually prefer to fudge the short rate. For many instruments, there may be some with saturated options such as residential MBS with very high- or very low-WAC collateral, prepayment penalties, commercial (non-prepayable) loans and deals, or static (non-MBS) bonds. They will be valued more accurately by the rate-fudging method rather than with antithetic reflection.

The ortho-normalization technique can apply to the entire simulation horizon (30 years or more) or for a much shorter, option-related, time window. For example, using this method for the first 10 years would bring a 90–95% improvement of accuracy for the method's maximum capacity. This observation allows one to reduce the number of paths for which ortho-normalization is feasible. For example, using monthly steps for the 30-year horizon, we have 360 steps and cannot use less than 360 paths to be able to ortho-normalize all the shocks. However, if we only seek to ortho-normalize the first 120 monthly shocks, we will be able to run fewer paths.

RMSE of OAS, bps

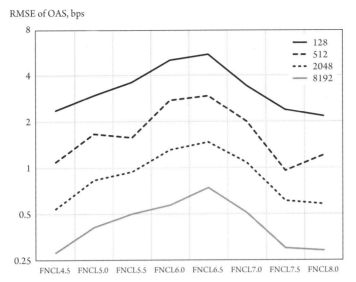

Figure 9.2 Accuracy of MC (Antithetic Reflection) for Various TBA Coupons and Number of Paths. Market as of Dec. 2007 (FN 30 rate = 5.4)

Figure 9.2 proves that Monte Carlo error declines with prepayment option cost. The largest error is seen for the coupon rate located at the steepest point of a refinancing S-curve (6.5 in our example). In contrast, both high and low coupons are close to saturation of the prepayment S-curve. The trend is similar for any number of paths and all the methods except for the plain Monte Carlo, which does not control the first moment, thereby causing a static, option-independent, bias.

VARIANCE REDUCTION TECHNIQUES: POST-PROCESSING

Post-processing usually includes correcting Monte Carlo averages or the weights themselves. One interesting example is the so-called *control variate method* widely used in financial engineering. This method improves on the Monte Carlo method by effectively re-weighing scenario results.

Traditionally, most authors describe this method in a rather rudimentary form (see, for example, Hull 2005). Let us consider the valuation of an MBS under some approximate method ("method"). We find another, usually simpler, instrument that closely resembles the MBS, but allows for a very accurate solution ("theory"); that instrument is called *control variate*. Then, for prices,

$$\begin{aligned} \text{MBS (theory)} = \text{MBS (method)} + \text{Control Variate} \\ \text{(theory)} - \text{Control Variate (method)} \end{aligned} \quad (9.13)$$

In other words, we correct the MBS value obtained by the approximate method using the error this method causes to the control variate. For example, Levin (2002) demonstrated how this approach can be used to value CMOs on grids, without simulations.

This trivial interpretation of the control variate technique has a limited practical value. First, it is usually not easy to find a very close analog for a complex instrument. Second, one needs to make sure that the correction could be done on a one-for-one basis, i.e. errors measured for the control variate are identical to those of the MBS. Glasserman (2004) describes a much richer approach when we apply a scenario-wise regression rather than formula (9.13). In order to describe the method, let us introduce some notations. Let y be a theoretical value of MBS (unknown) and x be a theoretical value of control variate (known precisely within the model); Y_k and X_k will be random values for scenario k generated by simulations without a bias; $\overline{y}$ and $\overline{x}$ will be the sample's averages, i.e. $\overline{y} = \dfrac{1}{N}\sum_{k=1}^{N} Y_k$, $\overline{x} = \dfrac{1}{N}\sum_{k=1}^{N} X_k$. Let us further assume that the vectors of random prices are linked via a simple linear regression:

$$Y_k = y + \beta(X_k - x), k = 1, \ldots, N \tag{9.14}$$

The MSE minimizing values for y and β solve the following linear equations:

$$y = \frac{1}{N}\sum_{k=1}^{N}[Y_k - \beta(X_k - x)] \equiv \overline{y} - \beta(\overline{x} - x) \tag{9.15}$$

$$\beta = \frac{\sum_{k=1}^{N}(Y_k - y)(X_k - x)}{\sum_{k=1}^{N}(X_k - x)^2} \tag{9.16}$$

Substituting (9.16) into (9.15) we obtain a linear equation for y:

$$y = \overline{y} - (\overline{x} - x)\frac{\sum_{k=1}^{N}(Y_k - y)(X_k - x)}{\sum_{k=1}^{N}(X_k - x)^2}$$

Resolving for y we note that our estimate of MBS' true price becomes a re-weighted average of scenario-wise values Y_k:

$$y = \sum_{k=1}^{N} w_k Y_k, \text{ where } w_k = \frac{1}{N}\frac{\sum_{i=1}^{N}(X_i - x)^2 / N - (X_k - x)(\overline{x} - x)}{\sum_{i=1}^{N}(X_i - x)^2 / N - (\overline{x} - x)^2}$$

$$\equiv \frac{1}{N} - \frac{(X_k - \overline{x})(\overline{x} - x)}{\sum_{i=1}^{N}(X_i - \overline{x})^2} \tag{9.17}$$

Note that the denominator is $\sum_{i=1}^{N}(X_i - x)^2 / N - (\bar{x} - x)^2 \equiv \sum_{i=1}^{N} X_i^2 / N - \bar{x}^2 \equiv \sum_{i=1}^{N}(X_i - \bar{x})^2 / N$, which is utilized in the last equality (9.17). It is easy to inspect that $\sum_{k=1}^{N} w_k = 1$, and see that, if the control variate was valued accurately by Monte Carlo, i.e. $\bar{x} = x$, then formula (9.17) would result in the simple averaging. If an error in the valuation of the control variate is detected, the weights will not be equal to each other. For example, if $\bar{x} > x$, all high-value control variate scenarios will be underweighted when computing y.

The control variate method presented above reduces the sampling error almost for sure. This is because we effectively project it into two orthogonal axes, one collinear to errors of the control variate (eliminated by the method), and one orthogonal to it. This can be shown mathematically. Given β, we can view the estimator (9.15) as $y(\beta)$; its variance is

$$Var\left[y(\beta)\right] = \frac{1}{N}Var(Y) - \frac{2}{N}\beta Cov(X,Y) + \frac{1}{N}\beta^2 Var(X)$$

and will be minimized at $\beta^* = Cov(X,Y)/Var(X)$, which is the theoretical limit of formula (9.16) for "practical β". Furthermore, that minimal variance will be equal to

$$Var\left[y(\beta^*)\right] = \frac{1}{N}Var(Y) - \frac{1}{N}\left[Cov(X,Y)\right]^2 / Var(X)$$

To compare, the plain Monte Carlo estimator $\bar{y}$ has a variance of $\frac{1}{N}Var(Y)$.

Hence, the use of control variate reduces the variance by the scale of

$$\frac{Var\left[y(\beta^*)\right]}{Var(\bar{y})} = 1 - \frac{\left[Cov(X,Y)\right]^2}{Var(X)Var(Y)} \equiv 1 - \rho_{X,Y}^2.$$

For a high correlation $\rho_{X,Y}$ (positive or negative) between the MBS in hand and the chosen control variate, the variance reduction will be strong enough to wipe out the entire error. If the correlation is zero, the initial Monte Carlo accuracy will be preserved. It is in sharp contrast to the rule (9.13), which can increase the error if the control variate is inadequate.[1]

---

[1] The variance reduction proof relies on the fact that β is known in advance. Since our β is assessed from the sample, it is random. This fact makes the statement of variance reduction imperfect, especially with a low N.

The method can be easily extended to the case of multiple control variates. Assume L different control variates (benchmark instruments) so that observations X_k, sample average $\bar{x}$ and theoretical price x becomes L-dimensional vectors. So does regression's slope β; we make all them bold in the following formulas:

$$Y_k = y + \beta^T \left(X_k - x \right), k = 1, \ldots, N$$

where, as in the single-dimensional case, y and β should be chosen to minimize the total MSE:

$$y = \bar{y} - \beta^T \left(\bar{x} - x \right)$$

$$\beta = V^{-1} \sum_{k=1}^{N} \left(Y_k - y \right) \left(X_k - x \right)$$

$V = \sum_{k=1}^{N} \left(X_k - x \right) \left(X_k - x \right)^T$ is the L-by-L symmetrical matrix of variances and convariances computed from the sample of control variates' prices. Excluding β we again express theoretical price y of MBS in the form of weighted average observations structurally similar to (9.17):

$$y = \sum_{k=1}^{N} w_k Y_k, \quad \text{where } w_k = \frac{1}{N} - \frac{\left(X_k - x \right)^T V^{-1} (\bar{x} - x)}{1 - N(\bar{x} - x)^T V^{-1} (\bar{x} - x)} \qquad (9.17\text{-m})$$

We compiled and presented the RMSE reduction scales for TBAs' simulations arising from the use of various At-the-Money (ATM) swaptions on the 10-year swap as control variates (Figure 9.3).

The accuracy improvement is moderate and not better than those provided by simpler pre-processing techniques we introduced in the previous section. However, aside from its role in variance reduction, the method of control variates can help identify instruments best replicating (hedging) the MBS. For example, our analysis allows for addressing the following question: Which swaption corrects MBS' errors the most? The answer shown in Figure 9.3 is not trivial: It is the one that expires in six years. Note, however, that an instrument providing the best correction is not necessarily the best hedge. As a counter-example, let us consider simulations with rate fudging and try employing option-free swaps as control variates to improve the accuracy. Of course, we will find no improvement despite the fact that swaps can certainly help to hedge the interest-rate risk found in MBS. Nevertheless, results in Figure 9.3 are interesting and informative.

RMSE reduction scale

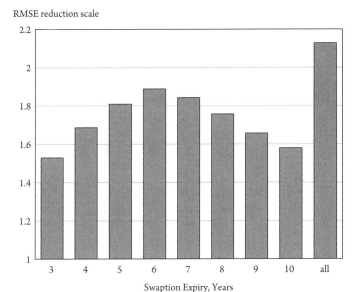

Swaption Expiry, Years

Figure 9.3 Error Reduction from Using Swaptions as Control Variates for TBAs. Error reduction scales are relative to the plain Monte Carlo and averaged across TBA coupons.

The control variate method does not alter the $N^{-\frac{1}{2}}$ convergence rate. Generally, using swaptions as control variates will not bring a sizable accuracy improvement if we complement Monte Carlo with simpler pre-processing techniques: rate fudging, antithetic reflection or ortho-normalization.

USING QUASI-RANDOM (SOBOL) SEQUENCES[2]

As we demonstrated at the beginning of this chapter, Monte Carlo method is essentially a way of numerical integration. We also showed that, if we could select grid points deterministically, the convergence rate would be higher than if we place them randomly. This is the idea behind Quasi-Monte Carlo methods (QMC). QMC approximates the integrand using carefully and deterministically chosen grid points that fill the multi-dimensional space uniformly. *Discrepancy* is a measure of deviation from uniformity; low-discrepancy points are desirable. Intuitively, low-discrepancy means that there should not be redundant points in small rectangles, nor should there be deficient points in relatively large rectangles.

[2] This section is based on work by Levy He of Andrew Davidson & Co.

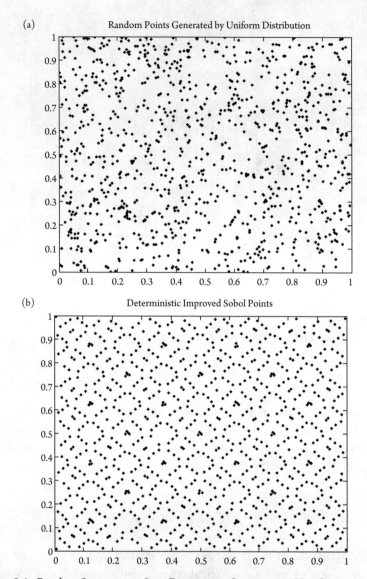

Figure 9.4 Random Sequences vs Low Discrepancy Sequences in Unit Square

Some good low-discrepancy sequences suggested by researchers are regular and improved Sobol sequences and generalized Faure sequences; see Papageorgiou and Traub (1996) and Joe and Kuo (2008). Figure 9.4 compares the filling of a 1-by-1 square by points generated (a) randomly and (b) using the deterministic Sobol sequence improved by Joe and Kuo.

There are limitations for the QMC, however. Although in optimal cases QMC's convergence rate could approach $O(N^{-1})$, the worst cases error for a d-dimensional problem is $O[(\log N)^d / N]$, which is faster than $O(N^{-\frac{1}{2}})$ associated

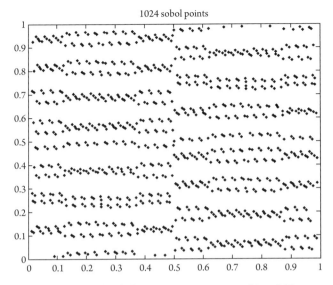

Figure 9.5 A 32-Dimensional Sobol Sequence: Dimensions 31 and 32

with the plain Monte Carlo in a low dimensional environment but is less effective or even worse in high dimensional problems. The difficulty is that low discrepancy sequences are no more uniform than random sequences in high dimensions, unless we use a very large number of points (Figure 9.5). Unfortunately, valuation problems in MBS valuation are indeed high dimensional as they require simulation of Brownian motions. We explain next how to reduce the effective dimensionality for Brownian motions.

Sobol Sequences with Brownian Bridges

Caflisch and Morokoff (1996) suggested using *Brownian bridges* so that the first few dimensions of a Sobol sequence mostly determine the interest-rate paths. A Brownian bridge is a stochastic process $B(t)$ whose probability distribution is conditional on a Brownian motion's $z(t)$ initial value and terminal value $z(t_1) = a, z(t_2) = b$. Through this technique, we can simulate the most important dimension first using the best Sobol numbers, and then fill in the details using conditional expectation and variance for the intermediate dimensions.

Consider a standard Brownian motion with $z(u) = x, z(s) = y, 0 \leq u < s$. Then, the Brownian bridge is a continuous, normally distributed, random process $B(t)$, $u \leq t \leq s$, with a linear expectation $\alpha(t)$ connecting the initial point (u, x) to the terminal point (s, y) and a parabolic variance $\beta(t)$:

$$\alpha = \frac{s-t}{s-u}x + \frac{t-u}{s-u}y, \quad \beta = \frac{(s-t)(t-u)}{s-u} \tag{9.18}$$

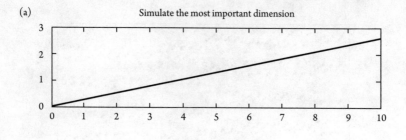

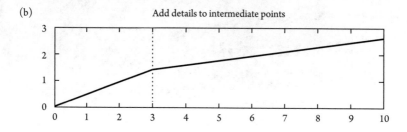

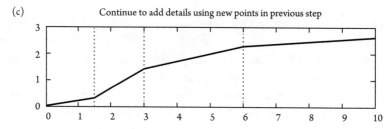

Figure 9.6 Procedure of Generalized Brownian Bridge Simulation

We can easily simulate a Brownian bridge at any time t between u and s by the following equation:

$$B(t) = \alpha(t) + \sqrt{(s-t)/(s-u)}z(t) \tag{9.19}$$

where $z(t)$ is the standard Brownian motion that starts from 0 at $t = u$. Therefore, the simulated value of $B(t)$ is influenced by the terminal values $z(u)$ and $z(s)$.

Figure 9.6 demonstrates a few steps in constructing a generalized Brownian bridge assuming the 10th year is the terminal point, followed by the 3rd year, then 1.5 year and the 6th year.

Sobol Sequences with Principle Component Analysis (PCA)

This method was first introduced by Acworth, Broadie and Glasserman (1998). Let us simulate a standard Brownian motion path as a discrete-time random walk: $z(t_1), z(t_2), \ldots, z(t_n)$. It is useful to visualize the sequential construction in a vector-matrix form:

$$
\begin{pmatrix} z(t_1) \\ z(t_2) \\ \vdots \\ z(t_n) \end{pmatrix} = A \begin{pmatrix} \Delta z_1 \\ \Delta z_2 \\ \vdots \\ \Delta z_n \end{pmatrix},
\tag{9.20}
$$

where Δz_i are independent random shocks drawn from the standard normal distribution, and A is an n by n matrix:

$$
A = \begin{pmatrix}
\sqrt{t_1} & 0 & 0 & \cdots & 0 \\
\sqrt{t_1} & \sqrt{t_2 - t_1} & 0 & \cdots & 0 \\
\sqrt{t_1} & \sqrt{t_2 - t_1} & \sqrt{t_3 - t_2} & \cdots & 0 \\
\sqrt{t_1} & \sqrt{t_2 - t_1} & \sqrt{t_3 - t_2} & \cdots & 0 \\
\sqrt{t_1} & \sqrt{t_2 - t_1} & \sqrt{t_3 - t_2} & \cdots & \sqrt{t_n - t_{n-1}}
\end{pmatrix}
\tag{9.21}
$$

Note that $AA^T = C$, the covariance matrix of vector $z = [z(t_1), z(t_2), \ldots, z(t_n)]^T$. Because a Gaussian process is completely specified by its covariance, any matrix B that satisfies $BB^T = C$ is a valid construction of the random walk (in fact, the Brownian Bridge technique is also a way of covariance matrix decomposition). We also know that the approximation error

$$
E \left\| z - \sum_{i=1}^{k} a_i \Delta z_i \right\|^2
\tag{9.22}
$$

from using just the first k numbers is minimized by using "principal components", i.e. the eigen-vectors that correspond to the largest eigen-values. Specifically, let us rank eigen-values of C in the descending order: $\lambda_1 > \lambda_2 > \cdots > \lambda_n > 0$ and set $a_i = \sqrt{\lambda_i} v_i, i = 1, \ldots, n$, where v_i are normalized eigenvectors ($\|v_i\| = 1$). In conclusion, we will choose $B = [\sqrt{\lambda_1} v_1 \quad \sqrt{\lambda_2} v_2 \quad \cdots \quad \sqrt{\lambda_n} v_n]$ in order to reduce the effective dimensionality.

Consider, for example, a random walk simulation over a progressively coarser time grid having 34 variable steps: The first two steps are 3 months each, next six are 6 months, and all the rest are 1 year. The eigenvalues of the covariance matrix are $\lambda_1 = 4506.89$, $\lambda_2 = 507.49$, $\lambda_3 = 187.69$, $\lambda_4 = 99.26$, $\lambda_5 = 61.91\ldots$ The variability explained by the first principal components are 80%, 89%, 93%, 95%, and 96%, correspondingly. This indicates that, although full construction of the path requires 34 normal random shocks, most of the variability of the paths can be determined using just a few of them.

The shortcoming of PCA is a computational cost that grows with the square of dimension of the covariance matrix. Several researchers have been focusing on reducing this computational cost. (See Akesson and Lehoczky 2000.)

Other Accuracy Improvements

We again consider assessing OAS accuracy for the same Fannie Mae 30-year TBA benchmarks we already referenced. We first note that the Moro inversion (1995) is used to transform the low discrepancy numbers into standard normal deviates, since it is reported that the Box-Muller algorithm damages the low discrepancy sequence properties (alters the order of the sequence or scrambles the sequence uniformity). In addition, the Box-Muller algorithm is slower than the Moro's inversion.

We then remark that, at high-dimensions, the Sobol points tend to repeat themselves across dimensions, resulting in high-dimensional clustering. The traditional solution is to discard an initial part of the sequence.[3] Another fact worth mentioning is that it will be trickier to measure the RMSE for deterministic low discrepancy sequences. Whereas Glasserman changes the parameters of the problem and runs QMC for 50 instances, Akesson and Lehoczky divide the Sobol sequence into 50,000 blocks of same size, then randomly selecting 50 without replacement. Our approach is to use distinct, non-overlapping and sequential subsequences. For example, we want to calculate the RMSE of 128 paths within 50 independent trials. For the first run, we use the first sub-sequence of length 128 (257th to 384th point); for the second run, we will use the 385th to 512th point, etc.

Figure 9.7 depicts accuracy comparison obtained via different methods. We show the plain Monte Carlo, its best improvement from the prior section (i.e. antithetic plus ortho-normalization), and two variations of quasi-random sequences.

---

[3]Glasserman [2004] recommends discarding 256 points although this is rather arbitrary and will affect results.

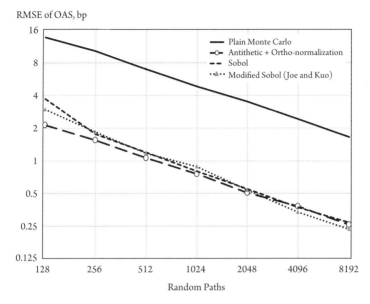

Figure 9.7   Error Comparison Using Pre-Processing Methods versus Sobol Sequences

The use of Sobol sequences reduces valuation error substantially and demonstrates the advantage of quasi-randomness over randomness. The error line has a somewhat steeper decline pointing to a faster than $O(N^{-\frac{1}{2}})$ convergence rate. At the same time, a combination of the efficient pre-processing methods of random shocks yields similar overall results. The modifications of the Sobol method (PCAs, Brownian Bridge) have not led to further error reductions in our simulation of interest rates over a sparsely branching probability tree. However, they provided modest improvements when simulating rates in a continuous space.

Financial engineers use a variety of methods to value mortgage-backed securities. The choice of methods requires a detailed understanding of the nature of the problem, the use of the model, computer capabilities and financial engineering techniques. While non-simulation techniques are useful for many problems, simulation based modeling provides the most flexible tool for MBS analysis.

10

Applications of the Option-Adjusted Spread Valuation Approach to Agency Mortgage-Backed Securities

Option-Adjusted Spread (OAS) is the expected additional (or subtractional) return to an investor taking all relevant risk factors into account. Chapter 4 introduced this approach, with a brief mention of its strengths and drawbacks. Chapters 8 and 9 provided recipes to compute MBS values using OAS or to perform the inverse calculation. Most MBS valuation systems revolve around this concept or its modifications.

There are three common applications of OAS valuation to agency MBS. The first is assessing the expected return given the market price of MBS. This exercise lets investors compare several investment candidates and decide which one is "cheap" on an OAS basis. Likewise, traders would like to sell instruments they feel are priced "rich."

The second application is valuing instruments that do not trade often and have no reliable market price. Examples include many rarely traded CMO tranches, unsecuritized loans, mortgage servicing rights (MSR) or so-called specified pools. In the latter case, despite the existence of an active market, models are heavily employed to price pools with known differences in characteristics (average loan size, FICO, loan-to-value ratio or LTV, etc.) relative to the to-be-announced (TBA) market. In each case, it is assumed that an analyst can come up with the right OAS level (e.g. using some benchmarks) to use to compute the price.

Finally, the OAS method can be employed to compute risk measures (such as effective duration) and related hedge ratios. For example, mortgage originators hire interest-risk managers—to take positions in the swap market or in the

TBA market in order to offset possible losses to the origination pipeline arising from an increase in interest rates. Measuring, monitoring, and hedging agency MBS risk should not be limited to interest rates, but should also include, for example, consideration of the exposure to a prepayment model's uncertainty (bias). Regardless of Deltas or Gammas measured, the use of OAS valuation usually assumes holding the OAS level unchanged when risk factors are stressed. This assumption will be challenged at the end of this chapter and will become an important motivation of the analysis presented in the following chapter.

THE ROLE OF INTEREST-RATE DISTRIBUTION

In chapter 5, we introduced several term-structure models and presented evidence that Gaussian models should generally be favored (except when interest rates are very low). How important is the selection of a rate model for the valuation of agency MBS?

In order to understand the role played by a term-structure model for the valuation of MBS, let us revisit its main purpose: capturing the cost of prepayment and other embedded options. If the prepayment speed did not depend on interest rates and coupon rates were always fixed, an MBS would be a static instrument. The value of such an instrument would become known with certainty by discounting its projected cash flows via observed market rates. It is the dependence of the cash flows on interest rates that makes MBS a dynamic financial instrument. Valuation results will vary depending primarily on the volatility specification within a chosen term-structure model.

Once the role of embedded option and volatility is understood, we can go one step further. As we know from the option theory, the dependence on volatility (Vega) reaches its maximum at-the-money, i.e., at the point where the underlying asset's price is equal to the option's strike. For an MBS, the concept of a prepayment option being in-, out-, or at-the-money is inexact and of an empirical nature. First, borrowers do not refinance all at once, so prepayment models assume an option exercise distributed over time. Second, a current-coupon (CC) pool is certainly out-of-the-money because borrowers who obtained a loan at the prevailing market rate have no incentive to refinance if that rate stays. It is natural to assume that the at-the-money point (ATM) is located at the center of the S-like refinancing curve, as shown in Figure 10.1.

In order to quantify the role of the term-structure model and its volatility specification, imagine what must happen to the market in order to move a given MBS toward the ATM point. For a discount MBS, a par-valued MBS, or even a modest-premium MBS, the mortgage rate must fall. For a high premium MBS to reach the ATM point, the rate must rise. Using these facts, let us compare a

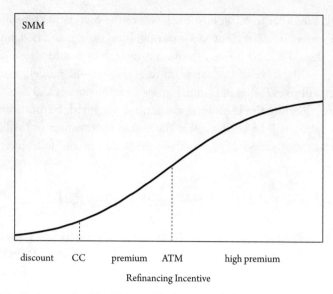

Figure 10.1 Understanding Key Points of Refinancing S-Curve

normal model to a lognormal model calibrated to the same forward curve and ATM volatility data. (Squared Gaussian model's results are expected to lie in between.) The absolute volatility of a lognormal rate model is proportional to the rate level; hence, it grows with the rate. In contrast, the absolute volatility of a normal model is independent of the rate's level.

Dependence of Option-Adjusted Spread on the Rate Model

Given market prices, the use of a lognormal model instead of a normal model will result in lower OAS levels for high-premium MBS and higher OAS levels for discount, current-coupon and moderate-premium MBS. This conclusion naturally flows from our rule formulated above: making absolute volatility higher or lower while moving the MBS towards the ATM point, we inflate or deflate the embedded option value that is exercised by the borrower against the investor.

Dependence of Option-Adjusted Duration on the Rate Model

It is rather easy to understand how an option-adjusted duration (OAD) will be affected by the rate model selection. If interest rates fall, the price will rise, but, additionally, a proportional volatility model will deflate the option. Hence, the

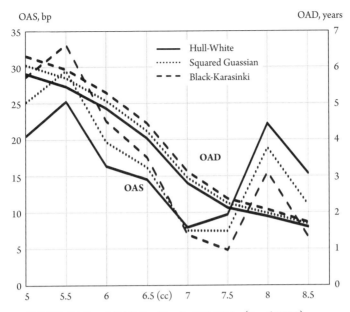

Figure 10.2 LIBOR OAS and OAD Profiles for FN TBAs (April 2002)

MBS price will inflate more. The opposite will occur if rates rise. Therefore, a lognormal model will generate longer effective duration, for all MBS coupons.

Figure 10.2 compares OAS and OAD generated with the use of various rate models. In April 2002, the current-coupon rate was close to 6.5%. The three OAS lines cross each other at a 7% point (priced at 102.2 by the TBA market) thereby suggesting that the ATM point was just 50 bps above the current-coupon rate. The OAD difference among the models is within 0.5 year, or 10% of its level.

The position of the ATM point is determined by the S-curve, but the price of that "ATM" TBA depends on other factors, most importantly, the prepayment speed projected at this central point. In order to explain this fact, we consider the much-slowed 2011 market, when both S-curves were somewhat shifted to the right and scaled down sizably in recognition of the stricter underwriting. Table 10.1 shows the OAS and OAD comparative results for March 2011. Now, the point at which the HW model and the BK model produce crossing OAS levels (TBA 5) is 90 bps above the market rate (4.11%). However, it is now equivalent to a five- (rather than two-) point premium due to the much-slower prepayment projection.

Although most mortgage instruments will look "shorter" under the HW model, there are some notable exceptions. As we explained above, the primary divergence of one model from another is found in differing volatility models. Since mortgage IOs and mortgage servicing rights (MSRs) have drastically changing convexity profiles, they will also have unsteady exposures to volatility,

Table 10.1 LIBOR OAS AND OAD PROFILES FOR FN TBAs (MARCH 2011)

3/18/2011	Price	LIBOR OAS			Effective Duration		
		HW	SqG	BK	HW	SqG	BK
3.5	95.34	27.63	41.11	44.35	6.70	7.45	7.62
4	99.31	20.19	32.97	34.78	6.05	6.71	6.75
4.5	102.41	18.30	30.04	29.78	5.07	5.63	5.75
5	105.08	13.19	19.77	16.65	4.27	4.65	4.99
5.5	107.25	14.04	17.14	12.98	3.47	3.75	4.11
6	109.00	28.14	29.28	25.81	3.51	3.74	4.15
6.5	112.19	19.07	17.71	16.11	3.48	3.66	3.98
7	113.86	43.20	40.25	38.94	3.59	3.77	3.98

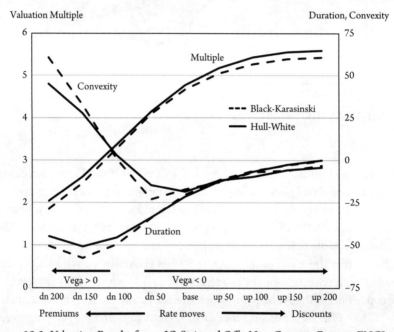

Figure 10.3 Valuation Results for an IO Stripped Off a New Current-Coupon FNCL pool

that is, Vega. For example, Vega is typically positive for an IO taken from a premium pool (case 1), negative for the one stripped off a discount pool (case 2), and about zero for the case when the pool's rate is at the center of a refinancing curve (slightly above par, case 3).[1] Therefore, the BK model will generally overstate the rate sensitivity for case 1, understate it for case 2, and will be close to the HW model in case 3 (Figure 10.3). When arriving at these conclusions, we kept

---

[1]This analysis is limited to the direct exposure to rate volatility and discards the strong indirect dependence via change in mortgage rates. See chapter 8 for a discussion of "full Vega."

in mind that an IO value, in contrast to regular MBS, grows with the rates. These interesting findings, though affecting Delta-hedging, do not contradict what is well known: IOs, POs, and MSRs are influenced greatly by prepayments and slightly by interest-rate models.

Can two different models be used for risk management: one for the assets, another for hedges? Suppose a mortgage desk blindly uses the BK model, whereas a swap desk trades with a skew. Unless the position is made Vega-neutral, differing volatility specifications in the models may considerably reduce hedge efficiency.

WHEN DOES THE NUMBER OF RATE FACTORS MATTER?

Limitations of single-factor modeling are well known—it is hard to believe that all rates are perfectly correlated. Recognizing that the fixed-income world is indeed multi-factor and that some instruments could have been valued differently had we used more realistic rate dynamics, we would like to compare the use of one- and two-factor term-structure models calibrated to the same forward curve and swaption volatility matrix. To simplify the analysis, we assume that this calibration is performed accurately and the marginal distribution of interest rates is the same for either model. The only difference between the two modeling families is that the two-factor model has the ability to change a curve's shape (twist).

Since a correctly calibrated two-factor model simulates rate collection in a much more realistic and accurate fashion than any single-factor model does, it seems at first glance that two- or more-factor modeling may reveal values and risks way beyond the primitive picture drawn by any single-factor model. As paradoxical as it may sound, it's easy to perceive an instrument as mispriced by a single-factor model. Most MBS by types—and an absolute majority of them—would not be valued materially differently, if we switched the business regimen to the use of the two-factor model. Whereas some instruments and exotic options certainly require two- or more-factor modeling, the most important role of a multi-factor model is assessing interest-rate risk, not finding today's value (or OAS).

Many practitioners mistakenly think that the value of the embedded prepayment option depends on the correlation between a long rate that drives the prepay speed and the short rate that is used for discounting. Hence, the use of a realistic two-factor model should deflate the prepay option and increase the value of MBS. If this common perception were right, it would affect European options too. Consider, for example, a European swaption. The exercise is triggered by the long swap rate; the discounting is done using an arbitrage-free sequence of the short rates, yet its price is known and independent of the rate-model selection. Levin (2001) has given a simple argument reminiscent of the classic Black-Scholes setting: If we model the prepay option as a sequence of European pay-offs on a single long rate and fix the volatility of this rate beforehand, we wouldn't find material dependence on the model specification for most MBS. This statement seems surprisingly robust: It holds true even if we relax stiff assumptions. For example, we may assume that prepay decisions are based on a "remaining-maturity" rate rather than on a single tenor.

Since the majority of commonly used practical models simulate prepay speeds as the sequence of European options on the MBS current market rate, volatility selection effectively "freezes" the value of a prepay option. This leaves much less freedom to deviate from the value given by a single-factor model tied to the same volatility source.

What would make the difference? To the extent MBS instruments are concerned, the answer is: *An asymmetric response to curve's twist.* For example, a prepay option may be triggered by the difference between two points of the curve, along with rate's level. If the dependence is linear, an MBS would lose and gain the same amount from steepening and flattening, thereby causing no need for a prepay option overhaul. It is only when the pay-off has an asymmetric dependence on the curve's shape that the curve's random twists change the value.

The *curve-at-origination* (CATO) prepay effect can serve as a good example. If the yield curve steepens from origination, homeowners who originally elected a fixed-rate mortgage may review their choice and switch to an ARM. If the curve flattens, they will not change their selection. Hence, CATO causes an asymmetric prepayment signal in response to a random twist.

Levin (ADPN Feb. 2005) documents valuation results for FRM and ARM passthroughs. The results prove that, without the CATO effect, both fixed-rate MBS and even hybrid ARMs are valued within 1 bp of OAS, that is, not beyond sampling accuracy, regardless of the number of factors and the inter-rate correlations. CATO causes a small (1–2 basis points) OAS difference between one- and two-factor worlds, which can be both positive and negative depending on the shape of the yield curve.

A much stronger example of the asymmetry can be found in *CMO floater and inverse floater tranches.* Suppose that x denotes a yield curve's random twist factor; without a loss of generality, we can center it on zero by interpreting x as the deviation of the curve's slope from its mean. Suppose further that the positive value of x corresponds to steepening. The value of a 1% fixed-rate IO will increase with x due to slower prepayments; let us write it down as $a + bx$ (where $b > 0$), ignoring higher-order terms. The actual floating coupon will change with x as $c + dx$

where d is positive (on average) for a short inverse floater (or a long floater) and is negative for a long inverse floater (or a short floater). We made this determination for the sign of d based on what part of the twisted yield curve plays the dominant role in rate resets. Hence, the total value of the IO will be $(a + bx)$ times $(c + dx)$. Taking mathematical expectation of this expression and keeping in mind that the expectation of x is zero, we get $ac + bd\sigma^2$, with the last term being missed by a single-factor model. Therefore, the slope's volatility (σ) boosts the value of a short inverse IO (or a long IO floater), which pays a higher rate longer and a lower rate shorter, i.e. it possesses a positive curve convexity. Vice versa, it deflates the value of a short IO floater (or a long inverse IO floater), which is negatively convex to the slope.

Table 10.2 presents comparative OAS levels for several inverse IO floaters taken from the Ginnie Mae Remic Trust 2005-008 deal and analyzed at origination, along with the deal's collateral. Since the two inter-rate correlation parameters employed as inputs do vary historically, we show results for several input sets. The "100/100" case is identical to the single-factor Hull-White model; we use it as the benchmark. Note that a low correlation pair (like "8/1") does not lead to the largest two-factor effect. In fact, such a set-up reduces the role of the short rate in the behavior of long rates. Like in the Hull-White case, one factor becomes either absent or dominated by the other. In between, we have true two-factor models with the "90/70" case being the closest to the 1995–2000 implied swap rates behavior (Levin 2001).

Table 10.2 confirms that inverse IOs with short projected lives (assessed along the forward-curve scenario) add OAS relative to the use of the Hull-White model. In contrast, long tranches lose. Collateral is barely affected by the choice of the model. We reiterate that every model we considered was calibrated to the same set of swap rates and ATM swaption volatilities. The accuracy of volatility calibration varied somewhat and could contribute slightly to the pricing results.

Table 10.2 OAS ADDED BY THE USE OF TWO-FACTOR GAUSSIAN MODEL (GNM 2005-008)

Tranche	Type (Intex)	Projected WAL	Correlation Input: 2-Year to Short Rate / 10-Year to Short Rate					Comment
			90/70	80/50	50/20	20/5	8/1	
			OAS Added by Two-Factor Model, bp					
DT	NTL_SEQ_INV_IO	1.43	48.9	82.5	105.6	67.8	40.5	short INV IO
SB	NTL_SEQ_INV_IO	8.96	−12.3	−16.9	−18.9	−14.0	−10.4	long INV IO
SD	NTL_SEQ_INV_IO	8.96	−13.8	−21.0	−23.9	−17.4	−12.2	long INV IO
TA	NTL_SEQ_INV_IO	1.43	48.3	77.8	95.0	61.4	37.6	short INV IO
COLLAT	PSEUDO	4.52	−0.1	−0.2	−0.3	−0.3	−0.1	collateral

Once the effect of using a two-factor model is proven for IO floaters, it can be extended to some other CMO tranches including the fixed-rate ones. Indeed, ignoring reset caps and floors, an inverse IO floater paying (c – LIBOR) should be valued as a premium of the regular tranche that pays a constant rate c and amortizes as the inverse IO in question (this identity is discussed later in this chapter). Hence, our conclusions apply to short (relative to collateral) and long fixed-rate CMO tranches as well: Given market premium price, short tranches should have higher OAS and long tranches should have lower OAS when using a two-factor model. The relative valuation of discounted tranches is opposite.

Hence, using the two-factor model may change the price of some CMOs. However, it simulates the dynamics of the historical curve three to four times more accurately than does a single-factor model (Levin 2001). Therefore, hedging against rate moves ("principal components") that stem from the two-factor view may be beneficial for maintaining a market-neutral position. As we demonstrated in this chapter, a single-factor pricing model can do very well, but a single-factor risk assessment that relies solely on the parallel-shock sensitivity is not a sound practice. The real choice remains between hedging principal components coming from a two- or three-factor model or using a set of "key rates." The former is quicker and more elegant; the latter is more accurate and time-consuming.

VALUING TBAS AND SPECIFIED POOLS

OAS models are actively utilized in selecting the cheapest pools to be delivered to TBA buyers, as well as setting market quotes for pools that possess preferred characteristics and deserve a premium called *pay-up*. Within the universe of pools eligible for delivery, TBA sellers normally favor (and TBA buyers should expect) the cheapest ones as confirmed by their lowest OAS levels. A pool's characteristics, both basic (weighted-average coupon or WAC, weighted-average maturity or WAM) and enhanced (average loan size, FICO, LTV, geography), can be key factors in the selection process.

Knowing TBA market quotes, both sellers and buyers can compute and screen OAS levels for a variety of pools available and eligible for delivery. For high-coupon (well above par) TBAs, one would normally expect the pools with the highest prepayment speed expectations to be delivered. Looking at a variation of the pricing formula (4.4p)

$$p(0) = E \int_0^T [c(t) - r(t) - OAS] e^{y(t)} dt + E[p(T) e^{y(T)}]$$

we see that, when $c > r + OAS$, price premium p is minimized for the highest amortization rate λ, leading to the strongest deflating factor $e^{y(t)}$. Similarly, we should expect to see pools with the slowest prepayment characteristics to be delivered as low-coupon (below par) TBAs.

Figure 10.4 explores OAS dependence on the pools' age, keeping market prices and gross rates fixed. We screen 2010–2011 origination vintages for September 2011 delivery. In panel (a), we disregarded the SATO effect, i.e. prepayment's dependence on whether the pool was originated above or at then-prevailing market rate (see Chapter 7 for a description of SATO). With the FNCL market rate at 3.25%, the cheapest FNCL 3.5 and 4.0 are brand new pools. As for larger-premium TBAs, 4.5 and 5.0, the lowest OAS will be reached at the age of four months. This is explained by a battle of two forces, aging and burnout. When a premium pool is new, it has not aged to be fast enough, but, when it is old, it may be already burnt. The minimum-OAS age depends on many factors, including propensity to refinance given the environment, quite stressed in 2011.

In panel (b), we added the SATO effect. As seen, SATO can be a strong factor, at times, changing the perception of cheapness. It appears that the FNCL 5.0 originated in 2010–2011 were well above prevailing rates, with SATO ranging from 60 bps (January 2010) to 160 bps (August 2011). Borrowers who agreed on an above-market rate may have had difficulties qualifying for a lower rate. With SATO factored in, 5% pools originated in April 2010 (age = 16 months) show the lowest OAS = 20 bps. Note that all premium pools originated in the fall of 2010 had high SATO and the related OAS spike (age = 10 months); they should be favored by buyers, but avoided by sellers.

Let us assume that the TBA market's participants have screened and selected the lowest-OAS pools. This selection makes other pools better than the TBAs and the practical question arises: "How much better?" For example, the 10-month aged pools shown in panel (b) of Figure 10.4 should be traded at a pay-up. Traditionally, pools with average low loan balance (LLB), low FICO, high LTV, originated in New York, Florida, or Texas are viewed as slow prepayers. Pools having lower GWAC (given net coupon) should prepay slower too. These examples demonstrate that a specified pool's pay-up can arise from both its basic fundamental characteristics (age, GWAC) and the enhanced borrower data. Furthermore, the perception of "slow" and "fast" factors changes with time. For example, California, normally a fast state, has many borrowers that, during the 2008–2010 financial troubles, found themselves underwater and unable to refinance. Some pools that feature a high percent of delinquent loans would traditionally be viewed as slow; in reality, GSEs' repurchase programs accelerated their liquidation.

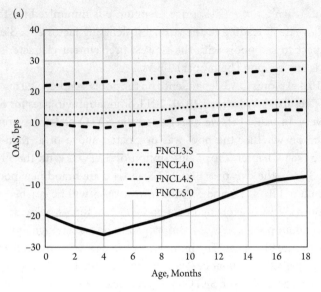

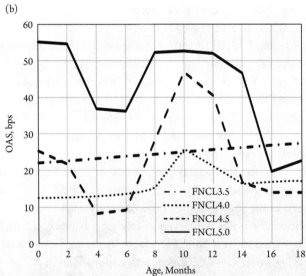

Figure 10.4 Computed OAS for TBAs as Function of Age for September 2011 Delivery

Theoretical pay-up is measured as the difference in price between the specified pool in question and a matching-coupon TBA, computed with the same OAS. That is, using a quoted TBA price, we first compute the OAS for pools likely to be delivered, and then utilize that OAS to value the specified pool.

Market pay-ups are often smaller than theoretical ones. The reason is that many investors buy pools with the intent to sell them. When selling the pool back to the market, they cannot be assured of a fair pay-up. This market inefficiency leads to the following problem: Suppose a pool bought at a pay-up will be held for some limited, investor-defined, period and sold at the TBA price. What is the fair pay-up now, given this adverse exit scenario? We define this measure as *practical pay-up*, which should be a function of the holding period, and is generally smaller than the theoretical pay-up.

How do we compute the practical pay-up, assuming that we know the holding period to be, say, six months? First, we compute theoretical pay-up, assuming the regular next-month settlement. Then, we compute theoretical pay-up using forward settlement in seven months. This is the pay-up we forfeit when selling the pool at the TBA forward price. Subtracting this forward pay-up scaled down for principal pay-off, amortization and discounting from the next-month theoretical pay-up, we obtain the practical pay-up we seek. We illustrate these computations in Table 10.3 using three hypothetical pools, a new pool, a low-loan balance pool, and a Florida discount pool.

The last column is computed as

$$Practical\ pay\text{-}up = Theoretical\ pay\text{-}up\left(next\ month\ settlement\right)$$

$$-\left[theoretical\ pay\text{-}up\ \left(7\ months\ settlement\right)\right]\times\left(pool\ factor\right)\times\left(discounting\right)$$

The new pool draws its pay-up from being early on the age ramp; in seven months, there will be little difference between it and the TBA. In contrast, the LLB pool's forward pay-up is still essential, although perhaps limited owing to the steep forward curve, making refinancing differences less important. A pool with a seemingly higher theoretical pay-up may end up with a lower practical pay-up. Once again, we emphasize the knowledge of the horizon as the key entry to this practical pay-up analysis. As for the Florida discount pool, it features a low

Table 10.3 PRACTICAL PAY-UP CALCULATIONS (JANUARY 13, 2005)

| Pool | Theoretical Pay-up, Decimals | | | | Pool Factor | Discounting | |
	Next Month	+ TBA Option	7 Months Fwd	+TBA Option	6-Months, 1-Month Fwd	6-Months, 1-Month Fwd	Practical Pay-up
New pool	0.20	0.20	0.00	0.00	0.88	0.97	0.20
LLB pool	0.30	0.30	0.15	0.15	0.88	0.97	0.17
FL disc pool	−1.00	0.00	−1.20	0.00	0.91	0.97	0.00

turnover rate and should be fair valued at a considerable *pay-down*. However, the
TBA delivery option allows for delivering this pool; hence, it cannot be marked
below the TBA price. This put option erases the pay-down.

Szakallas at el. (2006) summarized theoretical and practical pay-ups for various features and compared them with the market quotes during normal market
conditions. In some cases, the results of practical pay-up analysis were close to
market quotes, whereas in others they were somewhat apart. This should not surprise readers because we employ a particular modeling view, explained in this
chapter. As for the theoretical pay-up levels, they seem to be much above the
market, as we postulated.

The amount of pay-up depends on loan features and prepayment environment. By the end of 2012, about 40% of agency passthroughs were sold as specified pools rather than TBAs due to a high-premium state of the market coupled
with powerful prepayment-depressing regulation. One example is a so-called
HARP (Home Affordable Refinance Program) that allows high-LTV borrowers
to obtain new loan given proper payment history. Since such a privileged refinancing is allowed only once, high-HARP pools were considered slow and sold
at a considerable pay-up. According to Fuster *et al.* (2012), those pools, as well as
low-loan-size pools, could fetch 1.5 to 3 points over TBAs.

AN EFFECTIVE DURATION OVERVIEW

With several decades of combined MBS-related experience, we found computing effective duration (also known as option-adjusted duration, or OAD) to be
the main reason MBS risk managers employ OAS systems. OAD is measured as
logarithmic (relative) price sensitivity to a parallel change in interest-rate curve
(x) taken with the opposite sign

$$OAD = -\frac{d(LnP)}{dx} \equiv -\frac{1}{P}\frac{dP}{dx} \qquad (10.1)$$

and usually computed numerically using some (possibly, small) shock x. Often,
instead of OAD, analysts use Delta, which is the same measure without the divi-
sion by P. For example, a duration of four years means that price moves at the
pace of 4% *of its level* per each 1% of a rate's move. A Delta of four years means
that price moves at the pace of 4% *of the balance* per each 1% of rate's move. Delta
computed for one basis point of rate's move is termed *DV01*. Delta multiplied by
the MBS balance in dollars is called *dollar duration* (a portfolio's dollar durations
are additive).

Let us assume that we deal with a single-factor short rate model so that x is a parallel shift in $r(t)$, use formula (4.4p) for the price premium and compute Delta (dropping the terminal value at maturity):

$$
\begin{aligned}
Delta = -\frac{dp}{dr} = -\frac{d}{dr} \left\{ E \int_0^T [c(t) - r(t) - OAS] e^{y(t)} dt \right\} \\
= \underbrace{E \int_0^T e^{y(t)} dt}_{(A)\,annuity} - \underbrace{E \int_0^T \frac{d}{dr} c(t) e^{y(t)} dt}_{(B)\,floater\,offset} + \underbrace{E \int_0^T [c(t) - r(t) - OAS] e^{y(t)} t\,dt}_{(C)\,price\,premium\,effect} \\
+ \underbrace{E \int_0^T [c(t) - r(t) - OAS] e^{y(t)} \int_0^t \left[\frac{d}{dr} \lambda(\tau) \right] d\tau\,dt}_{(D)\,S\text{-}curve\,effect} \qquad (10.2)
\end{aligned}
$$

The first term (A), also known as *IO Multiple*, is simply the value of an annuity paying \$1 per annum and amortizing with MBS. For a fixed rate MBS, the second term (B) is zero, but, for a floater, it fully offsets the first term (A) if the coupon resets with the market rate, i.e. $(d/dr)c(t)=1$. The third term (C) arises due to price's premium (or discount) that will be contracted (or expanded) by a stronger (or weaker) discount factor $e^{y(t)}$. For a fixed-rate MBS, terms (A) and (C) together comprise *static duration*. Finally, the last term (D) links Delta to the prepay model's dependence on interest rates, that is, the S-curve. It is equal to zero for static instruments or perfect floaters. This term is similar to (C) except the force causing a stronger (or weaker) PV discounting is the rate-dependent balance's pay-off.

Before we proceed to a systematic classification of MBS classes and their special, duration-related, features, we will provide an overview of some fundamental factors affecting valuation modeling and option-adjusted duration (OAD) expectation, in particular.

Fundamental Factors

Given market conditions, OAD is influenced by the agency MBS (or CMO) type, prepayment model, interest-rate model, and pricing level.

The **prepayment modeling** aspect is somewhat understood by most practitioners. If OAD seems to be too long or too short, the prepayment speed will be the first suspect. However, one needs to understand clearly the difference between the static duration component and the dynamic effect produced by term (D) in (10.2). If we simply accelerate a prepayment model, we will reduce static duration due to the $e^{y(t)}$ factor, but not necessarily the full OAD. For example, the negative effective duration for IOs is explained by the dependence of prepayments on interest rates; should the S-curve totally flatten, OAD for an IO becomes positive. In order to realize the difference between static and dynamic duration terms, compare two S-curves in Figure 10.5 (this example taken from Levin (ADPN Jan. 2011).

The bold S-curve is never faster than the dashed S-curve. However, between the two models, an OAS system utilizing the bold S-curve never produces a longer effective duration, for *all rate incentives*. The logic of this paradoxical claim is as follows. We expect the OAD level to be almost identical in the two models except for the high-incentive zone (the large dot) that is associated with a high premium coupon located at or close to the full saturation of the refinancing curve. Such a high premium MBS can be viewed synthetically as a par-priced bond plus an IO paying a premium rate off the same principal balance. That IO has a negative OAD for the bold S-curve because it retains elasticity (higher market rates—lower prepayment speeds). The dashed S-curve becomes flat making the IO a static instrument with a positive duration. Once this is understood, it becomes clear why a slower S-curve retaining interest-rate dependence will generate a shorter OAD.

The **interest-rate model** is another driver explained earlier in this chapter. The use of a lognormal model typically inflates OAD relative to the normal model calibrated to the same market conditions because, when moving interest rates up

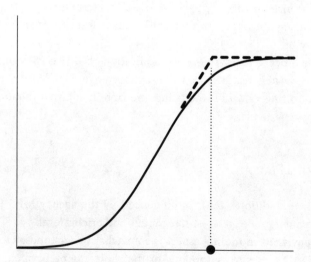

Figure 10.5 The Story of Two S-Curves

and down for the purpose of OAD computation, we inflate and deflate the option cost respectively. This causes an additional rate exposure of an investor's position.

The **pricing level** effect contained by terms (C) and, especially, (D) in (10.2) can be a strong force. The same MBS with same prepayment model and same interest-rate model, but priced at 80 will have a much longer effective duration than when it is priced at par. Assuming that $d\lambda/dr < 0$, price's discount ($c < r + OAS$) extends OAD; premium reduces it.

To appreciate this phenomenon, let us imagine that an MBS that looks like a 3-year zero-coupon bond in the base case, contracts becoming a 2-year bond in the down 1% rate scenario, and extends to a 4-year bond in the up 1% scenario. If the base discount rate is very high, say 30%, the 3-year bond is worth $100/(1+0.3)^3 = 45.52$, the 2-year bond is worth $100/(1+0.29)^2 = 60.09$, and the 4-year bond is worth $100/(1+0.31)^4 = 33.96$. Taking these three prices, we get a staggering OAD of 28.7 years. We would not have had such an effect had we used a much lower base rate, or removed the WAL sensitivity on interest rates. In short, discounting at a wide discount rate magnifies OAD when MBS changes its WAL, which is usually the case with MBS. A very good practical example would be POs that are deeply discounted and have a greater rate exposure than the collateral.

MBS Types

Below is a summary of "OAD laws" for commonly met agency MBS types and structures. We consider here passthroughs, IO/PO strips, and CMO tranches with a "passthrough-like" behavior (i.e. extend WAL with higher rates and slower prepayments). Various jumps found in CMOs can change the order of principal amortization. Hence, structural provisions can affect OAD levels considerably.

We separate this short section into Base Classes and Derived Classes; the latter can be created synthetically. We assume that a deal is backed by FRMs, but our conclusions will remain valid for ARMs, except the prepayment effect will normally have a weaker dependency on interest rates.

BASE CLASSES

A. *Fixed-rate MBS.* As already noted, OAD will generally be longer for discounts, shorter for premiums. High-premium old MBS are burnt and inelastic; they can actually have longer OAD than newer premium MBS that retain prepayment elasticity. OAD will be positive for most tranches, but can actually reach negative levels for high-coupon passthroughs and CMOs, as the excess IO contributes negatively.

B. *Fixed-rate IOs and POs.* Because of prepayment sensitivity to interest rates, OAD for an IO is expected to be negative. It will become less negative and can even become positive when an IO is taken from a deeply discounted pool (or a deep premium pool) where the prepay S-curve saturates, or when it flattens for other reasons.

  Given collateral characteristics, the IO coupon rate itself does not matter. POs behave opposite, usually with positive OAD.

C. *Perfect floaters.* These are bonds paying the exact market rate and resetting freely with the exact frequency of that market rate. Because such an instrument should be worth par regardless of the interest rates and prepayments, OAD will be zero. Note that, in (10.2), term (B) offsets term (A) whereas terms (C) and (D) are both zeros.

DERIVED (SYNTHETIC) CLASSES

D. *Premium/discount floaters.* A premium floater is the one resetting with a margin that exceeds market rate. This margin's cash flow constitutes an IO stream. Hence,

$$\text{Premium Floater} = \text{Perfect Floater} + \text{IO}$$

with a negative OAD unless the S-curve is flat.

E. *Floaters with caps and/or floors.* Caps will add positive Delta, floors will add negative Delta.

F. *IO floaters.* A perfect IO floater plus the matching PO constitute the perfect floater (Par):

$$\text{IO Floater} = \text{Par} - \text{PO}$$

Therefore, the Delta for IO floater is exactly same as the one for PO—except for the sign. Note that OADs will be different by the inverse scale of prices. If an IO floater is worth 20 and PO is worth 80, the OAD for the IO floater will be 4 times greater than the OAD for the PO.

G. *Inverse IO Floaters (IIO).* This is a difference between an IO and an IO Floater:

$$\text{IIO} = \text{IO} - \text{IO Floater} = \text{IO} + \text{PO} - \text{Par} = \text{“Bond”} - \text{Par}$$

using case F above, and where "Bond" refers to a tranche having the same principal decline as IIO and paying the fixed coupon from the IIO reset formula. For example, if IIO pays 7% – LIBOR, the Delta of this IIO will be the same as the Delta of a 7% bond.

If an IIO is leveraged, e.g. pays k times $(7\% - \text{LIBOR})$, Delta will be that of the matching 7% "Bond" times the leverage, but the duration remains the same as the IIO value scales up.

Without consideration of caps, floors and structural provisions, OAD for an IIO is expected to be positive. Usually, IIO have caps and floors matching, respectively, floors and caps of the IO Floater. IIO's cap is set assuming the index cannot fall below zero. In contrast, IIO's floor is a non-trivial derivative that is triggered when the index rises above a fixed rate. In the 7% – LIBOR formula, the floor will likely be set at 0. If LIBOR exceeds 7%, the IIO will pay nothing (instead of paying negative interest). Such a floor can induce a negative OAD component.

Although the Deltas of an IIO and the matching bond can be identical (as in a perfect theoretical case), the durations will differ by the pricing scale—much the same way it works for case F above.

THE EXPLANATORY POWER OF THE OPTION-ADJUSTED SPREAD METHOD

Within a typical function of risk management, the main question asked about agency-related valuation concerns Effective Duration. How good is one's model for producing sensible durations and hedge ratios? For the reason explained below, we would like to re-phrase this inquiry: How good is one's model in predicting price moves? In this section, we limit our analysis to the TBA market.

Understanding Option-Adjusted Spread Valuation Reports

We start with a common miscue in comparing an OAD to the measure of *Empirical Duration* that, in the opinion of some practitioners, shows the true rate sensitivity because it is model-free. In reality, Empirical Duration, usually computed over a short period (e.g. 60 business days, or 3 months), measures only an *unconditional dependence* on interest rates. This means that one regresses price-moves to rate-moves without paying any attention to possibly correlated moves in other pricing factors (such as curve's shape, volatility level, prepayment sentiments, or GSE's credit). For example, a fall in interest rates can be temporarily offset by a curve's steepening; the resultant effect on pricing premium TBAs may be close to zero.

The issues with Empirical Duration are not limited to premium TBAs, nor are they limited to duration's understatement. Effects can add up, too. For example, the Empirical Duration computed in August 2008 for TBA 4.5 showed a thundering 9-year level—likely because the housing turnover sentiments were gradually lowering as interest rates were rising. In contrast, Effective Duration assumes hypothetical changes in interest rates only, that is, it intends to measure a *conditional dependence*. Therefore, a quick and dirty evaluation of an OAS model's duration output is likely to fail.

How to Measure a "Pricing Miss"?

Let us consider periodic price moves of TBAs and compare them to what an OAS model would have predicted—had it known changes in economic factors it utilizes (interest rates, volatility) and TBA's characteristics (WAM, WAC). However, instead of rushing in and multiplying the reported Greeks by changes in the market, let's think a bit more about the task. The fundamental internal assumption that OAS models make is the constancy of OAS. It is applied to all calculations: for every path and every time step, for interest-rate shocks and computing other Greeks. Hence, had an OAS model perfectly predicted changes in price, we would not observe OAS changes from one analysis date to another. OAS changes absorb a price's misses: 10 bps of OAS change for a 4-year OAS Duration asset is reflective of a 40 bps of price change unexplained by the model, arising, possibly, from changes in prepayment sentiments, GSE creditworthiness, or the market's technicalities. Hence, we can construct a historical time series of price misses by simply using reported OAS changes and OAS Duration that translates OAS changes into the price's errors. This sequence can be further translated into various statistical measures. Table 10.4 contains statistics of computed R-squared and the correlation between model's misses and interest rates, using the eight-year long series of weekly measurements of AD&Co's OAS system.

First, let us pay attention to the R-squared in Table 10.4a. We use one of two common definitions, which is suitable when assessing the accuracy of a non-regression model (e.g. the OAS model).[2] As usual, a high R-squared means the model tracks price changes well. A low or negative R-squared means changes in price are not attributed to factors controlled by the model. For example, a

---

[2]This definition would be identical to R-sq = Var(Regression) / Var(Px Change) if we used an unconstrained linear regression to explain price changes. In all other cases, the two definitions differ.

Table 10.4a HISTORICAL R-SQUARED = 1 – Var(Price Miss)/Var(Price Change)

TBA Coupon	3.5	4	4.5	5	5.5	6	6.5
Mar-09 to Mar-11	78.8%	81.3%	78.9%	53.2%	40.4%	−57.0%	−116.8%
Jul-07 to Mar-09			63.7%	55.6%	47.6%	41.5%	41.4%
Sep-05 to Jul-07			94.2%	90.0%	90.6%	89.3%	77.9%
Mar-03 to Sep-05			89.4%	88.4%	85.6%	79.3%	61.3%
8-yr history			76.1%	70.5%	65.2%	49.6%	22.1%

Using AD&Co's OAS model

Table 10.4b CORRELATION BETWEEN PRICE MISS AND CURRENT-COUPON FN RATE

TBA Coupon	3.5	4	4.5	5	5.5	6	6.5
Mar-09 to Mar-11	9.7%	−8.5%	−5.6%	−0.7%	1.3%	5.7%	10.0%
Jul-07 to Mar-09			−15.2%	−15.9%	−15.6%	−15.3%	−12.6%
Sep-05 to Jul-07			−9.0%	−11.8%	−13.4%	−3.5%	−2.1%
Mar-03 to Sep-05			−2.1%	−11.7%	−12.1%	−10.1%	1.3%
8-yr history			−1.6%	−3.7%	−4.1%	−1.3%	0.5%

Using AD&Co's OAS model

dramatic TBA cheapening (LIBOR OAS widening) in 2008 should be seen on all professionally designed OAS models employed in the MBS industry. It was related to technicalities of MBS trading under the developing crisis, and the deteriorating GSE credit, but not the usual economic factors. The OAS tightening observed in 2010 also owes its existence to factors other than those considered by traditional OAS models.

Tables 10.4a proves that AD&Co's OAS model worked very well for a number of years prior to the financial crisis, explaining close to 90% of price variations. For every historical period, R-squared gradually fades as the TBA coupon increases. We should keep in mind that high-premium coupons are more technical, with price variations (i.e. the denominator in R-squared) being relatively small.

Even during the troubled years, AD&Co's OAS model kept tracking the TBA market satisfactorily well except for high-premium coupons, for which it stopped being a good predictor of market moves. This can be explained by:

a. Technical shifts in the marketplace: Prices for high-premium TBAs became more technical and less economically rational. TBA 6s and 6.5s were not originated in 2009–2011 nor actively traded, and, at times, were hard to find and deliver, sometimes resulting in stale prices.

b. Problems with adjusting prepayment models to the current environment, in general. Given the uncertainty in borrowers' ability to obtain new loans and GSE's repurchase actions, assessing the key factor for high-premium pools, the future prepayment speed, becomes difficult.

c. The level of interest rates has not been the leading risk factor in 2009–2011.

It is important to note that the OAS variations have weak correlations with interest rates (Table 10.4b). In other terms, the model does not have a strong directional bias that would disqualify it from its primary use—estimating interest-rate sensitivity. In fact, we should expect to see some directionality in traditional OAS models because they do not address the price of prepay modeling risk explained in the next chapter. Namely, we expect OAS to widen somewhat and absorb the rising refinancing risk for premium TBAs when rates drop (negative correlation). We expect OAS to widen and absorb the rising turnover risk for discount TBAs when rates rise (positive correlation).

DRAWBACKS OF THE OPTION-ADJUSTED SPREAD METHOD

These days, we can't imagine the MBS industry without the OAS method. Immensely popular and of great practical importance, it remains a somewhat ad-hoc approach. Most OAS systems quantify only the contribution made by random dynamics of interest rates. The introduction of an additional discount spread (i.e., OAS), if not for the reason of plain mispricing, is due to the existence of other risk factors that are hidden from the model. We complete this chapter with the discussion of OAS method issues commonly ignored, understated, or simply unknown to practitioners.

PREPAYMENT MODEL UNCERTAINTY

As we demonstrated in chapter 4, OAS can be interpreted as the *additional return expectation*—on top of the risk-free rate. Moreover, since OAS methods normally employ no-arbitrage rate models, the OAS can also be interpreted as a *guaranteed return*—if interest-rate risk is perfectly hedged. For example, if OAS = 100 basis points, an investor will earn the 1% spread for sure after hedging. Unfortunately, if the entire analysis relies on a prepayment model that may be biased or may become biased, the "sure return" is not that reassuring.

DIFFERING OPTION-ADJUSTED SPREAD LEVELS

MBS are priced at differing OAS levels, often leaving investors somewhat puzzled. "Does a cheap level of this MBS (wide spread) come from mispricing or does it come from missed valuation factors?" For example, IOs stripped from high WAC pools are almost always "cheaper" than matching POs. Both discount and high-premium TBAs are often "cheaper" (on an OAS basis) than par-coupon TBAs and small-premium TBAs. Illiquid CMO tranches and rarely traded mortgage assets like MSRs can also look "cheap."

This hurdle may become a dead-end when one would like to value instruments not marked by market makers. An example could be designing a pricing service MBS investors would like to employ. If it cannot be known in advance which and how additional risk factors have to be reflected in an MBS class that has not been traded lately, it becomes difficult to know which OAS level to start with.

Problems with Option-Adjusted Spread Constancy

The following example illustrates an issue with the fundamental assumption, the OAS constancy, made when computing Greeks (see Table 10.5).

Consider a pool stripped into IO and PO, with the former valued at 20 and the later valued at 80. We assume further that OAS levels for the IO and the PO are 400 bps and –100 bps, correspondingly. Weighing by market values, 0 is the expected portfolio's OAS. Let us consider a severe rate decline that made the IO valued at 10, PO at 95, and the total pool at 105. Assuming that both strips retain their respective OAS levels, we conclude that the OAS for the pool drops to -52 bps because the IO now becomes a much smaller part of the total. Therefore, the three members of valuation parity, IO + PO = Pool, cannot hold their OAS levels concurrently. Once this paradoxical fact is established for stripped derivatives, it can be extended to CMOs and synthetic instruments such as floaters and inverse IOs, tranches and their collateral, etc. Similarly, it can be shown that a portfolio cannot hold OAS over time when different instruments retire at different speeds, and as its composition changes.

These paradoxes shake one's faith in OAS. It appears that measuring effective duration, key rate durations, Vega, etc., by stressing market factors and holding OAS constant is ill-advised, as is applying the same OAS for the portfolio's cash flows projected at different timings. However, let us note that it would not be possible to construct a pricing paradox in Table 10.5 if the starting OAS levels were same. This point gives us a great hint at a possible solution to the problem

Table 10.5 A COUNTER-EXAMPLE TO THE OAS CONSTANCY
ASSUMPTION (IO + PO PARADOX)

		IO	PO	Total
	OAS 1, bp	400	–100	0
	Value 1	20	80	100
rates fell	Value 2	10	95	105
	OAS 2, bp	400	–100	–52

explored in the next chapter: Transform valuation problem so that MBS could be valued using the same spread to the same benchmark.

OAS models have been the working horses for agency MBS traders and analysts alike. However, these models generally rely on the unlikely assumption that prepayment models are true and unbiased, thus creating a variety of theoretical and practical issues. In the next chapter, we demonstrate how to improve on OAS modeling by taking prepayment-model risk into consideration.

11

Prepayment Risk Neutrality: The Concept of prOAS

This chapter focuses on a form of economic risk arising from the uncertainty of prepayment models, which is commonly missed by OAS systems. Unlike an efficiently exercised call option found in large corporate or agency bonds, the refinancing of a loan is decided by the individual borrower. We discussed this topic in chapter 7, where it was shown that the empirically observed refinancing option is exercised according to an S-like probability curve. Prepay modelers construct such a curve from empirical data, but it cannot be known with complete confidence. Over time, the exercise of prepay options can become more or less efficient; borrowers who could easily refinance in normal times find themselves ineligible during times of financial troubles and stricter regulation; new government programs may impose or lift prepayment restrictions, etc.

Prepayment model risk is one of the key reasons that agency MBS are valued at differing OAS levels. Even if all market participants agreed on a prepayment model, the very fact that they are exposed to that model's potential bias would force them to seek price breaks and compensation for the risk. In contrast, MBS that can be utilized to hedge (offset) the risk look rich on an OAS basis.

To illustrate the practical need to alter the traditional OAS method, let us consider a mega-fund that has $100B to invest in MBS. Using a model, a fund's manager identified an MBS (or an MBS class) that promises a wide +500 bps OAS. The fund has no problem with leveraging, and there is enough market size to execute the long strategy. The manager knows that if he hedges the interest-rate risk, the +500 bps additional return is guaranteed—assuming the prepayment model is right. This last assumption forces the manager to realize that a perfect hedge against interest-rate moves does not solve the model risk issue and the fund's investment may perform worse than expected if the prepay model turns out to be wrong. He (or she) starts thinking about hedging prepay model risk or, at least, adjusting return expectation....

This where the concept of MBS valuation adjusted for prepayment model risk becomes important.

PREPAY MODEL RISK IN THE MBS MARKETS

Table 11.1 shows that historical OAS profiles for Fannie Mae TBAs have not been flat; both high-premium and discount coupons are commonly valued cheaper than moderate premiums (usually those 50–150 bps above the prevailing par-coupon Fannie Mae TBA rate or FNCL index, bold numbers). Away from this richest point, above and below it, the OAS level increases almost monotonically. The only exception from this rule is observed for 2009 when the lowest coupon was the richest on an OAS basis.

This convex OAS pattern, measured through the history, can be explained by the following two-dimensional view of prepayment risk. Investors in premium MBS have those premiums at risk if the MBS retires faster than expected. They fear acceleration of the loan refinancing process above what the model promises, given the economic scenario. In contrast, investors in the discount sector do not care about refinancing. They would suffer losses if the housing turnover process were slower than the model assumes.

With the large variety of MBS types, structures and features, the fundamental products are residential loan pools themselves, not their derivatives like IOs, POs, or CMO tranches. Hence, the refinancing-turnover risk view we offer should explain the prevailing model risks for the mortgage market as a whole. The TBA market is one of the two major sources allowing us to gauge how MBS investors price prepay model risk.

Table 11.1 AVERAGE OAS LEVELS FOR FN TBAs (BY YEAR)

	FNCL rate	3.5	4	4.5	5	5.5	6	6.5	7	7.5	8
2003	5.13			38	31	27	**26**	42	47	71	76
2004	5.30			21	14	10	**2**	20	20	20	22
2005	5.39			−1	−3	−2	**−5**	16	18	14	21
2006	5.97			0	−5	−5	−9	**−10**	−8	40	25
2007	5.89			7	2	0	−4	**−10**	−32	51	102
2008	5.44			56	**45**	47	54	64	62	139	
2009	4.28		7	12	10	17	43	63	68		
2010	3.95	26	17	13	12	**5**	12	35			
2011	4.01	40	25	22	12	**9**	19				

Using AD&Co's OAS model

An alternative valuable source of information is the stripped derivatives market (Trust IOs and POs). Although this market is much smaller in comparison to TBAs, each investment instrument, an IO or a PO, is very sensitive (leveraged) to prepayment assumptions. Hence, one can read prepayment sentiments from market quotes and the related OAS levels. If an IO is priced cheaper (has a wider OAS) than the matching PO, it means the pool's prepayment speed is feared to exceed that of the model. It is most common that IOs stripped of premium pools look cheap and the matching POs look rich. In contrast, IOs stripped from low-coupon (discount) pools may look rich and even be valued at negative OAS. The very difference in OAS levels between IOs and POs suggests that a real-world prepayment model cannot be utilized to derive their Greeks, as we demonstrated at the end of chapter 10. Nor can we surely state if one of the two is a more attractive investment choice.

We will call a prepayment model that reflects real-world expectations a *physical* model, in contrast to a risk-neutral model. As there is great uncertainty in modeling prepayments, we cannot know the true physical model in advance, thus every physical model is likely to either be biased or to become biased.

What we can learn from these examples is that market views of prepayments can differ from any one physical view and this difference is manifested in MBS prices. The MBS market values prepayment modeling risk, that is, the risk that a model can have bias. By observing market prices, one can infer the directions of fears. However, we cannot distinguish between cases when prices reflect the risk that a prepay model may be become biased versus cases when a prepay model is already known to be biased. This is a very similar situation to equity derivatives or interest-rate derivatives where forward prices reflect both expectations and risk. The forward curve can steepen both due to the expectation that interest rates are going to rise and due to the inflation of the price of risk.

Another important point is that prepay model risk factors are directional. Holders of both IOs and POs are severely exposed to a prepayment model's uncertainty. However, one cannot expect to see a *concurrent* price break for both. If the market compensated just for bearing uncertainty and rewarded *both* IO and PO investors an extra return on that basis, one would simply combine the two to reduce (or even eliminate) the risk and earn more than the risk-free rate. In reality, the market's natural activity sets preferences and compensation for bearing a risk. If certain risky assets are cheap, their hedges must be expensive. Hence, in an IO + PO pair, only one instrument can look cheap and another must be rich—relative to the pool, on an OAS basis. Again, we find similarities to the swap market where positions of a fixed-leg payer and a fixed-leg receiver are opposite and equally risky, yet only one is rewarded and another is charged.

Finally, we view prepayment model risk as a risk that a model is biased or can become biased going forward; not the risk of random oscillations of monthly

CPRs over time; and not the risk of random CPRs arising from insufficiently large pools. Those types of uncertainties exist, but they can be diversified over time or via investing in a large number of small pools. Hence, a short-term investor or a small-pool investor should not expect special treatment; only a systematic risk, common for the market, is priced.

VALUATION WITH UNCERTAIN PREPAY MODEL

Above we set forth the following conjecture: two major prepayment sources, the refinancing process and the turnover process, are perceived to be risky by the mortgage market. To put it in simple practical terms, there exist two distinct market fears: refinancing understatement and turnover overstatement. Allowing the refinancing and the turnover processes to be randomly scaled we can extend the APD model (chapter 7) as follows:

$$ActiveSMM = \rho * RefiSMM + \tau * TurnoverSMM + \cdots$$

$$(11.1)$$

$$PassiveSMM = \beta * \rho * RefiSMM + \tau * TurnoverSMM + \cdots$$

where prepay scales, ρ and τ, are considered uncertain. We may posit various assumptions about random dynamics of ρ and τ. They can be viewed as diffusions (with volatilities σ_ρ and σ_τ respectively), random parameters, or of a hybrid type (i.e., diffusions with uncertain starting values). We also should allow for the correlation between the two factors. However, we will assume that ρ and τ are independent from interest rates. Indeed, if they were dependent, we could change the empirical prepayment model first—to fully reflect this relationship.

Let us apply the PDE (4.8rn) of chapter 4 assuming that the risky factor x is now a vector containing the rate factor (r), refinancing scales (ρ) and turnover scale (τ):

$$(r + prOAS)P = -\lambda P + c + \lambda$$

$$+ \frac{\partial P}{\partial t} + \mu_r \frac{\partial P}{\partial r} + \frac{1}{2}\sigma_r^2 \frac{\partial^2 P}{\partial r^2} + \mu_\rho \frac{\partial P}{\partial \rho} + \mu_\tau \frac{\partial P}{\partial \tau}$$

$$+ \frac{1}{2}\sigma_\rho^2 \frac{\partial^2 P}{\partial \rho^2} + \frac{1}{2}\sigma_\tau^2 \frac{\partial^2 P}{\partial \tau^2} + corr(\rho, \tau)\sigma_\rho \sigma_\tau \frac{\partial^2 P}{\partial \rho \partial \tau}$$

$$(11.2)$$

where *prOAS* denotes the new term, *prepayment-risk-and-option-adjusted spread*. This is the residual OAS after prepay model risks are accounted for. Following the spirit of chapter 4, we assume in (11.2) that the drifts of interest rates (μ_r), refinancing scale (μ_ρ) and turnover scale (μ_τ) are risk-neutral. This means that,

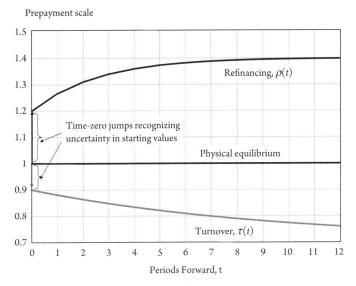

Figure 11.1 Expected Risk-Neutral Prepay Scales
Note: This figure is for illustration only and does not constitute an actual risk-neutral model

instead of accounting for the market price of each risk, we shift the distribution of risk factors. In the next section, we describe how to do this in practice using TBAs. We naturally call such a prepayment model risk-neutral if it has risk-neutral values of $\rho(t)$ and $\tau(t)$.

Figure 11.1 illustrates what risk-neutral values of $\rho(t)$ and $\tau(t)$ are expected to be for the general case when both initial values and future (mean reverting) paths are uncertain. For both scales, we expect 1.0 to the best-guess *physical* value. We can virtually "split" the risk between the initial risk and diffusion, and alter the rate of reversion. The dynamics shown in Figure 11.1 associate about half of refinancing risk with refinancing uncertainty already existing at time zero; the other half appears gradually. We are generally more certain about the starting turnover rate, and it may take a long time before future macroeconomic conditions will alter it, so a smaller portion of the total drift is present at time zero for the turnover risk component.

The cash flow based price representation (4.4) is not changing. This makes valuation with the risk-neutral model equally easy as the usual OAS method. We now assume that, aside from the interest-rate dynamics, there are other random factors, $\rho(t)$ and $\tau(t)$, properly specified.

Let us return to equation (11.2), which may look intimidating but is conceptually simple. The left-hand side is the expected return, which comprises the risk-free rate and the residual spread prOAS that is useful to reserve as any valuation theory may work imperfectly in practice. The right-hand side represents various mathematical terms of investment return coming from principal and interest cash flows and balance amortization $(c + \lambda - \lambda P)$, drifts of random factors, and several convexity terms. If we attempt to solve this PDE numerically, we will have to do this in the three- (or more-) dimensional state space of pricing factors (r, ρ, τ). This may prove to be impractical.

First, we can eliminate the drift terms by simply transforming the risk factors so that each is measured off its expected risk-neutral path. This transformation sets all drifts to zero. Second, we can either neglect the convexity terms arising due to volatility of $\rho(t)$ and $\tau(t)$ altogether or regard them approximately. Our experience suggests that, while risk-neutralization of prepay models is important, only a few instruments possess strong *prepayment convexity*, that is, asymmetry with respect to ρ and τ. One should realize the difference between price of risk and convexity. The price of risk compensates for bearing (possibly symmetric) uncertainty. In other words, gains and losses can be identical, but investors are adverse to the possibility of losses. Convexity terms arises when the pricing profile is nonlinear (convex or concave) with respect to a random factor thereby generating a systematic return component.

The approximate shortcut for solving PDE (11.2) numerically with all convexity terms accounted for is shown in A. Levin (ADQP 2004) and A. Levin and A. Davidson (2005). The idea is to differentiate (11.2) with respect to ρ and τ a necessary number of times and neglect the third-order derivatives. Let us assume that ρ and τ are indeed defined as deviations from their respective risk-neutral paths so that $\mu_\rho = \mu_\tau = 0$. Denote for brevity,

$$\frac{\partial P}{\partial \rho} \equiv P_\rho, \quad \frac{\partial P}{\partial \tau} \equiv P_\tau, \quad \frac{\partial^2 P}{\partial \rho^2} \equiv P_{\rho\rho}, \quad \frac{\partial^2 P}{\partial \tau^2} \equiv P_{\tau\tau}, \quad \frac{\partial^2 P}{\partial \rho \partial \tau} \equiv P_{\rho\tau}$$

We treat all them plus $P(t, r)$ as six unknown functions defined in the (t, r) space. The following set of equations (11.3) can be obtained from (11.2) by differentiating with respect to ρ:

$$\left(r + prOAS\right)P_\rho = -\lambda P_\rho - \lambda_\rho P + \lambda_\rho + \frac{\partial P_\rho}{\partial t} + \mu_r \frac{\partial P_\rho}{\partial r} + \frac{1}{2}\sigma_r^2 \frac{\partial^2 P_\rho}{\partial r^2} \qquad (11.3\rho)$$

Differentiating with respect to τ:

$$\left(r + prOAS\right)P_\tau = -\lambda P_\tau - \lambda_\tau P + \lambda_\tau + \frac{\partial P_\tau}{\partial t} + \mu_r \frac{\partial P_\tau}{\partial r} + \frac{1}{2}\sigma_r^2 \frac{\partial^2 P_\tau}{\partial r^2} \qquad (11.3\tau)$$

Differentiating with respect to ρ twice:

$$\left(r+prOAS\right)P_{\rho\rho}=-\lambda P_{\rho\rho}-2\lambda_{\rho}P_{\rho}+\frac{\partial P_{\rho\rho}}{\partial t}+\mu_{r}\frac{\partial P_{\rho\rho}}{\partial r}+\frac{1}{2}\sigma_{r}^{2}\frac{\partial^{2}P_{\rho\rho}}{\partial r^{2}} \qquad (11.3\rho\rho)$$

Differentiating with respect to τ twice:

$$\left(r+prOAS\right)P_{\tau\tau}=-\lambda P_{\tau\tau}-2\lambda_{\tau}P_{\tau}+\frac{\partial P_{\tau\tau}}{\partial t}+\mu_{r}\frac{\partial P_{\tau\tau}}{\partial r}+\frac{1}{2}\sigma_{r}^{2}\frac{\partial^{2}P_{\tau\tau}}{\partial r^{2}} \qquad (11.3\tau\tau)$$

Differentiating with respect to ρ and τ:

$$\left(r+prOAS\right)P_{\rho\tau}=-\lambda P_{\rho\tau}-\lambda_{\tau}P_{\rho}-\lambda_{\rho}P_{\tau}+\frac{\partial P_{\rho\tau}}{\partial t}+\mu_{r}\frac{\partial P_{\rho\tau}}{\partial r}+\frac{1}{2}\sigma_{r}^{2}\frac{\partial^{2}P_{\rho\tau}}{\partial r^{2}} \qquad (11.3\rho\tau)$$

We have to add terminal conditions

$$P(T,x)=1, P_{\rho}(T,x)=P_{\tau}(T,x)=P_{\rho\rho}(T,x)=P_{\tau\tau}(T,x)=P_{\rho\tau}(T,x)=0,$$

and solve the system of six PDEs (11.2), (11.3) on the (t, r) space. Note that although the additional five functions have the meaning of derivatives taken with respect to ρ and τ, the entire problem is solved without ρ and τ involved as state variables. First derivatives of the amortization speed λ with respect to ρ and τ, denoted $\lambda_{\rho}, \lambda_{\tau}$ in (11.3), are easily found from APD model's extended set-up (11.1): $\lambda_{\rho} = RefiSMM$ for Active part; $\lambda_{\rho} = \beta * RefiSMM$ for Passive part; $\lambda_{\tau} = TurnoverSMM$ for either part. The second derivatives of λ with respect to ρ and τ are all zeros.

Much as in the APD valuation scheme described in chapter 8, we value the active and passive parts of the pool separately, starting from maturity and going backward. For each time step, using PDEs (11.2), (11.3) we compute six functions rather than one. This certainly makes the process less speedy than in the simple case. However, the fact that the equations are solved on a low-dimensional grid that is not propagated to the dimensions of ρ and τ makes backward induction practically feasible. At the cost of additional computing time, equations (11.2) and (11.3) allow us to account for a prepayment convexity cost that, for TBAs, can reach a respectable level of five and more basis points.

One important special case arises when ρ and τ are risky parameters rather than processes. We can perceive it to be the case when $\sigma_{\rho}^{2}(t)$ and $\sigma_{\tau}^{2}(t)$ are Dirac functions, as it was done in chapter 4. The assumption means that these functions are zeros for $t > 0$, infinite at $t = 0$, and their integrals are equal to the variances of random scales ρ and τ, correspondingly. In the course of backward valuation, all prepayment convexity terms proportional to σ_ρ^2 and σ_τ^2 will be zero for $t > 0$ and the six unknown functions will change gradually as time t runs down from pool's maturity to the next-to-last step (next month from now). For the last step of the process, i.e. moving from $t = 1$ to $t = 0$, the convexity terms suddenly become infinite thereby inducing a finite shock to the six pricing functions.

CALIBRATION TO TBAS

From now on, we steer from the theoretical flow toward practical steps for using the prOAS model. We also describe problems the model may address and valuation results it generates. Assuming we know the stochastic physical patterns for the risk factors ρ and τ, we need to find their risk-neutral transforms. We restrict our focus to the case when ρ and τ are risky parameters, not processes, and the entire calibration process is limited to finding their best values using TBA market quotes. We can tune these constants to match market prices (or the desired prOAS targets), for a range of actively traded securities.

To find risk-neutral values for ρ and τ, we first need to define the appropriate target for prOAS. This target prOAS should reflect the spread on a similar security with no prepayment uncertainty. While assuming a zero prOAS to the swap curve may sound appropriate, we find that GSE debentures are a better benchmark as they have the same credit guarantee as GSE-backed MBS and carry no prepayment uncertainty.[1] Historically, LIBOR OAS levels for all coupons have been directional to the agency/swap spreads (Figure 11.2). Figure 11.3 confirms that these two spreads had strong historical correlation and it was, in fact, the TBA spread (measured for the current-coupon pool) that predicted the distress of GSEs' debentures in the fall of 2008.

Therefore, our conjecture seems to be supported by the empirical data and, without consideration of prepayment model risk, agency-backed MBS and agency-issued debentures, should be equally attractive to investors.

Let us return to risk-neutral calibration and select a day in history, August 29, 2003, for illustration. On that day, the mortgage current coupon rate was 5.67%, and there were both premium and discount TBAs in our benchmark sample

---

[1] Arguably, TBAs should trade even rich to the agency debts because they (a) have superior liquidity and (b) are collateralized, leading to a perception of higher credit quality. While a typical MBS is backed by residential properties, there exists no formal legal mechanism that provides any enhanced protection of an agency MBS beyond the guarantee of the agency. Given the drastic ongoing changes in the GSEs' status and role, we leave these points for future consideration.

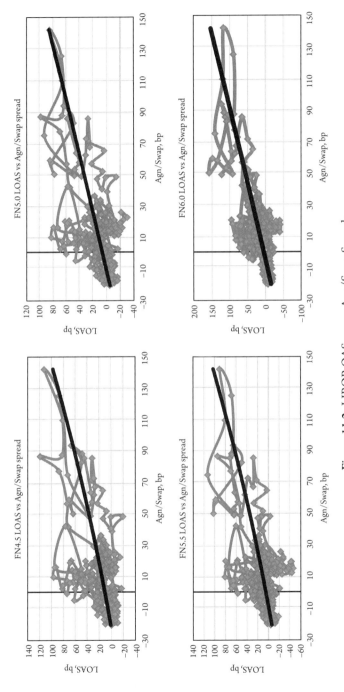

Figure 11.2 LIBOR OAS versus Agn/Swap Spreads

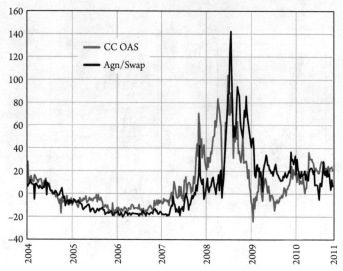

Figure 11.3 History of LIBOR OAS for the Current-Coupon (CC) TBA versus Agn/Swap Spread

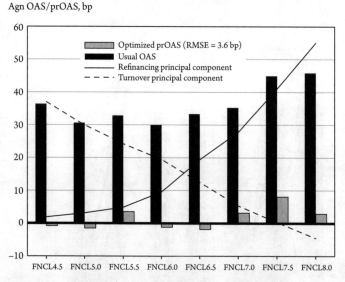

Figure 11.4 Risk-Neutral Calibration to TBAs as of August 29, 2003

with net coupons ranging from 4.5% to 8.0%. The risk-neutralization process is shown in Figure 11.4. First, we measured OAS to the agency debenture curve using the traditional valuation method, without any risk adjustment (black bars). We then employed the prOAS pricing method and selected $\rho = 1.50$

and $\tau = 0.65$ to minimize the prOAS levels (gray bars). As shown, the calibration worked fairly well across the range of TBAs having achieved a 3.6 basis point root-mean-squared accuracy in reaching the debenture (zero) prOAS target.

The lines drawn in Figure 11.4 show "principal components" of OAS. The solid line measures the difference between OAS and prOAS arising due to the refinancing risk. The dashed line shows the same for the turnover risk. Directionalities for both lines are apparent, but some interesting observations can be made. For example, the dashed line almost never leaves positive territory. Discounts would certainly lose value with slow turnover, but why will premiums suffer? The very steep yield curve is primarily responsible for this effect; slowing turnover pushes cash flows further out where discount rates are higher. It also slightly inflates the time value of the prepayment option.

HISTORICAL DYNAMICS OF RISK-NEUTRAL SCALES

Will the parameters of the prOAS model exhibit stability over time? Or, do we need to calibrate the model on a daily basis? While a goal of physical models is to stay steady, the concept of risk-neutrality is bound to changing market prices for benchmark instruments, which reflect the dynamics of market preferences for risk. Since the prOAS method is built on the idea of risk-neutrality, this model will require contemporaneous market information. This should be clear because market prices for TBAs may exhibit visible OAS tightening and widening over time (assuming an unchanged prepayment model). In this way, the market is sending us a message of changing perception of prepayment risk. A pronounced $\rho > 1$ refinancing scale indicates considerable risk of understated refinancing priced in by the MBS market. Likewise, a $\tau < 1$ turnover scale reflects a concern that the modeled turnover may be too fast. Close-to-1 scales suggest that the market does not reward for bearing the risk. This conjecture is borne out by examining the trends in risk-neutral scales at different dates, as shown in Figure 11.5 for some period of 2004 (the physical model remained unchanged). These scales are not constant and they show an exaggerated reaction to interest-rate dynamics.

As seen in Figure 11.5a the year 2004 started with concerns on both ends and ended with neither. We agree with Gabaix at al. (2004) and expressed similar views ourselves that the difference between the current coupon and the weighted average rate of outstanding MBS volume influences the risk. Hence, every sharp change in rates (marked by gray-shaded ovals) immediately violates market balance and inflates the risk. In contrast, a slow market drift does

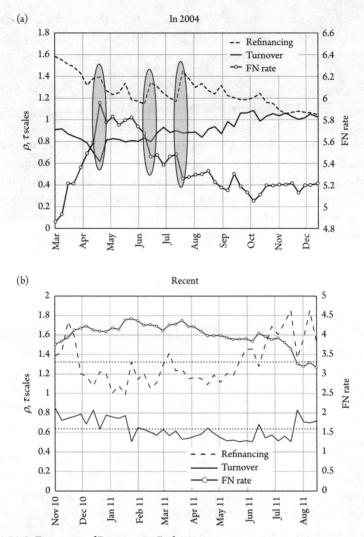

Figure 11.5 Dynamics of Prepayment Risk

not induce concerns. The uneventful fall of 2004 resulted in both tunings being stabilized close to their risk-less level, that is, 1.0.

Generally, risk-neutral dynamics of $\rho(t)$ and $\tau(t)$ is strongly mean reverting. Figure 11.5b shows that, despite a large short-term volatility that reflects constantly changing prepayment sentiments, in the absence of sharp changes in interest rates, the risk-neutral scales tend to be pulled back to some mean levels, usually $\rho > 1$, $\tau < 1$ depicted by the dotted lines.

VALUATION OF INTEREST-ONLY/PRINCIPAL-ONLY
STRIPS WITH PROAS

Within the traditional OAS valuation, either price or OAS should be given as input. Under the prOAS valuation, the role of OAS is performed by prOAS, a measure with less variability. The goal of prOAS pricing is to eliminate differences in OAS among instruments that are exposed to prepayment model risk in different ways. As we asserted earlier, the prOAS measure should value agency MBS flat to agency debentures. Therefore, once the risk factors are given their risk-neutral specifications, we can value other agency MBS, CMOs, or IO and PO strips much like swaptions, that is, looking at the benchmark rate and volatility structure, but without any knowledge of the traditional OAS.

The following two examples were constructed for our original publications on the prOAS method (see Levin ADQP 2004, Levin and Davidson 2005). Figure 11.6 shows valuation results for agency Trust IOs using risk-neutralized prepayment scales obtained from the calibration to Fannie Mae TBAs on May 30, 2003. The application of the prOAS method first leads to values[2] that are then converted into conventional OAS measures. The prOAS model explains IO "cheapness" (therefore, PO "richness") naturally and correctly predicts OAS level of (and above) 1000 basis points. Since POs stripped off premium pools should be looked at as hedges against refinancing risk, they have to be traded "rich." Our prOAS model successfully confirms this fact having virtually all OAS for Trust POs deep in the negative territory (not shown in Figure 11.6). Results in Figure 11.6 also provide some degree of confidence for managers of mortgage servicing rights (MSR) portfolios (not actively traded or frequently quoted)— they can employ the prOAS method to better assess the risk of their portfolios.

Given the low level of interest rates on May 30, 2003 (FN rate = 4.40%) and the overall premium state of the market, the entire risk perception evolved out of a refinancing/acceleration scare ($\rho = 1.52$, $\tau = 1.16$). Figure 11.6 proves that both the TBA market and the Trust IO market agreed with one another when incorporating this risk into pricing and the prices of IOs could be predicted using the information coming from interest rates and TBA prices.

In the summer months of 2003, rates rose sharply, pushing lower-coupon MBS (4.5s and 5s) into the discount territory. Figure 11.7 confirms that, by summer's end, the refinancing fear cooled off, leaving room for turnover concerns. As we explained, a slower-than-modeled turnover would result in a loss for a discount MBS holder. It is not surprising that the price for turnover risk, virtually non-existent in May 2003, later became sizable (Figure 11.4). What if we apply the

---

[2]To account for liquidity difference between IOs and TBAs, we applied 25 basis points prOAS.

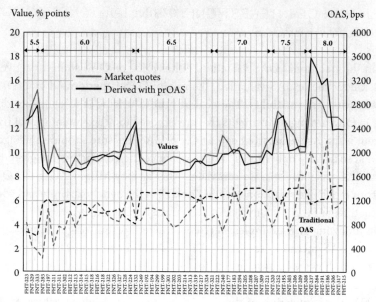

Figure 11.6 Trust IO Valuation as of May 30, 2003 (prOAS = 25 bps).
The prOAS model is calibrated to FNCL TBAs.

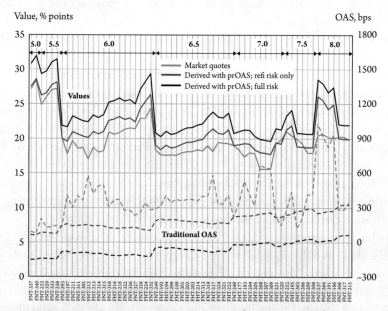

Figure 11.7 Trust IO Valuation as of August 29, 2003 (prOAS = 25 bps).
The prOAS model is calibrated to FNCL TBAs.

risk-neutral scales $\rho = 1.50$ and $\tau = 0.65$ we cited earlier, calibrated to the August 29, 2003 TBA market, to value Trust IOs? Figure 11.7 shows two stages in application of the prOAS model, valuation with refinancing-risk only, and with the total risk.

Comparing market prices and related OAS (light gray lines) with the valuation results under the prOAS model with refinancing risk only (dark gray lines) we see that the single-risk-factor prOAS model just slightly overstates values relatively to the actual market. It shows directionally correct OAS tendency (tighter spread for discount IOs, wider for premiums) and the magnitude. We could have brought this valuation exercise even closer to the actual market quotes if we had extended the single-risk-factor view to turnover as well. That is, by assuming that IO investors were provided incremental returns for turnover risk too.

Disaster strikes when we add the true turnover risk calibrated to the TBAs (black lines). Since IOs can be used as hedges against turnover risk, theory says that they should be penalized, not rewarded. An almost constant 250 basis points OAS reduction is seen as the result. Hence, on that day, the actual IO market did not seem to appreciate this theory. Price quotes were much lower than the full two-risk-factor prOAS model suggested they should have been. According to the arbitrage pricing theory, such mispricing should lead to an opportunity of constructing a fully hedged, risk-free portfolio that earns more than the risk-free rate.

After analyzing a large number of trading days, we believe that the severe TBA-IO dislocation is a rare event that usually coincides with a sharp surge of rates when the IO market, driven predominantly by acceleration fear, misses the hedging aspect against slowing down the housing turnover. For those market conditions, *there exists a theoretical opportunity to create a dynamically hedged mortgage portfolio that is prepay-model-neutral and earns an access return over funding rates*. However, it is vital to realize that the market value of this portfolio would remain exposed to the risk of further TBA-IO dislocation.

MODERNIZED GREEKS

Valuation adjusted for prepayment risk leads to different interest-rate sensitivity than the traditional one. Intuitively, premium passthroughs become less rate-sensitive because their risky spread "absorbs" interest-rate moves following the prepay option moneyness. Indeed, any rate fall elevates the refinancing risk and thereby inflates the traditional OAS; any rate rise reduces the risk and compresses the OAS. Since the discount MBS react inversely, they are more rate-sensitive under the constant-prOAS method than under the constant-OAS risk assessment. All these conclusions can be even easier explained by the transition from physical to risk-neutral prepayment model, faster for premiums and slower for discounts.

TBA Durations

Table 11.2 compares option-adjusted durations (OAD) with prepayment-risk-and-option-adjusted durations (prOAD) for several market days of history, including the two days of 2003 we already analyzed. On May 30, 2003, the entire TBA market looked faster on a prOAD basis than on an OAD basis. This is clearly related to the fear of acceleration above what models tend to produce. On August 29, 2003, prOADs were shorter for premiums and longer for discounts, in comparison to OADs. This is a more typical case.

For any particularly selected MBS, the dynamics of prOAD can be rather complicated. It depends on prepayment sentiments (hence, risk-neutral scales) and their role in valuation of that MBS. Often, but not always, $\rho > 1$ and $\tau < 1$ so that the risk-neutral prepayment model is faster than the physical model for premiums and slower for discounts. Hence, prOAD will exceed OAD when the pool

Table 11.2 FROM OAD TO PROAD: TBA DURATION DIFFERENCE

A. MARKET AS OF MAY 30, 2003 (FN RATE = 4.40%, ρ = 1.52, τ = 1.16)

	FN4.5	FN5.0	FN5.5	FN6.0	FN6.5	FN7.0	FN7.5	FN8.0
OAD	4.10	2.90	1.96	1.71	1.67	1.59	1.83	2.12
prOAD	3.42	2.03	1.07	0.77	0.80	0.90	1.11	1.28
Difference	−0.68	−0.83	−0.89	−0.94	−0.87	−0.69	−0.72	−0.84

Rates are low, all TBAs are at premium. Market fears refinancing tide, which indeed came in summer.

B. MARKET AS OF AUGUST 29, 2003 (FN RATE = 5.67%, ρ = 1.50, τ = 0.65)

	FN4.5	FN5.0	FN5.5	FN6.0	FN6.5	FN7.0	FN7.5	FN8.5
OAD	5.78	5.18	4.40	3.34	2.48	2.07	2.03	1.90
prOAD	6.11	5.44	4.54	3.32	2.35	1.98	1.81	1.68
Difference	0.33	0.26	0.14	−0.02	−0.13	−0.09	−0.22	−0.22

Market normalized having both premiums and discounts.

C. MARKET AS OF JUNE 6, 2011 (FN RATE = 3.90%, ρ = 1.33, τ = 0.51)

	FN3.5	FN4.0	FN4.5	FN5.0	FN5.5	FN6.0	FN6.5
OAD	6.07	4.91	4.01	2.74	2.55	2.74	2.16
prOAD	6.94	5.57	4.51	3.00	2.85	3.08	2.35
Difference	0.87	0.66	0.50	0.26	0.30	0.34	0.21

Rates are very low, most TBAs are at premium. However, base refinancing is suppressed and turnover risk dominates.

is at a discount; the opposite is correct when it is at a large premium. During normal times, refinancing speed for high-coupon MBS much exceeds and dominates a housing turnover rate. However, the actual refinancing rate during the 2008–2011 span has been very depressed, thereby making an uncharacteristically modest contribution to the overall speed. As a result, $\tau = 0.51$ offsets and prevails over the effect of $\rho = 1.33$ thereby extending prOAD over OAD for all coupons (Table 11.2-C).

The Interest Only/Principal Only Market Revisited

IOs, POs, and MSRs are important derivatives that leverage prepayment model risk. Their valuation is closely related to the concept of prepay risk-neutrality. Furthermore, if the TBA market and the IO/PO market do not agree with each other in understanding the risk, an arbitrage opportunity arises; we gave an example in the prior section. Instead of investigating arbitrage opportunities further, we focus on inspecting the role of risk-neutral prepayment modeling in pricing stripped derivatives and measuring their risk.

The first fact we present here is that, during normal times (i.e. $\rho > 1$), prOAD will be more negative than OAD for an IO. This can be easily proven using the following simplified logic. Let us consider valuation formula (4.4io) of chapter 4 with infinite maturity, constant amortization rate $\lambda(r)$, and a constant interest rate r:

$$P = \frac{c}{r + \lambda + prOAS}$$

Effective duration is going to be

$$D = -\frac{1}{P}\frac{dP}{dr} = \frac{1 + d\lambda/dr}{r + \lambda + prOAS} = \frac{P}{c}(1 + d\lambda/dr)$$

Let us further assume that $\lambda = \rho R(r) + \tau T$ where $R(r)$ is the baseline refinancing curve, a typically declining function of interest rate so that $dR/dr < 0$; T stands for the turnover rate and is assumed to be independent of r. Hence,

$$D = \frac{P}{c}\left(1 + \rho\frac{dR}{dr}\right) \tag{11.4}$$

which, given market price P, proves the point: selecting $\rho > 1$ shifts effective duration deeper to the negative territory. Although this "proof" is given merely as a conceptual illustration (in reality, the rates are random and the turnover rate T may somewhat depend on r), the practical conclusion can be confirmed. In

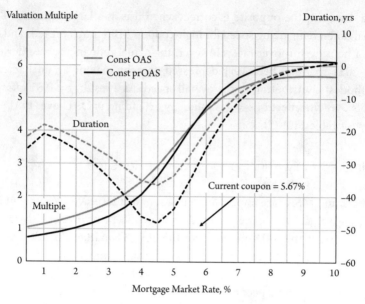

Figure 11.8 Valuation Profile for IO Using Two Methods (August 29, 2003)

Figure 11.8, we compare valuation profiles for an IO stripped off a 6.0%, just above current-coupon, pool. Valuation multiple represents the value of a 1% interest stream measured as P/c. We see that a constant-OAS valuation systematically understates rate sensitivity for all rate levels by as much as one-third. This implies, for example, that MSR managers would under-hedge if they employed the traditional constant-OAS duration.

These theoretical results have been validated using the volatile year 2003 as an example. We split the period from March to September into five short investment intervals featuring large market moves. For each period, one can compute price changes for the Trust IOs keeping OAS (or prOAS) constants and tracking moves in interest rates and volatilities. Then one can compare changes predicted by the model to the actual moves. Table 11.3 contains the results of this study.

For example, the MBS rate moved from 4.84% up to 5.37% between March 7 and March 21, 2003. This move induced a gain of 3.3 points, on average, for over 60 IOs frequently quoted by dealers. Keeping the starting OAS levels unchanged, we could predict only a 2.5-point move. The prOAS method served as a better predictor. We could expect a 3.6-point move (keeping long-term averaged risk-neutralized ρ and τ) or a 3.1-point move (re-calibrating risk-neutralized ρ and τ to each period). Therefore, either of the prOAS approaches would predict the average market move better than the OAS method. Furthermore, analyzing each of 60+ IOs involved in this analysis, we see that value prediction's accuracy improves for most of them.

Table 11.3 COMPARATIVE EXPLANATORY POWER OF OAS AND PROAS METHODS FOR LARGE TRUST IO MARKET MOVES
(60+ INSTRUMENTS)

Date	Days	FN Rate	Actual Value Move	Const OAS		Const prOAS Const RN Tunings		prOAS Beats OAS	Const prOAS Variable RN Tunings		prOAS Beats OAS
				value move	error	value move	error	%IOs	value move	error	%IOs
7-Mar-03		4.84									
21-Mar-03	14	5.37	3.3	2.5	-0.8	3.6	0.3	72.1%	3.1	-0.2	76.5%
30-May-03	70	4.41	-5.8	-4.1	1.7	-5.1	0.7	97.2%	-5.1	0.7	97.2%
15-Jul-03	46	5.08	3.9	2.6	-1.3	3.6	-0.4	94.3%	3.4	-0.5	97.1%
29-Aug-03	45	5.67	4.8	4.4	-0.4	6.9	2.1	28.6%	6.0	1.2	42.9%
30-Sep-03	32	5.01	-4.5	-3.1	1.3	-3.7	0.8	92.9%	-3.9	0.6	90.0%

The prOAS model is calibrated to the IO/PO parity.

For each of the five investment periods shown in Table 11.3, the constant OAS methodology understates the actual market move; in only one of these five periods, this methodology delivered a plausible prediction whereas the prOAS method performed poorly. This was precisely the period ending on August 29 when, as we showed, the IO market dislocated from TBAs and might lack financial rationale. For the other four periods, the application of either of two prOAS modeling versions would result in much more accurate predictions, both on average and across instruments. Table 11.3 also shows that constant recalibration of risk-neutral scales brings in just marginal benefits; the method can work reasonably well with averaged ρ and τ.

PRACTICAL BENEFITS AND IMPLICATIONS OF RISK-NEUTRAL PREPAYMENT MODELING

With the prOAS foundation explained, we finish this chapter with an overview of practical cases when an investor or risk manager would prefer this method to traditional OAS.

EXPECTED RETURN, MISPRICING, AND ARBITRAGE

Both OAS and prOAS can be interpreted as expected return spreads. In case of OAS, this expectation relies on the correctness of the prepayment model. In case of prOAS, the return expectation is free of the bias of any particular physical prepayment model. Since prOAS accounts for the price of prepay model risk as it is evidenced by the market (TBAs or IOs/POs), investors can lock into prOAS utilizing these instruments for hedging prepayment model risk (in addition to hedging interest-rate risk). In contrast, the expected return indicated by a traditional OAS may be eroded if the prepayment model risk is hedged.

Table 11.4 demonstrates how to spot an arbitrage and lock into profit. Let us first consider a 5.5% IO valued at +200 bps prOAS given that Fannie Mae TBA 5.0 (labeled as FN 5.0) is valued at –15 bps and FN 6.0 at –6 bps (Panel A), *using the same prepayment model*. At first, it seems that the IO is cheap, on an OAS basis. The problem, however, arises when we consider hedging prepay model risk. The IO (see the Unhedged Portfolio row) is exposed to both refinancing and, especially, the turnover scale. In fact, a 10% acceleration in the housing turnover will results in 3.3% loss of value.

Once we decide to hedge both dimensions of risk, selling a synthetic IO using the FN 6.0/5.0 swap comes to mind. Note that FN 6.0 is priced cheaper than FN 5.0 on an OAS basis, so that this hedging strategy calls for a return sacrifice. We computed the weights by minimizing the total prepay exposure while purposely keeping two TBA weights identical to one another. The resultant portfolio

Table 11.4 HEDGING A CHEAP IO

A. AN ARBITRAGE ILLUSION

Size	Position	Price	OAS	Refi Dur*	Turn Dur*
$100	FNT–350 IO	21.7	200	−0.8	−3.3
$466	FN 5.0	97.17	−15	−0.04	0.19
−$466	FN 6.0	101.11	**−5**	−0.07	0.03
Hedged	PORTFOLIO $	$3.34	−$0.01	−$0.02	$0.00
Unhedged	PORTFOLIO $	$21.70	$0.43	−$0.17	−$0.72

* per 10% of scale

B. REALISTIC ARBITRAGE

Size	Position	Price	OAS	Refi Dur*	Turn Dur*
$100	FNT–350 IO	21.7	200	−0.8	−3.3
$466	FN 5.0	97.17	−15	−0.04	0.19
−$466	FN 6.0	101.11	**−15**	−0.07	0.03
Hedged	PORTFOLIO $	$3.34	$0.46	−$0.02	$0.00
Unhedged	PORTFOLIO $	$21.70	$0.43	−$0.17	−$0.72

* per 10% of scale

requires $3.34 of investing, has a negligible residual prepay risk, but will return nothing above LIBOR. Hence, hedging prepay model risk out cancels projected earnings. We could have come to the same conclusion using the prOAS model, without constructing a TBA hedge. First, we risk-neutralize prepayment model using the TBA market; it would results in faster prepayments as evidenced by the OAS skew for the FN 5.0/6.0 pair. Then we would apply this model to the IO and find that derived prOAS is indeed close to zero.

In contrast, Panel B depicts a realistic arbitrage opportunity. The only difference from Panel A is the −15 bps OAS for FN 6.0 shown in bold instead of −5 bps (for simplicity, we keep prices from panel A). A wide OAS for the IO assumes compensation for bearing prepay model risk, but the flat OAS profile for TBAs suggests no such risk is priced in the TBA market. Now selling the synthetic IO does not only hedge prepay model risk out, but it also retains a considerable profitability of $0.46, or 14% annually above LIBOR. From the risk-neutral model standpoint, we should not expect to see acceleration over the physical model as the OAS profile is flat for key TBAs.

In both examples, the hedged portfolio certainly retains interest-rate risk, which can be hedged using usual rate derivatives; it causes no alterations of the profitability statement as we posited it against a no-arbitrage rate model. Also, our prepay hedge efficiency is limited to the assumptions made by the risk view we held. For example, we assumed that prepay model risk can be represented by two factors affecting all MBS instruments and that the risk found in the TBA market is the one affecting IOs. A dislocation of these two markets breaks the later assumption.

LESSONS OF RISK MANAGEMENT

We have already pointed out that valuation under a risk-neutral prepayment modeling alters effective durations and other Greeks. TBAs can look shorter or longer depending on coupon and prevailing prepayment concerns, whereas the dependence of IOs on interest rates is usually extended.

Table 11.4 illustrates another important lesson: In order to design an MBS portfolio that promises a steady, prepay-independent, return, prepayment model's uncertainty has to be explicitly hedged. This simple fact eludes many risk managers. Traditionally, they focus on hedging the interest-rate risk and refer to MBS widening to swaps as "basis risk." For example, adding a TBA to an IO (or MSR) will reduce the basis risk, from the traditional standpoint. Those who employ this risk management strategy think of basis widening or tightening as the only possible market moves and assume that IOs and TBAs must offset each other. This is a dangerous assumption as the notion of basis risk lacks financial meaning and cause. Can assets and hedges both lose? The events of 2003 showed they could—if the basis is widened on prepayment concerns. For the period leading up to May–June 2003, refinancing panic drove IOs down without an offsetting power of TBAs. OAS levels widened for all instruments making both assets and hedges decline. This is clearly seen in Table 11.2-A where risk-neutral refinancing and turnover scales are both found to be over 1.0 for what was essentially a premium-MBS market.

Instead of relying on the notion of basis risk, MBS investors and risk managers should treat risk-neutral ρ and τ as risk factors and control investment's exposure to them. Table 11.4 illustrates how to measure and hedge prepay model's exposures correctly. Only after the risk of shifting prepay model's scales is addressed, should the unexplained residual risk be further considered.

DESIGNING AND VALIDATING A MORTGAGE-BACKED SECURITIES VALUATION/PRICING SERVICE

Pricing services aid financial markets in discovering perceived values of instruments that are not immediately traded. For example, an investor in a CMO tranche may need to know its market price regardless of whether there have been recent trades or not. Pricing services are supposed to take available information about actual market trades and "extrapolate" it into a much larger universe of instruments. This extrapolation process usually involves modeling; for example, derived instruments can use OAS (Yield, BEEM, Z-Spread, etc.) levels derived from actual trades.

The theory of risk-neutral prepayment should influence the analytical process. We first select benchmark instruments that can be used to calibrate the model.

There are two powerful practical options: TBAs versus debenture, and IOs versus POs. In the former case, we deform a physical prepayment model so that the prOAS-to-agency curve is zero. In the latter case, we equate prOAS for IOs and POs, usually on average. The process transforms the prepayment model and establishes a pricing spread (prOAS) to use across instruments. We can apply this prOAS, with necessary practical adjustments,[3] and the risk-neutralized prepayment model to a vast universe of instruments lying well beyond the benchmark set. One example of this process was already illustrated in Figure 11.6 earlier: We were able to successfully predict prices of over 60 Trust IOs using just eight TBAs.

Using the risk-neutral prepayment modeling concept we introduced, MBS market participant can review and validate the job performed by a pricing service. This is the inverse problem to deriving prices. One can create a risk-neutral prepayment model and apply it to MBS of particular interest, using quotes from a pricing service. Derived prOAS levels will indicate if there exists a potential mispricing or arbitrage. A set of prOAS found in a tight range across a large universe of MBS would be an indication of market efficiency precluding an arbitrage. In contrast, large, unwarranted, deviations of prOAS from one instrument to another leaves questions. They can be an indication of either mispricing (the service did the job poorly) or arbitrage (prices are correct; the market has arbitrage opportunities).

CONCLUSION

MBS markets do price prepayment model risk, that is, the risk that projected prepayments are biased or can become biased going forward. We showed that this price of risk can be accounted for rather easily by deforming a physical prepayment model into a risk-neutral one. Typically, this process of risk-neutralization results in a faster refinancing and a slower turnover.

To find a risk-neutral transformation for agency MBS, one can target the TBA parity to GSE's debentures or the IO/PO parity. With the risk-neutral model, all benchmarks should look equally attractive to investors, on an OAS basis. This level of OAS is called prepayment-risk-and-option-adjusted spread (prOAS); this is simply an OAS computed with the risk-neutral prepayment model. The prOAS level points to the expected return spread, without reliance on a physical prepayment model. This approach explains many phenomena of the MBS markets, alters the Greeks, and is free from the drawbacks of traditional OAS

---

[3]For example, illiquid or odd-sized MBS may require add-on spreads.

models discussed in chapter 10. In its simple form (ignoring prepayment convexity terms), the prOAS method implementation requires no specialized software development and can still use the existing OAS analytical systems, but with altered prepayment scales.

HISTORICAL REMARKS

The first known work published on this subject is by O. Cheyette (1996). Subsequently, a Price-of-Risk-Constant (PORC) model by Bear Stearns' E. Cohler, M. Feldman, and B. Lancaster (1997) gained industry's recognition. While the goal of PORC was the same as ours—to account for prepay model risk—the means were different. The PORC authors proposed measuring pathwise exposure to a prepayment risk scale and did not consider the use of risk-neutral prepayment modeling. As a result, the implementation of PORC required developing specialized software, worked slowly, and suffered needlessly.

The prOAS approach described in this chapter follows A. Levin (ADQP 2004) and A. Levin and A. Davidson (2005). These publications have become known and gained followers (see A. Kolbe and R. Zagst 2008). Other important works on interpretation of OAS and prepay model risk belong to P. Kupiec and A. Kah (1999), and already cited X. Gabaix, A. Krishnamurthy and O. Vigneron (2007).

PART THREE

Modeling and Valuation of Non-Agency Mortgage-Backed Securities

12

Loan Level Modeling of Prepayment and Default

The next few chapters focus on the analysis of credit risk of mortgages and MBS. In order to do so, we need to extend modeling from the pool-level, total-terminations models of chapter 7. The analysis is extended in several dimensions. The subject of the analysis is prepayments and defaults, rather than total terminations. The focus goes from pools to loans. In addition to information about the mortgage contract terms such as coupon and amortization period, borrower and collateral characteristics are important in the analysis. Loan-level analysis also increases the focus on the delinquency status of the loans rather than just viewing loans as active or terminated.

MODEL OUTPUT

In order to perform credit analysis, we must also segment terminations from default from terminations due to prepayments. Unfortunately, the definitions of prepayment and default are not universally established. The confusion arises from the fact that the term "default" is not well defined. Technically, any time the borrower fails to make a payment under the mortgage note, there is a default. However, most investors think of a default in terms of a loan termination caused by a borrower's failure to pay, not the actual event of borrower default. That is, a default for the investor would be the termination of a loan that is caused by a failure to pay on the part of the borrower which often, but not always, leads to a payment of less than the full amount of principal outstanding. Different securities can have different rules as to when the investor would realize the loss or receive the recovered principle from a default termination. Additional confusion arises from the fact that for agency MBS, prepayment has always included defaults.

	Chapter 7	**Chapter 12**
Model Output	Total termination	Prepay
		Default
		Severity
		Delinquency
Granularity of Analysis	Pool	Loan
Data Elements	Mortgage note	Mortgage note
	Economic	Collateral
	"Enhanced" variables	Borrower
		Economic

One way of splitting terminations would be to split those that occur without loss and those that occur with loss. Only those with a loss would be called defaults. From a definitional sense this would create a clear delineation. However, many analysts also want to label loans that terminate after delinquency as defaults, thinking that even if there is no loss, a delinquent borrower has different economic motivations than a current borrower.

Another alternative would be to only include terminations that resulted from foreclosure as defaults. This has the problem that there may be short sales or other terminations that did not reach the foreclosure stage.

We introduce nomenclature here that is not standard in the industry to provide clarity on the definitions, and then link those terms back to commonly used metrics. For definitional purposes, we assume that terminations for mortgage contracts can be split between those that are *voluntary* and those that are *involuntary*. Generally a voluntary termination occurs when a borrower decides to fully prepay the mortgage due to the opportunity to refinance or due to moving.

An involuntary termination occurs when a borrower is unable to make the full payments. Involuntary prepayments could include some refinances, sales, or other terminations that do not result in losses. Involuntary terminations also include strategic defaults, where the borrower chooses to default even though they can afford the mortgage payments. One could argue that such terminations are not "involuntary," nevertheless we group them with the other loss-producing terminations. We generally include all terminations by delinquent borrowers in our definition of involuntary terminations.

Terminations are generally measured on a monthly basis as a percentage of the amortized outstanding balance. Here our approach differs from the industry's recommended approach. In the industry approach,[1] defaults and prepayments have different treatments, splitting loans into performing and non-performing. It

---

[1] See the SIFMA Standard Formulas in Uniform Practices for Clearance and Settlement of Mortgage-Backed Securities, available at: http://www.sifma.org/research/bookstore.aspx#Uniform Practices.

assumes that non-performing loans do not amortize and that defaults are measured against beginning of period balances rather than amortized balances. Our preference is to treat voluntary and involuntary terminations symmetrically and to incorporate the unpaid amortization into the loss amount. This approach fits well with situations where the servicer advances principal and interest for delinquent loans and then recovers the advances upon disposition of the property.

Total monthly terminations then equal the sum of voluntary and involuntary terminations. Annual terminations are computed from the monthly rates. Severity represents the amount of loss as a percentage of the involuntarily terminated balance.

Table 12.1 shows these definitions and the corresponding terms generally used by market participants. Monthly total terminations are often called *SMM*, or single monthly mortality. Annualized SMM is CPR or conditional prepayment rate. Note that CPR is generally used for total terminations despite the use of the word "prepayment" which some might equate to voluntary terminations. This is due to the widespread use of CPR for agency MBS where it reflects total terminations.

Voluntary terminations are distinguished by the use of the word "repayment." Thus there is a monthly repayment rate (mrr) and conditional repayment rate (crr) or alternatively voluntary prepayment rate (vpr). Involuntary terminations are usually called defaults resulting in monthly default rate (mdr) and annual default rate (cdr).

Monthly Computation:

$SMM = mttr = $ (Scheduled Balance – Actual Balance)/Scheduled Balance
Use $mvtr$ or vpr for Voluntary Terminations/Scheduled Balance
Use $mitr$ or mdr for Involuntary Terminations/Scheduled Balance

$$smm = mrr + mdr \, , mttr = mvtr + mitr$$

Annualization:

$$cpr = 1 - (1 - smm)^{12}$$

Generally, annualization occurs the same for each variable

$$axxx = 1 - (1 - mxxx)^{12}$$

Note therefore that annual rates do not add up: $cpr \neq cdr + crr$.

Table 12.1 MORTGAGE TERMINATION DEFINITIONS

Terminations	Standardized		Classic	
	Monthly	Annual	Monthly	Annual
Total	mttr	attr	SMM	CPR
Voluntary	mvtr	avtr	mrr	crr or vpr
Involuntary	mitr	aitr	mdr	cdr

Severity is computed by dividing the Total Loss on loan including costs by the Scheduled Balance at time of termination.

GRANULARITY OF ANALYSIS

Credit analysis is best performed at the loan level. Two pools can have the same average characteristics and have very different credit risk due to different distributions of loan-level characteristics. Pooling rules generally limit the range of coupon and amortization periods, but do not place as tight limits on credit variables such as LTV and credit score. The move from pool-level analysis to loan-level analysis increases the amount of data by several orders of magnitude as many pools can contain thousands of loans and generally there are more loan-level data elements.

Moving to loan-level analysis can help resolve two problems with pool data. First, loan data allows the observation of heterogeneity within a pool. This will reduce, but probably not eliminate, unobserved heterogeneity. Therefore, we still find the active/passive decomposition methods described in chapter 7 useful for loan models. Second, loan data allows us to observe the progression of loans through stages of delinquency. Not surprisingly, the performance of loans differs significantly between loans that are current versus delinquent.

Data Elements

At the loan level, there are potentially hundreds of variables that could be used to analyze mortgages. The American Securitization Forum (ASF) has proposed a list[2] of 157 data items that should be made available to investors at the origination of transaction. Origination data falls primarily into three categories: mortgage note, borrower and collateral.

MORTGAGE NOTE
Mortgage note data describes the borrower's payment commitment. Data includes the mortgage (or note) interest rate, the amount of the loan, the term of the loan, and the amortization period. For adjustable-rate loans, additional data is needed to describe the reset period, index, margin and limits on changes in the note rate, and payments.

[2]ASF RMBS Disclosure Package, July 15, 2009.

Borrower

Information about the borrower is primarily aimed at determining the borrower's general propensity and ability to make payments on this loan and on other financial obligations. The primary measure used is the FICO score. The FICO score is based upon the prior credit performance of the borrower and the borrowers existing credit lines. Other information about the borrower such as age, sex, marital status, and race might be useful to predict performance, but it could lead to prohibited discrimination and therefore is not used.

Borrower information about prior bankruptcies, employment history and assets is also used in the underwriting process. With the general failure of the private label securities market to produce well underwritten loans during the period leading up to the housing crisis, there is currently a focus on making more data available to investors to validate underwriting.

Collateral

The right to foreclose and use the home to settle an unpaid loan is what distinguishes mortgages from other loans. Therefore the characteristics of the home are important to credit analysis. Probably the most important feature of the collateral is the amount of the loan relative to the value of the home (LTV ratio). Investors are also interested in knowing whether or not there are additional liens on the property. The LTV including the second liens is called the total LTV (TLTV). Some have proposed that borrowers not be allowed to take on additional debt secured by their homes without permission of the first lien holder, as second liens appear to have been a significant contributor to mortgage defaults and to difficulty in loan resolutions after default.

The location of the home is also important because past and future home prices are largely tied to location. The LTV adjusted for changes in home prices is called the current LTV (CLTV). Also foreclosure laws and liquidation time lines vary significantly by location. Investors may also be concerned with the type of property, single family versus multiple units, and whether or not the borrower occupies the home.

Performance Data

Every month the borrower may choose to make its scheduled payment, an additional payment, fully pay off the loan, or not make any payment at all. This data is provided to investors and is used to update the amount of loan balance outstanding and the expected payments to the investors. Borrowers' failure to pay is also important to investors as it may be an indication of future losses. While borrower payments are generally required on a monthly basis, borrower delinquency is usually described as a number of days late. A borrower who has missed one payment is generally considered 30 days late, two payments, 60 days and so forth.

The mortgage servicer also reports if foreclosure proceedings have begun on a delinquent loan, if the property has been repossessed (real-estate owned or REO), or if there is a final disposition from a property sale. If there is not a full recovery, the servicer will report the amount of loss. The loss as a percentage of the outstanding balance is called the loss severity. Often servicers report losses on loans over several periods, both before and after the recognition of the termination of the loan. There may also be later recoveries of prior losses. This often complicates the reporting of loss severities. Loan loss severities are best reported by accumulating all of the losses and recoveries regardless of when they occurred to compute a single severity. For pools, it is generally best to report the losses and recoveries in the period they occurred, which may be different than the period that the termination is recorded. This can result in severities in excess of 100% or even negative severities, as the timing of losses may not match the timing of the associated defaults, but better matches the timing of cash flows to investors.

ASF recommends 205 data items that should be disclosed on a monthly basis. The monthly data items relate to loan payments, loan delinquency status, loan terminations, modifications, and costs associated with default and foreclosure.

General Economic Data

In order to forecast the performance of loans it is necessary to link the contract, borrower, and collateral information to economic variables. For most mortgage analysis, the primary economic variables are interest rates and home prices. Interest rates are generally the key to forecasting voluntary terminations and home prices are the key driver to changing levels of involuntary terminations and levels of loss severity.

Other economic variables such as the level of unemployment, housing activity, or changes in income may be useful in forecasting losses. Economic variables can be aggregated at the national, state, or local level. It often makes sense to consider both local and national economic factors.

An essential feature for the use of an economic factor in forecasting borrower behavior is that the economic factor can be analyzed to produce a forecast or a distribution of potential outcomes. While borrower defaults in a certain town may be related to a plant closing five years from now, it is unlikely that a specific forecast or even a specific distribution of probabilities can be constructed for that factor or for any individual factor.

APPROACHES TO CREDIT MODELING

There are four basic types of credit models commonly in use for mortgage-backed securities.

- Lifetime foreclosure frequency/loss severity
- Roll rate
- Hazard
- Dynamic transition

Traditionally, rating agencies and other market participants have used models to forecast **foreclosure frequency** over the **life** of the loan. These models take borrower and collateral characteristics and forecast what percentage of the loans are likely to experience foreclosure. Often separate models are computed for different loan types such as prime loans, alt-A loans, and subprime loans. The rating agencies would then calibrate these models to different economic environments to establish foreclosure frequencies for different rating categories. These models would be coupled with separate models for loss severity. Loss severities would also be linked to economic environments to produce different loss severities for different ratings categories. Higher rated bonds need to withstand greater levels of loss. Table 12.2 is an illustration of a foreclosure frequency and loss severity matrix showing the scenario that a bond of each rating category needs to survive.

The main advantage of this approach is that it provides a range of loss forecasts across economic environments. However it has several drawbacks. It does not provide an indication of timing of losses or any indication of timing or amount of repayments. Thus it is not very useful for generating cash flows or determining value. This method also is only valid at the time of origination of the loans, once loans have seasoned it does not indicate how to take advantage of additional information provided by current and prior delinquencies and paydowns.

Roll Rate models are the opposite end of the spectrum. They fully take into account the delinquency status of the loans and are effective for short-term forecasts. The basic concept is that all loans are put into buckets each month based upon their delinquency status. A transition rate is computed based on the average percentage of loans in that bucket that move into a different bucket during the next period.

Table 12.2 LIFETIME FORECLOSURE FREQUENCY, SEVERITY AND LOSS

Rating	Foreclosure Frequency	Loss Severity	Lifetime Loss
AAA	20%	60%	12.0%
AA	16%	55%	8.8%
A	10%	50%	5.0%
BBB	7%	45%	3.2%
BB	5%	40%	2.0%
B	3%	35%	1.1%

Table 12.3 ROLL RATE MATRIX, $[T]$

	Current	30	60	90/90+	Foreclose	REO	REO Sold	Prepay
Current	94%	5%						1%
30	50%	20%	25%					5%
60	20%	10%	20%	40%				10%
90	15%		10%	50%	20%			5%
Foreclose					90%	10%		
REO						75%	25%	
Sold							100%	
Prepay								100%

Table 12.3 is an example of a roll rate table (Markov chain). These transition rates can be viewed as a matrix $[T]$. The matrix $[T]$ can be applied to a vector d of the current delinquency status of the loans. By successive application of the matrix, it is possible to estimate the amount of loans that will prepay and be foreclosed during successive periods. For example, $[T] \times [T] \times [T] \times d$ would give the status of the loans after three periods.

The roll rate approach gets its name from how the loans "roll" from one status to another. Since this approach captures current delinquency status and average roll rates, it usually can produce good short-term forecasts as it typicallytakes several months for loans to move through the delinquency and foreclosure process. Note, however, that this approach does not fully utilize detailed loan characteristics. Some firms produce separate matrices for different loan types to address this shortcoming. Another shortcoming is that it does not take different economic environments into account, thus making it less useful as a long-term forecasting tool.

Hazard models are econometric models that expand upon the foreclosure frequency models by incorporating the timing of terminations, and they address prepayments and defaults.

One of the earliest academic models combining prepayments and defaults is Deng et al. (2000). Another good example of a hazard model approach is the Pennington-Cross model. Pennington-Cross estimates a competing risks proportional hazard model, which includes unobserved heterogeneity. This type of model builds upon similar models for total terminations, described in chapter 7, by allowing two types of terminations, prepayments and defaults, and recognizing that each loan can only terminate by either prepayment or default, whichever comes first.

Pennington-Cross (2003) defines the time to prepayment as T_p and the time to default as T_d. These random variables that have a continuous probability distribution defined as $f(t_w)$, where t_w is a realization of $T_w (w = p, d)$. The joint survivor function for loan j is then $S_j(t_p, t_d) = pr(T_p > t_p, T_d > t_d)$ and has the following form:

$$S_j(t_p, t_d) = exp\left[-\theta_p \sum_{t=0}^{t_p} exp(\beta'_p x_{jt}) - \theta_d \sum_{t=0}^{t_d} exp(\beta'_d x_{jt})\right].$$

where the x_{jt} are characteristics of loan j at time t, β's are the weights of the characteristics and θ's are positive coefficients.

These types of model offer the advantage of dealing directly with the timing and interaction of prepayment and default events. They also allow for explicit treatment of time dependent economic variables such as interest rates and home prices and addresses unobserved heterogeneity. One disadvantage of these models is that the statistical complexity limits the use of some of the non-linear techniques described in chapter 7. More importantly, these models do not incorporate any of the delinquency status information. Therefore, they are less useful for seasoned pools of loans. While it may be possible to add delinquency status as one of the loan level variables, this turns out to be a poor approach.

Finally, **dynamic transition** models represent a combination of the three methods described previously. These models begin with the assignment of models into delinquency statuses. Transitions from one status to another are modeled using dynamic models. These can be simple logistic regressions, proportional hazard models, or more complex non-linear formulations that incorporate unobserved heterogeneity.

By using the loan status as the starting point these models are useful for seasoned, as well as new pools of loans. This approach also allows for the explicit forecasting of the timing of prepayments and defaults. It also allows for the incorporation of time dependent economic variables. The main downside of this approach is that it entails substantially more work because separate models need to be computed for each transition.

Perhaps the earliest use of this approach for mortgages can be found in Smith et al. (1996); another source describing this method is Kaskowitz et al. (2002).

The implementation of this approach generally involves grouping several loan delinquency statuses together and using relatively simple functional forms for some of the less important and less variable transitions. This is the approach that we have used at Andrew Davidson & Co since 2007. We call this model Loan Dynamics. It is described in Ching (ADQP 2008) and used in Levin and Davidson (2008).

A Dynamic Transition Model

Figure 12.1 is a schematic of the loan statuses and transitions utilized in the model. There are three statuses for active loans: current, delinquent, and severely

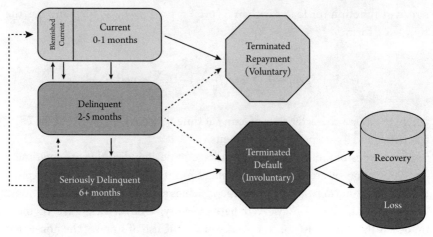

Figure 12.1 Dynamic Transition Model Schematic

delinquent, notated as C, D, and S. Each status represents a range of delinquency periods. C is for loans that are current or not more than one month delinquent. D is for loans that are at least two but not more than five months delinquent. S is for loans that are six or more months delinquent. There are two ways for loans to terminate: termination by repayment (voluntary termination) and termination by default (involuntary termination). Blemished current (BC) represents a special status. In this status, loans which transitioned from delinquent back to current retain the taint of delinquency and are modeled separately. Otherwise we do not distinguish loans by the path they take to get to a particular status.

Loans can transition between any of the active statuses and can terminate in either of the termination statuses. For example, the transition from current to delinquent is called CtoD. Similarly, the transition from current to terminated is called CtoT. The most important transitions are shown with solid lines. Less important transitions are shown in dotted lines. Unlikely or impossible transitions are not shown. Transition probabilities from each status must add to 100%, as in the roll rate model. In most cases the highest probability is for a loan to stay in the same status from one month to the next. Transitions are applied to starting delinquency balances as in the Roll Rate Model above. Each transition rate is a separate model. We will describe these models below. For example the CtoT model is much like the prepayment model described in Chapter 7. Other transitions may be simple hazard functions or use other functional forms. The result is a dynamic roll rate matrix as shown in Table 12.4 as opposed to the static roll rates in Table 12.3.

Table 12.5 shows some of the key transitions in the model and the key variables. Each transition is created as a dynamic function of both loan characteristics

Table 12.4 DYNAMIC ROLL RATE MATRIX

	C	BC	D	S	T
C	1-a-b		a(X)		b(X)
BC		1-c-d	c(X)		d(X)
D		e(X)	1-e-f-g	f(X)	g(X)
S		h(X)		1-h-i	i(X)

Probability of loss = j(X)
Severity = k(X)

and economic variables. In this way, transition rates can change as economic conditions vary. In Table 12.5 pluses and minuses are used to show the direction of the effect. Stronger effects are shown with multiple pluses or minuses. Several important transitions are discussed below.

CtoT: Current to Terminated (Voluntary)

The CtoT transition is the voluntary repayment transition. For many loans this is the most important transition, and thus modeling CtoT is much like modeling total terminations as described in chapter 7. Just like total terminations, CtoT is driven by housing turnover and by the borrowers' incentive to refinance. The borrowers' credit characteristics also affect ability to refinance with higher LTVs, lower credit scores and declining home prices all negatively affecting voluntary terminations.

Figure 12.2 is an example of how credit variables, in this case borrower credit scores, affect voluntary prepayments. The *x*-axis shows the incentive to prepay based upon the ratio of the borrower's current payment to the new payment after refinancing. With higher incentives, borrower repayment rates increase. Borrowers with lower credit scores have a muted response. These borrowers require a greater incentive to repay their loans and the pace of repayment is lower than borrowers with higher credit scores.

CtoD: Current to Delinquent

The value of the transition approach can be understood when comparing CtoT to CtoD. The factors that lead to termination via voluntary prepayment are largely opposite to those leading to delinquency. Borrowers with lower credit scores and higher loan-to-value ratios are more likely to become delinquent. Declining home prices can lead to significant increases in the rate of delinquency. Borrowers do not ruthlessly exercise their option to stop making mortgage payments based solely upon the value of their home relative to the loans. There are other costs to foreclosure and other benefits to a home that are not captured by the LTV.

Table 12.5 Characteristics of Key Transitions

Transition	Name	Monthly Rate Range	Borrower Credit Score	Collateral LTV	Geo	Contract Coupon	Maturity	Economics Rates (lower)	HPA (lower)
CtoT	Repayment	0.5–15%	+	–		++	+	++	–
CtoD	Delinquency	0–4%	– –	+	✓				++
DtoC	Cure	0–20%	–	–				+	–
DtoS	Serious DQ	15–30%	+	+					
StoT	Foreclosure	3–5%	–		✓		+		+
Loss	Severity	0–100%	–	+	✓	+			++

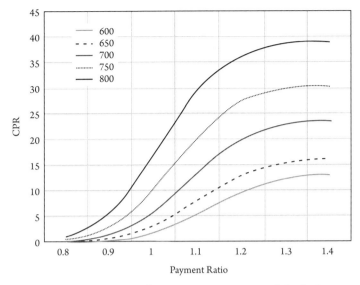

Figure 12.2 Model CtoT Interaction between Rate Incentive and Credit Score

The CtoD transition generally follows the same pattern as the Vasicek default in chapter 1. But like CtoT, delinquencies don't rise to 100% and are affected by more than just the LTV.

A simple functional form for the CtoD transition is

$$a * N(b * Current\ LTV + c * FICO - d)$$

Figure 12.3 seems to indicate that a linear function like

$$MAX(0, -(FICO - 710) * (1.5 / 60) + (LTV - 50) * (2 / 20))$$

would be a good fit, however we find that such a formula does not perform well especially at the high quality end of the spectrum where the delinquency rate is low but not zero.

As both CtoT and CtoD reduce the amount of current loans outstanding, the two transitions act as competing risks. Higher levels of repayment reduce the number of loans that can default. Thus, if interest rates fall, the total lifetime amount of default and loss is likely to be much lower than in rising interest-rate environments. The reduction in losses from higher voluntary terminations is not exactly proportional to the decline in balance from voluntary terminations as often the borrowers who are most likely to default are least able to refinance. From a theoretical standpoint, it might make sense to fit both CtoT and CtoD models jointly in a competing risk framework.

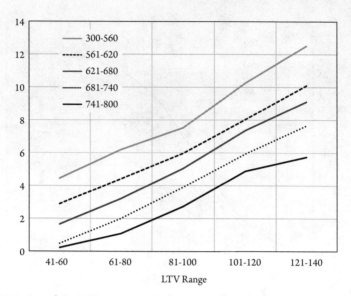

Figure 12.3 Actual CtoD Transition Rates by LTV and Credit Score

DtoC: Cure

Not all borrowers who become delinquent eventually default. In fact, in many economic environments, most borrowers cure from delinquency and become current again. The transition approach reveals another insight. Common sense would indicate that borrowers with higher credit scores would be less likely to become delinquent and more likely to cure, or become current once delinquent. It turns out that the actual result is counterintuitive. High credit score borrowers are indeed less likely to become delinquent, but once delinquent they are **less** likely to cure. On the other hand, borrowers with lower credit scores are more likely to cure from delinquency.

The explanation for this counterintuitive result is that high credit score borrowers would likely exhaust financial resources before becoming delinquent while lower credit score borrowers frequently miss payments and then find a way to recover. Figure 12.4 shows this for Alt-A loans (loans with limited documentation to supposedly high credit quality borrowers) during 2008 which was a period of rising delinquencies and defaults.

BCtoD: Redefault

We have found that despite becoming current, borrowers who have previous delinquencies do not exhibit the same performance as borrowers with no prior delinquencies. Therefore, we segment the current status into always current and blemished current. Figure 12.5 shows the surprising results. It is not surprising that the recidivism rate, that is, prior delinquent loans becoming delinquent

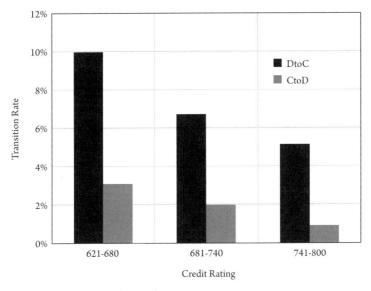

Figure 12.4 Default and Cure by Credit Rating

again, is higher than the delinquency rate for loans that have never been delinquent. However, it is surprising that the pattern of delinquency is very different. For never delinquent loans, higher loan-to-value ratios are related to higher delinquency. For blemished current, the pattern is flat or even reversed with lower LTV loans showing higher recidivism.

When the CtoD rate of blemished current are viewed based on number of months since cure from delinquency, a familiar pattern emerges. Figure 12.6 shows the rate of blemished current loans returning to delinquent status. The CtoD rate is high at first and then declines as the balance declines. Thus these loans exhibit unobserved heterogeneity and produce a pattern much like prepayment burnout. The loans that remain current after some time have a lower rate of re-default. It seems that borrowers who make payments for two to three years after curing behave almost as if they did not become delinquent in the first place.

StoT: Foreclosure

The determination of transition rate from Seriously Delinquent to Terminated (StoT) is dominated by the amount of time to complete the foreclosure process. As a result of the housing crisis and the large volume of loans experiencing foreclosure, these times rose dramatically from 2002 to 2012. Foreclosure time lines rose from four months for foreclosures completed in 2002 to 29 months for foreclosures completed in the first half of 2012 as shown in Figure 12.7. Foreclosure

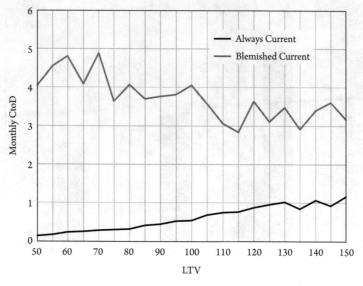

Figure 12.5 CtoD versus BCtoD by LTV

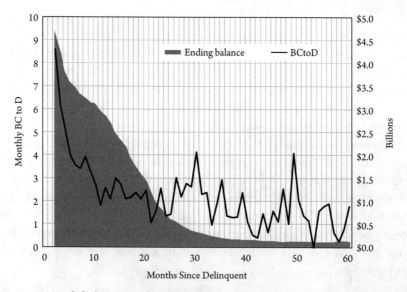

Figure 12.6 Redefault Rate Looks Like Burnout

time lines also vary significantly by state as shown in Figure 12.8. Some states require the use of the court system for foreclosures; these are called *judicial states*, these are shown in gray, in Figure 12.8. For foreclosures completed in 2011 the difference in time lines was about 6.5 months.

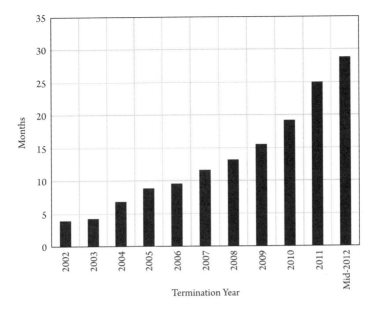

Figure 12.7 Change in Foreclosure Time Lines

ESTIMATION OF SEVERITY

While many loans terminate out of delinquent statuses, not all terminate with a loss. If the value of the home exceeds the value of the loan, then it may be possible to terminate without a foreclosure sale, or even if there is a foreclosure sale the proceeds might be sufficient to fully pay off the loan. In some ways, it is possible to view foreclosure as a put option where the borrower puts the home back to the lender. The severity can be thought of as the payoff of that option.

In computing severity, we need to consider that the actual value of the home will not exactly match the estimated value of the home based on market indices. In order to address this issue, we model loan-loss severity in an option valuation framework and assume that there is uncertainty about the actual value of the borrower's home. Borrowers with home values lower than average will be more likely to be foreclosed with losses and borrowers with higher than average value homes will be less likely to foreclose and will not produce losses. Therefore the average severity of a pool of loans will not equal the average value of the loan less the average value of the homes for terminated loans.

In Figure 12.9 we assume that the original LTV of the home was 90%. If the home falls in value by 10%, according to regional index, then the home value equals the loan value. At this point, we would expect no foreclosures and no

F2011

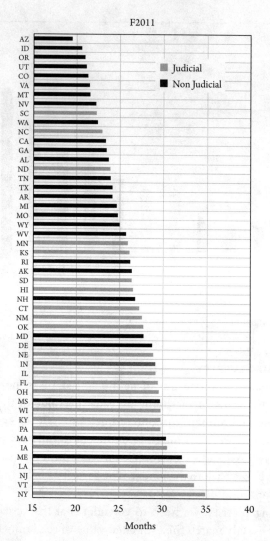

Figure 12.8 Foreclosure Time Lines by State

losses. However, due to the variability in the values of individual loans there is a 50% probability that some loans will be underwater and will generate losses. Thus, the expected severity is about 5% on the 50% of loans that are expected to take losses. As home prices fall further the probability of loss rises to 100% and there is less difference between the intrinsic severity and the option-based severity.

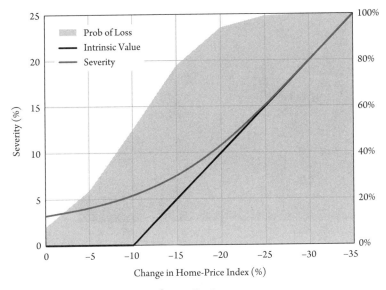

Figure 12.9 Loss Severity Computed as an Option

PROBABILITY MAPS

A credit model such as the dynamic transition model presented here does not say whether or not a particular loan will prepay or default. Rather it presents a set of probabilities of the state of the loan over time based upon an assumed economic environment. Figures 12.10a and 12.10b show the probability maps for a loan which started as a current loan and a loan which starts as a delinquent loan. In all other respects the two loans are assumed to be identical and they face the identical economic environment.

Over time each loan has varying probabilities of transitioning between the various delinquency statuses. Probability accumulates in the terminating states of voluntary and involuntary terminations as terminated loans cannot become active again.

These figures also demonstrate the importance of understanding the updated delinquency status. The delinquent loan has about four times the likelihood of involuntary termination as the current loan.

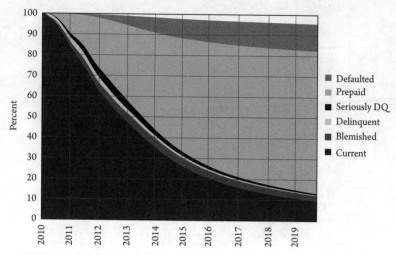

Figure 12.10a Probability Map of a Current Loan

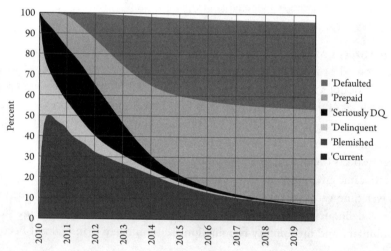

Figure 12.10b Probability Map of Delinquent Loan

CONCLUSION

Dynamic Transition based models such as the one described in this chapter present an effective means of describing voluntary and involuntary prepayments. They incorporate loan-level data about the loans at origination and can also utilize updated economic data and loan delinquency data. As described in the next chapter, these models can be combined with dynamic models of the economy that incorporate interest rates and home prices and can be used to generate, analyze and value cash flows for complex mortgage securitizations.

13

The Concept of Credit Option-Adjusted Spread

With the past growth of the non-agency mortgage market and the large volume of distressed MBS created by the mortgage crisis that began in 2007, finding fair economic value of credit-sensitive mortgage-backed securities has become a crucial ingredient in the functioning of capital markets. In the late 1990s, credit modeling attracted the attention of the academic world, first with applications to corporate liabilities. Leading researchers known for their works in asset pricing, options, and interest rates, switched their focus to modeling credit events (see Duffie and Garleanu 2001). However, the modeling of borrower options demonstrated in chapters 7 and 12 generally involved both theoretical and empirical analysis as the behavior of borrowers could not be completely determined by purely theoretical considerations. Furthermore, modeling defaults and losses in pools of homeowners demands more data than modeling prepayments and is most accurately predicted at the loan-level.

Until the mid-2000s, the primary holders of credit risk in the mortgage market were depository institutions, through their lending and portfolio activities, the government sponsored enterprises (GSEs)—Fannie Mae and Freddie Mac and the Mortgage Insurance companies. Credit modeling was performed at these institutions and at the major rating agencies. With the exception of the GSE and Mortgage Insurance companies, these generally focused on setting loan loss reserves and capital levels rather than the fair value of credit sensitive instruments. In the years leading to the financial crisis, several major Wall Street firms and independent analytical firms built credit valuation models.

Symptomatically, the risk-bearing party in the non-agency securities market, MBS investors, had been traditionally relying on external modeling efforts. For example, an AA-rated MBS tranche investor would employ the discount spread commonly used in the AA fixed income market and apply it for otherwise loss-free cash flow of the tranche. The credit crisis that began in 2007 highlighted the trouble of overreliance on credit rating labels and spreads. It appeared that AA and even AAA ratings did not grant close-to-ultimate protection anymore. Even if a reasonable expectation of losses does not trigger a senior tranche's write-down in a stable economic environment, a further deterioration of market conditions might produce losses. Davidson's "Six Degrees of Separation," written in 2007 (ADPN Aug. 2007) and reproduced in chapter 17, describes the mechanics and flaws of mortgage origination, underwriting, and investment and the roles of all parties involved in the crisis.

Two important points should be brought up here. First, it is the investor who should do the homework in obtaining the collateral data and forecasting delinquencies, defaults, and losses and deriving economic values. Second, a single baseline forecast does not earn an "A"; the MBS/ABS market values tranches considering all possible, perhaps remote, losses. We discuss this aspect in the next section and show why a stochastic modeling approach is necessary to explain market prices.

THE NECESSITY OF STOCHASTIC MODELING OF LOSSES

In this section, we provide a few important mortgage industry examples where the probability distribution of losses needs to be known to find the economic value of financial instruments.

DEFAULT OPTION MODELING

Much like prepayment, default on a loan is an option. A borrower in a grim financial situation (unable to make payments) can either sell the house or walk away. The decision depends on the amount of borrower's equity, which is a function of the house's price. Given this optional nature of the default, that is, a put option on the property, default rates and losses have to depend on home prices nonlinearly. To continue the parallel with the refinancing option (a call), the default option is not exercised efficiently and its laws can be best seen throughout the prism of empirical modeling. Common refinancing patterns suggest negative convexity of MBS prices with respect to interest rates; we assert positive convexity of losses (and still negative convexity of prices) with respect to home prices.

What follows from this option-like argument is that the expected default rates and losses in a cohort of loans cannot be accurately assessed using a single forecast. Examples shown in this and other chapters of this book demonstrate that static forecasts materially understate mathematical expectation of losses.

SUBPRIME MORTGAGE-BASED SECURITIES

Let us assume that a subprime MBS deal is made of three protected tranches or classes, a senior tranche, a mezzanine tranche, and a junior tranche. Suppose further that the credit enhancement structure protects the junior tranche up to 10% of collateral loss, the mezzanine tranche up to 20%, and the senior tranche up to 30%. What this means is that a collateral loss of, say, 5% will not be propagated into these three classes and will be absorbed by subordinate classes. A 15% collateral loss will considerably reduce cash flow to the junior tranche, but will not cause any loss of the mezzanine and senior classes. A 25% loss will cause principal write-downs on everything but the senior tranche, etc.

At first glance, all an investor needs to know is a single number, the projected collateral loss. However, one can find that the market prices of all tranches are somewhat discounted for losses, albeit to various extents. No single loss scenario can explain the market values across the capital structure. This mystery disappears if we start viewing the loss as a random number. Instead of assuming that the loss can be either 5%, 15% or 25%, we assume that there exists some probability of a 5% loss, a 15% loss, and a 25% loss, that is, the loss is subject to some probability distribution. This randomness can be easily associated both with market factors (described in the next section) and the model's uncertainty itself.

L. Gauthier (2003) suggested recovering the loss distribution using market prices across the credit structure. Suppose we work with a grid of loss scenarios, ranked from lowest to highest. Each loss level results in some prices of MBS tranches. We then seek probability for the scenarios so that the weighted prices for the tranche set best match actual market prices. This approach is a low-cost effort because it requires no loss modeling and it recovers probability distribution of defaults and losses directly from observed market prices. As attractive as this method sounds, it again out-sources the actual modeling work and views it as granted. For example, in the fall of 2007, MBS prices were unstable, suggesting that the market makers lost firm views on future losses. The other issue with the Gauthier model is that it requires the user to construct each scenario grid point by linking losses to prepayments and delinquencies and expressing them as time-dependent vectors, i.e. somewhat arbitrarily. The timing of prepayments and losses are important too, but cannot be accurately predicted without modeling.

Mortgage Insurance, Guarantees, Losses, and Capital Requirements

The insurance business requires the protection seller to maintain sufficient capital to cover possible losses. Therefore, the physical expectation of the losses represents only part of insurance coverage and premium. The additional capital maintained to cover losses above the expected level can only earn the risk-free rate, thereby leading to "capital charge" (see chapter 4). This charge depends on the loss distribution, protection depth, return on capital, and the insurance coverage. GSEs could charge the highest premium because they provide full protection against loss,[1] but in practice, GSE operate using artificially low capital, which allows them to reduce the premium.

A similar argument applies to other participants of the MBS and ABS markets. CDS protection sellers are insurers of MBS tranches rather than loans. Mortgage originators that keep unsecuritized mortgage loans on their balance sheet set aside a so-called reserve for losses. We outlined the capital charge-based valuation in chapter 4. In essence, we showed how financial business logic contributes to the definition of price of risk and, therefore, to risk-neutrality of losses.

Exposure to Interest Rates

The default and loss rates cannot be considered independent of interest rates. Historical analysis points to a negative correlation between mortgage rates and the systematic component of home-price appreciation (HPA). This fact suggests that losses in MBS pools should rise and fall with interest rates. Hence, the interest-rate exposure of subprime MBS is different from the one established without credit modeling. The negative relationship between HPA and interest rates may look both counterintuitive and contradictory to simple statistical measurements. We discuss this topic in detail in chapter 14.

Is the Loss Stream an Interest Only or a Principal Only?

When a loss model is replaced by the "equivalent" discounting, a certain assumption is made: the loss stream looks like an IO. Indeed, an annual loss at a constant rate of 1% of the remaining principle is equivalent to a 100 bps additional discount spread, from the pricing standpoint. Above we mentioned that, if rates change, losses would change too, so the usual OAS method does not give us an accurate rate exposure. However, are losses an IO at all?

If a part of the collateral pool is already severely delinquent, it will likely to go through foreclosure, regardless of the interest rate. Hence, the loss stream of this

---

[1]A part of an agency-guarantee premium is related to the liquidity advantage of the agency MBS; another part, since 2012, is directed to sponsor payroll taxes.

kind resembles a PO, not an IO. Furthermore, unlike a PO, the liquidation time is not driven by interest rates. Therefore, losses steaming from severely delinquent loans look more like a portfolio of zero-coupon bonds with positive 0.5 year to 2.0 year duration (compare this to the typical duration range of IOs). It turns out that, to capture the interest-rate exposure correctly, a good model must relate the nature of losses to collateral's delinquency composition.

FACTORS AND INGREDIENTS OF A CREDIT OPTION-ADJUSTED SPREAD PROCESS

The concept of "Credit OAS" refers to an extension of the OAS method that involves an explicit model of credit events–delinquencies, defaults and losses– and their influence on cash flows. In other words, instead of generating loss-free cash flow for an MBS and discounting this cash flow with a purposely-inflated "credit spread," we delve into full credit modeling of the underlying collateral. For structured deals, the losses are translated into a tranche's write-downs and interest shortfalls. The cash flows generated this way are finally discounted using discount rates plus OAS that is similar in level to the OAS of credit-perfect instruments.

A well-designed valuation system should employ random factors that follow risk-neutral dynamics. Randomization of future events in our case must include prepayments, defaults and losses, rate resets and deal triggers. In particular, market randomness leads to random losses, that is, we will simulate the loss' probability distribution. On the other hand, subjective views of these probabilities by a particular empirical modeler will rarely generate accurate market prices. Empirical modeling, fair or biased, lacks the market price of risk. As we showed for the mortgage insurance example, the expected loss is only a part of the insurance premium. This leads to the problem of defining risk-neutral conditions imposed on the factors' behavior that we discuss throughout the chapter.

Market factors employed for this modeling certainly include, but are not limited to, interest rates. Interpretation of the default option as a put on property suggests that a relevant home-price indicator (index) must be included too. Another good candidate would be the unemployment rate because borrowers who lost their income may likely become delinquent. For example, a Deutsche Bank model presented by Patruno et al. (2006) employs a joint simulation of these three factors. A list of relevant economic factors can be long, but even if they all were known, the default and losses could only be predicted approximately. This simple example illustrates that a model's systematic error (bias) represents an important risk factor itself. It is not a random oscillation of outcomes around modeled forecasts that the market needs to price–they are diversified over time. Nor is it the deviations of a single loan's behavior from the average, which is diversified in large pools. It is the risk that a model understates the default rates and losses systematically that concerns investors.

In our work at AD&Co, we consider it most practical to use interest rates and home prices as key factors in Credit OAS. We clearly realize the need to employ a risk-neutral model for prepayments, defaults, and losses, but this goal can and should be reached via the alteration of a reasonably well-designed empirical model. The theoretical argument we made in chapter 4 and in our works on prepayment risk-neutrality, as explained in chapter 11, is that a risky return generated by any factor (e.g., a model's parameter) can be exactly replicated via altering this factor's drift (or value). Therefore, a risk-neutral transformation can be done via model's "tuning" to market prices of MBS benchmarks. Figure 13.1 presents main ingredients of the Credit OAS approach.

All OAS systems designed for MBS use some type of risk-neutral models of the interest rate term structure. Term structure modeling is a well-developed area of financial engineering; a good model should be calibrated to market instruments (rates, options) that are relevant to the MBS funding and optionality. We explained various forms of risk-neutral term structure modeling in chapters 5 and 6. A Home-Price Appreciation (HPA) model was also discussed in chapter 6, with a link to the market of forwards and futures on residential property indices. In the absence of the forward market, one can start from a physical HPA model described further in chapter 14. Modeling borrowers' default and losses constituted the essence of chapter 12. We focus the remainder of this chapter on the specifics of valuation, the risk-neutralization process, and the results one should anticipate from using a Credit OAS approach.

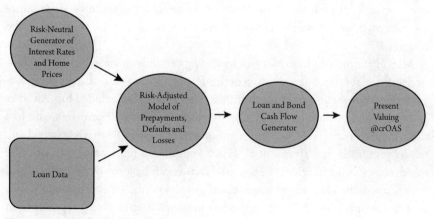

Figure 13.1 Credit OAS Method

SETTING UP THE CREDIT OPTION-ADJUSTED SPREAD CALCULATIONS AND MONTE CARLO RECIPES

Once we define a "risk-neutral" evolution of interest rates and home prices, along with cash flows $CF(t)$ contingent upon these processes, the economic value of a T-maturity instrument is defined according to the continuous-finance formula (4.4d) of chapter 4, which we reproduce below with minor notation changes and assuming no remaining balance at time T:

$$p = E \int_0^T [c(t) - d(t) - R(t)] e^{y(t)} dt \qquad (13.1)$$

where

$$dy = -(R + \lambda) dt,$$

$$R = r + crOAS$$

In this formula, p denotes price premium (or discount), c is the coupon rate, d is the loss rate, λ is total amortization rate that includes both prepayments and defaults. Finally, $crOAS$ stands for "Credit OAS," i.e. residual discount spread. Despite the name, $crOAS$ does not carry credit risk anymore because we impair the cash flow explicitly; it is merely a measure of technical conditions (financing or liquidity) or mispricing. Calculations of economic values using $crOAS$ as well as iterating for $crOAS$ using known prices is done via formula (13.1). Generally, instruments traded at a wider $crOAS$ are considered "cheap." Exposure to interest rates and HPA rates will be measured using a constant $crOAS$.

Formula (13.1) can be interpreted as the pricing formula for a regular, non-amortizing, non-defaulting, bond that pays the coupon of $c + \lambda - d$ in the economy functioning under a $r + \lambda$ risk-free rate. Therefore, the amortization rate λ is additive to both the paid rate and the discount rate whereas the loss rate d is subtracted from the paid rate—as we would expect. A bond will be valued at par, regardless of the interest rates and amortization, if it pays a perfect floater, $c = r + m$, indexed to the short rate r with the margin m exactly equal to the expected loss rate d. This is the case of most subprime MBS deals at origination. Once the expectation of losses or liquidity (reflected in $crOAS$) change, the bond will be valued at premium or discount, which become a function of interest rates and amortization. The loss stream itself is valued at

$$L = E \int_0^T d(t) e^{y(t)} dt \qquad (13.2)$$

If all the rates are constants and the instrument is perpetuity, then the integrals are taken easily:

$$P \equiv p+1 = \frac{\lambda+c-d}{\lambda+r+crOAS}, \quad L = \frac{d}{\lambda+r+crOAS}$$

The number of mathematical "states" describing the interest rates, home prices, credit model and cash flows is rather high, making random simulations the only candidate for a credit OAS pricing scheme. The number of random "forces" is limited to those driving interest rates, the HPA diffusion and the HPA jumps (introduced in chapter 6, but explained in further detail in chapter 14). For example, the use of a single-factor term-structure model and a national home-price index (HPI) will ultimately require us to simulate three random shocks concurrently. Because many non-agency MBS are complex in structure and cash flow rules and backed by heterogeneous collateral groups, realistic applications of the credit OAS method limit the number of paths severely. We have revisited the Monte Carlo recipes introduced and proven useful in chapter 9. We compared the accuracy of three main methods: rate fudging, antithetic reflection, and ortho-normalization (moment-matching), as well as their combinations. For reader's convenience, below is a brief summary of those methods.

Antithetic reflection splits all random shocks into "odd" and "even," with one group being a mirror reflection of another. If w_1, w_2, ... are random shocks applied for the first path of any economic variable, for period 1, 2, etc., then we apply $-w_1$, $-w_2$, ... for the second path. The method guarantees a symmetric distribution and no bias in shocks, but achieves these features by making only half of the paths truly independent.

Paths "fudging." Using some rudimentary theoretical information (such as the knowledge of market's discount factors) one can add artificial adjustments to the random processes that "center" them on correct values. Consider, for example, a Monte Carlo method for interest-rate derivatives. Adding a "fudge factor" to the short-rate paths to ensure exact values for the discount factors is a simple and effective technique. Similarly, adjustments can be made to long rates and shocks generated for the HPA diffusion and jumps. In comparison to antithetic reflection, this method does not double the number of random paths although does not result in theoretical symmetry of the sample.

Ortho-normalization of random shocks. If shocks are scaled to 1 and made orthogonal to each other, we ensure that the random paths follow the correct volatility patterns, which is critical for option pricing. This technique can be classified as the moment matching as per Glasserman (2004). We first start with random numbers, then apply the Gram-Schmidt method to transform them into properly scaled, serially independent samples. All the second moments, the standard deviation of every variable, in particular, exactly match theoretical levels. Shocks used to generate the interest rates, the HPA diffusion, and the HPA jumps, are not correlated with one another (of course, the HPA process is linked to the interest-rate process by construction). The number of paths required to achieve ortho-normalization of all the shocks should, at least, be equal to the number of shocks. For example, when using 34 branching points for the short rate, HPA diffusion and HPA jump, we must generate 102 or more random paths, to achieve a full ortho-normalization. If we combine this method with antithetic reflection, the required number of paths should double. If the number of paths is chosen to be small, one can apply a limited-length ortho-normalization to some number of the nearest branching points.

Comparison of Monte Carlo Methods

Figure 13.2 illustrates comparison of loan valuation accuracy obtained by different methods. We considered subprime loans differing in credit-quality impairment (FICO score), originated in December 2007 with Loan-To-Value Ratio (LTV) of 90% thereby facing considerable losses in the housing market's downturn. We averaged the results and, as in chapter 9, presented them with the axes drawn to the log-2 scale. We can see that ortho-normalization brings the strongest benefits followed by antithetic reflection and rate fudging, which is not very influential. This ranking contrasts to the similar comparison presented

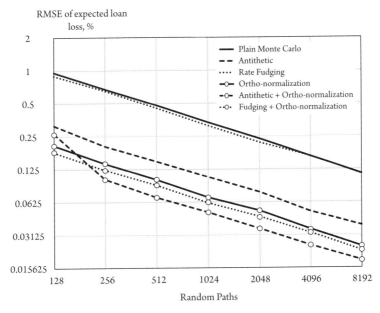

Figure 13.2 Comparative Accuracy of Loan Valuation with Losses

in chapter 9 for agency TBAs where ortho-normalization was shown to be the weakest force of the three. Rate fudging was found to be a good method for TBAs where there are no losses and exact discounting is important. This is not the case with credit analysis when the promised principal and interest may not be paid and the loss expectation is more important than discounting.

Seed shuffling. If all we need is to assess expected loss or the price of a large loan portfolio, there is a very simple and effective method: Use a few Monte Carlo paths per position but start each position's run from a random seed. It turns out that, from the portfolio's standpoint, this approach is equivalent in accuracy to many independent Monte Carlo runs. The efficiency depends on the homogeneity of loans. Imagine, for example, that collateral is made of 1,000 perfectly identical loans. Then, running two random paths per loan seeded randomly is equivalent to running 2,000 random paths, from the portfolio standpoint. In contrast, running two random, but *same*, paths per loan, is no different than running only two paths for portfolio. Even if loans are somewhat heterogeneous, using random seeding will be as accurate for each loan, and more accurate for the portfolio's summary than using same-seeding. Furthermore, if the collateral was made of one million loans (rather than one thousand), we might even extend our faith in Monte Carlo and, instead of running two randomly seeded paths per each loan, apply them to few thousand randomly chosen loans.

Table 13.1 demonstrates that using just few paths per loan, *different* for each loan, allows us to assess the expected losses rather accurately for both 1749 fixed-rate loans and 2546 ARMs of the subprime CWH07008 deal issued by

Table 13.1 Monte-Carlo Convergence (Expected Losses) for CWH07008

A. At Origination

Accurate	Fixed-Rate Loans 6.928		Adjustable-Rate Loans 6.107	
	Random seed	Same seed	Random seed	Same seed
100 paths per loan	6.933	6.901	6.111	6.074
20 paths per loan	6.977	6.857	6.122	6.069
10 paths per loan	6.983	6.727	6.139	5.936
2 paths per loan	6.876	5.495	6.068	5.301

B. In 2011

Accurate	Fixed-Rate Loans 46.989		Adjustable-Rate Loans 52.590	
	Random seed	Same seed	Random seed	Same seed
100 paths per loan	46.534	46.175	52.279	52.222
20 paths per loan	47.456	48.269	52.934	53.473
10 paths per loan	47.270	42.718	52.743	48.472
2 paths per loan	45.652	42.950	52.239	49.259

Countrywide in 2007. In contrast, using few, but *same*, paths for each loan is less accurate.

This "seed-shuffling" method benefits from error diversification—much like investing in many independent stocks. It also suggests that a typical senior manager's dream of seeing every position priced "consistently" against same set of paths will likely reduce the accuracy in risk measurements. Unless positions need to be accurately valued themselves and versus each other (e.g., asset versus hedge, specified pool versus TBA), using same paths for every position is not computationally advantageous. When measuring duration, convexity and other Greeks, we must keep the initial seed unchanged, but can change it going from one position to another.

Loan clustering. Analyzing very large loan cohorts or structured deals using a loan-level Monte Carlo is computationally costly. The best assessment of losses and their distribution does require loan-level modeling, but there are alternatives to a direct stochastic simulation of each line item. Instead, we can first employ a single market scenario to compute prepayments, default and losses, for every loan. Using these measures ("scores") we can cluster loans so that they are grouped into few internally homogeneous groups. In a very simple case, we can use the lone loss score and create two loan groups–similar to "active" and "passive" groups of the APD prepayment model (see chapter 7).

Clustering is a field that lies between computer sciences and statistics. It employs both established theoretical facts and proven numerical processes (usually, iterations). For example, the optimal cluster is such that each loan is "closer" to its own center (called "centroid") than to other centers. Our study, which is beyond the scope of this book, proves that using only two loan groups clustered by the loss score that comes from a simple static analysis is a reasonable method. If we ran a full Monte Carlo with this two-group surrogate, we would assess collateral's loss distribution with suitable 3–5% accuracy. A three-group formation warrants further accuracy improvement, albeit a rather moderate one. In contrast, using only one cluster, i.e. the single weighted-average line leads to an unsatisfactorily large error of 20–25% and more. Since default and loss rates are usually non-linear functions of loan characteristics, loan aggregation may require using certain "convexity adjustment" rules.

WHERE DOES RISK-NEUTRAL DISTRIBUTION OF LOSSES COME FROM?

Risk-neutralization of a loss model, i.e. embedding necessary market risks and expectations, is a challenging problem. Unlike the agency MBS market, full of actively traded instruments (TBAs, specified pools, IO/PO strips, many CMO tranches), the non-agency MBS market is much sparser, less liquid, and exposed to more risk factors. The risk is not limited to interest rates, but includes home prices and related economic factors that may trigger borrowers decisions (like employment). Even if the rate process and the home-price processes are properly risk-adjusted, the loss model itself remains a source of risk. This uncertainty is similar to the one we described in chapter 11 for agency prepayment modeling.

This section essentially considers three alternatives in risk-neutralizing loss models:

- Using HPI derivatives markets (introduced in chapter 6)
- Applying a concept of capital charge (introduced in chapter 4)
- Deriving an implied model using ABX prices

The first two methods have already been introduced in mathematical details and we will review them briefly. The third option is perhaps the most important one and will be discussed at length below.

Home-Price Appreciation Derivative Markets

One developing source of home-price risk neutrality is the real estate derivatives' markets that we described in chapter 6. These markets (if they grow sufficiently large) could be used by mortgage insurers and GSEs, MBS investors and CDS protection sellers, and homebuilders to hedge exposures to home prices as well as to speculate. In order to execute hedge strategies, an HPA hedge ratio has to be measured first. Much like in the case of interest-rate risk, the Credit OAS method should deliver all the relevant Greeks.

In chapter 6, we demonstrated how to construct a risk-neutral HPI process using today's continuous forward curve $F(0, T)$ and forward volatility function $\sigma(t, T)$. The derivations assumed continuous trading in time and expiration. Despite its mathematical attractiveness, this approach stands on an unrealistic foundation in practice. Given the weakness and illiquidity of HPI derivative markets, most of the information necessary for risk-neutralization of the HPI process needs to be borrowed from an empirical model, as the one to be introduced in chapter 14. In fact, it is most convenient to start from an empirical model and tune it so that the forward curve implied by that model would pass through traded points. It may require alignments of both short-term and long-term HPAs.

Even if it is feasible to risk-neutralize an HPI process, this step does not exhaust all dimensions of uncertainties. The market's view of losses may differ from anyone's subjective view, both in physical expectation and in adding the price of risk.

Therefore, having risk-neutral processes of interest rates and home prices may be insufficient for the Credit OAS method to function accurately.

Capital Charge and Loss-Distribution Method

In chapter 4, we introduced a risk adjustment method that draws on the economics of loan insurance, in the absence of hedging instruments. We considered the position of a loan insurer (limited insurance coverage), GSE (unlimited insurance) or CDS protection seller that is interested in estimating the premium (p) that needs to be charged to make the business profitable. The insurer must charge more than the expectation of losses (μ) in the real world. By definition, insurance provides protection against worse-than-average events, so capital (c) must be maintained to back the obligation. This capital must stand ready and can earn only the risk-free rate (r), which is much less than a return on capital target (R). We further assumed that the insurance covers some maximal rate of loss, l_{max}. This consideration has led to the following answer:

$$p(1+r)=\mu+(l_{max}-\mu)\frac{R-r}{1+R} \qquad (13.3)$$

Formula (13.3) gives us the insurance premium that minimizes the insurer's capital. This is a risk-adjusted price of credit losses stated in the form of "expected loss plus capital charge." It allows for a convenient practical adaptation of the risk-neutral modeling method. Imagine that loss is a linear function of a random variable x, be it a home-price index or another risk factor, $l(x) = \mu + x$, within reasonable range of values of that factor; assume x is centered on zero. Let us further assume that the coverage is stated as a number k of standard deviations of x, i.e. $l_{max} - \mu \equiv k\sigma_x$. Hence, formula (13.3) can be rewritten as

$$p(1+r)=\mu+k\sigma_x\frac{R-r}{1+R} \qquad (13.3')$$

Let us introduce a new risk factor $\tilde{x}=x+k\sigma_x(R-r)/(1+R)$, i.e. simply shift the distribution of x by a constant. Now, with x replaced by $\tilde{x}$, the loss expectation of $l(\tilde{x})$ will be exactly equal to the expression $(13.3')$. As in other places of the book where we employed this method, its practical power comes from the fact that one does not need to know every parameter entering the formula, i.e. R, r, k, μ and σ_x. The loans' quality or characteristics do not enter this transformation either, which is performed over the risk factor. Nor would it matter whether we value loan losses or any of their derivatives (MBS tranches, ABX).

We simply need to find p from the insurance market; that p becomes discounted risk-neutral loss-rate $l(t)$.

This great practical convenience comes at a cost: Assumptions we had to make may be unreliable. Mortgage insurance quotes may not be widely available and, in case of GSE guarantees, do not represent efficient markets; investors may not find the cost of mortgage insurance perfectly correlating with expectation of MBS losses. However, the method may be suitable for finding the economic value of illiquid financial instruments, or when it is hard to find an established security benchmark market.

Implied Versus Modeled Distributions of Losses

As we mentioned at the beginning of the chapter, to assess expected credit losses to any ABS, the entire probability distribution of collateral has to be known. First, we attempt to recover the loss distribution using prices of tranches via the Gauthier (2003) scenario grid method. We work with nine different classes, M1 through M9 of the CWH07008 subprime deal that were priced by the market in May of 2007. We then construct 20 credit scenarios, ranging from ultimately optimistic (no new defaults) to unreasonably pessimistic. Our assumptions about prepayment scale, default and loss severity rates for every scenario are somewhat arbitrary, but appeal to financial intuition, although is not based on any model. For example, we couple lower prepayment scales with higher default rates; the exact definition of the credit scenario grid should not affect our results materially. For each credit scenario, we run a usual OAS model that involves stochastic interest rates and prepayments, but apply constant default and loss severity rates. Since we account for losses directly by altering the cash flows, the OAS level we employ should match that of agency MBS adjusted with appropriately chosen liquidity difference. At the end of this step, we computed the entire scenario-by-tranche pricing matrix; it is schematically shown in Figure 13.3 (with OAS set to 50 basis points for all nine tranches).

We then start interpreting credit scenarios as random, having certain probabilities that total 100%. With this view in mind, the price of each tranche will certainly be equal to the probability-weighted scenario prices. We finally find an optimal probability distribution of our credit scenarios so that the computed prices best approximate known market quotes. Instead of assigning each scenario an independent probability value, we may prefer to parameterize the distribution using the Vasicek loss model (1987, 1991) or our adaptation called "3-part Vasicek model" explained further in chapter 15. Figure 13.3 shows the optimal probability; most tranches came out reasonably close to the actual market prices (average root-mean-squared error is just 0.43%).

	Scales in order of increasing losses							Tranches' OAS Prices			
Scenario	default	severity	prepay	delinquency	recovery	cumulative loss %	Optimal probability	M1	M2	...	M9
1	0.00	0.00	1.00	0.00	1.0	0.00%	0.00%	100.495	100.586	...	108.690
2	0.25	0.94	0.95	0.50	1.0	1.46%	1.03%	100.469	100.560	...	108.632
3	0.50	0.96	0.90	0.60	1.0	2.97%	9.02%	100.441	100.531	...	108.470
4	0.75	0.98	0.85	0.80	1.0	4.55%	19.73%	100.445	100.532	...	107.271
5	1.00	1.00	0.80	1.00	1.0	6.20%	16.30%	100.433	100.477	...	106.907
6	1.10	1.02	0.78	1.05	1.0	7.01%	8.91%	100.642	100.751	...	113.392
7	1.20	1.04	0.75	1.10	1.0	7.85%	8.16%	100.522	100.765	...	121.313
8	1.30	1.06	0.73	1.15	1.0	8.73%	7.21%	100.523	100.735	...	122.864
9	1.40	1.08	0.70	1.20	1.0	9.64%	6.18%	100.535	100.757	...	101.670
10	1.50	1.10	0.68	1.25	1.0	10.60%	5.17%	100.549	100.791	...	59.592
11	1.60	1.12	0.65	1.30	1.0	11.60%	4.22%	100.565	100.834	...	38.608
12	1.70	1.14	0.63	1.35	1.0	12.64%	3.38%	100.583	100.887	...	30.724
13	1.80	1.16	0.60	1.40	1.0	13.72%	2.67%	100.603	100.950	...	27.710
14	1.90	1.18	0.58	1.45	1.0	14.84%	2.07%	100.629	101.022	...	25.870
15	2.00	1.20	0.55	1.50	1.0	16.00%	3.66%	100.665	101.096	...	24.480
16	2.50	1.22	0.53	1.55	1.0	18.65%	1.90%	100.772	95.375	...	21.238
17	3.00	1.24	0.50	1.60	1.0	20.99%	0.33%	100.3593	52.815	...	19.195
18	3.50	1.26	0.48	1.65	1.0	23.07%	0.05%	85.522	23.295	...	17.679
19	4.00	1.28	0.45	1.70	1.0	24.94%	0.01%	50.708	19.500	...	16.474
20	5.00	1.30	0.40	1.80	1.0	27.71%	0.00%	20.263	16.820	...	14.798
					Probability Weighted	7.84%	100.00%	100.506	100.370	...	93.042
					Quoted Market Price			99.973	99.860	...	93.167
					Mispricing			0.532	0.510	...	-0.125

optimize

minimize

per bond mispricing	0.43

Figure 13.3 Implied Default Model Setup (May 2007)

So far, our exercise has not involved the method of Credit OAS; we simply inferred loss probabilities from bond prices. Let us now apply the Credit OAS method and measure the loss distribution coming from it. Moreover, we are interested in changing characteristics of the model in such a way as to approximate the distribution shown in Figure 13.3. In order to find the closest match, we may need to tune a number of parameters of the model such as HPA model dials, a default rate scale, a severity scale, etc. To simplify, we restrict our interference with only one dial; Figure 13.4 depicts the distribution of losses arising from using different long-term HPA rates. Had we lowered the long-term level of HPA to about 2%, the distribution of losses would have somewhat approached to the implied distribution. This is an important result attesting feasibility of our approach. In short, a stochastic world presented by our Credit OAS model is easily deformable to an adequate market view of the distribution of losses, at the time of analysis.

Having established the risk-neutral transformation, we can use it for other ABS deals. At first glance, the level of 2% long-term HPA rate may seem modest. Upon deeper review, it does not appear to be erroneous. First, we expected the risk-neutral HPA assumption to be worse than what can be gleaned from empirical expectation: it must include the price of risk, which we quantify in the next section. Second, we should attribute some of the pessimism of the 2007 market to short-term forecasts, which we left unaltered in this case study. Had we

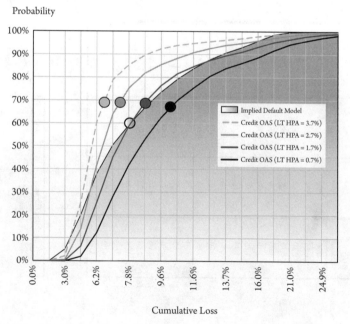

Figure 13.4 Risk-Neutralization of Loss Distribution in Credit OAS (May 2007)

included the short-term HPA into our best-fit search, we would have certainly come up with a more optimistic long-term HPA. The tuning recommendations, however, change with the market as demonstrated in the next section.

CALIBRATION TO DISTRESSED ABX PRICES

The example using tranche prices for inferring collateral loss distribution that we presented in the previous section, assumed a known crOAS level of 50 basis points. Such an approach is suitable when the market is active, liquid and when financing can be easily obtained. We call the values derived using these assumptions *intrinsic values*. They represent the economic value of cash flows generated by an MBS adjusted for economic risks and cost of hedging, but not for technical factors such as illiquidity and lack of financing. In mid-2007, the non-agency market started to lose liquidity and investors were no longer able to obtain necessary financing. Not only did this development inflate the crOAS levels, *it made them unknown.*

We now demonstrate how both implied loss distribution *and* crOAS can be calibrated to market prices using a case study of the SASC 2006-BC4 subprime deal, a member of the ABX 07-1 index. We compare valuation of its four tranches that differ in credit protection, a senior tranche (A5) and three mezzanines (M2, M5, M8) on September 28, 2007.

With the regular OAS method, the losses are not regarded at all, so that the OAS metric "absorbs" them. With the Credit OAS method, we simulate prepayments, defaults, and losses via AD&Co's Loan Dynamics Model (LDM) introduced in chapter 12, and apply two loss-controlled tunings— the short-term HPA rate and the long-term HPA rate of the HPA stochastic simulator explained further in chapter 14. In performing this analysis, we pursued a meaningful pattern of liquidity spreads across the deal's tranches and in essence determined the collateral loss distribution endogenously. We assumed that crOAS (i.e., the technical spread left after economic risks are fully accounted for) should be comparable across the deal's tranches, perhaps, somewhat wider for the junior, less liquid, bonds. We did not, however, say in advance, what crOAS should be.

THE METHOD
Our approach can be conceptualized as the following. For N instruments taken from *the same deal* we have N known market prices $P(i)$, hence, N equations:

$$F[crOAS(i), Collateral\,Loss] = P(i), \quad i = 1, \ldots, N$$

with $N + 1$ unknowns: N levels of crOAS and one common *Collateral Loss* factor that affects random distribution of losses. Of course, the exact timing of loss can be another factor, which may play some role (i.e. *Collateral Loss* may be formalized as a vector of factors), but this is not essential for the conceptual understanding of our approach. We add $N - 1$ economic conditions such as $crOAS(1) = crOAS(2) = \cdots = crOAS(N)$, or, more generally, postulate an appropriate relationship that reflects market liquidity and financing conditions.

We now have $2N-1$ equations with only $N + 1$ unknowns. We may deem the market's quotes reasonable, if we can solve this over-defined system with reasonable accuracy. Note that if $N = 1$, the problem is actually under-defined (i.e., we can't separate liquidity from credit for 1 tranche) and, if $N = 2$, the solution will be exact.

The method allows us to

a) judge the reasonableness of market quotes,
b) separate technical factors from credit losses, and
c) construct intrinsic values from market quotes thereby avoiding a subjective view of losses.

RESULTS

Table 13.2 attests the completion of our goals. With the short-term HPA of −11.5% and the long-term HPA of 4.7%, the crOAS came out in comparable size among the four tranches generally following the pattern of our technical preference, with accuracy.

It is important to realize that we were not at liberty to alter the HPA assumptions considerably, nor were the LDM-produced loss assumptions critical. In essence, we relied on the fact that the A5 tranche was not expected to lose, whereas the M5 and M8 tranches were very sensitive to loss assumptions. Hence, the system of equations we considered in the process of calibration indeed had a realistic-looking solution.

With the loss model properly tuned, we can apply a crOAS of 50 bps to produce the intrinsic values (last column in Table 13.2). One can view this modest crOAS as the historical pre-crisis level reflective of normal liquidity and funding. The difference between the computed intrinsic marks and the market prices can be interpreted as "technical distress"; it varied from 6 to 20 pricing points.

The mark-to-market method looks magically attractive because it starts with actual market prices that reflect an impaired market's technicalities and ends up with economic values, with a moderate use of modeling assumptions. It is somewhat time-consuming, however, as the loss assumptions of a deal must be endogenously calibrated to market prices. In chapter 15, we introduce a shorter path

Table 13.2 Valuation Measures of SASC 2006-BC4 (September 28, 2007)

Tranche	Market Price	OAS (no loss)	Calibrated Credit OAS Model		
			crOAS	PV of loss	Intrinsic Value*
A5	92.27	312	254	0	98.80
M2	75.43	737	511	2.1	95.83
M5	65.44	876	378	17.3	76.96
M8	37.13	2,030	480	57.6	53.11

*Intrinsic value is computed at $crOAS = 50$ bps.

using a Vasicek-like theoretical distribution. Historical time series of intrinsic values for the tranches of the SAS06BC4 deal can be found in Levin (ADPN Oct. 2008). Applications of risk-neutralization using ABX prices to different historical periods are found in Levin and Davidson (2008) and Levin (ADPN Feb. 2009, Apr. 2009).

WHY DO WE NEED CREDIT OPTION-ADJUSTED SPREAD?

The concept of Credit OAS revolves around coupled simulations of interest rates and home prices. It is imperative for explaining prices of traded ABS, CDS, and loan protections rationally. The Credit OAS approach requires a risk-neutral stochastic model of home prices, a model of defaults and losses (theoretical or empirical), and a rigorous and efficient valuation scheme. The risk-neutral assumptions can be derived from concurrently observed prices of ABS tranches up and down the credit structure. An attractive alternative is to provide theoretical premiums for GSE loan guarantees, mortgage insurance, or CDS based on expected losses and capital requirements. Once the risk-neutral model is established, it can be used to price other credit-sensitive instruments ("derivatives").

The model can be employed for both liquid and illiquid markets. Even distressed-market prices can be explained by a combination of modeled losses (under risk-neutral interest rates and home prices) and a properly selected credit OAS level, that is, technical spread. Next we summarize what one can expect from using a Credit OAS modeling framework.

Loan Values and Losses

Borrower default is an option. This option's pay-off is convex with respect to economic factors such as home prices. In other words, we should expect a larger average loss in a stochastic simulation relative to a single economic scenario (forward curve, determinist HPI). This "stochastic loss ratio" will always be above 1.0 and can be as much as 5.0 for loans originated in volatile geographical areas (e.g., California, see further in chapter 20). Naturally, the Credit OAS method will produce a lower loan value than a single-scenario view.

Loan aggregation for the purpose of credit analysis should be done with care and may result in a severe bias. An "average" loan taken from a good-quality pool is likely to understate losses produced using the full loan-level analysis because most losses may come from the *worst* loans.[2]

VALUES AND LOSSES OF MORTGAGE-BASED SECURITIES TRANCHES

In order to explain market quotes for tranches taken from the same deal, a stochastic framework is necessary. Much like in the loan case, there is a non-linear relationship between expected principal write-downs and economic factors. However, a loan default resembles a regular *put option* on property and its payoff gradually rises with home prices falling. In contrast, many MBS tranches resemble *digital options*: principal losses are either not taken at all or taken in full. For mezzanine and other thin tranches, the distance between life and death is a short one: Once they start losing principal, they may lose it all quickly.

Digital options are also non-linear in the underlying factors, but their convexity is determined by the option's "moneyness." In-the-money options are negatively convex whereas out-of-the-money options are positively convex. This concept can be easily employed to interpret Credit OAS results. Senior, well protected, tranches will look worse under the Credit OAS valuation whereas junior tranches will look better in comparison to the traditional single-scenario analysis. As a senior tranche may not lose any principal at all in the single-scenario, its losses become possible when economic conditions deteriorate. In contrast, junior tranches may be projected to lose their entire principal in the single scenario, but may save some of it if home prices improve. Of course, "senior" and "junior" classes should be treated relative to the economic environment. At the height of the credit crisis (first quarter of 2009), many non-agency MBS tranches were projected to lose principal and some original "senior" classes were viewed as almost certainly losing it.

---

[2]For a very bad quality pool, the effect of aggregation can theoretically be opposite, as most borrowers are expected to default and there are few better ones that will not. However, such deals almost never get securitized because issuers would rather create "barbells" that underperform the averages.

THE GREEKS

The Greeks will depend strongly on the modeling details (such as the link between interest rates and home prices), vary widely from model to model, and will unlikely be close to the measures computed using the traditional OAS approach. The following factors extend interest-rate dependence (Effective Duration) of non-agency MBS.

A. The S-curve of the refinancing model. For agency MBS, the S-curve determines whether principal cash flow will be paid sooner or later. For non-agencies, it often determines whether principal cash flow will be paid or lost: The more likely borrowers can refinance their loans, the less likely they are to default. In a high-rate environment, losses are more likely to occur and non-agency MBS values will decline more than those for a comparable agency MBS.

B. Dependence of home prices on interest rates. If we assume that the two major factors are negatively correlated for the lifespan of credit events, losses will grow faster with interest rates and Effective Duration will naturally increase. Should we be making the opposite conjecture, the full interest-rate sensitivity will be lower. The negative correlation is documented and featured in the HPI model introduced in chapter 14; it can be explained by an affordability argument. Nevertheless, there were periods when rate were rising due to economic improvements thereby confusing the matter.

These examples show that the full MBS exposure to interest rate may be difficult to know. The authors found a great deal of disagreement in the investors community over how Effective Duration for non-agency MBS should be measured and what modeling assumptions have to be made. However, the interest-rate hedging dilemma may be not as difficult to resolve. Well-protected deals and tranches will not be very sensitive to the home-price dependence on interest rates. Those that will be, may be more severely exposed to credit risk itself than to the interest-rate level. They may not even need a rate-risk hedging as it will not reduce the overall risk materially. We discuss priority of risk factors further in chapter 19.

C. The role of crOAS level. Even with losses explicitly modeled, the levels of crOAS found after risk-neutralization of losses will be typically larger than those for agency MBS. In other words, due to illiquidity and financing restrictions, non-agency MBS will be additionally discounted. This causes a possible duration's extension effect, similar to A above. When rates rise and pool's life extend, the same crOAS will cause a drop in value.

THE CREDIT OPTION-ADJUSTED SPREAD SIGNAL

The levels of crOAS (computed after necessary risk adjustments) is an indication of technical distress (liquidity and financing), but not a reflection of expected loss. In chapter 18, we will present historical analysis of crOAS for the SASC 2006-BC4 deal between 2007 and 2011, clearly showing that it spiked during the extreme lack of liquidity and financing (end of 2008) and not necessarily when the implied loss expectation peaked (March 2011). For the same reason, levels of crOAS found for prime, Alt-A, and subprime deals will not differ as much as their loss levels. The same is also true about senior, mezzanine, and junior tranches. The crOAS will differ only to the extent deals and tranches differ in non-modeled technical factors.

14

Empirical Modeling of Home Prices

The 2008–2009 financial crisis in the United States was triggered, in large part, by a housing price bubble that collapsed. Unsound mortgage programs caused massive borrower delinquencies and drastic losses to investors, while cash-constrained homeowners who had bet on refinancing or selling their homes at a profit became unable to do so. Hence, it is not an overstatement to view the value of residential properties as an enormously important economic indicator. In the previous chapter, we introduced the concept of Credit OAS for MBS valuation, using interest rates and home prices as two major factors.

Already in 2004–2005, leading economists generally agreed that the growth of home prices outpaced household income and rent. Shiller (2005, 2008) expressed concerns that the country's mindset "over-encouraged" home ownership and warned of an upcoming collapse. Interestingly enough, his prediction, while correct in principal and directionality, was not correct on the timing of when this would happen. Similarly, unlike many others on Wall Street, Weaver (2007) overall correctly predicted the decline of home prices between mid-2007 and mid-2008. However, her main argument—the ratio of mortgage payments to household income exceeded its historical equilibrium—could be made in the 1970s and 1980s when a severe lack of affordability had not led to a housing market decline.

One lesson we learned from these examples is that one should regard home prices as random processes; modeling these processes is the subject of this chapter. As we established in the previous chapter, producing a model that can be used to value MBS requires considering a range of possible outcomes, not just a single path. In fact, our approach to modeling HPI has similarities (and dissimilarities) to models for other assets, as we discuss further. Home prices are volatile, and the realized volatility has a unique pattern and carries important information.

Home-price modeling can use purely economic reasoning, statistical evidence, or it can be tied to traded-financial contracts thereby becoming "risk-neutral." In the United States, such contracts became available to both risk management and speculation in 2006 (Case-Shiller futures) and 2007 (Radar Logic's PRX forwards). Taking a bet on the direction of home prices does not require buying or selling residential properties anymore. One can simply take a long or a short position in an index in the form of a futures contract (even an option) or an over-the-counter forward contract. Their use in risk-neutral home-price modeling was explained in chapter 6.

If HPI forwards and futures can be viewed as vanilla contracts, losses in residential loans and in MBS should be viewed as "exotic" derivatives. From a practical standpoint, the interpretation of MBS as derivatives of home prices may at best indicate the direction of informational flow; the US MBS market is huge and incomparable in size and importance to the tiny market of explicitly traded HPI derivatives. Rather than viewing HPI models in isolation, the modeling approach we describe here is just a part of more general non-agency MBS valuation and affects our focus on HPI modeling. For our purposes, the two-to-five-year horizon of home prices matters the most for assessing the MBS default option since borrowers who establish a long unblemished payment history rarely default.

HISTORICAL PROPERTIES OF HPI AND HPA

The Diffusion + White Noise Pattern of the HPA

If we take an HPI index, compute periodic returns and annualize them, we obtain the Home-Price Appreciation (HPA) measure. The U.S. HPA rate published by Federal Housing Finance Agency (FHFA) is shown in Figure 14.1 going back to 1975. Along with the national HPA, we depict the behavior of the MBS current-coupon rate.

The purpose of showing both indices on the same plot is two-fold: to assess a visual correlation (if any), and to compare the two distinctly different types of dynamics. It is clear that the MBS rate is continuous whereas the HPA rate is not. The latter seems to contain random "jumps" or "shocks" that occur around otherwise continuously changing mean levels. A white noise + diffusion pattern seems to resemble the dynamics of the HPA rate reasonably well. We can prove this by measuring an empirical standard deviation function of horizon and an autocorrelation function of lag (Figure 14.2).

The bars in Figure 14.2 are taken from the empirical data; we compute these statistics for generally overlapping intervals, but with an adjustment for actual degrees of freedom.

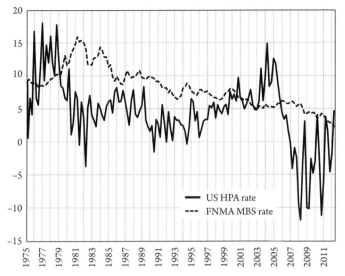

Figure 14.1 The FHFA US HPA Rate versus the MBS Rate Since 1975
The MBS rate: Bloomberg (since 1984), extrapolated via 10-year CMT before 1984.

Had $HPA(t)$ been a continuous random process, both statistics would have been continuous functions. In reality, an apparent discontinuity exists between $t = 0$ and $t = 1$ that lets us statistically assess the size of random shocks. Without the white noise, it would not be possible to explain a sizable short-dated uncertainty in the HPA $(t = 1)$ and the drop in the autocorrelation function.

Lines in Figure 14.2 reflect the theoretical combination of white noise (normal "jumps" when observed in discrete time) and a first-order mean-reverting diffusion (JD1, punctured line) or a second-order mean-reverting diffusion (JD2, solid line). Let σ_d and σ_w be the volatility of the HPA diffusion and the magnitude of the white noise, respectively, and a be the diffusion's mean reversion. Then, the theoretical statistics for the JD1 pattern depicted in Figure 14.2 as a function of $t > 0$ are

$$stdev\left[HPA(t)\right] = \left[\sigma_d^2 \frac{1 - e^{-2at}}{2a} + \sigma_w^2\right]^{\frac{1}{2}}$$

$$Corr\left[HPA(T), HPA(t + T)\right] \underset{T \to \infty}{\to} e^{-at} \frac{1}{1 + 2a\sigma_w^2 / \sigma_d^2}$$

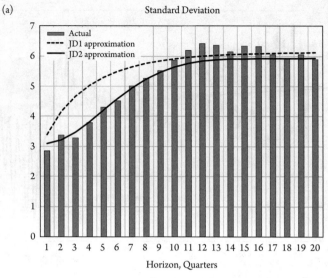

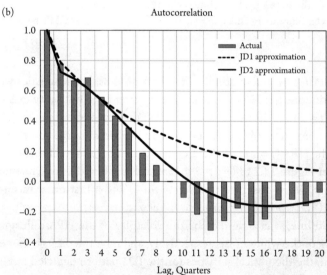

Figure 14.2 Empirical versus Theoretical Unconditional Statistics of the US HPA

Similarly, let the second-order diffusion have a pair of complex eigen-values, $\alpha \pm i\beta$ with a negative α. Then, the theoretical statistics for the JD2 pattern will be

$$stdev\left[HPA(t)\right]=\left\{\frac{\sigma_d^2}{4\beta^2}\left[\frac{e^{2\alpha t}-1}{\alpha}-\frac{\alpha\left(e^{2\alpha t}cos2\beta t-1\right)+\beta e^{2\alpha t}sin2\beta t}{\alpha^2+\beta^2}\right]+\sigma_w^2\right\}^{\frac{1}{2}}$$

$$Corr\left[HPA(T),HPA(t+T)\right] \xrightarrow[T\to\infty]{} \frac{e^{\alpha t}\left(cos\beta t - \frac{\alpha}{\beta}sin\beta t\right)}{1-4\alpha(\alpha^2+\beta^2)\sigma_w^2/\sigma_d^2}$$

As demonstrated by Figure 14.2, the JD2 model with optimally selected parameters approximates empirical standard deviation and autocorrelation well. Note that the empirical data exhibits an oscillatory behavior well matched by a second-order oscillator, but not feasible in the first-order model. For example, the empirical autocorrelation function turns negative for remote time lags suggesting an "overshooting" when responding to a disturbance in the initial condition. This cannot be observed in the JD1 model, the autocorrelation function of which is always positive. In the next two subsections, we attempt to explain the causes for the diffusion + white noise pattern and the oscillatory behavior.

Home Prices versus Dynamic Assets

The existence of immediate shocks in the HPA series should not be unexpected although seems to have eluded many researchers who tend to treat an HPA as a continuous process, a forecast of which can start from the last observation. Indeed, an HPA is the return rate of an HPI index. Recall that, in the real world, the log-price X of a diffusive asset should follow the stochastic differential equation,

$$dX = \mu dt + \sigma dz \tag{14.1}$$

where σ is volatility, μ is drift, and z is the Brownian motion. The latter is the integral of white noise (w), a mathematical limit for normally distributed, uncorrelated shocks. Let us denote the annualized return on X as $x = dX/dt$. Then

$$x = \mu + \sigma w \tag{14.2}$$

or "diffusion + white noise." The first term in (14.2) determines the expected return. The white noise is the source of the immediate randomness. Therefore, if the HPI's time series represents values of an asset or an index, its return rate (the HPA) must be compliant with the "diffusion + white noise" form. This proves that our modeling guess was a good one, and, when looking at Figure 14.1, our vision does not malfunction. It is now clear why the MBS rates shown in Figure 14.1 are continuous: They represent *expected* (not actual) returns on an MBS and are therefore chiefly diffusive.

We borrowed the dynamic asset's pricing setup to explain the discontinuous nature of an HPA. It does not mean that we must treat an HPI as a traded-and-stored asset nor the risk-neutral μ must be equal to the risk-free rate. In fact, we cannot trade a storable asset for an HPI value, a point that was explained in chapter 6.

The Oscillator Property

Why do the stochastic properties of historical HPA resemble those of an oscillator? Here is a rather simple economic postulate: Home prices cannot drift (lead or lag) away from other economic indicators forever. Hence, the direction of HPA depends on whether the HPI is too high or too low. Therefore, the first derivative of HPA should depend on the attained value of HPI (HPA's integral) thereby making the (HPA, HPI) system akin to the mechanical spring-and-mass oscillator $dx = \cdots -k(X - X_{eq})dt$ with $dX = xdt$. In this relationship, log-HPI (X) is a "coordinate" whereas HPA (x) is "speed." Without dampening and random terms, X will perpetually oscillate around its "equilibrium" (X_{eq}).

The best-fit JD2 model depicted in Figure 14.2 has a pair of $-0.38 \pm 0.77i$ (1/yr) complex eigen-values pointing to an 8.1-year periodicity with a 2.6-year time decay. It should be understood, however, that, once we specify the dynamics and role of the explicit economic factors (such as income and interest rates), the optimal parameters change.

The oscillatory-behavior model we advocate is rather different from the popular concept of "business cycles" that have haunted many economists. A stable two-dimensional system with complex eigen-roots has dampening forces (frictions); we cannot predict its phase without the knowledge of external forces. We do not at all suggest that peaks and troughs of an HPI can be predicted by cycles.

INFLATION, INTEREST RATES, AND THE CONCEPT OF "SOFT" EQUILIBRIUM

How do interest rates affect home prices? This question seems to be a puzzling one and has been answered differently by different researchers. First, let us start with an objective statistical measure, a cross-correlation function between the logarithm of total mortgage payment rate and the FHFA HPA rate measured as a function of time lag (Figure 14.3).

The correlation is apparently negative for the near term and turns positive for the long run. Here is our possible explanation of this dynamic: A decline in MBS

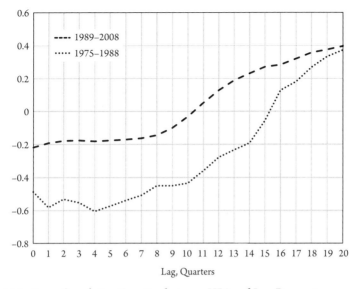

Figure 14.3 Cross-Correlation Function between HPA and Log-Payment

rate improves housing affordability, but is paired with reduced long-term inflation, hence, long-term HPA.

Note that Figure 14.3 depicts two lines for two non-overlapping historical intervals. The strength of the correlation has apparently changed historically. Recall
that the correlation is a measure of *linear* relationship for *stationary* processes.
With the changing relationship, the long-term correlation can be artificially low.
Had we depicted the 1975–2008 cross-correlations, we would have witnessed a
misleadingly low level that could have discouraged some analysts from looking
any further at the HPA dependence on interest rates. In fact, this relationship
exists and, *when stationary*, exhibits a steady pattern, proven by Figure 14.3.

Let us elaborate on the assumption that, over a long run, home prices cannot lead or lag other economic indicators, most importantly, household income.
Historical data seems to confirm this statement. During the 33-year period
(1975–2008), the FHFA HPI grew at the average annual rate of 5.33% whereas
the national household income grew only at a 4.37% rate. However, with declined
mortgage rates, the standard mortgage payments grew at a pace of only 4.11% per
year, i.e. close to income. Postulating that the loan payment should constitute a
constant part of the household income, we derive an equilibrium level of HPI
(denoted HPIeq) as (in logarithms)

$$HPIeq = Income - Payment\ Rate + const \qquad (14.3)$$

As we argue a little further, we may not need to know the constant to build a
decent model. Let us subtract Income from HPIeq and call this difference "real

HPI equilibrium." Relationship (14.3) suggests that the derivative of this measure with respect to time must offset the derivative of Payment Rate. This introduces the explicit relationship between the log of real equilibrium and the mortgage rate; it is nearly linear within a limited region of MBS rates. For example, with the base loan rate of 5% to 6%, a 1% shift causes approximately an 11% shock to the equilibrium. The relationship weakens somewhat as the loan rate gets higher.

How can HPIeq affect HPI? It is unlikely that the equilibrium, being a function of mortgage rates, can immediately affect HPI. Had it been this way, historical volatility of HPI would have been much higher. A more plausible assumption is that a change in mortgage rate immediately affects the *HPI equilibrium*, but not the *immediate HPI*. This disturbance will affect HPI gradually, after some transient process. When the mortgage rate and household income stay constant, the HPI equilibrium will not change.

Having postulated the existence of equilibrium, we face the challenge of determining it. How much of its disposable income should an average U.S. household allocate for mortgage payments? California pays more than the rest of the country, and mortgage originators use a higher underwriting threshold. While the right guess can very well be 30%, 35%, or 40%, this uncertainty itself points to a dramatic dispersion of HPI equilibrium effectively invalidating an otherwise well-designed HPI model. We show in the next section that one can "soften" the concept of equilibrium by accounting only for its dependence on changing interest rates and household income, but not the knowledge of a constant shown in formula (14.3). To put this simply, we will formulate a model that measures and employs only $dHPI_{eq}/dt$ and not HPI_{eq} itself.

Later in the book (see chapter 16) we demonstrate that the bubble and the collapse of the housing market in the US was triggered by a severe proliferation of affordable lending in 2002–2006 followed by its sudden death. Nevada, Arizona, California and Florida saw the most of this action and experienced the largest HPI decline. Not only does this explain the roots of the financial crisis that followed, but it also proves that the effective *financing rate*, be it conventionally published or actually computed, plays a role in the home-price dynamics we described above. Financing cost includes more than just loan payments, but we defer details until chapter 16.

THE HPA STOCHASTIC SIMULATOR

In this section, we formally describe our model's construct intended for physical modeling of HPA. We also review the necessary statistical technique. The next section discusses forecasts the model generates.

Model Equations

As before, we denote $x(t)$ the HPA rate, $X(t)$ the log-HPI, $w(t)$ the white noise that produces normally distributed, serially uncorrelated, HPA increments seen as normal shocks in discrete time. We represent the HPA as a sum of continuous diffusion, white noise and income inflation ($iinf$).

$$x(t) = x_1(t) + \sigma_w w(t) + iinf(t) \tag{14.4}$$

where $x_1(t)$ follows a second-order linear system of stochastic differential equations that is analogous to the spring-mass oscillator with friction and random forces:

$$\dot{x}_1 = x_2 + k_1 \dot{X}_{eq} \tag{14.5-1}$$

$$\dot{x}_2 = -ax_2 - bx_1 + k_3 \dot{X}_{eq} + \sigma_d w_d \tag{14.5-2}$$

For brevity, equations (14.5) are written in "engineering" notations, with the dot denoting time derivatives. The HPA diffusion is disturbed by another white noise w_d (independent of w, interest rate and income) and the derivative of log-HPI equilibrium that is measured via the financing rate. The pair of SDEs (14.5) describes a stable process if $a > 0$, $b > 0$ and becomes an oscillator when $a^2 < 4b$.

Changes in the HPI equilibrium affect the HPA diffusion's first and second derivative via the coefficients' k's. With a non-zero k_1, a change in mortgage rate results in an immediate change in x_1, hence, the HPA. Aside from the above stated inequalities, coefficients should be bound by one equality condition. To show this, let us assume that there are no random forces and the mortgage rate drifts very weakly, at a constant pace that is much slower than the transients of the model (14.5). In this case, we expect the HPA diffusion to converge to $\dot{X}_{eq}$ as $t \to \infty$ so that the HPI eventually follows HPIeq. This consideration imposes another constraint on the model's parameters: $ak_1 + k_3 = b$.

The interest rates enter the HPA model via two terms: income inflation and the time derivative of X_{eq}. We often refer to $x_1(\dot{X}_{eq})$ as the "affordability effect"; it can be generated by setting both white noises to zero. In contrast, the $x_1(w_d)$ term generated without $\dot{X}_{eq}$ is sometimes referred to as "HPA diffusion." This term is due to economic forces other than inflation, interest rates and is independent of them. General economic conditions, unemployment not reflected in the household income, or prevailing speculation can cause large HPI deviations from the equilibrium. Figure 14.4 presents the HPA modeling process as a flowchart.

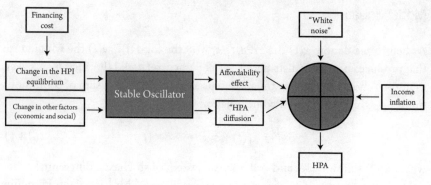

Figure 14.4 Flowchart of the HPA Model

In the complete absence of random forces and change of equilibrium, our HPA will follow a second-order ODE. In particular, it will be continuously differentiable, i.e. bound not only to the previous value, but to its derivative too. Such a model can maintain momentum and explain why HPA may continue to grow or decline after the HPI equilibrium passed. This useful feature lets us properly initialize a forecast using historical series.

The Dataset and Adjustments

Unless we state otherwise, most of the modeling observations and results will refer to a quarterly FHFA 25-MSA composite index that we computed ourselves. We use the MSAs (metropolitan statistical areas) and the weights published by Radar Logic and apply them to the FHFA historical purchase-only HPIs. At the time of this writing, FHFA did not have purchase-only HPI series for all MSAs, so we interpolated them by combining the available purchase-only state series and the total-transaction series published at both state and MSA levels. This approach presents advantages over using the FHFA US index or the RPX25 index outright. The RPX index family itself, while informative, does not extend deeply into history. The FHFA US index is not representative for MBS analytical purposes because it underweighs regions with a disproportionally modest volume of conforming loans (e.g., California).

The other adjustment we made was to recognize the proliferation of "affordable" loan programs such as Option ARMs and IO ARMs that give borrowers the dubious privilege of making small payments and not amortizing the balance. Coupled with the compromised underwriting of subprime and Alt-A loans when borrowers were not required to pay their fair share of the credit risk, and were not required to make prudent down-payments (20%), these practices effectively lowered the available financing rate. Although the resultant rate is difficult to assess and requires a specialized data study presented later in Chapter 16, it is safe to assume that, in 2002–2006, the total cost of financing fell sizably in some areas. This assumption can be backed by a geographical comparison: While 40–50% of Californians had been lured into "affordable" products, most Ohioans borrowed conventionally. Coincidentally, California, but not Ohio, experienced a pronounced bubble followed by a housing market collapse. Hence, we have to consider two interest-rate factors: the usual conventional rate and the suppressed one that existed in 2002–2006, that we depict in some exhibits that follow. The latter, as shown further, explains the rise and decline of the housing market well.

Statistical Technique and the Use of Kalman Filtration

Let us re-write the system of differential equations (14.4)–(14.5) in an approximate discrete vector-matrix form (h is a time step):

$$X_k = FX_{k-1} + w_k + u_k \tag{14.6}$$

$$x_k = HX_k + v_k + iinf_k \tag{14.7}$$

where, for our two-dimensional diffusion, X, w, u are vectors of state variables, disturbance and external forces, respectively, F is a square matrix, and H is a row-vector:

$$X = \begin{bmatrix} x_1 \\ x_2 \end{bmatrix}, w = \begin{bmatrix} 0 \\ \sigma_d w_d \sqrt{h} \end{bmatrix}, u = \begin{bmatrix} hk_1 \dot{X}_{eq} \\ hk_3 \dot{X}_{eq} \end{bmatrix}, F = \begin{bmatrix} 1 & h \\ -bh & 1-ah \end{bmatrix}, H = \begin{bmatrix} 1 & 0 \end{bmatrix}$$

We observe the HPA rate x_k disturbed by unobservable state vector X, random shocks $v_k = \sigma_w w_k \sqrt{h}$ and observable income inflation $iinf_k$. If the time step h is small, the discrete system (14.6)–(14.7) approximates the continuous system (14.4)–(14.5) well. If the time step is not small, parameters a, b, etc. of the discrete model may have to be somewhat different from those of the continuous model.

Before we attempt to optimize the model to best-fit historical data, we need to recognize the existence of two unobservable random forces, w and w_d. Even if we knew all of the model's parameters, determining historical $w(t)$ and $w_d(t)$ would remain an ambiguous task. In essence, we want to split one process into two, a problem that can be solved by the linear Kalman filter. Under the assumption that the coefficients in equations (14.6)–(14.7) are known, the filter maximizes the conditional log-likelihood function with respect to discrete realization of w and w_d. For each time period, it is done in two steps.

Predict. We first forecast the HPA diffusion vector $\hat{X}_{k|k-1}$ using the $(k-1)$th estimate $\hat{X}_{k-1|k-1}$, available interest rates and by setting $w_{dk} = 0$:

$$\hat{X}_{k|k-1} = F\hat{X}_{k-1|k-1} + u_k$$

We also update the error covariance matrix (estimating accuracy of state variables)

$$P_{k|k-1} = FP_{k-1|k-1}F^T + Q$$

where Q is the covariance matrix of w, i.e. $Q = \begin{bmatrix} 0 & 0 \\ 0 & h\sigma_d^2 \end{bmatrix}$

Update. Using actual HPA observation x_k, we can update our estimates of the state vector X and the covariance matrix P:

$$\hat{y}_k = x_k - H\hat{X}_{k|k-1} - iinf_k \text{ (residual's measurement)}$$

$$S_k = HP_{k|k-1}H^T + h\sigma_w^2 \text{ (residual's covariance)}$$

$$K_k = P_{k|k-1}H / S_k \text{ (optimal gain)}$$

$$\hat{X}_{k|k} = \hat{X}_{k|k-1} + K_k \hat{y}_k \text{ (updated state estimate)}$$

$$P_{k|k} = (I - K_k H)P_{k|k-1} \text{ (update estimate covariance)}$$

This Predict-Update Kalman algorithm is well known and cited here following a Wikipedia article on Kalman filtering; another good reference is the D. Simon (2006) book. It is proven to minimize the Euclidean error norm: $E||X_k - \hat{X}_{k|k}||^2$. At each step, one can back the shocks $\hat{w}_k$ and $\hat{w}_{dk}$ from the values of estimated state variables.

The Kalman filter possesses another, less known, useful practical feature: It allows theoretical prediction of variances and covariances of all variables involved in the process. For example, the variance of $\hat{w}_k$ and $\hat{w}_{dk}$ coming out of the Kalman filtration will not be equal to 1, but can be expressed via other statistics. If the process x_k, X_k indeed follows equations (14.6), (14.7), then the empirical statistics will asymptotically converge to theoretical ones listed below:

$$h\sigma_d^2 E\left(\hat{w}_d^2\right) \to K_{2k}^2\left(P_{11k|k-1} + h\sigma_w^2\right)$$

$$h\sigma_w^2 \, E\!\left(\hat{w}^2\right) \to (1-K_{1k})^2\!\left(P_{11k|k-1}+h\sigma_w^2\right)$$

These conditions can be complemented by a variety of other trivial requirements such as zero correlation between $\hat{w}_k$ and $\hat{w}_{k-i}$ for various $i > 0$ or their independence from the interest rate and inflation terms. Using these properties, one can optimize the model by forcing these important theoretical statistics to match their respective empirically computed counterparts. Therefore, we employ Kalman filtering both as a signal observer and as a model estimator.

If we apply the Kalman filter to a stable linear dynamic system with constant coefficients, the elements of matrix P, vector K, and scalar S gradually stabilize and stop changing between time steps. Since we normally do not have reliable initial conditions for the state estimates, it makes sense to start the filtration process ahead of the model's estimation window. Figure 14.5 depicts outputs of the filtering process with optimized parameters. Filtration starts with a somewhat frivolous initial condition $\hat{X}_{0|0}$ in 1984, but only the 1989–2008 dataset is used for estimation.

The white-noise process (Figure 14.5b) exhibits apparent heteroskedasticity. The rate-related HPA factor's bubble (Figure 14.5a) owes its existence to the artificially inflated affordability during the 2002–2006 period that we discussed above. Once borrowers no longer had access to high LTV loans, option ARMs etc., the HPI equilibrium fell dragging HPA down. Hence, our model links both the formation of the housing bubble and, especially, its subsequent collapse to the birth and death of "affordable" lending.

HPI FORECASTS, BUBBLE, AND DECLINE

A good model validation test should include a comparison of retrospective forecasts to actual data. Note that "forecasting" for statistical models usually means computing mathematically expected values. Since the HPA to HPI transformation is nonlinear, it is easier for us to compute the median path that does not need to be adjusted for convexity. The following three exhibits depict the forecasts that we would have made had we been using the model on Dec. 2008, Dec. 2005, and Dec. 2002, respectively. For example, observing the index up to Dec. 2008 we would have predicted its further decline by 17% with the trough reached in September 2011 (Figure 14.6). When forming these forecasts, we turned both w and w_d to zero, set the MBS rate to its Dec. 2008 level and assumed that inflation will slowly grow from 1% per year to 4% per year. The initial conditions for x_1, x_2 were given by the Kalman filter. We compare the forecast to the RPX forward market quotes observed on 12/31/08, 3/31/09 and 6/30/09, for each year-end settlement (bars).

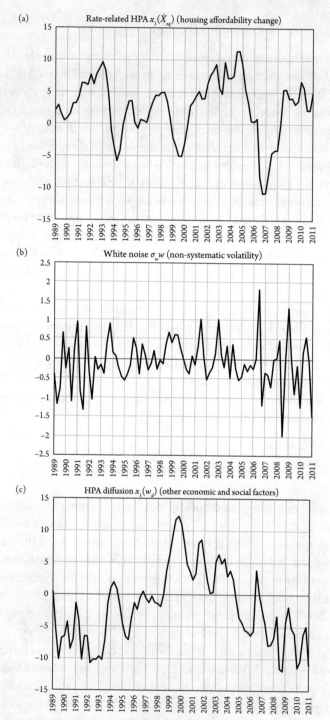

Figure 14.5 Composition of the Historical 25-MSA HPA (Results of Kalman Filtering)

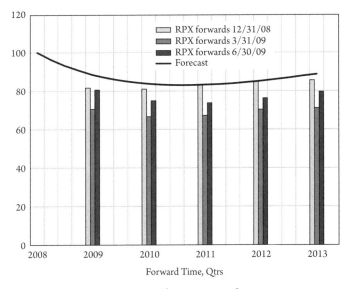

Figure 14.6 FHFA-25MSA HPI Forecast from 2008–End

Apparently, the market views change from better to worse and back. As we should have expected, our forecast is more optimistic than the forward market. First, we are using a physical model whereas forward quotes reflect the price of risk. Second, our modeling object—the FHFA composite—should look better than the corresponding RPX. The FHFA HPI data is compiled using transactions backed by conforming loans. In contrast, the RPX HPI includes properties backed by subprime loans and has more distressed sales, hence, deeper declines.

Was the model forecasting the HPI decline? Figure 14.7 suggests that had the model used the 30-year conforming rate as the financing basis, it would have expected housing prices to continue to grow, albeit at a slower pace (dashed line).

This would be the "soft landing" scenario that many economists anticipated. It is only if we consider that many borrowers were lured into cheap financing or were granted compromised underwriting shortcuts during the prior years, can we explain what happened. Assuming that the solid line represents the effective financing rate, artificially lowered in 2002–2005 and suddenly brought up to reality in 2006, we sent the model a signal of a substantial affordability decline. The model accepts this signal, keeps HPA momentum for a while, but shifts its gears downward (solid line). This $HPI(t)$ path the model predicted matches well to what really happened (bars in Figure 14.7), perhaps not without some luck as we compare a median path to the reality, i.e. a unique realization of randomness. Later in the book (chapter 16) we will establish that affordability was indeed high through 2006, once we consider other costs: the cost of smaller-than-normal

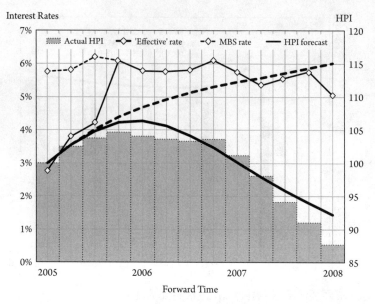

Figure 14.7 FHFA-25MSA HPI Forecast versus Actual from 2005–End

down payment and the cost of credit risk under-pricing. Hence, the "effective rate" in Figure 14.7 is a reflection of blended borrower cost rather than mortgage rates alone.

Figure 14.8 continues our exploration into historical forecasting by depicting two lines the model could be producing at 2002-end. It predicted a relatively fast HPI growth of 37% in 3 years even if the MBS rate was the true indicator of lending (punctured lines). With "affordable" lending, the effective financing rate was as much as 3% lower, and the model forecasted a 57% HPI growth in 2002–2005 (the HPI had actually grown by 47%). The ratio of these two HPI forecasts is $1.57/1.37 = 1.15$; hence, the model attributes 15% of the HPI to the proliferation of affordable lending.

Therefore, our modeling work suggests that the catalyst of the housing crisis was not the bubble alone. The total-cost door slammed into the face of existing and potentially new low-down-payment, Option ARM, IO ARM and subprime borrowers drastically reduced the affordability-based HPI equilibrium.

Since Kalman filtering determines the initial conditions, suddenly improved or deteriorated HPI historical data materially affects both the short-term and long-term HPI outlook. Quantification of this effect is important from a risk-measurement standpoint. If the HPI random process was a Brownian motion, (or a martingale, in general) any change in its observed initial condition would be equally propagated forward. In our model, only the white-noise component of the HPA moves future HPI 1-per-1. Disturbances of the HPA diffusion

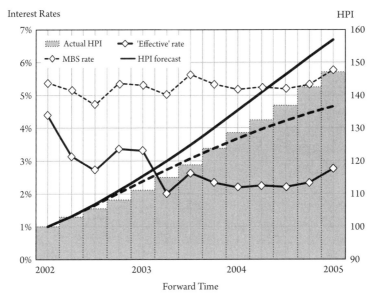

Figure 14.8 FHFA-25MSA HPI Forecast versus Actual from 2002–End

part will cause some greater change in HPI. This feature of the model agrees with historically realized volatility of forward prices cited in the next section.

Figure 14.9 depicts the HPI effect of a 1% HPI sudden shock. The Kalman filter optimally splits this "surprise" into HPA diffusion and white noise. As seen, the long-term HPI forecast shifts by more than 1% and varies from region to region. This pattern agrees with the traders' views illustrated by Figure 6.1 in chapter 6: HPA surprises are enlarged in forward quotes.

The lines depicted in Figure 14.9 come from sub-optimal geographical modeling for Los Angeles (LA), Miami (MIA), New York (NY), and Phoenix (PX). Naturally, indices featuring relatively large white noise (e.g., PX) will change their forecasts less than indices having relatively large HPA diffusion (e.g., 25MSA Composite).

AVERAGE VOLATILITY

Conditional versus Unconditional Measures

Let us compare the empirically assessed realized volatility to the one implied by the model. Our focus, however, will not be on testing the volatility function, but rather the average volatility measured between t and $t + \tau$ as a function of τ. Namely, we will compute the HPI's τ-long logarithmic increments as long

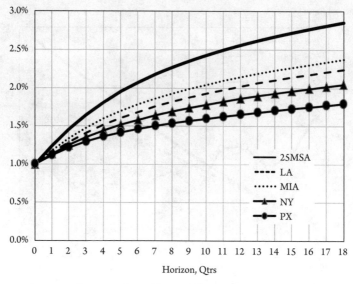

Figure 14.9 Forecast Change Followed by a 1% Sudden HPI Shock

as observations exist. The standard deviation of this measure divided by the square-root of τ has the same meaning as the average (Black) volatility between t and $t + \tau$:

$$\sigma_{avg}(\tau) = stdev\left\{ ln\frac{HPI(t+\tau)}{HPI(t)} \right\} / \sqrt{\tau} \qquad (14.8)$$

This measure can be computed both analytically (using the HPI model's equations) and empirically. In the latter case, we deal with an unconditional standard deviation in (14.8) whereas in the former case one can compute both unconditional and conditional (given an initial point) statistics. In order to explain how it can be accomplished analytically, let us consider the discrete system (14.6), (14.7) and find the covariance matrix:

$$E\left[\mathbf{X}_k \mathbf{X}_k^T \right] = E\left[\left(\mathbf{F}\mathbf{X}_{k-1} + \mathbf{w}_k + \mathbf{u}_k \right)\left(\mathbf{X}_{k-1}^T \mathbf{F}^T + \mathbf{w}_k^T + \mathbf{u}_k^T \right) \right]$$

$$= \mathbf{F}E\left[\mathbf{X}_{k-1} \mathbf{X}_{k-1}^T \right] \mathbf{F}^T + E\left[\mathbf{w}_k \mathbf{w}_k^T \right] + E\left[\mathbf{u}\mathbf{u}_k^T \right] \qquad (14.9)$$

In deriving this relationship, we accounted for mutual independence of $\mathbf{X}_{k-1}$, $\mathbf{u}_k$, and $\mathbf{w}_k$. Therefore, the covariance matrix can be computed iteratively, starting from $k = 1$ without simulations. In (14.9), matrices $E[\,\boldsymbol{w}_k \boldsymbol{w}_k^T\,]$ and $E[\,\boldsymbol{u}_k \boldsymbol{u}_k^T\,]$ serve as "inputs" to the process. They are

$$E[\,\boldsymbol{w}_k \boldsymbol{w}_k^T\,] = h\sigma_w^2 \begin{bmatrix} 0 & 0 \\ 0 & 1 \end{bmatrix}, \quad E[\,\boldsymbol{u}_k \boldsymbol{u}_k^T\,] = h\sigma_{pmt}^2 \begin{bmatrix} (k_1)^2 & k_3 k_1 \\ k_1 k_3 & (k_3)^2 \end{bmatrix}$$

where σ_{pmt} is proportional to the volatility of the loan payment due to the volatility of the financing rate. We can extend the method to compute variances of HPA (x_k) and log-HPI (X_k). Note that income inflation may be correlated to the change in financing rate.

Conditional statistics. The iterative process (14.9) must start with some initial condition for $E[\,\boldsymbol{X}_0 \boldsymbol{X}_0^T\,]$. If we clearly observe today's vector $\boldsymbol{X}_0$, it has a zero variance. This case corresponds to computing the conditional average volatility. We can even consider the uncertainty in $\boldsymbol{X}_0$ estimated by the Kalman filter and stored in matrix $\boldsymbol{P}_{kk}$.

Unconditional statistics. In order to apply this method to computing the unconditional volatility, we assume that we are dealing with a stationary random process, so that $E[\,\boldsymbol{X}_0 \boldsymbol{X}_0^T\,]$ is the same as unconditional $E[\,\boldsymbol{X}_k \boldsymbol{X}_k^T\,]$ measured for large k. Our point of interest becomes not the variance for log-HPI (i.e. X_k), but rather for $X_k - X_0$.

Figures 14.10-A, B depict a family of $\sigma_{avg}(\tau)$ measures computed using the model's equations. We show the white noise, HPA diffusion, and interest rate related components (due to affordability, inflation, and the total) separately as well as the Pythagorean sum. Figure 14.10-B also shows the empirical (1989–2008) measure, for comparison.

Naturally, the unconditional average volatility is larger than the conditional one, for any horizon. The difference between these two is particularly sizable for shorter horizons. When we know the initial conditions with certainty, the short-term uncertainty is mainly due to white noise. Over a longer term, it loses importance. However, with the unconditional statistics, white noise contributes weakly even for the 1-quarter period. Indeed, the unconditional uncertainty of $HPI(t + 1)/HPI(t)$ is the same as the unconditional uncertainly of HPA (just over 3% annualized, revisit Figure 14.2), which far exceeds the white noise piece (just over 1% annualized).

It is evident that, for longer-term horizons, the HPA diffusion term dominates. To some extent, the effects of income inflation and housing affordability partially offset each other, thereby reducing the resultant dependence on interest rates. When computing model-implied statistics in Figure 14.10, we assumed a 75% correlation between the inflation rate and mortgage financing rate. Empirically, these two rates show a much lower correlation when measured over a short

(a)

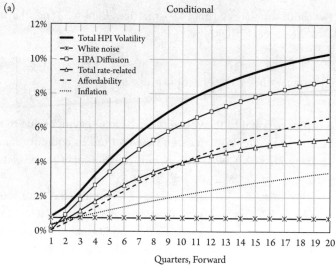

(b)

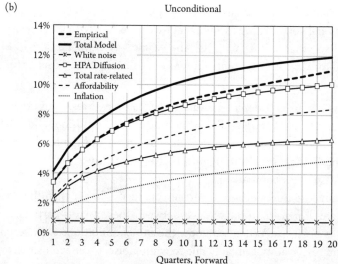

Figure 14.10 Average Annualized HPI Volatility

period as generally do the short and long rates. However, mortgage rates correlate with a longer-term expectation of inflation and the level we used may be justified. At times, housing financing rates may depart from income inflation as in 2002–2006 when the housing market went into a bubble. When this happens, financing rates may become a greater factor of risk and a much greater contributor to the HPI volatility than Figure 14.10 shows.

How can we relate these volatility measures to the valuation of HPI options? In Chapter 6, we demonstrated that the local volatility structure $\sigma(t, T)$ of forward prices dictates volatility $\sigma(t, t)$ of the risk-neutral spot HPI process. Hence, if we could continuously trade in forwards or futures, the HPI options would have very low volatility limited to the white noise. In reality, according to TFS, a traded platform for CS futures and options, in January 2009, dealers offered 1-year options on the 10-city CS Composite index at a 9% implied volatility. This level is comparable with the empirical $\sigma(t, T)$ estimate in the 6%–12% range that we cited in chapter 6. One explanation we can give here is that the assumption of continuous trading we made for the purpose of risk-neutral derivations in chapter 6 is unrealistic for residential derivatives. With a low liquidity and an intimidating bid-ask spread, market participants cannot take full advantage of the known HPI drift. Therefore, the drift's uncertainty must also be reflected in the risk-neutral model.

Random Paths Generation

Figure 14.11 depicts 100 random paths generated for the 25-MSA Composite HPI on May 2013 when it is set to 100%. The bold solid line shows the deterministic path assuming forward interest rates, without innovations of diffusion $(w_d = 0)$ and white noise $(w = 0)$. The bold dotted line is for the sample's average. The interest rates used for this sample are those from the matching-date Squared Guassian rate model (see Figure 5.7 of chapter 5). The random-path generation is conditional on knowing today's vector X_0.

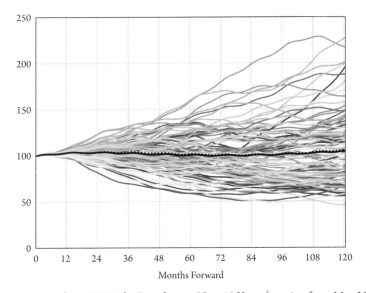

Figure 14.11 Random HPI Paths Sample over Next 10 Years (starting from May 2013)

There are several interesting observations that follow this exhibit. First, the HPI averaged forecast is rather flat for an extended period: Mathematical expectation of the HPI in ten years is just 6% above the starting value. This can be explained by the steep forward curve of interest rates. Because higher mortgage rates depress housing affordability, using the forward rates limits potential growth in HPI, at least, until the force of higher inflation takes over. Had we continued HPI paths beyond the ten-year horizon, we would have reached forward annual level of growth of about 3.0%.

The forward-curve HPI and the average HPI look surprisingly close to each other. This may be a coincidental result of two convexity adjustments almost offsetting each other. First, the HPI function of the cumulative HPA is exponential so that, in the presence of volatility, averaged HPI should clearly be greater than the forward-curve HPI. On the other hand, averaged interest rates are higher than the forward rates (see chapter 5) due to its own convexity adjustment; that one causes mortgage rates to evolve higher, hence, reduces the HPI.

Finally, the collective visual mop-like image of random HPI scenarios does not resemble those of stocks or stock indices. This fact may seem to contradict the point we made earlier in the chapter where we explained why the HPA signal is discontinuous. However, Figure 14.11 agrees with Figure 14.10-A that clearly demonstrates that the conditional HPI volatility is small in the short-term and grows significantly with time horizon.

The Geographical Angle

If our modeling views of the home-price evolution are valid, we expect them to stay valid across geographical regions, states and MSAs. Figure 14.12 depicts the unconditional average volatility measured for the United States, New York, California's large cities, and Cleveland, Ohio.

We can make a couple of interesting observations:

1. Densely populated urban areas are the leading source of U.S. housing market volatility. Compare the 25-MSA Composite to the FHFA US average, for example. Volatility ranges drastically across regions and indices, from 2% to nearly 20%. We can explain this empirical fact by an inelastic supply of housing (see chapter 16).
2. The Case-Shiller indices are somewhat more volatile than the region-matching FHFA indices. As we explain in the Appendix, the CS family likely accounts for more distressed sales (foreclosures), and includes transactions backed by subprime loans with borrowers unable or unwilling to maintain homes (A. Leventus, August 2008).

How does the model explain a super-low realized volatility of Cleveland in comparison to the much higher theoretical levels shown earlier in Figure 14.10? One explanation comes from the fact that, with lower or non-existing white noise and HPA diffusion components, and local income inflation partially offsetting

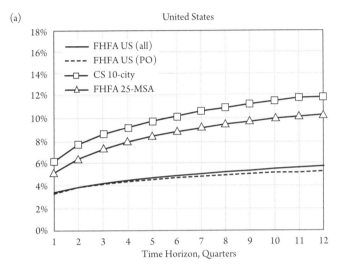

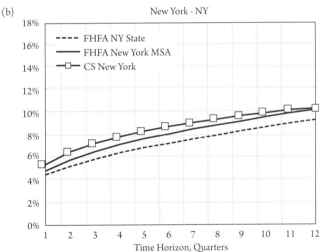

Figure 14.12 Empirical Unconditional Volatility: Indices and Geography

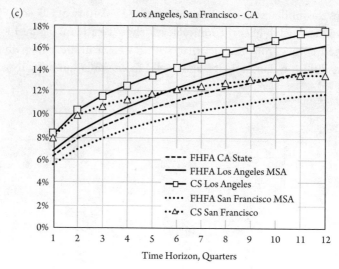

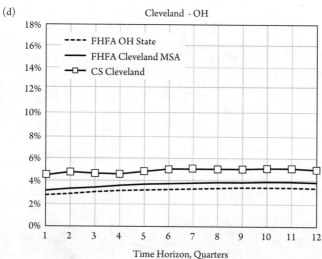

Figure 14.12 Empirical Unconditional Volatility: Indices and Geography (Continued)

mortgage rates, the interest-rate part of the HPI can have relatively low volatility, too. Another explanation is that cities like Cleveland and Pittsburgh borrowed mostly conventionally and never experienced a bubble (we will revisit this point in chapter 16). Hence, the interest rate related HPI could actually differ in volatility across the United States.

GEOGRAPHICAL MODELING

Our goal is to forecast and simulate HPAs and HPIs at the state level and the MSA level, i.e. to construct a geographical HPI model. One option is to apply the modeling concept we described in this chapter to every geographical area. This approach would lead us to a stochastic model with a very large (over 400) number of partially dependent factors. Even if such a model could be constructed in a reliable way, its use would require considerable computing resources, both memory and processing time.

An attractive alternative is to restrict the full-scale dynamic modeling to several "core" indices. Then, we can regress HPAs of 400+ geographical areas (states and MSAs) against the few core HPA indices, thereby creating a much-reduced modeling framework. We conducted an empirical study that showed that this reduced form of geographical model is as accurate as the full one. The question this fact poses is "How to select the core?" In selecting five core indices, the 25-MSA Composite, Los Angeles (LA), Miami (MIA), New York (NY), and Phoenix (PX), we assumed that the RPX market would help us align empirical HPI modeling to the observed forward curves. Although the geographical part of the RPX trading has never caught the wind, the approach was meaningful. We describe below how using just a few core indices can create a localized home-price model.

Core HPI Models

We apply our modeling method explained in this chapter to the five core indices. In order to simplify this phase of modeling and achieve some other desired properties, we purposely retain the 25 MSA Composite's model structure and parameters that are responsible for the dynamics and the propagation of the interest-rate effect (a, b, k_1, k_3). For each of four other regions, we optimize only white noise's size σ_w, HPA diffusion's volatility σ_d, and exposure to affordable lending discount (set to 1.0 for the Composite model).

Because we fixed some parameters to match the Composite, our four geographical models become suboptimal. The last column of Table 14.1 depicts the

Table 14.1 OPTIMIZATION RESULTS FOR FIVE CORE MODELS

	Jump	Diffusion	Beta	ADCO score
25 MSA	1.54	2.63	1.00	0.25
LA	3.79	3.18	1.72	0.37
MIA	2.90	3.93	2.38	0.37
NY	2.76	2.18	0.43	0.40
PX	4.90	4.98	2.55	0.39

Table 14.2 Cross-Correlation Matrix

	25 MSA	LA	MIA	NY	PX
25 MSA	100.0%	73.0%	55.7%	55.5%	53.7%
LA	73.0%	100.0%	39.8%	25.7%	37.5%
MIA	55.7%	39.8%	100.0%	37.7%	33.6%
NY	55.5%	25.7%	37.7%	100.0%	23.6%
PX	53.7%	37.5%	33.6%	23.6%	100.0%

internally used, best-fit statistical score (the lower, the better) computed for the regional optimization. By definition, the Composite model was optimal to the selected reduced-rate history and has the lowest score.

As seen, regions vary in volatility and exposure to affordable lending. PX is clearly the most volatile followed by LA and MIA. These three regions also exhibit about twice-larger dependence on the reduced-rate financing than the Composite whereas NY looks immune. This matches the perceived proliferation of affordable lending. The ADCO score measures look satisfactory relative to the Composite, given the statement of optimization problem.

Table 14.2 exhibits the correlation matrix for random geographical shocks.

Historical Regressions for Derived MSAs

For the chosen five-index geographical core, our model for 436 indices [including MSAs, MSA Divisions (MSADs), 50 states, D.C., and the United States (national index)] employs the following regression to determine HPA for the k-th derived index:

$$HPA_k(t) - F(t) = \sum_{i=1}^{5} \beta_{ki} \left[HPA_i^{core}(t) - F(t) \right], k = 1, \ldots, 436 \quad (14.10)$$

where $F(t)$ is a common factor explained below. Some of the Betas can be negative; however, we constrained the regression so that the Composite's Beta is non-negative. All HPAs used in this formula are seasonally adjusted; local seasonality should be added on the top of (14.10).

As seen, we build the regression for the deviations of all HPAs off the common factor F. In essence, one can view the local HPI as a regression against six indices: five core HPIs and F. The use of the common factor improves the regression's accuracy and allows for one useful property: All derived HPAs will move in unison if we change F. It is important to realize that F enters modeling of all core indices. Although there is a freedom in selecting F, it is natural to associate it

Table 14.3 Historical R-Squared for HPA Regressions

	5-index Core		9-index Core	
	States	**MSAs**	**States**	**MSAs**
Weighted R-sq	75%	69%	80%	76%
Loan % of R-sq > 60%	78%	74%	83%	81%

HPAs net of the common factor, weighted by balances.

with the national affordability factor and income inflation. For example, when we change interest rates, this change will affect all MSAs synchronously.

It is essential to construct local HPIs from seasonally adjusted core HPAs. Had we not done so, seasonality would drive the regression's coefficients (Betas). For example, seasonality of the U.S. national index is comparable to that of the 25-MSA Composite. However, the latter is about twice as volatile. Hence, if we regress the seasonally adjusted US HPA against the seasonally adjusted Composite, the Beta is expected to be around 0.5. If we performed the same operation with seasonally unadjusted HPAs, the Beta would be much higher thereby setting up a wrong volatility model.

Table 14.3 reports the quality of historical regressions using the five-index core and the nine-index core; the latter adds Chicago, Detroit, Washington (D.C.), and Oakland.

Note that the reported R-squared levels somewhat understate the actual quality of modeling. We computed them for HPAs *net of F*, hence, variability explained by *F* is not included in R-squared. The extension of our geographical core from five to nine indices improves R-squared by 5% to 7%. Many small MSAs show modest levels of R-squared, but the majority of loans and balances are covered by the local HPI regressions with R-squared exceeding 60%; those that are not, use the national index. In chapter 20, we will demonstrate that a localized HPI model affects expectations of loan losses.

US HPI INDICES

We conclude this chapter with a brief description of US HPI Indices.

FHFA (OFHEO) Indices

FHFA, formerly known as Office of Federal Housing Enterprise Oversight (OFHEO), compiles a family of HPIs going back to 1975. These indices are computed using the repeat-sale method and published quarterly. Due to its method, the index computation requires that a property be sold twice; the index is recomputed retroactively (e.g. a property sold in 1980 and then in 2000 affects the index value for the entire historical period between the sales). The index is published with (approximately) a two-month lag, and covers the U.S., its nine Census Bureau divisions, each of 50 states, and Metropolitan Statistical Areas (MSAs) or Divisions that have at least 15,000 transactions over prior 10 years (294 MSAs in May of 2009).

FHFA derives its family of HPIs by the virtue of being the regulator of Fannie Mae and Freddie Mac, the U.S. mortgage agencies. Therefore, FHFA HPIs are based on home sales and appraisals secured by conforming loans only. For these reasons, the FHFA indices are the least volatile among the HPIs and may understate home-price decline in a time of crisis.

Along with traditionally published quarterly data, FHFA now produces monthly estimates as well. It publishes both all-transaction indices and purchase-only indices, with and without seasonal adjustments.

The Case-Shiller Indices

The repeat sales methodology we mentioned above belongs to Karl Case and Robert Shiller. S&P computes HPI for 20 metropolitan regions across the U.S. along with two composites. Indices are published on the last Tuesday of each month with a two-month lag, using a three-month moving average. In addition, a broader US composite index is computed and published quarterly. The Case-Shiller indices include distressed sales (foreclosures), but filter out outliers that may point to a physical change of property. They go back to January of 1987 (albeit not for all regions); all CS indices are set to 100 on January 2000.

The Case-Shiller repeat-sales method is also employed by Fiserv, a company that computes and maintains the CS indices covering thousands of zip codes and metro areas, but not all. However, it is the S&P 10-city family of Case-Shiller indices that is traded at the CME.

The Core Logic Indices

Like FHFA and CS, the family of Core Logic's home-price indices utilizes the repeat-sales method (weighted by value). The source of raw data is public records. Indices are produced for twelve tiers including distressed versus non-distressed transactions, various property types, conforming loans versus non-conforming loans.

Core Logic updates HPI monthly with a four-week lag, with history going back to 1976. It stands out in geographical coverage: In addition to the U.S. states and MSAs, separate HPIs are computed for almost 1,200 counties and 7,000 zip codes.

Core Logic acquired Case-Shiller indices from Fiserv on March 20, 2013.

The Radar Logic Indices (RPX)

While the Case-Shiller method controls the quality of traded homes by using a pair of sales for the same property, Radar Logic does this differently: It computes and publishes indices as a price per square foot; see Arthur and Kagarlis (2008). Radar Logic publishes its indices *daily*, with a 63-day lag. Along with daily indices, the RPX family includes a seven-day and a 28-day averages that aggregate transactions. The standard geographic coverage is limited to 25 MSAs and a composite; an additional subscription gains access to a number of smaller MSAs and Manhattan Condominium indices. Radar Logic's HPIs include all transactions and are not seasonally adjusted.

The RPX family of indices (the 28-day version) is employed for the forward and futures residential derivative markets.

The National Association of Realtors Indices

The National Association of Realtors (NAR) publishes indices of all transactions gathered from Multiple Listing Services (not listed transactions are excluded). The index is published monthly at the national and census region levels and quarterly for more than 150 metropolitan areas. The day of publication—around the 25th of the next month—makes NAR indices the timeliest information about housing market conditions available.

NAR indices are expressed via the median dollar figures, but do not provide a home-quality control, e.g., a change in size of homes sold next month from the previous month may send a false signal of change in the HPI.

15

Credit Analysis on a Scenario Grid and Analytical Shortcuts

The method we introduce in this chapter was initially designed to serve as a dynamic alternative to traditional credit ratings. We call this alternative measure Breakpoint Ratio. While presenting an effective numerical process of computing it in this chapter, we develop a richer method that utilizes a rather routine set of credit scenarios to produce comprehensive credit risk reports, assess the likelihood of certain losses and even value non-agency MBS without simulations. In essence, we describe an intuitive and practical shortcut to complex non-agency MBS analyses, which is used in the next part of the book.

BREAKPOINT RATIO AND SCENARIO GRID

We will start describing our method with the introduction of several key terms.

Credit scenario is a deterministic scenario featuring certain projections of economic factors (interest rates, home prices) and model's stresses (scales, shifts, etc.). A base-case scenario is the one practitioner subjectively views as the most likely one to occur.

Breakpoint scenario is a market scenario, out of a sorted set, that forces a non-agency bond to lose its first dollar of principal. This term can be generalized to describe a scenario causing a bond to lose exactly 5% of principal, 25% of principal, and so on.

Breakpoint Ratio (BPR) is a metric such as collateral loss, conditional default rate (CDR) or monthly default rate (MDR), measured for the breakpoint scenario relative to the base case. This is an estimate of distance-to-default and is the basis for dynamic rating. If the base-case collateral loss is estimated at 10%, and a bond's breakpoint collateral loss is 20%, the Breakpoint Ratio for this bond is 2.0.

Unlike agency ratings, Breakpoint Ratios change continuously. They reflect the dynamics of interest rates and home prices, as well as monthly updated delinquency composition. A shrinking ratio points to credit deterioration in advance of an official downgrade. For example, a AAA mezzanine bond backed by an Alt-A collateral of option ARMs was put on negative watch earlier in 2008. By the time it happened, the Breakpoint Ratio already had fallen to 0.65 and the bond was projected to lose over 20% of its principal on our model. Some AAA bonds we analyzed still maintained their initial rating, but our assessment of the Breakpoint Ratio, in a 0.8–1.5 range, indicated that future write-downs were not unlikely.

One can consider several possible definitions for the Breakpoint Ratio:

A. The explicit MDR vector scale that breaks the bond.

    This simple and easy-to-understand measure is almost model-free and closely related to the Vasicek distribution scale (see below). Its downside is that not all senior bonds can break even under 100% MDR if the loss severity is not large enough.

B. Collateral cumulative loss scale, i.e., a ratio of collateral loss that breaks the bond to the collateral loss under the base case ("Simple BP Ratio"— see Table 15.1).

    This measure is rather robust, too. Its main disadvantage is that the risk of losing on the same scale is not equally presented in different pools. Let us compare two hypothetical deals, one new (no delinquencies) and another one very seasoned with lots of delinquent loans (hence, with high certainty of losses). A Breakpoint Ratio of 2.0 should point to a higher risk level for the new deal than for the old one.

C. Collateral cumulative loss scale computed for current loans only ("Extended BP Ratio"—see Table 15.1). This metric is free of the issue pointed out for B, although it assumes certainty of losses from delinquent loans.

D. User-defined, grid-specific, scale of the base case that inflicts principal loss.

Table 15.1 EXAMPLES OF BREAKPOINT RATIO COMPUTATION

Deal ID	Bond	(A) Breakpoint Future Loss	(B) Expected Collateral Loss	(D) Expected Collateral Losses for Current Loans	A/B Simple BP Ratio	[A–(B–D)]/D Extended BP Ratio
NAA06AR1	IVA	21,803,054	12,277,706	5,942,971	1.78	2.60
CWF05025	A11	13,585,643	9,184,583	8,807,148	1.48	1.50
DAA05006	IIA3	32,020,475	19,607,642	16,446,564	1.63	1.75
WFM07010	IA22	60,598,456	80,537,621	80,488,665	0.75	0.75

Measures presented in Table 15.1 have been compiled using the LoanDynamics model (LDM) introduced in chapter 12. The first bond (IVA) has a simple BPR of 1.78, which, simply interpreted, says that losses on the entire collateral of the deal would have to be 1.78 times greater than the expected losses for this bond to reach a breakpoint. The Extended BPR suggests that the expected losses of the currently performing loans would have to be 2.6 times their expected losses for the bond to risk a principal write-down. In contrast, the last bond in the table (IA22) has a very low BPR, simple and extended. According to the Simple and Extended BPRs, only 75% of the expected collateral losses would have to occur for this bond to break.

Naturally, the Extended BPR is always larger than the Simple BPR if a bond does not break at the base case; it is smaller if a bond breaks. These two measures are close to one another for new bonds—like the last bond in Table 15.1.

For portfolios of MBS or ABS, Breakpoint Ratios cannot and should not be aggregated. For example, if one possesses a portfolio of equally weighted bonds from Table 15.1, the averaged BP Ratio will surely exceed 1.0. However, the IA22 bond, hence the entire portfolio, does lose in the base case, so the average BPR is rather misleading. The portfolio's histogram of Breakpoint Ratios would be a more useful sketch of credit risk—see example in Levin (2008).

How would we calculate the Breakpoint Ratio? We would have to iterate over a set of credit scenarios until the bond's write-down becomes equal to the target level such as one dollar (with some accuracy). In the process, we have to inspect the results of these iterations, which, if not discarded, can become a good credit risk report. Therefore, instead of starting with the Breakpoint Ratio search, we first define a grid of stress scenarios (MDR scales, and/or Severity scales, and/or HPA assumptions, etc.) sorted in order of increasing losses that may be of interest for credit risk management. Each scale is a simple multiple of a vector (MDR, Severity) otherwise computed by the LDM. For each of the scenarios, we generate prepayments, defaults, losses, and bond write-downs. We can even enumerate and interpolate scenarios in a customized fashion. For example, Scenario 3 can be viewed as the base case. Scenarios 4 through 11 feature user-defined

Table 15.2 BREAKPOINT GRID OF MDR SCALE

	Input		Output				
	Scenario	MDR scale	Cumulative Writedown	Cumulative Loss	Cumulative Default	Average CDR	Simple BPR
	1	0	0	0	0	0	0
	2	0.5	0	2.8	13.6	2.4	0.57
Base case	3	1	0	4.9	23.4	4.6	1.00
	4	1.5	0.01	6.5	31.0	6.5	1.34
	5	2	0.11	7.9	37.2	8.4	1.62
	6	2.5	0.44	9.0	42.4	10.1	1.86
	7	3	1.03	10.0	46.7	11.8	2.06
	8	3.5	1.68	10.9	50.4	13.4	2.24
	9	4	2.35	11.6	53.6	15.9	2.4
	10	4.5	2.98	12.3	56.5	16.3	2.53
	11	5	3.59	12.9	59.0	17.7	2.66
Breakpoint	3.9	1.46	0.01	6.4	30.4	6.4	1.31

combinations of inflated MDR scale, and/or severity scale, and/or home price shifts, etc., growing in pessimism. Then, a breakpoint "scenario 3.9" (Table 15.2) can be interpreted as an "interpolated" scenario.

This process delivers a valuable risk metrics and, at the same time, narrows the search interval for the Breakpoint. For example, Table 15.2 shows a Breakpoint Grid set in scale of base-case MDR vector predicted by the LDM. Once each grid point was analyzed, the Breakpoint search was performed between scenario scales 1.0 and 1.5.

Note that the simple collateral loss ratio grows more slowly than the MDR scale does. Collateral life contracts with faster termination, both voluntary and mandatory. Therefore, the cumulative default rate (percentage of loans defaulted) and the cumulative collateral loss cannot grow with the exact pace of CDR. This explains why the Breakpoint Scale is 1.46 whereas the Simple BP Ratio is only 1.31.

Table 15.3 depicts the Breakpoint Grid construction using the same MDR shocks as in Table 15.2 and a combination of two home-price appreciation (HPA) shocks, the short-term shift and the long-term shift. The shifts are additive to the initial HPA $x_1(0)$ and income inflation, respectively, for the HPI model introduced in chapter 14. Note that the short-term HPA rate is an instantaneous annualized rate and is not equal to the first-year HPA rate, which is affected by both short-term HPA and long-term HPA. The cumulative loss and default levels for Breakpoints shown in Tables 15.2 and 15.3 are comparable to each other although not identical due to some difference in predicted vectors. Note that the BP Ratio is now slightly larger than the Scenario Scale at Breakpoint. When loan losses are convex in home prices, they can be built up faster.

Table 15.3 Breakpoint Grid Including HPA Shocks

	Input				Output				
Scenario	MDR scale	Yr1 HPA	Yr2 HPA	Long-term HPA	Cum Writedown	Cum Loss	Cum Default	Avg CDR	Simple BP Ratio
1	0	1	4.9	5.2	0	0	0	0	0
2	0.5	-0.7	4	4.7	0	2.2	12.4	2.3	0.46
3 (Base case)	1	-2.5	3	4.2	0	4.9	23.4	4.6	1
4	1.5	-4.2	2	3.7	0.28	8.5	34.3	7.1	1.75
5	2	-6	1.1	3.2	3.77	13.8	45.6	10	2.84
6	2.5	-7.8	0.1	2.7	10.1	20.9	56.8	13.1	4.31
7	3	-9.5	-0.8	2.2	17.27	28.2	65.9	16.5	5.81
8	3.5	-11.3	-1.8	1.7	22.72	33.4	71.8	19.4	6.88
9	4	-13	-2.8	1.2	26.51	36.7	75.7	22	7.56
10	4.5	-14.8	-3.7	0.7	29.18	39.1	78.5	24.3	8.05
11	5	-16.6	-4.7	0.2	31.27	40.8	80.7	26.4	8.41
Breakpoint	3.6 / 1.46	-3.5	2.4	3.9	0.01	6.6	28.9	5.8	1.35

Unlike BPRs, other Breakpoint Grid results can be aggregated for a portfolio, but we first need to make sure that each scenario point is common for every position. At first glance, it seems that constructing the grid in terms of a common factor (like a single home price index, HPI) makes more sense than using an MDR scale. However, if we extend the notion of "common market risk factor" and include model risk, we start to understand that an MDR (as well as severity or prepay speeds) scale can serve the purpose.

In chapter 19, we analyze the use of BPR during the 2008-2009 credit crisis and show that BPR could serve an advanced signal of trouble and it predicted and preceded bonds' actual downgrading by the traditional credit agencies.

ASSIGNING PROBABILITIES TO SCENARIOS

Can we assign each of the credit scenarios a probability? In order to achieve this goal, we normally employ a model randomly simulating interest rates and home prices ("Credit OAS") introduced in chapter 13. Alternatively, we can adapt a simpler and intuitive analytical approach offered by O. Vasicek (1987, 1991) that we introduced in chapter 1.

In order to explain this approach, let us start with consideration of a single loan. Let us assume that the loan is observed over a one-year period and can default with a probability of p. We can view the actual default rate for this loan as a random binary number, which is equal to either 100% (with probability of p) or 0% (with probability of $1 - p$). The entire distribution is therefore defined by one number, p. In particular, this distribution has a mean of p and a variance of $p(1 - p)$.

Let us now switch to a very large cohort of identical loans, each defaulting with probability of p. If the borrowers' default decisions are perfectly correlated to one another, the distribution of the total default rate will not differ from that of a single loan. On the other hand, if individual defaults are totally independent, the entire distribution of the default rate collapses to one point, p, due to the complete diversification of idiosyncratic causes. This is the base case scenario case.

O. Vasicek constructed a theoretical distribution of the infinite cohort default rate (x) as a function of two parameters, the mean default rate p of individual borrowers and correlation between borrowers' asset values, Rho. The Vasicek formula is

$$W(x) = N\left[\frac{\sqrt{1 - Rho}\, N^{-1}(x) - N^{-1}(p)}{\sqrt{Rho}}\right]$$

where, as usual, N stands for the cumulative standard normal distribution. Vasicek characterized the distribution as "highly skewed," which is correct unless

$p = 0.5$ in which case it becomes symmetrical. Correlation between individual borrowers' default decisions can be explained by their dependence on common market factors. As we mentioned, these factors can be a common HPI index or a common model error.

There exists a slightly more convenient form for Vasicek probability distribution that utilizes the median default rate p_{med} rather than the mean rate p:

$$W(x) = N\left[\sqrt{1-Rho}\, \frac{N^{-1}(x) - N^{-1}(p_{med})}{\sqrt{Rho}} \right]$$

The convenience of using the median rate is due to the ability to obtain it more accurately from scenario analysis. Assume that the default rate x depends monotonically on a single global economic factor, set to its median at the base case. Under this assumption, the base case scenario analysis delivers the median default rate p_{med}. Then, $W(x) = N(0) = 0.5$ for that scenario. Although default models depend on a large number of factors (note that each dynamic economic factor can actually be viewed as a 360-month or longer vector), the assumption that the base case scenario approximates the median default rate is plausible. In contrast, it is not usually possible to infer the mean rate p directly from the base case.

The Vasicek distribution is almost model-free (under several very simplified and practically unrealistic assumptions) in that it does not require explaining loan defaults via complex modeling. We do not need to know which factors affect individual defaults, their volatilities, etc. Everything is given in terms of p_{med} and Rho. Median default rate p_{med} can be taken from the LDM's base case whereas the correlation parameter Rho can be recovered from the way the market prices ABS capital structures as explained in chapter 13. According to our firm's own research, the ABS-implied correlation parameter typically varies between 6% and 15%, but it was higher in 2008-2009. An alternative way of getting correlation can be based on statistics of empirical losses (see Mashayekhi and Wang 2008). The Vasicek model underlies the Basel II accord, and the 15% level is elected there as the standard for MBS (Fitch Ratings 2008).

The original Vasicek model is a one-period model. Hence, we face a challenge to properly interpret default rates x and p_{med}. They can be viewed as monthly rates (MDR), annual rates (CDR) or even cumulative rates. For the reason explained in the next section, the latter may be an advantageous choice. Figure 15.1 depicts the probability of exceeding cumulative defaults associated with the MDR scales from Table 15.2, for three different correlation parameters, 5%, 10%, and 15%; a higher correlation leads to a fatter tail.

In addition to the probability of exceeding each of the stressed levels, we can compute the probability of reaching a breakpoint. For example, the CDR-based BPR of 1.46 shown in Table 15.2 corresponds to the $x = 30.4\%$ cumulative

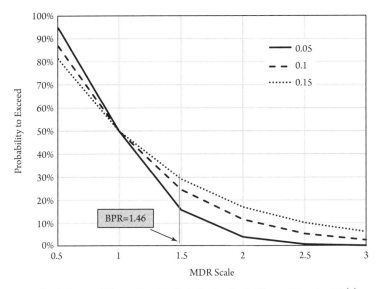

Figure 15.1 Probability of Exceeding Default Scales for Different Rho, $1 - W(x)$

default and would point to 18% to 31% probability-to-exceed, depending on correlation Rho.

After we assign probabilities to each scenario, we can compute many measures requiring weighting the results, such as computing average loss, defaults or even price. Before we show how to use this exciting feature, we introduce a simple, but essential improvement, to the Vasicek model.

THE 3-GROUP VASICEK MODEL'S EXTENSION

The Vasicek loss theory assumes that loans are equally likely to default and pool's default rate may range between 0 and 100%. This is hardly a case for non-agency MBS. A typically seasoned pool has loans that are severely delinquent (belongs to the "S" status, see chapter 12) and very likely to default. On the other hand, some loans will very unlikely or never default. Those occupying their own residence and the financially affluent may disregard an opportunity for a strategic default—even if home prices fell well below loan balances. Hence, the entire range of default rates observed in actual pools underlying non-agency MBS may be limited and the extreme values can be easily found from the same scenario grid.

Consider, for example, Table 15.3 and assume that scenarios 2 and 11 deliver the extreme values of cumulative default rates, $p_{min} = 12.4\%$, $p_{max} = 80.7\%$. This means that 12.4% of borrowers (by balance) will always default and 100%–80.7% = 19.3% will never default. Let us assume further that the remaining

68.3% of the pool are homogeneous and subject to the Vasicek distribution. Parameter p_{med} of that distribution (previously thought to be 23.4% from the base case scenario) is actually

$$p_{med} = \frac{p_{base\,case} - p_{min}}{p_{max} - p_{min}} = 16.1\%$$

It is now simple to assign probabilities to scenarios using the Vasicek formula with modified parameters. The default rate x used in the formula will now be the transformed rate:

$$x = \frac{x_{scenario} - p_{min}}{p_{max} - p_{min}}$$

We provide and discuss here only two illustrative examples for brevity. In each case, we compare a Vasicek-like probability assignment to a large number of Monte-Carlo simulations of interest rates and home prices. The scenario grid employed was limited to the same factors: optimistic scenarios featured lower interest rates and higher home prices, pessimistic scenarios were constructed in the opposite way. The extreme scenarios were not set to be realistic, but rather to explore the full range of default rates generated by the loan-level model introduced in chapter 12.

Example 1. Cusip 76110WF35 is a senior tranche of a protected ("wrapped") second lien deal RFC04KS9 (class AII4); we removed the contractual protection to enable losses. Figure 15.2 compares the histograms of cumulative defaults compiled using 2,000 Monte-Carlo simulations (40 minutes to complete) and a Vasicek-like theoretical probability density functions (computed in 40 seconds). The grid's base-case default rate was $p_{base\,case}$ = 47.4%, the minimal rate was p_{min} = 35.4%, and the maximal rate was p_{max} = 70.6%. As shown in Figure 15.2, the shape and the tail of the 3-group version resemble the Monte Carlo results much better than those of the traditional Vasicek model. The best fit seems to require selecting the correlation parameter Rho to be around 20%.

As importantly, the 3-group Vasicek approximation is much more reasonable in assessing tails of losses (not shown). For example, Monte-Carlo simulations produced cumulative default rates ranging from 35.6% to 65.4%. This is just inside the range generated by the 3-group Vasicek distribution (35.4% to 70.6%). In contrast, the regular Vasicek distribution is valued between 0 and 100% as we already pointed out. The 3-group version is also more accurate in assessing the distribution of the bond's principal write-down including its two most important statistics, expectation and standard deviation, as well as the tail. For example, Monte-Carlo produced principal write-downs ranging from 0% to

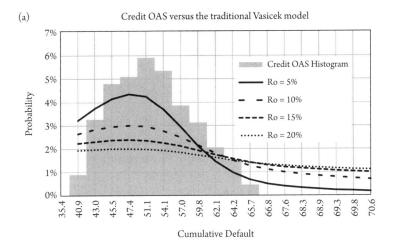

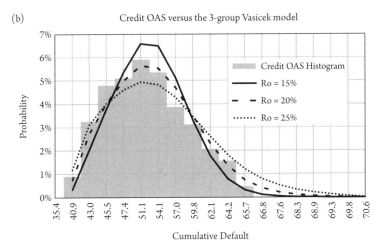

Figure 15.2 Comparative Probability Density Functions for 76110WF35

37%. The 3-group method agrees with Monte-Carlo by giving a very small probability (within 0.1%) for the bond loss to exceed 37%. In contrast, the standard Vasicek method assesses this probability as 1% to 13% depending on Rho.

Example 2. Cusip 68389BAB9 is a usual senior tranche of the subprime deal OOHE0603 (class IIA2). We selected it for two reasons. First, this deal is projected to experience a very large 76.2% base-case cumulative default (that is, over ¾ of loans go into default). Second, the tranche remains very well protected: only 27 random paths out of 2,000 caused its principal write-down, with the weighted-average loss of a tiny 0.04%, but the maximal loss of 7.43%. This side of analysis is particularly difficult to replicate because some of the credit-grid scenarios did produce material bond losses, up to 17% in size. Hence, we may wonder how the 3-group approximation performs in these circumstances and whether it "figures" to assign very low odds to large bond losses. Like in Example 1, we start with constructing the Breakpoint grid and finding parameters of the 3-group Vasicek distribution: $p_{base\ case}$ = 76.2%, p_{min} = 63.9%, and p_{max} = 87.0%. We then compare the results of Monte Carlo simulations to theoretical distributions (Figure 15.3).

Again, the 3-group approximation seems to do a much better job, mostly by limiting the default rate. Like in the previous example, the best fit is seen when correlation parameter Rho is close to the 20% range although the shape of the density function may be slightly off.

Now we turn our attention to bond losses. Table 15.4 lists some key statistics backing the 3-group approximation. Though losses are over-stated, they

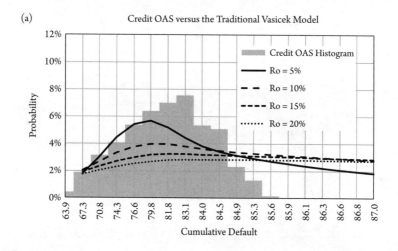

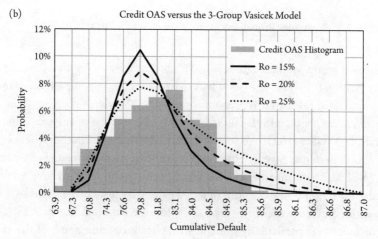

Figure 15.3 Comparative Probability Density Functions for 68389BAB9

Table 15.4 COMPARATIVE STATISTICS OF BOND LOSS (CUSIP 68389BAB9)

	MC	Vasicek with different Rho				3-group Vasicek with different Rho		
		5%	10%	15%	20%	15%	20%	25%
Average	0.04%	1.54%	2.96%	3.86%	4.48%	0.24%	0.44%	0.67%
Stdev	0.41%	4.13%	5.84%	6.61%	7.05%	1.06%	1.57%	2.07%
P(loss> 7.43%)*	0.0%	9.0%	18.0%	24.5%	27.0%	0.50%	1.50%	3.00%

* maximal loss of Monte Carlo

are much closer to simulations for the 3-group version than for the traditional Vasicek model.

In most cases, the 3-group Vasicek model is a better approximation than the traditional Vasicek model. The correlation parameter Rho is larger and more intuitively appealing because the distribution, by construction, spans a narrower range of possible default rates.

MBS VALUATION USING SCENARIO GRID

Once we assigned probability to each of the credit scenarios, we can proceed to solving many problems including the MBS valuation.

Computing the Price

Let us assume we use K scenarios and denote CDF_k to be the 3-group Vasicek cumulative distribution function assigned to the k-th scenario so that $CDF_0 = 0$, $CDF_K = 1$; P_k the present value of cash flows for that scenario using a desired yield or discount spread, and the bond's price is approximated as

$$P = \frac{1}{2}\sum_{k=1}^{K-1}\left(P_k + P_{k+1}\right)\left(CDF_{k+1} - CDF_k\right) \qquad (15.1)$$

Formula (15.1) can be viewed as an alternative to Monte Carlo simulations. W. Searle (ADPN May 2009) analyzed a 3-group Vasicek probability approximation for a variety of non-agency deals and found it generally suitable. His study spanned the most common collateral types: Subprime, Alt-A (FRM and ARM), Prime (FRM and ARM), and Option ARMs, with tranches ranged from super-senior to subordinate mezzanines. Searle finds that $Rho = 30\%$ best fits Monte Carlo valuation results (2,000 paths). Table 15.5 compares the two

Table 15.5 COMPARISON OF MONTE CARLO AND 3-GROUP VASICEK PRICES, R_{HO} = 30%

		Price			Tranche Loss					
					Average		Minimum		Maximum	
		MC	3-g V	diff	MC	3-g V	MC	3-g V	MC	3-g V
WFMBS 2006-9	1A31	96.82	98.88	2.06	1.5	1.3	0.0	0.0	8.6	10.2
	1A32	86.13	85.73	-0.40	21.8	21.8	0.0	0.0	72.8	81.9
	B1	34.01	31.71	-2.30	87.0	86.2	11.1	0.0	98.2	98.1
	B2	12.89	13.15	0.26	99.0	98.5	98.6	65.8	99.2	99.3
CWHL 2006-HYB2	2A1B	94.96	94.44	-0.52	5.5	5.4	0.1	0.0	11.9	12.7
	2A2	36.92	37.33	0.41	71.4	70.5	63.1	48.5	75.6	80.1
	M	5.82	5.40	-0.42	99.9	99.9	99.9	99.9	99.9	99.9
	B1	3.25	2.83	-0.42	99.9	99.9	99.9	99.9	99.9	99.9
JPALT 2006-S3	A3A	97.59	99.47	1.89	3.7	2.8	0.0	0.0	23.4	28.3
	A4	88.60	89.43	0.83	17.7	17.6	0.0	0.0	48.2	50.5
	A5	84.83	84.15	-0.68	30.3	27.4	1.4	0.5	59.0	60.6
	A6	97.45	98.17	0.72	5.2	4.6	0.0	0.0	16.2	18.7
	A7	45.10	46.85	1.75	68.8	66.3	33.9	8.7	88.8	91.5
	M1	11.60	11.44	-0.17	100.0	100.0	100.0	100.0	100.0	100.0
SARM 2006-11	1A1	83.67	83.74	0.08	9.0	8.5	1.2	-0.2	20.5	18.6
	1A2	26.66	26.70	0.04	75.3	75.3	61.5	55.8	83.9	86.6
	M1	1.74	1.80	0.06	100.0	100.0	100.0	100.0	100.0	100.0
	M2	1.26	1.30	0.04	100.0	100.0	100.0	100.0	100.0	100.0
SASC 2006-BC4	A4	73.65	72.91	-0.74	18.2	18.3	0.0	0.0	58.9	60.4
	A5	31.57	33.77	2.20	91.9	90.3	15.0	0.0	100.0	100.0
	M1	3.80	4.12	0.32	100.0	99.6	100.0	75.9	100.0	100.0
	M4	1.63	1.67	0.04	100.0	100.0	100.0	100.0	100.0	100.0
INDX 2006-AR6	2A1A	72.45	72.84	0.39	25.0	24.3	12.3	9.8	34.1	31.6
	2A1B	32.12	32.22	0.09	69.6	69.6	65.8	63.5	72.9	74.2
	2A1C	17.93	17.88	-0.05	83.6	83.7	81.4	80.3	85.1	86.9
	M1	1.49	1.58	0.09	100.0	100.0	100.0	100.0	100.0	100.0

pricing methods, using a spread of 300 bps over LIBOR. In most cases, the accuracy delivered by the 3-group Vasicek approximation ("3-g V") is well within trading ranges. Some bonds that feature a wider loss distribution (e.g. SASC 2006-BC4 A5 that can lose from 15% to 100% of its principal) are approximated less accurately, but the knowledge of their market value is much less certain too.

Finding the crOAS

Above we assumed the discount spread was known. Realistically speaking, most practitioners start their analyses using market quotes obtained from dealers or pricing sources. Iterations for crOAS can be obtained using a method similar to the one we showed for Monte Carlo (chapter 9). Let CF_{kt} denote the cash flow generated for the k-th scenario, t periods from now. Assuming continuous compounding one can factor out the *crOAS* terms in formula (15.1):

$$P \cong \frac{1}{2} \sum_{k=0}^{K-1} (CDF_{k+1} - CDF_k) \sum_{t=1}^{T} e^{-t^* crOAS} (PV_{kt} + PV_{k+1,t}) \qquad (15.2)$$

where PV_{kt} is the present value of time-t cashflow assuming $crOAS = 0$:

$$PV_{kt} = (CF_{kt}) exp \left[-\sum_{t=0}^{t-1} \frac{r_{k\tau}}{12} \right]$$

Formula (15.2) allows for iterating without re-generating cash flows. All we have to do is to compute and store KT elements of the PV_{kt} array that requires no knowledge of *crOAS*. The Newton-Raphson process we described in chapter 9 is a suitable, quickly converging, method for finding *crOAS*.

A K-scenario grid pricing method is not more accurate than the one using K-paths Monte Carlo simulations. Nor does it result in more accurate Greeks. However, it has advantages that we describe in the remainder of this chapter.

Valuation with Models' Uncertainties

In the previous section, we limited the scenario grid to shifts in economic factors (interest rates and home prices) so we could compare the grid-based results to Monte Carlo simulations. In reality, a credit model is a source of additional risk by itself: Even when we stress economic factors adversely, the model may still understate potential losses. To account for a model's errors and biases, we include

Table 15.6 EXAMPLE OF SCENARIO GRID WITH ECONOMIC AND
MODEL'S STRESSES

Scenario	Model Stresses			Economic Stresses		
	MDR scale	Severity scale	Prepay scale	Short-term HPA shift	Long-term HPA shift	Interest-Rate Shift
1	0.875	0.875	1.25	14	1.75	−125
2	0.9	0.9	1.2	12	1.5	−100
3	0.925	0.925	1.15	10	1.25	−75
4	0.95	0.95	1.1	8	1	−50
5	0.9625	0.9625	1.075	6	0.75	−37.5
6	0.975	0.975	1.05	4	0.5	−25
7	0.9875	0.9875	1.025	2	0.25	−12.5
8	1	1	1	0	0	0
9	1.0125	1.0125	0.975	−2	−0.25	12.5
10	1.025	1.025	0.95	−4	−0.5	25
11	1.0375	1.0375	0.925	−6	−0.75	37.5
12	1.05	1.05	0.9	−8	−1	50
13	1.0625	1.0625	0.875	−10	−1.25	62.5
14	1.075	1.075	0.85	−12	−1.5	75
15	1.1	1.1	0.8	−14	−1.75	100
16	1.125	1.125	0.75	−16	−2	125
17	1.15	1.15	0.7	−18	−2.25	150
18	1.175	1.175	0.65	−20	−2.5	175
19	1.2	1.2	0.6	−22	−2.75	200
20	1.225	1.225	0.55	−24	−3	225

prepayment, default, and severity scales as grid factors stressed concurrently with rates and home prices. Table 15.6 contains 20 scenarios with economic factors deteriorating from top to bottom and the loan loss model getting stressed in the same direction concurrently.

With scaling of the model, a grid-based analysis features an effectively wider range of outcomes. As a result, well-protected tranches lose more; junior tranches projected to lose their entire principal boost the recovery odds. For example, tranche A4 of the SASC 2006-BC4 deal loses 8 points of value under the same crOAS; tranches A5 and M1 gain 9 points and 11 points respectively. Even tranche M4, which looked certain to lose its entire principal on the economic-factor grid, had a slim chance of recovery once we included the stresses on the model.

RISK-NEUTRALIZATION USING THE SCENARIO GRID METHOD

We introduced a method of finding risk-neutral distribution of losses in chapter 13 ("implied loss" method). In short, we concurrently valued several tranches from the same non-agency deal and searched for parameters of distribution so that the weighted PVs best approximate observed market prices. The scenario grid method lets us accomplish this goal rather easily. The most time-consuming computational step in a non-agency MBS analysis is the cash flow generation: It includes a loan-level analysis, combining loan's results and generating cash flows (principal-interest-losses) for every tranche. Once cash flows are generated, their post-processing can be arranged quickly. For example, in formula (15.2), Vasicek's parameters, p_{med} and *Rho* enter only CDFs. Furthermore, the *crOAS* term enters cash flow-independent factors of (15.2). These observations allow us to perform a risk-neutral parameter search after the cash flow generation phase is complete.

As an example, let us revisit the SASC 2006-BC4 subprime deal as of March 29, 2011. Using three tranches (A2, A3 and A4), we solve for the three unknowns, a common level of *crOAS*, and parameters p_{med} and *Rho* entering the 3-part Vasicek distribution so that probability-weighted prices match the market prices precisely. Table 15.7 summarizes the results.

Using the first and the last scenario, we compute the extreme default rates, p_{min} = 55.7% and p_{max} = 89.0% for the pool, hence, the risk-neutral median default rate p_{med} = (79.9%–55.7%)/(89.0%–55.7%) = 72.7% to use in the Vasicek distribution.

The physical model's crOAS profile is rising with credit losses; lower tranches have wider spreads. Risk-neutralization finds the solution using a common crOAS of 156 basis points, a higher median default rate, but a lower correlation. The two probability density functions are depicted in Figure 15.4, along with credit losses. Risk-neutralization moves the median economic scenario from "Scenario 8" having a default rate of 74.8% (left bold dot) to "Scenario 11.6" with a default rate of 79.9%, or almost four grid-steps to the right (right bold dot).

Table 15.7 RISK-NEUTRALIZATION RESULTS FOR SASC 2006-BC4

Tranche	Price	Physical Model $P_{base case}$ = 74.8%, Rho = 30%		Risk-Neutral Model $P_{base case}$ = 79.9%, Rho = 24.7%	
		crOAS, bp	Credit Loss* %	crOAS, bp	Credit Loss* %
A2	99.59	113.3	0.0	156	0.0
A3	92.64	336.8	0.6	156	1.4
A4	52.09	491.0	26.5	156	41.6
Collateral			48.3		54.3

*Credit loss is the total of principal write-down discounted at bond's coupon rate

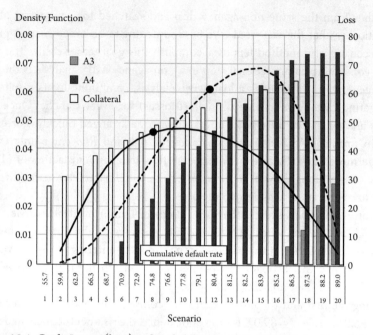

Figure 15.4 Credit Losses (bars) and Probability Density of Cumulative Default Rate Physical Model's PDF—solid line; Risk-Neutral Model's PDF—dash line

This risk-neutralization process separates market-implied credit losses from technical factors measured by the *crOAS*. For example, Table 15.7 above, shows that the risk-neutral model is more conservative, from the credit standpoint. The shift in the loss distribution increased the averaged collateral loss from 48.3% to 54.3%, a chance for credit loss, hence, price discounts for tranches A3 and A4. With larger credit losses, it was not necessary anymore to apply wide *crOAS* levels in order to match market prices. As for A2, this class is not projected to experience a loss in any scenario we considered, but it becomes slightly "longer" when the economy deteriorates. This can explain a small gain in value so that its *crOAS* actually increases somewhat after the risk-neutral transformation.

Interpretations and Extensions

In the above example, we considered only three classes taken from the same deal and solved for three unknowns. We could use more tranches and approximate the designed (e.g. flat) crOAS, on average. We would not be able to make the crOAS levels exactly identical for all tranches considered, but we would considerably reduce the difference and the seemingly existing arbitrage.

Generally and often, a risk-neutral loss model is more conservative than an empirical model backed by data. The price of risk inclusion is the main systemic bias found in risk-neutral models. As most of the RMBS market, as a whole, is long credit losses, it is natural to assume it expects an additional return for bearing the risk that a loss model is (or may become) too optimistic. To most practitioners, this additional return is shown as an inflated *crOAS*, but, after a loss model is risk-neutralized, it will be the loss level, not a discount spread, that explains the difference in market prices of senior, mezzanine, and junior classes.

We demonstrated how to deform a loss model on a scenario grid using one subprime deal. We can give a different convenient interpretation to the result. Instead of focusing our attention on the fact that the median default should move from 74.8% to 79.9% (an observation limited to one deal), we can say that the median economic scenario implied by market prices is "scenario 11.6" of the scenario grid (Figure 15.4). This statement can be utilized for valuation of many other deals, without calibrating each of them.

In principle, the best information for constructing a risk-neutral loss distribution and a *crOAS* level comes from prices of the ABX and PrimeX family of indices. Since each index is made up of a fair number of deals, computational efforts may be significant. Carrying out the analysis on a scenario grid saves considerable time relative to the straight use of Monte Carlo simulations. Once the median scenario is found and the best correlation Rho is determined, we know the market-implied loss distribution in terms of economic scenarios.

Selection of a market-implied correlation Rho may vary with deal types. Typically, subprime deals consist of a large number of geographically diversified loans. In contrast, prime deals may be made of fewer, high quality, jumbo-size loans with a large California concentration. In the Vasicek theory, Rho represents the correlation between asset values that trigger individual defaults; we should expect Rho to be higher for the prime RMBS market than for the subprime one.

PART FOUR

Analysis of the 2008–2009 Financial Crisis

16

Lesson #1: The Role of Financing and Affordability in the Formation of Housing Prices

Why did home prices in the United States grow by 50% in just a three-year period (2004-2006)? What forces inflated the housing bubble? And what caused the subsequent national-scale collapse of the housing market that was tightly coupled with economic recession? Was this dynamic caused by the economic recession or was it the cause? Could the HPI model introduced in chapter 14 have predicted these dramatic events?

One of the most complex and controversial subjects of home-price modeling is the role of financing, interest rates in particular. Unlike other goods we buy, most real estate acquisitions are funded by loans. In chapter 14, we used interest rates as an indicator of affordability and as a force of inflation. When rates grow, affordability and home values decline. However, over a long period, higher interest rates paired with higher income inflation will ultimately push housing values up. This pattern is backed by empirical data, which shows that the Home-Price Appreciation (HPA) rate is negatively correlated to the loan payment rate, both immediately and for up to three to four years after: The correlation turns positive after that.

The concept of HPI equilibrium is closely related to financing terms, which go beyond a merely stated loan rate. It can be presented as a dragon having three heads:

- Loan rate
- Down payment
- Mispriced risk

This chapter follows Levin and Davidson (ADQP 2012), which analyzes the history of the mid-2000s housing bubble and the subsequent decline to reveal the role contributed by each of the constituent components. Our conclusions generally agree with academic studies that seek the root of the crisis in availability of credit stemming primarily from unregulated non-agency securitization (e.g. Levitin and Wachter 2012).

THE ROLE OF THE DOWN PAYMENT (EQUITY)

Along with entering into a loan, borrowers need to come up with equity, or "borrow" a down payment at an "equity" rate. If we blend the loan rate (payable on debt) with equity rates (applied to down payment), we may have a better gauge of what the loan really costs. For example, combining a traditional 20% down payment at a 20% return-on-equity (ROE) rate (20.08% payment rate assuming the 30-year amortization) with an 80% debt at a 6% rate (7.3% payment rate), gives us 9.9% of an annual payment measured off the full price of a home. If the loan rate drops to 4% (5.8% payment rate), then the total combined cost will go down to 8.7%. In this example, loan payments fall by 20%, but the equity-adjusted cost moved down only 12%, as seen in Table 16.1.

Naturally, a reduced requirement for a down payment will be shown as a lower equity cost on borrower balance sheet—even with an unchanged loan rate. If, in the above example, we replaced the 20% down payment with a 10% down payment, the total cost would drop from 9.9% to 8.7% or by 13% (Table 16.2).

Table 16.1 COMPUTATIONS OF TOTAL BORROWER COST FOR
TWO LEVELS OF LOAN RATE

	OLD	NEW	Change
Loan Rate/Payment	6.0% / 7.3%	4.0% / 5.8%	–20%
Loan (CLTV)	80%	80%	
Equity Rate/Payment	20.0% / 20.08%	20.0% / 20.08%	
Equity (down-payment)	20%	20%	
Total (Blended) Cost	**9.9%**	**8.7%**	**–12%**

Table 16.2 COMPUTATIONS OF TOTAL BORROWER COST FOR
TWO LEVELS OF DOWN PAYMENT

	OLD	NEW	Change
Loan Rate/Payment	6.0% / 7.3%	6.0% / 7.3%	
Loan (CLTV)	80%	90%	+10%
Equity Rate/Payment	20.0% / 20.08%	20.0% / 20.08%	
Equity (down-payment)	20%	10%	–10%
Total (Blended) Cost	**9.9%**	**8.7%**	**–13%**

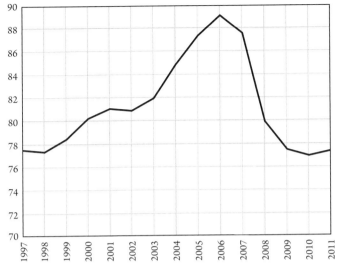

Figure 16.1   Historical Combined LTV at Origination (US average, purchase)
Pre-2008: Non-agency loans; 2008–2011: Agency loans.
Sources: Intex, Freddie Mac, AD&Co

This gives us a hint of what happened in the 2000s. During the housing bubble, the CLTV rate on non-agency loans used to purchase homes rose significantly (see Figure 16.1). That trend was reversed in 2008–2011 (for that period, the data in Figure 16.1 reflects agency loans used to purchase homes rather than non-agency loans, given the lack of new non-agency origination).

Using the concept of the equity cost, we can quantify that the shift in down payment alone moved the combined borrower cost down from 2000 to 2006 and up since 2006. This dynamic, shown in Figure 16.2, contributed to the HPI moves we observed. The drop in interest rates was largely offset by the increase in down-payment cost. Therefore, even in a falling interest-rate environment, housing could become less affordable. By the end of 2011, the loan cost constituted only about 50% of the blended cost.

RATES AND RISK

A historical chart of blended financing rates would not yield sufficient information without also considering loan quality. A large pool of subprime borrowers that is projected to lose 20% of its principal over a five-year average life can be viewed as losing 4% per annum. If that pool has a 7% WAC, it will effectively be paying only 3%—if we attempt to monetize borrowers' economics (regardless of

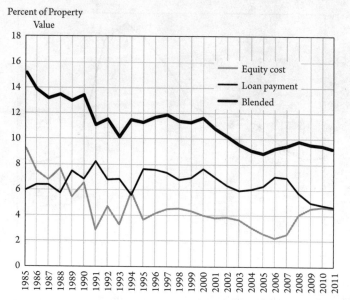

Figure 16.2   Equity Cost and Loan Payment (US average)

whether the investor is protected by loan insurance or not). Such a loan instinctively catches borrowers' attention even if they cannot assess their own credit risk objectively. This example shows that an undervalued risk may lead to a strong demand to buy homes. It is the loss-adjusted rate that matters for modeling the borrower incentive. Creating financing privileges and loopholes for weak borrowers stimulates them and inflates demands for housing.

Figure 16.3 presents impressive qualitative evidence that the explosion of non-prime origination in the years leading to the crisis coincides with the housing bubble.

Measuring Credit Risk Under-Pricing

How can we determine whether the credit risk was or was not correctly priced in newly originated loans? We conducted the following historical study. For each non-agency origination quarterly cohort, starting from 2000, we ran our Credit OAS model (read chapter 13) to assess expected loan losses and (after dividing by the projected WAL) annualizing them. This approach utilized the model of borrower behavior explained in chapter 12 and the risk-neutralized (conservative) Home-Price Simulation model. Results are shown in Figure 16.4.

Figure 16.4b shows that, before 2004, risk-adjusted rates had been strikingly similar among Prime, Alt-A and Subprime loans, suggesting that the risk had

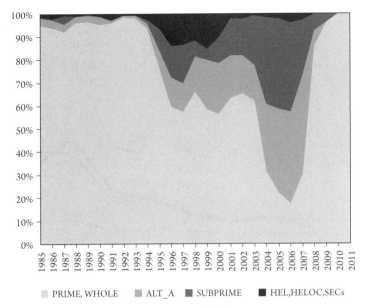

Figure 16.3 Non-Agency Origination by Loan Shelf
Source: Intex, AD&Co

been priced fairly. Since 2004, the lower quality loans were under-priced, with the loss-adjusted rate falling below that of top-quality loans.

The Causes of Risk Under-Pricing

We have further analyzed the cause of this phenomenon in detail. We found that the credit-risk mispricing could be attributed to

a) uneconomically low loan origination rates for Alt-A and subprime loans
b) the growing percentage of ARMs and Option ARMs (see the next section)
c) the increase of Combined LTV

with the worsened *ex-ante* HPI outlook inappropriately priced into non-conventional products. In particular, we see that the reduced down payment standards affected both the equity cost and the expected credit losses, effectively reducing the borrower cost in each case.

The critical economic driver, the Home-Price Appreciation (HPA) outlook, is shown in Table 16.3. In forming this assumption, our model introduced in chapter 14 reacts to the observed HPA trend and statistically separates systematic

(a)

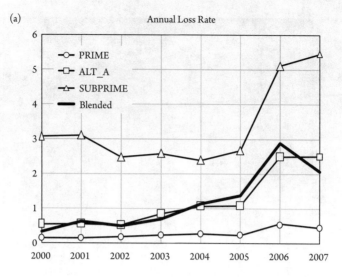

(b)

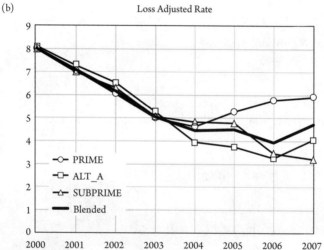

Figure 16.4 Projected Credit Losses and Rates (US)

Table 16.3 Forward, Risk-Adjusted HPA Outlook*

	2000	2001	2002	2003	2004	2005	2006	2007
2-yr cumulative %	11.5	12.8	12.8	8.0	9.3	4.1	−11.8	−10.7
5-yr cumulative %	28.4	26.0	22.0	11.5	14.3	9.3	−11.8	−10.5

*Produced by the AD&Co HPI model (see chapter 14) for the 25-MSA Composite index using forward interest rates at each analysis date and a constant risk adjustment for HPA. These are median scenarios shown for illustration purposes; the actual Credit OAS model (see chapter 13) works with random interest rates and HPA paths.

(diffusive) terms from non-systematic (jumpy) terms. It also gauges the total cost of financing that affects changes in HPI equilibrium. In particular, the worsening in the HPI outlook from 2004 to 2005 and again from 2005 to 2006 was mostly due to the trend in HPA. The fact that the HPA stopped growing suggests a reversion in the second-order differential equations that describe the HPA diffusion term in the model. In contrast, the persistent pessimism through 2007 was caused by the quick increase in financing costs that occurred when poorly underwritten loan products ceased to exist and the low down-payment regime ended.

Table 16.4 lists results of the retrospective analysis by loan type and by origination shelf. It shows some of the key variables that affect credit cost. In general, there was an increase in CLTV in many of the segments and a move toward riskier, lower loss-adjusted rates and products.

In the beginning of the 2000s, the spread of the blended rate of non-prime loans above the prime-borrower rate was in the 50–100 bps range for Alt-A borrowers and about 300 bps for subprime borrowers. These spreads did not widen and, in some cases, tightened by 2006—contrary to the worsening dynamics of our HPA outlook.

A rising share of non-prime ARMs and Option ARMs that offered below-market introductory rates was another problem. Even with comparable FICO and LTV levels, ARMs are proven to be riskier products relative to FRMs due to both the reset-related payment shocks and the way borrowers are self-selected and qualified for the product. In addition, the quality of so-called Alt-A loans deteriorated as evidenced by the falling percent of fully documented loans.

Table 16.4 CREDIT-RISK MISPRICING IN DETAIL (HISTORICAL AVERAGES FOR US PURCHASE LOANS)

		2000	2001	2002	2003	2004	2005	2006	2007
PRIME FRM	Share, %	66.0	51.3	45.6	35.0	10.8	10.6	11.6	29.8
Input Data	FICO	695	709	714	737	744	745	744	748
	CLTV	74.5	76.7	77.4	78.1	77.3	80.9	83.5	84.9
	FULL DOC %	65.2	71.8	62.3	57.1	46.2	41.5	40.4	40.9
	Rate	8.23	7.37	6.79	5.88	5.90	5.90	6.50	6.41
Results	Annual Loss	0.07	0.07	0.09	0.07	0.07	0.10	0.30	0.25
	Loss Adjusted Rate	8.16	7.29	6.69	5.81	5.83	5.80	6.19	6.16

(*Continued*)

Table 16.4 CREDIT-RISK MISPRICING IN DETAIL (CONTINUED)

		2000	2001	2002	2003	2004	2005	2006	2007
PRIME ARM*	Share, %	17.3	12.2	23.4	30.4	26.6	16.2	13.0	13.3
Input Data	FICO	711	724	730	737	737	744	742	750
	CLTV	81.1	71.9	77.7	81.6	82.8	81.1	81.3	81.6
	FULL DOC %	22.6	52.7	42.6	46.3	48.1	43.7	42.2	38.6
	Rate	7.86	6.45	5.10	4.35	4.44	5.25	6.20	6.30
Results	Annual Loss	0.41	0.43	0.38	0.37	0.35	0.26	0.63	0.55
	Loss Adjusted Rate	7.45	6.02	4.73	3.98	4.09	5.00	5.57	5.75

*Including a small share of Option ARMs

		2000	2001	2002	2003	2004	2005	2006	2007
ALT-A FRM	Share, %	8.9	21.6	15.5	12.9	9.1	10.3	13.3	16.1
Input Data	FICO	675	697	707	710	715	723	716	722
	CLTV	77.9	77.4	79.6	81.5	83.7	87.9	90.1	89.6
	FULL DOC %	38.2	28.6	33.5	30.1	29.4	25.2	16.6	20.2
	Rate	9.11	7.96	7.32	6.47	6.47	6.43	7.16	7.12
Results	Annual Loss	0.60	0.54	0.39	0.45	0.37	0.38	1.12	1.26
	Loss Adjusted Rate	8.50	7.42	6.93	6.01	6.10	6.05	6.04	5.86

		2000	2001	2002	2003	2004	2005	2006	2007
ALT-A ARM*	Share, %	1.4	1.4	3.6	6.1	19.5	19.1	17.0	16.1
Input Data	FICO	676	708	713	703	710	714	712	718
	CLTV	78.4	79.5	75.5	81.5	87.0	89.1	91.8	91.6
	FULL DOC %	9.8	70.2	45.4	35.1	29.8	23.9	14.1	14.0
	Rate	7.30	6.63	6.32	5.76	5.56	6.13	7.14	7.44
Results	Annual Loss	0.21	1.20	1.26	1.70	1.51	1.16	2.69	2.95
	Loss Adjusted Rate	7.09	5.44	5.06	4.07	4.04	4.97	4.45	4.50

*Excluding Option ARMs

Table 16.4 CREDIT-RISK MISPRICING IN DETAIL (CONTINUED)

		2000	2001	2002	2003	2004	2005	2006	2007
ALT-A Option ARM	Share, %	0.4	0.0	0.2	0.5	5.8	10.8	11.4	9.3
Input Data	FICO	711		696	710	727	723	723	727
	CLTV	77.5		76.3	76.0	78.4	82.6	85.2	85.3
	FULL DOC %	18.4		17.9	19.5	23.3	16.6	10.4	10.6
	Rate	4.27		4.55	2.52	1.72	1.72	2.70	4.82
Results	Annual Loss	0.88		1.07	1.30	1.06	1.45	3.04	2.59
	Loss Adjusted Rate	3.39		3.49	1.22	0.67	0.28	-0.34	2.24

		2000	2001	2002	2003	2004	2005	2006	2007
SUBPRIME FRM	Share, %	1.8	3.9	2.8	4.1	4.7	4.9	6.5	2.9
Input Data	FICO	590	613	636	656	659	658	650	640
	CLTV	89.1	94.5	93.8	87.3	84.7	91.9	94.1	92.7
	FULL DOC %	30.0	29.4	44.5	42.1	42.0	38.9	40.3	54.8
	Rate	11.14	10.26	9.32	8.16	8.04	8.55	9.44	9.61
Results	Annual Loss	2.17	1.61	0.74	0.78	0.72	0.67	1.68	2.39
	Loss Adjusted Rate	8.97	8.65	8.59	7.38	7.32	7.88	7.75	7.22

		2000	2001	2002	2003	2004	2005	2006	2007
SUBPRIME ARM*	Share, %	4.1	9.6	8.9	11.0	23.6	28.1	27.3	12.4
Input Data	FICO	593	598	619	631	648	646	642	638
	CLTV	92.0	92.7	91.7	89.3	88.5	91.5	92.2	91.0
	FULL DOC %	37.5	25.8	47.4	46.0	43.5	37.8	33.6	40.9
	Rate	11.10	10.22	8.79	7.70	7.28	7.45	8.58	8.68
Results	Annual Loss	3.66	3.87	3.32	3.50	3.04	3.20	6.04	6.01
	Loss Adjusted Rate	7.43	6.35	5.47	4.21	4.23	4.25	2.53	2.67

* Including a small share of Option ARMs

Sources: Intex and AD&Co

Finally, in retrospect, there was obviously a gross misperception of the direction of home prices. With an expectation of positive HPA, defects in the design of many loan products, which turned out to be toxic, might not have been so evident (e.g. Option ARMs or subprime loans).

Interestingly, FICO scores did not deteriorate, and mostly improved, in each loan category. Whether this was an objective trend or, more likely, a scoring system's compromise, it might have sent a false signal to originators, who started to believe that borrowers became more creditworthy. This, in turn, further encouraged lending in high-risk products.

All-in Cost

With the loss component detected, we now can compute the all-in cost rate (Figure 16.5):

All-in Borrower Cost = Loan payment + Loss rate (negative) + Equity cost

The blended lines in Figure 16.5 clearly depict the mid-2000s "dent" in effective cost despite an increase in loan rates. It was caused by the plummeted equity cost and the increased credit risk under-pricing. The effect is seen to be somewhat stronger in California, which originated more Option ARMs and non-standard loans in general (read the next sections). The existence of the dent in financing cost history was predicted in chapter 14 and shown to have matched the actual HPI dynamics fairly well.

THE ROLE OF OPTION ARMS

Figure 16.6 depicts origination by loan type and shows two prominent periods that saw 10%+ negative amortization ARMs. First, they were COFI ARMs, designed to match banks' liabilities. Negative amortization was an innocent by-product feature arising from the mismatch between frequent interest resets and less frequent payment resets. In contrast, the second wave of "negam" innovation was malignant by design. Homeowners-to-be had incentive to increase their debt in hope to sell homes later at a higher price and pay off the loan.

The negative amortization volume also has a remarkable coincidence with HPI booms and busts, although it remains a chicken-and-egg dilemma. Option ARMs could only be offered with confidence that home prices would grow. The low-cost financing they offer propels the HPI further. Once it reaches its peak, Option ARMs stopped being offered. Their death caused the HPI to decline deeper as new homebuyers could not afford prices paid by previous owners who used Option ARMs.

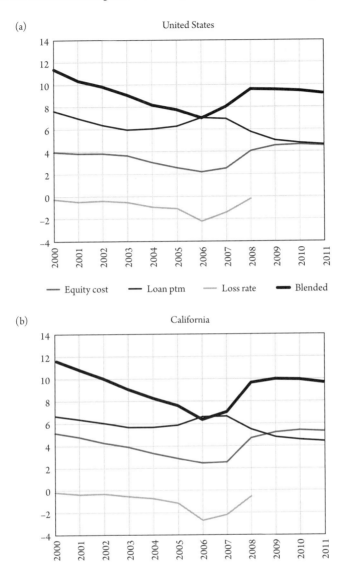

Figure 16.5   All-in Cost of Borrowing (non-agency loans, % of property value)

GEOGRAPHICAL ANGLE

The housing bubble and decline were most prominent in California, Nevada, Florida and Arizona. Figure 16.7, taken from Levin (ADCP 2010), shows the connection between these HPI anomalies and the proliferation of "affordable" lending programs. It is evident that the four states that experienced the largest plunge are those that abused the affordable lending programs (Nevada, Arizona, Florida, and

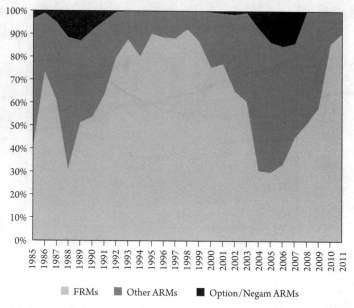

Figure 16.6   Non-Agency Origination by Loan Type

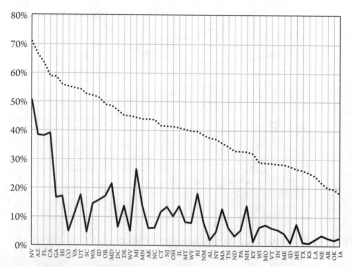

Figure 16.7   Affordable Lending versus HPI Decline
Dotted line: Share of Option ARMs + IO ARMs for Prime + Alt-A originations during
2002–2006; Solid line: Decline from the peak to first trough (2009Q1)

California). Overall, the correlation between affordable lending and HPI decline is evident although other factors may have played a certain role, too (e.g., severe stumbling of the automotive industry in Michigan). Berkovec et al. (2013) also argue that loan features evading normal amortization is the first most important explanatory variable in matching bubble and bust, across geographical regions.

Figure 16.8 demonstrates the last quarter-century history of non-conventional origination in California and its relationship to HPA. This state was the

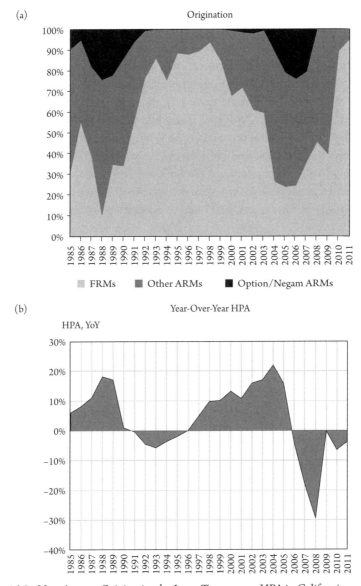

(a)   Origination

FRMs   Other ARMs   Option/Negam ARMs

(b)   Year-Over-Year HPA

HPA, YoY

Figure 16.8 Non-Agency Origination by Loan Type versus HPA in California

motherland of COFI ARMs in the second half of 1980s and it had the Option ARMs share exceeding 20% of its 2005–2007 loans. The COFI ARM origination caused a modest HPI decline in the 1990s, but the proliferation of Option ARM was really poisoned.

NATIONAL AND REGIONAL MARKET COMPOSITION

Before we proceed to reporting our actual results that explain historical events via change of housing affordability, we need to pay attention to the mortgage market's composition in the area in question. We should account for the shares of government (GNMA) loans, conforming (GSE) loans and non-conforming (non-agency) loans. Those main loan types have existed for many years, but different regions featured their distinctly differing and dynamically changing shares. For example, California loans had been mostly non-conforming due to their size until 2008. Figure 16.9-US reports composition of the national mortgage market and blended costs we assess for GNMA, GSE and non-agency loans. Figure 16.9-CA shows same for California where composition has obviously shifted in recent years with the increase of conforming limit. Figure 16.9-TX depicts Texas where majority of origination was backed by GNMA or the GSEs—even in mid-2000s. In compiling the data for these charts, we neglected credit risk under-pricing for GNMA and GSE loans and utilized origination data from Mortgage Market Statistical Annual (2012). Although this may seem as being a frivolous shortcut to avoid complexity, the quality of GSE loans has been very high as of late and the points paid by borrowers to obtain FHA loans may be viewed a fair compensation of the high-LTV related credit risk.[1]

As seen from Figure 16.9, the cost of conforming loans has been notably stable despite the interest-rate volatility because CLTV at origination was lower when rates were lower, thereby inflating the equity cost and offsetting the decline in loan cost. As for the loans guaranteed by GNMA, we see their rates falling as well, but without an equity cost offset, as the original LTV has been quite stable in the narrow 93–95 range over the last decade. The main driver that differentiated the regions was the dynamic of non-agency market share: This is where the all-in cost dropped the most by mid-2000s. California, a predominantly non-agency state, followed the trend, whereas Texas did not and dodged the bubble.

---

[1]At the time of this writing, we have not analyzed the credit risk of government loans.

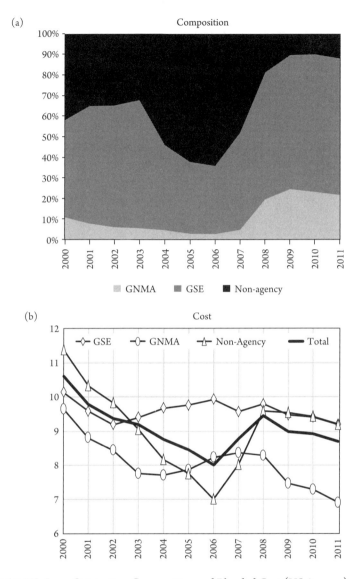

Figure 16.9-US Loan Origination Composition and Blended Cost (US Average)

AFFORDABILITY INDEX AND HPI EQUILIBRIUM

Having computed an all-in borrower cost, we are now in position to define the Affordability Index, or, equivalently, affordability-based home-price equilibrium. The Affordability Index is the ratio of household income to the annual borrowing cost:

$$\text{Affordability Index} = \text{Income} / (\text{All-in Cost} * \text{HPI})$$

(a)

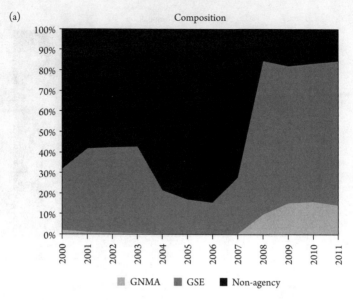

(b)

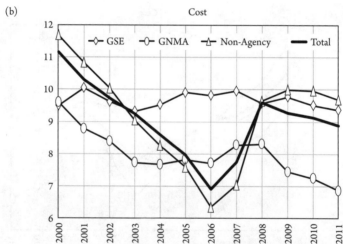

Figure 16.9-CA Loan Origination Composition and Blended Cost (California)

HPI equilibrium is defined as the HPI level that keeps the Affordability Index constant using the above formula. We depict the Affordability Index relative to its 2000 level (i.e., in 2000 earned dollars) in Figure 16.10.

If home price exactly followed the cost of borrowing and income, the Affordability Index would stay constant. In Figure 16.10, we see that our All-in cost was much less volatile than the standard measure (advocated by the National Association of Realtors, NAR) that considers only loan payments. Equivalently, our affordability-linked HPI equilibrium, unlike the standard one, was a much

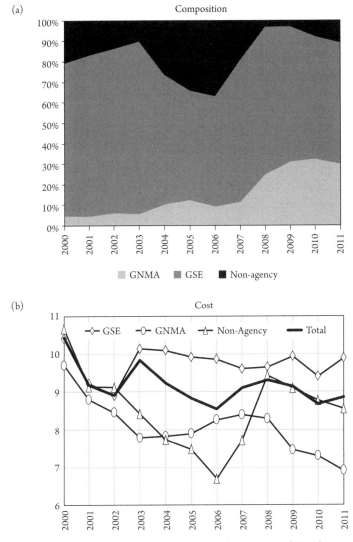

Figure 16.9-TX Loan Origination Composition and Blended Cost (Texas)

better predictor of HPI trends and levels (Figure 16.11). We observe that our HPI equilibrium was quite predictive of actual home prices, although other factors also contributed to the HPI dynamics. Such factors were classified in chapter 14 as "HPA jumps" (non-systematic randomness) and "HPA diffusion" (systematic randomness). For example, the HPI equilibrium derived straight from our affordability index would understate the housing bubble both in the United States (on average) and in California. It can be explained by the fact that we excluded forward HPA expectation from affordability thereby ignoring speculative optimism.

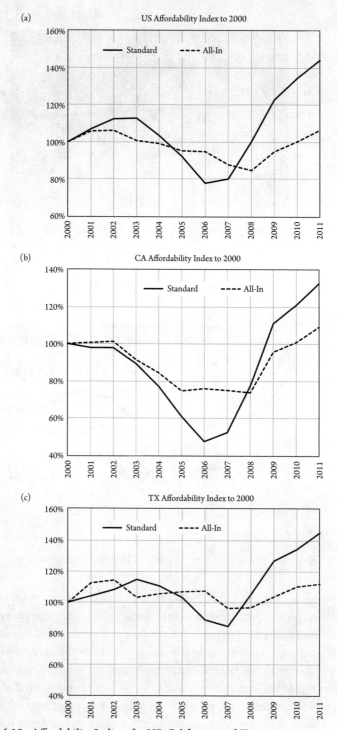

Figure 16.10   Affordability Indices for US, California, and Texas

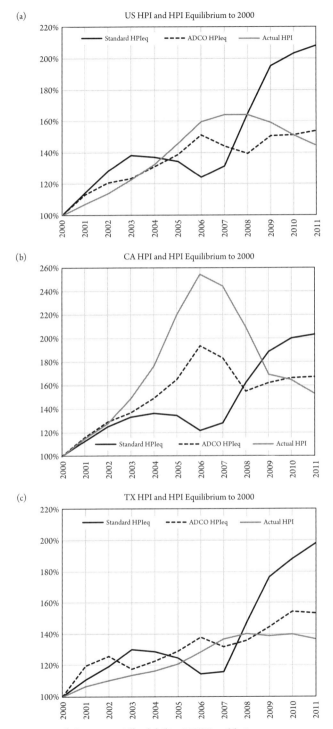

Figure 16.11   HPI and Constant-Affordability HPI Equilibrium

Not surprisingly, home prices overgrew the objective equilibriums in mid-2000s in California and the United States.

According to the NAR, 2012 was the year of record-high affordability[2]; this agrees with the Standard HPIeq lines in Figure 16.11. Our index does not share this view. Once we consider currently existing high down payment and strict credit requirements, the HPI equilibrium is found just above observed home prices.

HPI EQUILIBRIUM AND A DEMAND-SUPPLY ARGUMENT

In general, HPI volatility is known to be stronger in densely populated areas such as major MSAs. For example, we show in chapter 14 (Figure 14.12) that the HPI volatility measured for the Composite of 25 largest MSAs is almost twice as large as the HPI volatility for the United States; San Francisco and Los Angeles are more volatile than the state of California; the New York MSA is more volatile than the state of New York. We contend that these observations can be backed by demand-supply curves for the housing market. In essence, the ability to meet growing demand by new construction reduces potential HPI appreciation. In contrast, areas lacking free land (e.g. dense MSAs) can see HPI moving stronger in each direction. We illustrate this important point using Figure 16.12, depicting hypothetical demand-supply (y-axis) against HPI (the x-axis).

Demand (D) Supply (S)

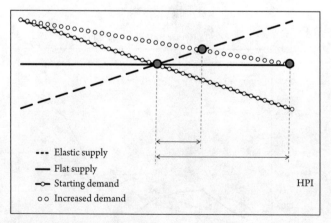

Figure 16.12   Demand-Supply Curves

[2] http://www.realtor.org/news-releases/2012/03/housing-affordability-index-hits-record-high

Let us start with some demand curve, a decreasing function of home prices ("Starting Demand"). If financing conditions improve, the line scales up ("Increased Demand"). How much will this improved affordability increase home prices? The answer depends on the supply curve. In large MSAs offering no or limited new construction, that curve can be relatively flat ("Flat Supply"). This means that homeowners intending to sell homes will do so no matter what the price is. Many of them expect to buy another property so their gain on one transaction offsets the loss on the other. Of course, a perfectly flat curve is an over-simplification as there will be some homeowners not selling at low price, e.g. investors.

If new construction is possible, housing supply will ultimately rise ("Elastic Supply"). As seen in Figure 16.12, the HPI shift will be larger in the case of a flat, or less elastic, supply. It is therefore important not only to measure housing affordability, but also to quantify its role in formation of the HPI equilibrium, i.e. the intersection of that region demand and supply lines.

The exact position of demand-supply lines is unlikely going to be known in practical modeling. However, one can assume that the HPI equilibrium is formed using some parameterized relationship and calibrate parameters using historical data.

CONCLUSION

Mortgage rates alone do not paint a complete picture of borrowers' economics. The rates should be credit-adjusted and blended with the cost of equity, i.e. down payments. These factors, analyzed retrospectively, can reveal the causes of the housing boom and decline. Proliferation of non-standard lending programs such as payment-reducing ARMs and negatively amortizing Option ARMs, non-prime loans, high-CLTV loans, and other loans with underpriced credit risk were significant contributors to the crisis. Lowered down-payments and loosened credit standards increased demand and cause the bubble. The reverse process led to the collapse of the housing market. With the demand-supply argument, we showed that changing financing conditions played larger roles in formation of housing prices in densely populated areas.

Aside from the fact that the shape of HPI equilibrium we constructed resembles the actual bubble-decline pattern, we would like to mention some other facts supporting our views.

1. In recent years, loan origination shifted from GSEs to GNMA, the Federal Housing Administration (FHA), in particular. This GNMA-sponsored,

high-LTV origination has grown to approximately 25% of total.[3] It is evident that the low down-payment requirement made those loans popular.

2. According to our all-in cost formula and its translation into the Affordability Index, the relative role of interest rates is higher when the role of equity cost is lower. As seen from Figure 16.5, in 2006, loan payments constituted close to 100% of the total cost (with the equity cost being essentially offset by the risk under-pricing). By the end of 2011, loan payments constituted only 50% of the total cost and were rather modest by historical standards. This explains why the record-low interest rates alone do not impress borrowers and do not propel home prices up.

3. Following a similar train of thought, with the small equity cost in mid-2000s, the relative importance of risk-adjusted loan rate was high. Therefore, risk under-pricing played a strong role in borrower decisions. We think that if originators were to offer subprime loans in 2011–2012 at a low rate, it would not lead to a substantial surge in demand due to the severe equity requirement.

[3] A rough estimate. Weighted average OLTV of GNMA loans has been 91%; combined OLTV is not available.

17

Lesson #2: The Collateralized Debt Obligation Calamity and Six Degrees of Separation

Volumes have been written on the Mortgage-Backed Securities Crisis of 2007 and the ensuing Financial Crisis that began in the fall of 2008. The twin crises produced a massive drop in home prices, the near collapse of the financial system, and a devastating increase in unemployment. A by-product of the crisis was that the once vibrant non-agency mortgage-backed securities market became dormant, or perhaps even died. From the crisis through 2012 there were only a few non-agency MBS transactions, primarily those sponsored by the REIT Redwood Trust.

The non-agency mortgage was at the epicenter of the housing boom and bust. As we discussed in the previous chapter, the wide availability of mortgage credit with low down payments to borrowers with poor payment histories contributed to the run-up in home prices. Moreover, many of these loans were poorly underwritten, so that many borrowers who were given loans did not even meet the *relaxed* loan requirements. The demise of the non-agency mortgage market caused home prices to tumble as servicers sold foreclosed properties, but probably more importantly, the flow of easy money was shut down, putting the inflated home prices out of the reach of potential homeowners.

In this chapter we look at two components of the failure of this market; in both cases the failure takes place at the intersection of financial theory and agency theory. In the first case we look at CDOs, or collateralized debt obligations. The process of creating CDOs magnified the separation of functions in the mortgage market and produced a situation where no one was looking at the quality of the loans being originated. Further, the fundamental structure of CDOs was incompatible with financial theory on diversification.

The second case is the failure of representations and warranties to ensure appropriate underwriting quality as originators were not sufficiently motivated to produce loans that met underwriting requirements. This failure arose from the compound option nature of the representation and warranty exercise.

Securitization is the process by which loan investment is separated from loan origination. Through this separation, securitization provides the economy with certain benefits. One clear benefit of securitization is increasing the availability of capital beyond the capacity of the loan originators. Securitization also offers the benefit of spreading risk and allowing more market participants the ability to impact the pricing of assets. However, the separation of origination and investment can become counterproductive if the link becomes too attenuated, and excessive risk seeps into the markets.

THE FAILURE OF CDOS

While the causes of the twin crises are many, the CDO was a key player in the non-agency mortgage drama. CDOs are built upon the same principles as the non-agency mortgage-backed securities. Rather than the collateral for the transaction being mortgage loans, the collateral for the CDO is other bonds. CDOs comprising predominantly bonds from subprime mortgage-backed securities were called ABS CDOs. Transactions backed by single-A and double-A MBS were called high-grade ABS CDOs, and transactions backed by BBB MBS were called Mezzanine, or Mezz ABS CDOs. According to Adelson and Jacob (2008), by 2005, CDOs were "the sole investors for subordinate credit risk in subprime mortgage ABS."

As discussed in chapter 2, ABS stands for Asset-Backed Securities and arises from the tradition at many Wall Street firms of having separate trading desks for prime MBS and subprime MBS. The subprime mortgage market grew out of second lien mortgages, some open ended, (called HELOCs, home equity line of credit) and closed-end seconds (HELs). These instruments were generally traded and structured by the same people who were responsible for auto loan and credit card securitizations. Over time the market grew to encompass first lien mortgages to borrowers with poor credit histories.

CDOs were based upon the simple idea that in a diversified pool of bonds, not all bonds would default at the same time and that even when some bonds defaulted, there would be substantial recovery of principal. Therefore, even in a portfolio of BBB-rated bonds there were some cash flows that would be available even in an AAA scenario. These cash flows could be used to create AAA bonds from a pool of BBB bonds. Whether this was brilliant financial engineering, wishful thinking, deceptive financial alchemy, or perhaps some combination of all three, depended on the details of how the deals were constructed.

In the end, nearly all of the ABS CDOs failed, leaving behind losses of $420 billion on $641 billion of issuance according to Cordell et al. (2011). The fundamental flaws of the ABS CDOs can be understood based on the principles discussed in this book. The key insights are:

1. The idiosyncratic risk of individual loans is largely diversified in creating MBS.
2. It is difficult to further diversify a portfolio of bonds with diversified collateral of similar loans.
3. The structuring of ABS BBB bonds made it likely that in a stress scenario there would be little or no recovery of principal.

In retrospect, the flaws of CDOs seem so obvious that it seems incredible that they could have grown to be such a large portion of the market. It appears that firms were willing to put short-term profits ahead of long-term viability. Investors were not focused on analyzing CDOs, but on adding investments with higher than average yields. CDO managers were not focused on the quality of the loans but only on the ratings. Rating agencies were not focused on the quality of the loans, but on the stated characteristics. Underwriters were not focused on the risks of the products they were creating for themselves and their customers but on short-term profits. Everyone was happy to continue a profitable operation.

Davidson wrote about this in August 2007 in "Six Degrees of Separation" (ADPN, Aug. 2007) just as the market was collapsing. A version of this article is reproduced here:

SIX DEGREES OF SEPARATION

In the simplest terms, what went wrong in the subprime mortgage market is that the people responsible for making loans had too little financial interest in the performance of those loans and the people with financial interest in the loans had too little involvement in the how the loans were made.

The capital markets are a wonderful vehicle for transferring risk and providing capital to lending activities. But when the transfer of risk leads to a lack of diligence, markets become dysfunctional. To see how this can happen, let's start with the most basic lending transactions.

Zero Degrees of Separation

For much of the last century, it was the Savings and Loans, or "Thrifts" that provided the bulk of the mortgage loans. In the traditional lending model, the Thrift raised money via deposits from its customers and then lent that money to other customers for home purchases. If the borrower was unable to make its mortgage payments, the Thrift would suffer the consequences directly. With the advent of deposit insurance, the depositors were protected and the only risk was to the capital of the institution. With limited risk management capability and limited ability to raise deposits outside of their home markets, Thrifts were subject to a boom and bust cycle that meant that capital flows for mortgage lending were uneven.

One Degree of Separation

The secondary market for mortgages was developed to separate the process of creating loans from the capital required to fund the loans. In the secondary market, the risk of borrower default would be transferred to an investor. Investors for the most part however, were unwilling to take on the risk of borrowers they did not know. To facilitate the availability of capital, Ginnie Mae, Fannie Mae and Freddie Mac were established. Without getting into the full history or details, the main impact of these agencies was to take on the credit risk of borrowers and allow other financial market participants to provide the funding for the mortgages.

These agencies, as well as the mortgage insurance companies, bore the risk of default. To protect themselves, they established underwriting criteria for the types of loans they would own or guarantee. While they did not originate loans (and are prohibited from doing so), they are actively involved in monitoring the process of loan origination.

To further insure the performance of purchased loans, the mortgage market has developed the practice of requiring "Representations and Warranties" on purchased loans. These reps and warrants as they are called, are designed to insure that the loans sold meet the guidelines of the purchasers. This is because mortgage market participants have long recognized that there is substantial risk in acquiring loans originated by someone else. An essential component in having valuable reps and warrants is that the provider of those promises has sufficient capital to back up their obligations to repurchase loans subsequently determined to be inconsistent with the reps and warrants. A financial guarantee from an insolvent provider has no value.

Six Degrees of Separation

The current secondary market for non-agency mortgages, including subprime mortgages has many participants and a great separation of the origination process from the investment process. Each participant has a specialized role. Specialization serves the market well, as at allows each function to be performed efficiently. Specialization, however also means that risk creation and risk taking are separated.

In simplified form, the process can be described as involving:

- A borrower—who wants a loan for home purchase or refinance
- A broker—who works with the borrower and lenders to arrange a loan
- A mortgage banker—who funds the loan and then sells the loan
- An aggregator—(often a broker-dealer) who buys loans and then packages the loans into a securitization that are sold to investors.
- A CDO manager—who buys a portfolio of mortgage-backed securities and issues debt
- An investor—who buys the CDO debt

Two additional participants are also involved:

- A servicer—who keeps the loan documents and collects the payments from the borrower
- A rating agency—that places a rating on the mortgage securities and on the CDO debt

This description is obviously a simplification of a more complex process. For example, CDOs were not the only purchasers of risk in the subprime market. They were, however, a dominant player, with some estimating that they bought about 70% of the lower rated classes of subprime mortgage securitizations. What is clear even from this simplified process is that the investor in the CDO bond has attenuated contact to the borrower. While six degrees of separation creates a smaller global community, it is not sufficiently close to insure a good mortgage origination process.

When is a Door not a Door?
One of my favorite riddles from childhood is "When is a door not a door?" The answer is: "When it's a jar (ajar)."

That is the problem with the current secondary market, especially for subprime loans: no one is the gatekeeper, shutting the door on uneconomic loans. The ultimate CDO investor placed his trust in the first loss investor, the rating agencies and the CDO manager, and in each case that trust was misplaced.

In the secondary market, mortgage transactions are generally structured so that someone at zero or one degree of separation would take the first slice of credit risk and thus insure that loans were originated properly. In the subprime market, however it was possible to originate loans and sell them at such a high price, that even if the mortgage banker or aggregator retained a first loss piece (or residual) the transaction could be profitable even if the loans did not perform well. Furthermore, the terms of the residuals were set so that the owner of the residual might receive a substantial portion of their cash flows before the full extent of losses were known.

Rating agencies set criteria to establish credit enhancement levels that ultimately led to ratings on bonds. The rating agencies generally rely on historical statistical analysis to set ratings. The rating agencies also generally rely on numeric descriptions of loans like loan-to-value ratios and debt-to-income ratios to make their determinations. Rating agencies generally do not review loans files or "re-underwrite" loans. Rating agencies also do not share in the economic costs of loan defaults. The rating agencies' methodology allowed for the inclusion of loans of dubious quality into subprime mortgage pools, including low documentation loans for borrowers with poor payment histories without the offsetting requirement of high down payments.

The rating agencies also established criteria for Collateralized Debt Obligations that allowed CDO managers to produce very highly leveraged portfolios of subprime mortgage securities. The basic mechanism for this was a model that predicted that the performance of subprime mortgage pools were not likely to be highly correlated. That is, defaults in one pool were not likely to occur at the same time as defaults in another pool. This assumption was at best optimistic and most likely just wrong.

In the CDO market, the rating agencies have a unique position. In most of their other ratings business, a company or a transaction exists or is likely to occur and the rating agency reviews that company or transaction and establishes ratings. In the CDO market, the criteria of the rating agency determine whether or not the transaction will occur. Let me explain further. A CDO is like a financial institution. It buys assets and issues debt. If the rating agency establishes criteria that allow the institution to borrow money at a low enough rate or at high enough leverage, then the CDO can purchase assets more competitively than other financial institutions. If the CDO has a higher cost of debt or lower leverage, then it will be at a disadvantage to other buyers and will not be brought into existence. If the CDO is created, the rating agency is compensated for its ratings. If the CDO is not created, there is no compensation. My view is that there are very few institutions that can remain objective given such a compensation scheme.

CDO investors also relied upon the CDO manager to guide them in the dangerous waters of mortgage investing. Here again investors were not well served by the compensation scheme. In many cases, CDO managers receive fees that are independent of the performance of the deals they manage. While CDO managers sometimes keep an equity interest in the transactions they manage, often the deals are structured in such a way that the equity of the deal can return the initial equity investment even if some of the bonds have losses. Moreover, many of the CDOs were managed by start-up firms with little or no capital at risk.

Willing Suspension of Disbelief

CDO investors were not blind to the additional risks posed by CDO investing. CDOs generally provided higher yields than similarly rated bonds and it is an extremely naïve, and to my mind, rare, investor who thinks they get higher returns without incremental risk. It is not unusual, however, for investors not to realize the magnitude of additional risk they bear for a modest incremental return. Ultimately it is investors who will bear the losses and investors must bear the bulk of the burden in evaluating their investments. There were clear warning signs for several years as to the problems and risk of investing in subprime mortgages. Nevertheless, investors continued to invest in this sector as the risks grew and rewards decreased.

Now What?

As expressed herein, the primary problem facing the subprime market is a failure of industrial organization. The key risk takers in the market, the CDO investor, were too far from the origination process. Moreover, they probably didn't even realize that they were the key risk takers. At the origination end, without the discipline of a skeptical buyer, abuses grew. The buyer was not sufficiently concerned with the process of loan origination and the broker was not subject to sufficient constraints. Stories abound on the amount of fraud and predatory lending. The mortgage investor was like an absentee landlord. Without supervision and oversight, there is no constraint on an unscrupulous originator.

As the problems of the mortgage market are in industrial organization, the solutions must also reside there. To some extent markets are self-correcting, but markets have surprisingly short memories and seemed to be easily fooled by structural innovations that obfuscate risk. Therefore, without some institutional changes, these problems are likely to reemerge.

Some have proposed greater regulation of mortgage origination practices such as limiting the types of loans allowed or establishing minimum underwriting requirements. However, solutions which address allowable loan types, underwriting requirements may be counterproductive since they may limit the availability of credit to those who need it and deserve it. They lead to innovation focused on circumventing regulation rather than in providing credit. Also such regulations have the greatest impact on closely regulated institutions such as banks, which for the most part were not engaged in the egregious subprime practices.

I believe regulatory action should be directed at reducing the separation between origination and investment. Capital is the key to this process. Fundamentally, there was too little capital at risk in key parts of the mortgage origination and investment chain.

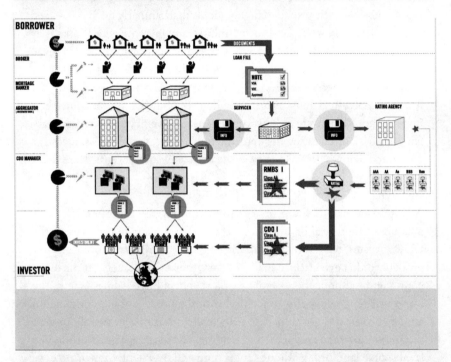

CONCEPTUAL FLAW OF ABS CDOS

The organizations and institutions described above engaged in the issuance of CDOs despite serious conceptual flaws. It should have been clear to investment bankers, rating agencies and CDO managers, if not investors, that the AAA bonds issued by the CDOs were likely to fail at much lower levels of economic stress than other AAA bonds.

Rating agencies established rules for rating of MBS and ABS deals; these rules essentially established breakpoints (as defined in chapter 15) for different rating categories. These rating categories are roughly related to the rating agency's perceptions of the probability of reaching these breakpoints. Generally BBB breakpoints have an (ex-ante) probability of about 5%–10% and AAA break-points have a probability of less than 0.5%.

Rating agency approaches generally focused primarily on the breakpoint and the probability of loss, rather than the expected loss or the tail risk (expected shortfall). Therefore, deals were mostly structured with bonds at many rating categories, so that the below cash flows could be split into eight or more rating categories. The impact of this is that each bond was "thin" in that there was only a small difference between the scenario of first loss and the scenario where the principal was wiped out.

As we have seen, a diversified portfolio of MBS follows the Vasicek theory, so there is a common factor among the loans. Figure 17.1 shows the loss pro-file of a single bond as a function of standard deviations of the common factor. You can think of the common factor as the average home price change for the loans in the deal. An MBS deal is structured by creating a series of bonds that are exposed to losses at different levels of loss on the underlying collateral. The loss on the underlying collateral follows the familiar S-curve when parameterized by the common factor.

Figure 17.1 shows for our sample deal ("Deal A") that as the common factor reaches 1.25 standard deviations, which has about a 10% probability, loss levels on the underlying mortgage collateral rises to 14% and the BBB takes losses. As these bonds are thin, it only takes a small increase in losses above the BBB level to create near 100% loss in principal. This can be seen by picturing three or more

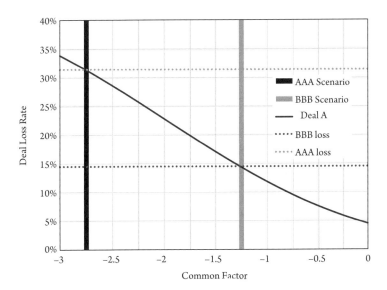

Figure 17.1 MBS Deal with Common Factor

cutoffs for BBB+, A, and AA bonds between the BBB and AAA scenarios. The AAA level is set at 0.3% probability and is triggered when the common factor declines by 2.75 standard deviations and the collateral loss level reaches 32%.

Now imagine several similar bonds from three different deals, A, B and C. Each deal will have its own common factor, but the losses on the underlying collateral will have a similar profile relative to its own common factor. Thus there will be several different S-curves of losses on the underlying collateral. Each deal will have multiple bonds and each will have its own trigger points for losses on BBB and AAA bonds.

Note, however, that the common factor for one deal might not be exactly the same as for the other deals. Over time, there might be some separation of the common factors of the three deals relative to each other. This is shown in Figure 17.2, with the factors for Deal B and Deal C shifted by one quarter of a standard deviation.

The point where there is a default on the BBB bond from Deal A is shown by the vertical line at –1.25 standard deviation line for Deal A. At this point, there is also a default on the BBB from Deal C as its collateral loss exceeds 14%, but there is no default on the BBB from Deal B. Thus it appears that there is some diversification of risk between the BBB deals.

The point where Deal A reaches its AAA scenario is at –2.75 standard deviations and where losses on the collateral reach 32%. At this point the BBB bonds from Deals B and C are also well over their BBB loss threshold of 14%. Therefore, once we reach the AAA scenario there is no longer a benefit to diversification for BBB bonds. In other words, no BBB bonds survive a AAA loss scenario for the

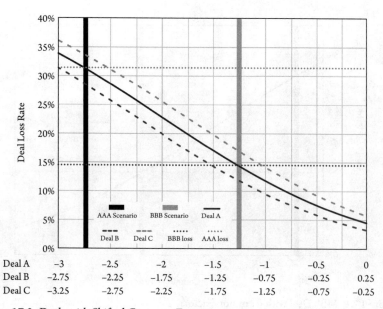

Deal A	–3	–2.5	–2	–1.5	–1	–0.5	0
Deal B	–2.75	–2.25	–1.75	–1.25	–0.75	–0.25	0.25
Deal C	–3.25	–2.75	–2.25	–1.75	–1.25	–0.75	–0.25

Figure 17.2 Deals with Shifted Common Factors

other deals. This would imply that there is no method to construct AAA bonds from a portfolio of similar BBB bonds.

Even if we assume a very large difference in the ultimate performance of the underlying common factors, it is unlikely that the Deal B and Deal C BBB bonds will not default when Deal A reaches the AAA scenario. In Figure 17.3 we show the driving factors differing by 1 standard deviation. Since there are no principal cash flows available from the portfolio of the BBB bonds from Deals A, B and C, it is not possible to construct a AAA bond of any significant size. That is, the BBB bonds are wiped out before reaching the AAA scenario. The only way to construct AAA bonds from BBB bonds would be to use bonds that have very low correlations between their common factors and low severities in the AAA scenario.

The MBS/ABS deals generally had a geographically diversified portfolio of loans as collateral. In addition, they were constructed largely of loans from the same time period, using similar underwriting requirements and with similar geographical representation. Often deals with different underwriters contained loans originated by the same firms. In this situation, it was extremely unlikely that there would be a significant difference between the underlying common factors for the various deals.

In addition to assuming that the risk of BBB bonds was diversifiable in the AAA scenario, CDO analytics also generally used simplified severity assumptions for the bond default assuming anywhere from 30% to 60% severity. In the AAA scenario, most BBB bonds would not only default, but would lose their entire principal.

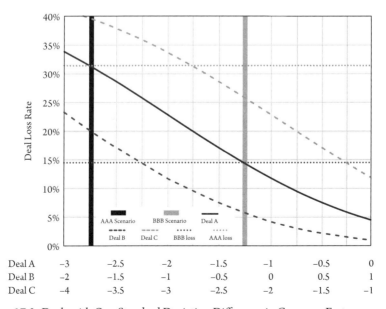

Deal A	−3	−2.5	−2	−1.5	−1	−0.5	0
Deal B	−2	−1.5	−1	−0.5	0	0.5	1
Deal C	−4	−3.5	−3	−2.5	−2	−1.5	−1

Figure 17.3 Deals with One Standard Deviation Difference in Common Factors

To make matters worse, these CDOs also contained a large percentage of other CDO bonds, making these in part CDO^2 or *CDO-squared*. As with the underlying ABS deals, the performance of the CDOs used as collateral, was almost sure to be highly correlated with the other CDO bonds and the other ABS in the deal.

As the underlying MBS/ABS bonds already represented diversified portfolios of loans and the CDOs represented diversified portfolios of bonds, it would be difficult to further diversify risk, especially in the more severe stress scenarios.

While CDOs contributed to the mispricing of risk in the BBB ABS market, it is also important to keep in mind that the economics of the CDO was not so much based upon the expected losses of the underlying bonds, but from the advantage of creating higher rated bonds from lower rated bonds. Although the yield spreads on CDO bonds were higher than the spreads on similarly rated bonds used as collateral, the advantage came from treating "BBB" cash flows of the underlying bonds as "AAA" cash flows of the CDO.

Some CDO managers and rating agencies have claimed that poor underwriting and fraud were the cause of the losses on the CDOs rather than the flawed structure of the transactions. This charge is disingenuous in two ways. First, the structures would have failed even if loans did not have poor underwriting. Second, it was precisely the CDOs and rating agencies that produced the conditions that lead to a lack of due diligence and declining loan quality, as described in "Six Degrees of Separation."

It is also interesting to note that some of the largest losses in the CDO market hit the firms that were originating these transactions, indicating either that they did not understand the risk they were creating or that they put short-term profits ahead of the long-term viability of their firms.

Alan Greenspan spoke about this:

"I made a mistake in presuming that the self-interest of organizations, specifically bank and others, were such that they were best capable of protecting their own shareholders and their equity in the firms. So the problem here is something which looked to be a very solid edifice, and, indeed a critical pillar to market competition and free markets, did break down."

> —Alan Greenspan at Congressional Committee for Oversight and Government
> Reform on October 23, 2008

FAILURE OF REPRESENTATIONS AND WARRANTIES

Representations and Warranties are designed to insure that originators produce loans that meet the promised underwriting standards. During the financial crisis this mechanism failed to produce high quality loans. For example, at the start of 2013, Bank of America agreed to a $10 billion settlement of its representation and warranty obligations to Fannie Mae. This represented only a fraction of the total claims. To date most of the claims related to the non-agency mortgage market have not been settled. A more effective system would not be focused on settling rep and warrant claims, rather it would be focused on eliminating violations at the outset of the origination process.

Reps and Warrants as Options

Representations and Warranties (reps and warrants or R&W) generally allow the buyer of a loan to put the loan back to the seller if they find that the loan did not meet the promised characteristics. Reps and warrants generally insure conformity with underwriting guidelines such as verification of borrower income and the use of appropriate home appraisals. The value of the R&W as a put can be expressed via $P(L, X, T, \sigma)$, the value of an American Put Option with loan value L, exercise price $X = 100$, time to maturity of T and volatility σ of market price of the loan.

However, exercise is uncertain since the investor is uncertain as to whether or not there is a violation of the R&W, the determination of the violation is costly

$$R = \pi_v P(L, X, T, \sigma) - \gamma \qquad (17.1)$$

where

π_v is the probability of a violation of the R&W, γ is the cost of determining if there is a violation and enforcing the violation. Note that, cost γ is incurred for every loan, but the put is only exercised for the proportion π_v with R&W violations.

As it is costly to perform the analysis to determine if there is a violation, the value of the put may be less than the cost of analysis if

1. The value of L is close to X, that is, there is not much pay-off, even with the known violation and the exercise price, which is usually par.
2. The percentage of loans analyzed with violations is low.
3. The cost of analysis is high.

Thus, not only is the rep and warrant an option, the decision whether or not to determine whether or not a loan violated the R&W is also an option, essentially a call option on the right to buy the put at price γ. The average intrinsic value of the option will be positive when:

$$R = \pi_v(X - L) > \gamma \qquad (17.2)$$

As a result, investors generally wait until there is a default before determining if there is a violation of the rep and warrant. For defaulted loans, both $D \equiv \mathrm{Max}(0, X - L)$ and π_v, the percentage of loans with violations are usually larger than for performing loans. Note also that the value of the put option is affected by any change in the value of the loan, not just those characteristics related to the R&W violation.

Since exercise of the R&W option is often delayed until default, the equity of the seller/warranty provider becomes important. Proceeds from exercise of the put will be limited by the equity of the counterparty. We can write this as:

$$R = \mathrm{Min}(E, \pi_v D) - \gamma \qquad (17.3)$$

Where E is the equity of the provider of the rep and warrant, for an individual loan. Suppose the firm originated N loans with total equity E_0. The amount of equity available for each loan would be:

$$E = E_0 / N \qquad (17.4)$$

Thus, the greater the number of loans, the less equity available to satisfy each repurchase requirement.

$$R = \mathrm{Min}(E_0 / N, \pi_v D) - \gamma \qquad (17.5)$$

As the investor retains the right as to whether to perform the analysis of violations and enforce the reps and warrants through repurchase, the intrinsic value of the Rep and Warrant can be written as:

$$R = \mathrm{Max}\left[0, \mathrm{Min}(E_0 / N, \pi_v D) - \gamma\right] \qquad (17.6)$$

We can see from equation (17.6) that R&W enforcement is a complex compound option, reflecting the investors call option to research, the originators limitation of liability allowing a put at its equity value, and the originators ability to put the loans to investor, all subject to the valuation of discount for mortgages loans that violate reps and warrants.

During a time period when defaults are low, perhaps due to rising home prices, the investor will not incur the costs of determining violations thus deferring exercise of the put option until a time period when defaults are high. Thus the number of loans subject to potential repurchase N can increase significantly, so that any potential recovery would be split among more loans. Just when the investor finds it profitable to enforce the repurchase obligation is when they are most likely to find that the originator no longer has the financial capacity to meet the obligation. As rep and warrant enforcement is unlikely in good housing markets and the originating firm will have reduced equity during down markets, the repurchase obligation provides little incentive for firms to originate loans that meet the rep and warranty requirements. Thus it is not surprising that a large housing boom lead to a significant decline in loan origination practices.

A Penalty for Violations

Due to the flaws of the current repurchase approach to enforcement of reps and warrants, a better form for the enforcement would be to provide a penalty, Δ, for a violation, regardless of the value of the loan which replaces the put option in formula (17.1) so formula (17.5) becomes:

$$R = Min\left(E_0 / N, \pi_v \Delta\right) - \gamma \qquad (17.7)$$

If Δ is large enough, the firm will have the incentive to investigate violations. The value of the (17.7) is positive only if

$$\pi_v \Delta > \gamma \qquad (17.8)$$

and capital will not limit the payoff only if

$$E_0 / N > \pi_v \Delta \qquad (17.9)$$

With this formulation we can construct a reasonable penalty and establish an appropriate level of capital. Let, $\bar{\pi}_v$ be maximum acceptable violation rate and $\hat{\pi}_v$ be the capital requirement violation rate, $\hat{\pi}_v > \bar{\pi}_v$. Then we can set required penalty

$$\bar{\Delta} \equiv \gamma / \bar{\pi}_v \qquad (17.10)$$

in this way, the penalty covers the cost of re-underwriting. A lower acceptable violation rate translates into a larger penalty.

The capital requirement can be set to cover the expected penalty such that :

$$\bar{E}_0 \equiv N \hat{\pi}_v \bar{\Delta} = \gamma N \frac{\hat{\pi}_v}{\bar{\pi}_v} \qquad (17.11)$$

As $\hat{\pi}_v / \bar{\pi}_v$ is greater than 1,

$$\overline{E_0} > \gamma N \tag{17.12}$$

That is, the amount of capital is determined by the cost of screening for R&W violations and the number of loans that are subject to R&W obligations. The capital requirement can be set to a multiple of this level to provide greater protection and at the same time the total capital requirement can be limited by keeping the time period under which the investor can collect the penalty to a short time period, thereby reducing N.

For example, if the cost of an evaluation is 0.2% of the loan amount and the allowed violation rate is 1%, then the penalty should be at least 20% of the loan amount. If the violation rate for capital purposes is 5%, or five times the allowed violation rate, the total capital required would only be 1% of the originated loan balance. Firms will have sufficient equity to compensate the investor for the cost of determining the violation, but will find it hard to originate failing loans profitably because each loan with a violation will face a 20% penalty. The investor can determine $\bar{\pi}_v$ on a sample of loans much smaller than N, but if there are violations, it will claim the penalty on all $N\pi_v$ loans. The investing firm might plan on a 5% sample of the loans and would then incur a 0.01% (one basis point) cost on all loans that would be factored into the purchase price. If the actual violation rate on that sample exceeds 1% then the investing firm would perform an analysis of all loans so as to maximize the penalty. They might also choose not to continue buying loans from the poorly performing originator.

In addition to the problems of optional exercise, Reps and Warrants also suffer from additional structural weaknesses. First the R&W are generally made by the seller of loans to a buyer of loans. When there are multiple owners in the chain of transfer, the ultimate investor does not have a direct relationship with the originator of the loan. Also in securitizations there may not be a party to the transaction who has the explicit responsibility to enforce the reps and warrants.

We believe an origination certificate, that created a direct liability of the originator, had specific penalties for non-compliance, required repurchase of loans with violations and was backed by demonstrated financial capability would greatly reduce the volume of loans that violated the intended underwriting requirements.

Comparison of Alternatives

With Dodd-Frank, Congress regulation, attempted to address some of the issues of poor loan quality through the idea of risk-retention, or skin-in-the-game. The skin-in-the-game approach would require security issuers to retain vertical, horizontal or hybrid positions in the capital structure of the securities they issue. This is an indirect approach to controlling origination risk as it relies on the security issuer managing its exposure to originators, presumably using some other mechanism; it only has a direct bearing on origination risk when the originator is the security issuer.

We can compare the current repurchase obligation, the origination certificate and risk retention.[1] It is worth noting that these policy options have very different forms of *fraud penalty*, i.e. the losses that the seller would incur in the event of loan fraud. The penalties are (1) proportional to all losses under the skin-in-the-game proposal, and only apply in the event of credit losses, so that in good states of the economy the penalty for fraud can be close to zero, (2) limited to loan put-back under the standard rep-and-warrant approach and can in principle apply regardless of whether there are any credit losses and (3) would consist of loan put-back plus a fine under the origination certificate, and as with the standard approach apply regardless of whether or not the fraud results in a credit event.

Both the origination certificate and the traditional R&W violation based re-purchase approach directly address and separate origination risk from other forms of credit risk. (These risks were discussed in chapter 2.) In contrast, requiring originators to hold vertical or horizontal slices of capital-structure risk means they must hold capital not just for origination risk, but also for other forms of credit risk. In addition, when the security issuer is one or more steps removed from the origination process, requiring the issuer to hold both origination and economic credit risk means that the issuer will have to fall back on legal protections it obtained in its purchase contracts. Since the chain of loan sellers could potentially be long, it is clear that the origination certificate is nothing but a standardized mechanism to allow these legal protections to transfer with the loans without any loss of "legal fidelity." Therefore, we believe that the origination certificate is the most direct approach to address origination risk.

We believe that the directness with which the certificate addresses origination risk and its enhanced transferability implies that it is also a more robust approach. For example, Fannie Mae and Freddie Mac have greater ability to enforce representations and warranties than typically found in private-label securities. This is because the GSEs generally deal directly with the firm who originated the loans, they have rights to seize servicing, they have an ongoing relationship with the seller of loans and they have minimum capital requirements. Additionally, they typically do not re-sell loans for others to securitize. Therefore, the traditional R&W enforcement approach favors the agency securitization model.

---

[1]See Davidson and Belbase (ADPN, Sept. 2010) for a cost comparison of these approaches.

On the other hand, the origination certificate approach would function equally well regardless of whether agency securitization or non-agency securitization dominated. We also note that the transferability of a standardized origination certificate would also permit multiple degrees of separation between origina-tors and security issuers, allowing a range of industrial organization models for non-agency securitization.

Next, we consider the recourse that borrowers have in the event that their legal protections (e.g. fair lending, usury, predatory lending) are violated under the different models. Under both the skin-in-the-game approach and the traditional R&W enforcement approach, there is no standard recourse for borrowers to fol-low. If the responsibilities for those violations have been assigned to the issuer or any intermediary other than the originator, then those responsible for those violations have their liability capped at the premium over par at which the loans were first sold. If those liabilities have remained with the originator, then the bor-rower has no recourse in the event of originator bankruptcy. We believe that the origination certificate rectifies both of these shortcomings. For example, penal-ties for particular types of violations could be specified, with the explicit penal-ties potentially much larger than in the other approach. We believe this flexibility would ultimately benefit borrowers.

Solutions Deal Structures

The traditional senior/subordinated structures contributed to the meltdown. The beauty of the senior/subordinated structure is that the credit quality of the senior classes is based on the quality of the underlying assets, not on the guaranty of any third party. In principle, the diversity of loans in a pool should create a bet-ter quality guaranty than even a highly rated corporate guarantor.

The structure works by locking the subordinate investments in place until the senior classes are assured of full payment. To increase the value of the subordinate investments, structures have been devised that allow payments to subordinate investors when that subordination is no longer needed. Herein lies the problem. Issuers, investment bankers, and investors in subordinate classes are always seek-ing to reduce the amount of credit enhancement and increase the early cash flow to subordinate classes. This has lead to complex overcollateralization targets, multiple triggers, and early step-down dates. These structures are designed to meet specific rating agency scenarios and may not provide the desired protection in real world scenarios.

In addition, the ratings process has led to the creation of very "thin" classes of subordinate bonds. Some bonds may make up only a small percentage of the total collateral, so when losses rise they can face a complete loss of principal over a very small range of performance change. This makes these bonds extremely difficult to analyze as they may be worth near par or near zero. The securitization market would function more smoothly if these classes were less complex and were not so finely divided. The "gaming" of rating agency models by underwriters needs to be eliminated.

These problems were aggravated by the lack of investor capacity to perform independent investment analysis. While there may not be a way to force investors not to rely on ratings in making investment decisions, it may be possible to increase the amount of information available to investors to improve the quality of their decision-making. Over the past few years, too many bonds were sold with insufficient information for investors to form independent views on performance. Ratings should not be a safe harbor against independent analysis. Without detailed loan level information, clear underwriting criteria, and assurances against fraud, it is nearly impossible to form an independent view of a security.

In this book, we have introduced a wide range of analytical tools to assist in the analysis of credit sensitive bonds. Any of these methods would have clearly indicated the inadequacy of credit enhancement and the risks to subordinate bonds and CDOs. Investors who use tools like these will not be dependent on outdated and inadequate rating methodologies. The investor's motto should be: If you can't assess, don't invest.

CONCLUSION

The standard for assessing securitization must be that it benefits borrowers and investors. The other participants in securitization should be compensated for adding value for borrowers and investors. If securitization does not primarily benefit borrowers and investors rather than intermediaries and service providers, then it will ultimately fail.

At the loan origination stage of the securitization process, there was a continuous lowering of credit standards, misrepresentations, and outright fraud. Too many mortgage loans, which only benefitted the loan brokers, were securitized. This flawed origination process was ignored by the security underwriters, regulators, and ultimate investors.

In the middle of the process, we saw the creation of complex structures that shifted value from higher rated bonds to lower rated bonds. Step downs, triggers, and credit enhancement targets may be good tools to make securitization structures more efficient, but when they allow credit enhancement to leak out of a structure in a manner that is not transparent to investors, they become counterproductive. Further, the re-securitization of mortgage bonds into collateralized debt obligations (CDOs) can create instruments with risks and values that cannot be precisely assessed using current analytical capabilities.

In the final stage of the securitization process, investors were too reliant on rating agency assessments. This created a herd mentality that served to reduce the intensity of critical assessment of investment risks. Bonds often traded at yield spreads that seemed to be driven solely by rating. Such pricing would imply that the rating agencies always got their assessment right and that market participants had no additional insights into the pricing of assets.

As a final note, the cost of securitization must be reduced. The securitization process is overly complex; it involves too many parties and lacks sufficient standardization. Investors face a myriad of issuers, definitions, and structures. Each transaction must be analyzed individually, not just from the collateral point of view, but from the point of view of structure and service providers. All of this complexity increases legal costs, operating costs, and marketing costs.

No matter what changes are implemented, there will still be volatility, losses, and probably even asset bubbles. However, if the securitization process is restructured with the idea that it should benefit borrowers and investors first, then, rather than being a destabilizing force, securitization can once again add value to the economy.

18

Lesson #3: Fair versus Intrinsic Valuation under Market Duress

In mid-2007, prices for mortgage-backed securities fell dramatically. Some market participants assumed that this was a direct indication of cash flow losses investors were expected to take from borrowers' defaults. As we mentioned in chapter 13, along with a credit crisis (loan non-payment), the years of 2007–2009 saw an enormous technical deterioration of the MBS market. Transactions gradually became rare, market prices became unknown. Those transactions that occurred were usually carried at low price levels, often by investors that were forced to liquidate their MBS positions.

These developments not only caused panic, they also led to an accounting dilemma for institutions that did not plan to sell the MBS they held. They faced a challenge of determining "Fair Value" of portfolios made largely of instruments not frequently traded by the market or traded at undesirably low levels. The use of market prices might indicate that the firm had insufficient assets to meet its liabilities, hence, has failed. Yet a cash flow analysis would indicate that the firm had excess capital, but ignored the changing dynamics of the market and opportunity costs.

In this chapter, we demonstrate how different value measures can be utilized in the absence of reliable market quotes and how models can help assign reasonable values to MBS. We will prove that the non-agency MBS pricing distress of 2008–2009 for many high grade sectors was largely of a technical nature, primarily, due to the lack of funding (leveraging) and not the expected loss in cash flows. We will re-use the concept of intrinsic valuation introduced in chapter 13 and show its advantages for investors who are not forced sellers.

INTRINSIC VALUE AND FAIR VALUE ACCOUNTING

The traditional accounting approach to fair value according to FASB statements of accounting principles was

- Assets are probable future economic benefits obtained or controlled by a particular entity as a result of past transactions or events.
- A fair value measurement reflects current market participant assumptions about the future inflows associated with an asset (future economic benefits).
- A quoted price in an active market provides the most reliable evidence of fair value and shall be used to measure fair value whenever available.

These accounting concepts are only loosely related to the economic and financial concepts we have presented in this book. The ambiguity of the accounting concepts made it difficult to apply these rules during the financial crisis.

Throughout the book, we show that the fundamental uncertainty of the behavior of borrowers coupled with the uncertainty of economic factors, such as interest rates and home prices, creates the need for a sophisticated framework for mortgage analytics. The accounting rules do not reflect recognition of these uncertainties. For example, while accounting rules recognized that outcomes are subject to random variation, hence the use of the term *probable*, they did not directly assess the impact of uncertainty on valuation. The definition seems to say that market values are based upon the most likely outcome.

As we pointed out in chapter 4, market prices are not measures of probable "real-life" outcomes. Instead, market prices reflect expectations of "risk-neutral distributions" of outcomes. Furthermore, a spread used for discounting cash flows to achieve present values, can reflect the availability of leverage and the liquidity of an asset. Market prices are dynamic, not just because of economic changes, but also because of the fundamental uncertainty of outcomes and changing risk premium for bearing that uncertainty.

The returns earned by firms from investments are a result of their ability to assess and bear the uncertainty associated with their investments. While changes in economic conditions that affect cash flows are likely to affect all investors, some investors have reduced exposure to changing technical factors, financing and liquidity. For these firms, the use of market based fair values might present a misleading assessment of their financial condition.

Accounting policy should recognize that non-active markets could become distressed and in such instances market prices might not be reflective of "fair value." The financial crisis demonstrated that traditional accounting principles were inadequate. Over a dramatic period of reassessment during 2008 and 2009, the accounting rules were revamped to better address the concepts of risk and market prices. In order to understand the limitations of the accounting approach to fair value and the changes to the rules during the crisis period, it is useful to think about three aspects of analysis:

Scenarios: Single likely scenario vs. distribution of outcomes
Framework: Real life (physical) vs. risk-neutral assumptions
Discounting: Risk-free rate, coupon rate or other rate

Table 18.1 shows how they can be combined to produce different measures of value. Here we will focus on four measures and likely choices that play a role in the accounting discussions.

Table 18.1 ACCOUNTING MEASURES AND RELATED ASSUMPTIONS

Measure	Framework	Scenarios	Discounting
Market value	Risk Neutral	Stochastic	Market spread
Intrinsic value	Risk Neutral	Stochastic	Non-distress spread
Par less mean expected loss	Physical	Stochastic	Original spread
Incurred loss amount	Physical	Median	Original spread

Market value is the price of a security, thus it reflects the market choice for all three variables: risk-neutral framework, stochastic scenarios and discounting at market rates. It is the appropriate measure of the "liquidation" value of a security.

Intrinsic value replaces the market spread with a non-distressed spread, but retains a risk-neutral framework and stochastic scenarios. Intrinsic value may be the best measure of the value of a security if a firm can afford to hold the position through a crisis period. Intrinsic value reflects the cost of risk and hedging, but not the cost of illiquidity or lack of financing. We will focus on this measure later in the chapter.

Par less mean expected loss utilizes a non-distressed spread like intrinsic value, but uses a physical framework. This metric does not reflect the cost of risk or changes in the yield curve, but it does reflect future expected cash flows.

The **incurred loss amount** is a static measure of physical losses, with discounting generally at a non-distressed rate. This represents the losses along a single path. Such an approach cannot reflect a "value" for a security, but might provide insight into potential losses assuming there is no further change in the economic environment. As such, it might only be useful within an accounting system that does not recognize risk and uncertainty.

Table 18.2 shows the prices of the SASC 2006-BC4 tranches during the financial crisis. We can see three paths that bonds followed. The most senior bonds (A2, A3) fell in price substantially during the crisis, but later recovered their value. The more junior bonds (M1-M8) lost value early in the crisis and

Table 18.2 MARKET PRICES OF TRANCHES OF SASC 2006-BC4

	Sep-07	Nov-08	Apr-10	Mar-11	Nov-12
A2	99.04	91.59	95.91	99.59	Paid off
A3	97.65	73.91	85.63	92.64	97.95
A4	95.23	47.09	35.70	52.09	44.57
A5	92.2	25.44	12.65	25.62	12.64
M1	81.92	13.18	0.67	1.00	0.14
M2	75.43	5.47	0.22	0.15	Paid off
M5	65.44	1.56			Paid off
M8	37.13	0.83			Paid off

never recovered. The bonds in the middle (A4, A5) vacillated in value through the period, generated a significant amount of cash flow, but are unlikely to fully recover the principal investment.

DYNAMICS OF DISTRESS MEASURED

In this section, we demonstrate how to separate expected losses from technical factors and how to explain the enormously widened levels of crOAS since 2007. For the details of our approach, we refer readers to chapter 13 where we introduced the concept of Credit OAS, the crOAS measure and the concept of risk-neutralization of losses. In short, we simulate interest rates and home prices, generate random cash flows from loans (including prepayments and defaults) and bonds, and discount them by adding a common spread (crOAS) on the top of risk-free rates. Furthermore, we adjust our subjective loss model to make the crOAS profile either flat or a function of tranches' perceived liquidity across the capital structure of benchmark deals, usually members of the ABX indices. This means the investor would not prefer one tranche to another as long as the adjusted (risk-neutralized) model accounts for economic risks and model risks.

We have been using SASC 2006-BC4 deal as the risk-neutralization benchmark, since the birth of the Credit OAS method.[1] Historical results are compiled and shown in Table 18.3 with the tranche set utilized for risk-neutralization shifting somewhat as losses penetrated the capital structure (reported losses and defaults are simulation averages, off outstanding balances).

Prior to the crisis and through most of 2007, we had viewed the crOAS level of 50 bps as a reasonable input for valuation. The Sep-end 2007 point was the first time it became apparent that the non-agency market had widened for technical reasons. As seen from Table 18.3, the crOAS varied widely, with no

[1]Using the entire ABX index is another alternative, which has its own issues. It is more time-consuming and limited to the few tranches quoted, with some of them being credit IOs.

Table 18.3 HISTORICAL LEVELS OF crOAS AND PROJECTED LOSSES OF THE
SASC 2006-BC4 DEAL

Period	Tranches employed	crOAS, bps	Loss/Defaults		Publication (see ADPN)
			Physical	Risk-Neutral	
Sep-end, 2007	A5 thru M8	250–500	N/A	19.9/53.5	Feb. 2008
Nov-end, 2008	A4 thru M2	1600–2000	47.4/72.4	42.0/66.5	Feb. 2009
Apr-end, 2010	A2 thru A5	700–1000	46.2/71.6	62.1/73.1	N/A
Mar-end, 2011	A2 thru A5	150–200	57.6/75.0	67.5/83.2	Apr. 2011

direct relationship to credit losses. In fact, the Mar-end 2011 point shows both a strong crOAS tightening and severe loss expectancy for the deal. In contrast, the Nov-end 2008 point, just after the failure of Lehman Brothers, marked the worst technical conditions, but far from the worst credit outlook. That point of history presents two questions:

1. How could MBS be valued at a spread level most commonly found in equities (15–20%)?
2. Why was the risk-neutralized model less conservative than the physical model?

Levin (ADPN Apr. 2009) provides explanations. As we noted, crOAS reflects financing and liquidity conditions, possibly distressed. If investors cannot finance a non-agency MBS, they do not have leverage. Hence, the investment makes sense only if an ROE target can be achieved outright, without leverage. As for question 2, nothing in the pricing theory states that a risk-neutral model must be more conservative than a subjective physical model. Even with a positive price of credit risk, expectation of losses made by AD&Co or any particular modeler may differ from others or from the market's average. In fact, our model has been rather consistent in computing expected losses over time—compare the Nov-end 2008 with the Apr-end 2010 rows.

Table 18.3 proves that, from 2008 to 2010, financing and liquidity improved somewhat and the crOAS levels roughly halved. Finally, the technical situation continued to improve though 2010 and the first months of 2011. As for the collateral loss outlook, it continued to worsen, although with respect to the faded deal's outstanding balance. As of Mar-2011, according to Intex, the deal's actual loss reached about 21% of its original balance, with 51% of its current balance being delinquent and HPI-Updated LTV being equal to 107.7%.

Analyzing crOAS over time, we can come to rather important conclusions. First, the crOAS dynamics was objective and not strongly influenced by our modeling choices because we altered the model to flatten the crOAS profile. Second, it was reflective of changing impaired funding (inability to obtain leverage), and liquidity (bid-ask difference), but not reflective of expected credit losses.

INTRINSIC VALUATION

If an MBS investor does not intend to sell, the economic value of the expected cash flow will serve a better basis of valuation than unreliable market quotes. We introduced intrinsic valuation in chapter 13 assuming that it reflects all economic risks, but not technical risks. We therefore start with risk-neutralizing a loss model as we did before. Instead of using often-inflated levels of crOAS, we use much more moderate levels that are typical for a normally functioning market. Whereas it may be not easy to pinpoint the right number, a range of 50 to 100 basis points can be deemed acceptable. Table 18.4 presents valuation results for the same SASC 2006-BC4 deal's tranches at Nov-end 2008.

We will discuss two methods of computing intrinsic value. In the first, intrinsic value is computed using a risk-neutralized loss model, calibrated to market prices of tranches, but with cash flows discounted at a much tighter crOAS of 100 basis points. We call this process *Intrinsic Mark-to-Market Valuation*. Intrinsic values will change with economic factors such as interest-rate risk, prepayment-model risk and credit risk. For example, they fall if an HPI outlook worsens and are typically in line with loss expectations. They are predictive of path-wise projected cash flows and a cost of risk hedging reflected in the risk-neutral loss model. The credit loss expectation includes the cost of hedging, feasible or virtual (shorting one tranche versus another). However, intrinsic values do not absorb technical distress.

This important point can be illustrated using retrospectively computed intrinsic values for the same deal. Let us ignore benchmark market quotes and instead

Table 18.4 Valuation Metrics of the Credit OAS Model with Implied Losses (Nov. 28, 2008)

| Bond | Market | | Loss | | Intrinsic Value |
	Price	crOAS	Static	Avg	(To Market's Model)
A4	47.09	1835	0.0	2.5	94.17
A5	25.44	1959	0.0	43.3	75.21
M1	13.18	1574	71.0	76.3	32.31
M2	5.47	2064	100.0	95.2	11.27
Collateral			40.2	42.0	

Market Price is by a pricing service. The "avg" loss measure is Monte Carlo average, not discounted.

attempt to infer risk-adjusted home price dynamics aligning our stochastic model with the RPX forward prices. We call this second process *Intrinsic Mark-to-Model Valuation*. The computed intrinsic values (dots) along with market prices (bars) are shown in Figure 18.1 in a historical retrospective, for the one-year period starting September of 2007.

The mezzanine bonds show good overall correlation between our intrinsic values and the market quotes with major changes occurring synchronously or within one month. By the end of the period, the senior A5 tranche remained relatively well protected, from the credit-modeling viewpoint. For higher-rated bonds, intrinsic marks lie visibly above market prices with the ratio of two increasing as the technical duress developed. We explain these observations by the view that expected economic losses were smaller than the losses coming from the lack of funding and liquidity. In contrast, for lower-rated bonds, projected loss or recovery of the principal were key pricing factors.

The intrinsic mark-to-model method is a more practical and faster method than the intrinsic mark-to-market's model, but it relies on a model more heavily. The differences between dots and bars can be explained by the technical duress, but also by the prepayment and credit assumptions employed within the borrower behavior model (as well as by odd market quotes).

Regardless of its form, intrinsic valuation is a strong candidate for accounting value as it is reflective of objective economic costs, but is immune to technical duress that does not affect investors until they sell MBS. In some cases of distress, intrinsic values can predict dynamics of market prices. For example, our intrinsic

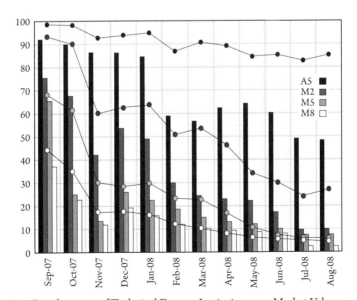

Figure 18.1 Development of Technical Duress: Intrinsic versus Market Values

value measured in November 2008 provided a good indication of potential price recovery for senior bonds. The intrinsic value recognized that the market was pricing with an enormous equity-like 16–20% yield. As the technical conditions gradually improved, the A2 and A3 bonds recovered. The intrinsic value model also recognized the severe permanent deterioration in the value of the M1 and M2 bond that did not recover. As for the A4 and A5 bonds, intrinsic values measured in November 2008 probably overstated their potential due to the additional home price deterioration that followed. By November 2008, home prices had fallen by about 12% from their peak in 2006. Due to the ongoing financial crisis, home prices fell an additional 10% relative to the peak, contributing to the underperformance of the bonds.

From an economic standpoint, it is important to recognize that the largest principal amount is concentrated in the senior bonds, therefore the difference between the market value and the intrinsic value on those bonds represents a significant impact on the value of the institutions that hold those assets. In addition, most of the mezzanine bonds were held in CDOs. A clear delineation between the decline in value of the CDOs (which was permanent) and the decline in value of the senior tranches of MBS deals (which was mostly temporary) would have been valuable information to investors and regulators.[2]

DEVELOPMENT OF ACCOUNT RULES FOR FAIR VALUE

FASB Statement 157, which was adopted in 2006 on the eve of the financial crisis and became effective just as the mortgage market was melting down in 2007, recognized that risk represented a component of securities valuation: "This Statement clarifies that market participant assumptions include assumptions about risk. . . . A fair value measurement should include an adjustment for risk if market participants would include one in pricing the related asset or liability. . . . "

While this recognition of risk was part of an evolution of fair value accounting, the financial turmoil of 2008 and 2009 led to significant changes in the account rules. Statement 157-e expanded the definition of not active markets and distressed valuation to include factors that are not directly related to trading volume, but rather to changes in risk premiums and liquidity premiums. The following is an extract:

---

[2]Due to the accounting rules in place in November of 2008, it took some time to sort this out.

- Indexes that previously were highly correlated with the fair values of the asset are demonstrably uncorrelated with recent fair values.
- Abnormal (or significant increases in) liquidity risk premiums or implied yields for quoted prices when compared with reasonable estimates (using realistic assumptions) of credit and other nonperformance risk for the asset class.
- Abnormally wide bid-ask spread or significant increases in the bid-ask spread.

With these expansions of the definition of not active markets, firms were allowed, indeed encouraged, to make adjustments to market prices to reflect changes in risk.

When making a determination of fair value, Statement 157-3 also required that firms could estimate a price for an "orderly transaction." The price at which such a transaction would be executed should reflect a "reasonable risk premium." Such risk premiums were clearly differentiated from the "abnormal liquidity risk premiums" that lead to the classification of the market as "not active."

In addition to these substantial changes in rules for determining fair value, FASB went further (FASB 115-2 and 124-2) and changed the rules for impairment. For bonds with other than temporary impairment (OTTI), it was no longer necessary to take the full adjustment of fair value into income. Instead, only the incurred loss, or loss in a probable or base case scenario was recognized on the income statement. Any additional decrease in fair value beyond the probable loss would be recognized in other comprehensive income (OCI).

The combined effect of these changes was to remove the presumption that "a quoted price in an active market provides the most reliable evidence of fair value." Instead, accounting rules recognized that market prices, at least under some circumstances, did not reflect the probable future benefit of an asset.

Based on our experience with clients for whom we performed fair value and OTTI analysis, the adoption of these changes to accounting rules had a significant positive effect on reducing distress in the financial markets. While, some people have cited the release of the stress test results by the Fed in the same period as the cause of the calming of the markets, we believe the change in the account rules was a more significant event.

CRITICAL EVALUATION OF ACCOUNT RULES

Even with these changes, we do not believe that the current accounting rules represent an enlightened view of pricing mechanisms and the appropriate reporting of risk and return. Ideally, accounting models should recognize that market prices are not market participant forecasts of future cash flows. Rather, market prices reflect market participant requirements to earn returns as compensation for the uncertainty of future cash flows, based upon their funding costs, including capital requirements and the anticipated costs (including transactions costs) associated with the investment of the marginal investor. As the costs and benefits may vary significantly from firm to firm, there is no assurance that market price reflects "probable" outcomes for any given firm.

Income and return on investment are ultimately determined as the uncertainty of investment is resolved within the context of the firms overall strategy and asset liability mix. Accounting statements are far from providing information about this process. This does not mean that there is not a role for Fair Value and Mark-to-Market accounting, but it does mean that guidance should be provided in a way that is more consistent with economic reality. For example, if a firm is unable to hold an asset it should show assets at market price, even if that is a distressed price.

If a firm can demonstrate the ability to hold an asset, it should impair the asset based upon "expected losses"[3] and value the assets using an intrinsic value approach. Where possible, expected losses should be reconciled to current market values by segmenting changes in value due to yield spread, and risk adjusted loss assumptions.

Impairments due to "distressed markets" should be reversed when the conditions that created the distress are resolved. The ability of a firm to capture the value of the asset is a firm specific determination based upon their on-going ability to hold the asset.

In chapter 3, we described different types of financial institutions and their constraints. A hedge fund utilizing repo financing may have a much lower ability to retain an asset through a period of turmoil than a depository or an insurance company with more stable liabilities. Forcing the depository to mark down assets based on the financing requirements of a hedge fund can introduce unnecessary instability into the financial system.

A more general accounting theory would address the interaction of assets and liabilities and the amount of risk borne by an institution. Parallel market value

---

[3]FASB issued "Proposed Accounting Standards Update" December 20, 2012 on Financial Instruments—Credit Losses (Subtopic 825-15) that moves in this direction.

and cost based accounting (adjusted for changes in expected losses) might provide a better indication of the level of risk bearing and a firm's ability to weather adversity.

As losses on individual assets are uncertain, loss reserves should be established for portfolios of similar assets. The current OTTI and Fair Value rules achieve much of these goals, but via a convoluted logic. As an alternative, we recommend side by side Fair Value and Cost based measures of company value.[4] Fair value reflects the current pricing of uncertainty in the market. (Intrinsic Value should be used when a firm has the ability to hold an asset and the market pricing reflects technical distress.) Cost based measures show how companies have entered into risk bearing transactions. Side by side comparison of these measures would provide a more complete picture of the prospects of a company.

[4]See Davidson (ADPN Apr. 2004).

Building a Healthy Housing Finance System

19

How to Measure Risk, Rank Deals, and Set Aside Capital

The financial crisis of 2007–2009 convincingly revealed problems with the usual methods of measuring and managing risk and our reliance on traditional credit ratings. Many MBS investors only manage interest-rate exposure, which might only partially (and often insignificantly) reduce the overall risk.

Over-reliance on the credit ratings issued by the major rating agencies (S&P, Moody's, and Fitch) was another problem. Credit risk was viewed as something external, principally unimportant, barely measurable and non-hedgeable. Capital was assigned based on credit ratings, that is, the job done by S&P, Moody's, and Fitch, and did not serve as dynamic measures. During the crisis, most non-agency MBS were downgraded, but only after their outlook had already worsened dramatically. With each downgrade, often too late, investors assumed further impairments of their positions and capital evaporation, but some downgrades could have been anticipated if the credit risk was dynamically monitored.

Diligent interest-rate risk management was not the solution as the risk was not in this dimension. This development has led to a number of important questions we address in this chapter. How should one measure MBS risk? How important is it to hedge interest-rate risk? How can one produce a dynamic credit ranking internally, without reliance on the work done by the credit rating agencies? How should capital requirements be determined?

MORTGAGE-BACKED SECURITIES RISK CLASSIFICATION

Before risk-management decisions are made, it is useful to understand and classify risk factors. Very much in the spirit of this book, we will split the total risk into (A) interest-rate risk, (B) HPI risk, (C) model risk, and (D) residual spread risk. Each risk factor represents an *unexpected move*. For example, the expected credit loss is not a risk in our classification—much like the exercise of an in-the-money option according to the model. Each risk group can be further sliced into sub-factors as explained below.

Interest-rate risk includes unexpected moves of a benchmark curve (such as LIBOR or Treasury) as well as changes in that curve's volatility. In chapter 5, we demonstrated that a two-factor view of the curve risk could be supported by its historical principal components. Empirical magnitudes of those components can be employed to simulate rate scenarios or applied analytically as explained in the next section.

Independently, the level of overall volatility of interest rates as measured by a model-specific volatility index could also serve as a risk factor. It is important to stress that this factor is defined within specification of the chosen term-structure model. For example, using the Hull-White rate model, we assume that the absolute volatility is specified and stays rate-independent. It is that volatility index that represents a sub-factor of risk, not the widely quoted Black volatility, which will move in the opposite direction of interest rates under the Hull-White model.

Home-price risk includes unexpected changes in loss distribution, including mathematical expectation or a base case scenario, which come from shocks to a home-price factor or factors. HPI modeling approaches introduced in chapters 6 and 14 can serve as a foundation for credit risk quantification. Sub-factors can include short-term and long-term HPA rates viewed as independent risk factors.

Interest rates and home prices are economic factors.

Model risk represented a novel focus of this book. We view the assumptions made in designing prepayment and default option models as sources of uncertainty priced by the market. We demonstrated this view in chapters 11 and 13. For example, we could see how the prepayment model risk is priced in the TBA market, the stripped derivatives market, and quantified the volatility of the turnover scale and the refinancing scale. These volatilities may reflect shifts in both actual prepayment sentiments and the prices of risk.

A well-understood model risk should be favored over more mechanical and less rigorous measure of *mortgage basis risk* as we pointed out in chapter 11. Similarly, an empirical loss model, as the one introduced in Chapter 12, can be viewed as a source of uncertainty.

Finally, **residual spread risk** reflects a change in liquidity or financing conditions that is not reflected in economic risks or costs of their hedging. As showed in chapter 18, the 2008 MBS duress was caused by the lack or absence of financing, not the credit losses alone. The volatility of spread can be assessed empirically, although as the events of 2007–2009 demonstrated, it is hard to rely on those measures. Nevertheless, this factor is the residual one, after main economic factors are considered. For example, any widening or tightening caused by a change in prepayment sentiments (factor C) or credit losses (factors B and C) *will not* be counted as the spread risk, under our classification.

The risk factors, if desired, can be modeled and viewed as mutually uncorrelated. This statement is not a frivolous simplification: If factors X and Y have a correlation of ρ, one can replace Y with another mathematical factor Y' so that $Y' = Y - (\rho\sigma_Y/\sigma_X)X$ is not correlated with X. This method, known as the Gram-Schmidt orthogonalization, leads to a set of uncorrelated factors. For example, let us assume that the prepayment model risk is shown to be correlated with interest rates. This means that the prepayment model's error has interest-rate directionality. In this example, we would like to alter the prepayment model first so that interest rates are reflected without a bias and the model risk becomes independent.

Another important example of factor interaction is the inclusion of interest rates in home-price modeling. To follow the idea of factor separation, the rate-dependent component of HPI has to be classified as an interest-rate risk factor. This is true to our risk factor definition as the change in HPI, given a change in interest rates, represents an *expected factor*, hence, not a source of additional credit risk. If necessary or desired, it is, of course, possible to keep the inter-factor correlation; this will require a slight modification in computing and reporting. In the next three sections, we demonstrate how an MBS risk can be measured.

THEORETICAL (DELTA-GAMMA) VALUE-AT-RISK

Value-at-Risk (VaR) is a popular and well-known concept widely used for trading accounts. Its purpose is to assess short-term risk, namely the maximum loss given some confidence level. The "Delta-Gamma" approximation we describe here has some practical advantages over an empirical assessment of VaR. It is closely related to the outputs typically available from an OAS model (Durations, Convexities) and allows for a straight-forward quantification of constituent risk factors. It does not require a position (or portfolio) in question to have historical price volatility data and can apply to both old and newly issued MBS.

The Methodology

Let us assume that our instrument (strategy, portfolio) is exposed to a factor x having known standard deviation σ over user-selected time horizon. First, we measure Duration (D) and Convexity (C) of our instrument with respect to x. Then, we postulate that price $P(x)$ is quadratic in x:

$$P = P_0\left(1 - Dx + 0.5Cx^2\right) \tag{19.1}$$

Let us define the short-term risk as the expected loss of investment return plus one standard deviation. Assuming that, over a short time horizon, risk factors are normally distributed and a monotonic relationship between risk factors and price holds within the probable region of x, this measure is equivalent to the VaR at a 84% confidence (denoted VaR_{84} hereinafter). It can be computed as one standard deviation of value—approximately $|D|\sigma$—plus the average convexity loss of $-0.5C\sigma^2$. This simple definition allows for scaling the standard deviation contribution by any factor—if one prefers a more conservative VaR confidence. Note that, for a short investment horizon:

A. The distribution of price is close to normal. Hence, VaR at any confidence can be linked to a multiple of standard deviation and the convexity term.
B. D and C computed now with respect to risk factors, hold in the near future.
C. Volatility of cash flow is not essential; a return's uncertainty is firmly linked to that of price and not the income.
D. MBS portfolio amortization is small and deterministic.

Neglecting C for the moment, we can state that $|D|\sigma$ represents one standard deviation of the instrument's price caused by the volatility of x. For illustration, if a rate's volatility is 100 basis points per year, and that rate is a Brownian motion, then σ will be close to 14 basis points per week. With a 4.0-year Effective Duration, a TBA will have a $4.0 * 0.14\% = 0.56\%$ weekly price volatility. This is how much the TBA can lose, with an 84% confidence. For, the three-month period (13 weeks), VaR_{84} will become 2.02% although such an assessment can be deemed less accurate given the relatively long horizon, random amortization, changing Duration and the presence of Convexity (estimated below).

If an MBS is exposed to several independent risk factors, then the respected standard deviations can be added using the Pythagorean rule ("Total Quadratic Risk"): $\sqrt{D_1^2\sigma_1^2 + D_2^2\sigma_2^2 + \cdots}$. In particular, the largest risk, if it exists, will dominate. As we have already pointed out, a risk model can be designed with independent risk factors by choice.

For many short-term risk calculations, the Duration terms dominate whereas Convexities contribute insignificantly. Occasionally, one can face a situation when Convexity cannot be neglected. For example, convexity risk rises in prominence with an extending time horizon, or when the directional risk is already Delta-hedged.

If the $P(x)$ remains monotonic within a reasonable region of x, the VAR_{84} can be assessed rather easily.

For one-factor case:

$$VaR_{84} = -0.5C\sigma^2 + \sqrt{D^2\sigma^2 + 0.5C^2\sigma^4} \qquad (19.2)$$

For the case of n independent factors:

$$VaR_{84} = -0.5\sum_i C_i\sigma_i^2 + \sqrt{\sum_i (D_i^2\sigma_i^2 + 0.5C_i^2\sigma_i^4)} \qquad (19.2\text{-m})$$

Note that the three terms shown in these formulas are of different magnitude in σ. Assuming σ is small, the leading term is that of Duration (linear in σ). The next in importance is the convexity term, quadratic in σ. Finally, the smallest term is the duration-correcting convexity term under the radical (assuming a non-zero D).

In order to assess the magnitude of these convexity terms, let us revisit the example of a four-year duration TBA. Assuming a negative-2 convexity, our one-week standard deviation becomes 56.1 bps, i.e. immaterially up from the 56 bps we had before. However, due to the negative convexity, we expect to lose 1.9 bps, on average. The total VaR$_{84}$ is now 58 bps. As for the three-month horizon, the total VaR$_{84}$ becomes 2.31% (up from 2.02%), i.e. convexity terms inflate interest-rate risk by 14%.

The Time Aspect of Risk

In the numerical example given above, we assumed that interest rates follow the pattern of a Brownian motion. As such, the risk should grow in proportion to the square-root of time (ignoring convexity). It is known, however, that interest rates are stable, hence, mean-reverting—albeit at a slow pace. Other factors may be even more strongly mean reverting.

One example is prepayment model risk. Any announcement of government activity related to credit eligibility or economic policies nowadays can swing prepay outlook. Figure 19.1 depicts a historical example of risk-neutral Refinancing and Turnover scales of the same physical model.

Prepayment scales are rather volatile, especially Refinancing, but this volatility is "front-loaded." One reason is that an empirical model is usually designed using some historical interval and fitting on-average. Therefore, those models can be biased at any point of time and the bias is likely to persist. This is in a sharp contrast to interest rates, accurately known on any analysis date. Statistical analysis confirms that, whereas volatility of Refinancing is 21% per week, its mean reversion is 33% per week (1,716% per year). That makes annualized volatility 30.2%, that is, much below what the square-root rule would imply. For the Turnover, the strength of mean reversion is even more impressive: 80% per week or 4,160%

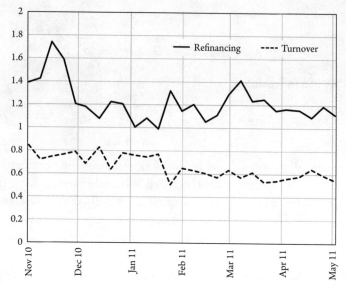

Figure 19.1 Historical Risk-Neutral Refinancing and Turnover Scales

per year. The annualized volatility is 16.1% with most of it (14.4%) shown in one week.

Assuming a linear, single-dimensional Ornstein-Ulenbeck pattern, we can connect standard deviation $\sigma(t)$ at horizon t (in years) to the annualized volatility $\sigma(1)$ as

$$\sigma(t) = \sigma(1)\left(\frac{1-e^{-2at}}{1-e^{-2a}}\right)^{1/2}$$

where a is the mean reversion per year. Hence, if volatility is quoted in an annual form, one can easily assess standard deviation in one week, one month, etc.

If mean reversion a is 0, $\sigma(t)$ becomes proportional to $\sqrt{t}$ (after taking the limit to resolve a 0/0 uncertainty). However, if a is infinite, then $\sigma(t)=\sigma(1)$ for any $t > 0$. Figure 19.2 depicts the $\sigma(t)/\sigma(1)$ ratio as a function of a.

As seen, the stronger the mean reversion is, the closer the standard deviation becomes to the mathematical step-function. This observation explains different weights of factors contributing to the total VaR computed over different horizons.

Volatility Assumptions

In order for the theoretical VaR method to work, not only do we need to compute Deltas and Gammas, but we also have to know stochastic properties of risk

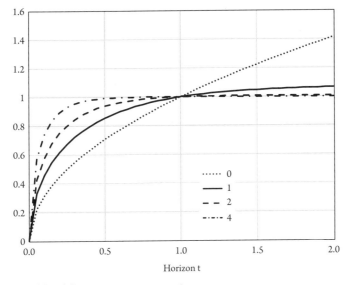

Figure 19.2 $\sigma(t)/\sigma(1)$ Ratio as a Function of a

factors; volatilities, mean reversions, mutual correlations (if any). Below we explain the source of this information.

Interest-Rate Risk. Volatility of the "parallel" change pattern can be easily implied by the swaption volatility matrix. In chapter 5, we introduced several single-factor short-rate models and their calibration processes. They allow for finding the best short-rate volatility parameter and the mean-reversion constant. Note that none of those models implies a strictly parallel shift in the yield curve with the exception of the Hull-White model with zero mean reversion. In most cases, using a mean-reverting model leads to a volatility structure falling with maturity.

Volatility of the slope change can be found from empirical observations. One way is to find the second largest principal component of the curve moves, see A. Levin (2001), J. James and N. Webber (2000). Note that the propensity to twist changes with time. For example, in 2007 all rates were falling while the shape of the curve remained essentially flat. In 2008–2009, short rates declined more than long rates. At the time of this writing (first quarter of 2013), the curve had experienced a considerable steepening and, with the Fed's intent not to raise rates, the curve's shape can easily change in either direction. Our analysis is based on the pattern of steepening/flattening depicted in Figure 5.10 (chapter 5).

Finally, interest-rate volatility can be measured using equivalent volatility constants observed over a recent historical interval.

Home-Price Risk. Having introduced a stochastic home-price model in chapter 14, we can use its parameters to form the short-term HPI uncertainty necessary to compute theoretical VaR. Since we advocated using a two-dimensional HPA model, the Ornstein-Ulenbeck pattern can be viewed as an approximation.

Prepayment and Credit Model Risk. For the agency MBS market, one can quantify prepay model risk via calibrating the prepay model to the TBA/agency debt parity and measuring stochastic properties of thus obtained refinancing scale and turnover scale. We refer to Figure 19.1 as an example of relevant empirical data. Aside from both scales exhibiting strong mean reversions, they are negatively correlated.

The volatility of a credit model can be expressed via two main factors, the default rate scale and the severity scale. For example, annual volatility of 20% means that we allow each scale to be within 20% of the model, with 68% confidence, for the 1-year horizon. Often, the designers of financial models can assess their accuracy. For example, the residual terms of credit models and their stochastic properties point to volatility and mean-reversion constants we employ ("expert estimate").

Spread (OAS Level) Risk. This is the risk of the OAS level changing after all economic factors have been accounted for. It is the residual risk that reflects the volatility of technical factors (financing and liquidity) both for the MBS market as a whole, and for particular asset types. Note that this risk, while certainly existing, should be deemed free of contributions made by changing prepayment views; those are absorbed by the prepayment model risk. Hence, we expect the spread risk to be generally less important than a traditional risk analysis would show.

Table 19.1 contains an example of volatility assumptions. We also compute standard deviations of each factor for four different time horizons ranging from one day to three months. As we explained above, a strong mean reversion makes the standard deviation resemble the step-function. For example, uncertainties of prepayment scales are of the same order of magnitude whether we use a one-week horizon or a three-month horizon. In contrast, no-mean-reverting factors or weakly mean-reverting factors follow the famous square root of time rule: The risk in three months is roughly 3.5 times greater than the risk in one week.

Results

The MBS world features a vast variety of underlying characteristics and structuring features. Any one of the four risk factors can dominate the others for certain asset types and it is impossible to discard any of them in advance. Whereas most hedging activity is aimed at interest-rate risk (IRR) reduction, this is not the only factor and, sometimes, not the leading factor. Furthermore, even when it is

Table 19.1 Volatility Assumptions for Theoretical VaR Analysis (as of March, 2011)

Factors	Annual Volatility	Mean Reversion %	1-day STDEV	1-wk STDEV	1-mo STDEV	3-mo STDEV	Comments
Interest-rate risk							
IR level, bp	108.3	0.4	6.7	15.1	31.3	54.2	Calibration to swaptions
IR slope	0.7	0.0	0.04	0.10	0.20	0.35	Scale of twist factor, Fig.5.10
Vega, %	20	10	1.3	2.9	6.0	10.4	Expert estimate
Home-price risk							
HPA jump, %	0.8	Infinity	0.8	0.8	0.8	0.8	Model, Ch.14
HPA diffusion, %	3.1	0	0.19	0.42	0.88	1.53	Model, Ch.14, approximation**
Model risk							
Refinance Scale, %	30.2	1716	10.6	21.0	29.3	30.2	Empirical estimate*
Turnover Scale, %	16.1	4160	8.4	14.4	16.1	16.1	Empirical estimate*
MDR Scale, %	20	500	3.9	8.4	15.0	19.2	Expert estimate
Severity Scale, %	20	500	3.9	8.4	15.0	19.2	Expert estimate
Spread risk							
MBS prOAS, bp	30	20	2.0	4.6	9.5	16.1	Empirical estimate
ABS crOAS, bp	300	20	20	46	95	161	Empirical estimate

* A negative 50% correlation between Refinance Scale and Turnover Scale is assumed.

** Equates the diffusion-related HPI volatility for 3-mo horizon to that of the actual HPI model.

the leading exposure, its elimination causes a weaker overall risk reduction than many practitioners expect.

In order to demonstrate the method and results it may produce, we compare four asset classes we studied in this book: agency TBAs, Trust IOs, non-agency Prime MBS, and subprime MBS. Figure 19.3 shows the VAR$_{84}$ levels, with factor separation including the IRR contribution.

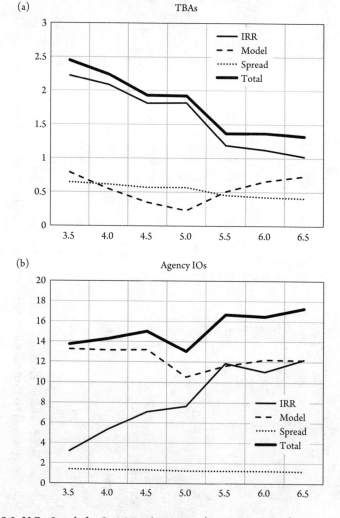

Figure 19.3 VaR$_{84}$ Levels for One-Month Horizon (as of March 2011)

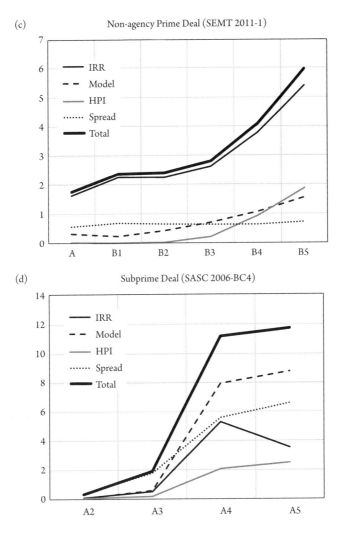

Figure 19.3 VaR$_{84}$ Levels for One-Month Horizon (as of March 2011) (Continued)

In terms of the overall VaR, the IO group is the most risky, followed by the subprime deal, the prime deal and the TBAs. Note that VaR measures a value uncertainty, not a loss expectation; therefore, the risk ranking may be counter-intuitive. As far as the constituent components are concerned, interest-rate risk seems to be important, indeed, at first glance. The subprime bond floaters case is an obvious exception when the credit model risk and the spread risk are more important. In addition, the model risk is sizable and may even exceed the IRR for IOs and high-premium TBAs. As for the home-price risk, it may seem to be relatively modest with the exception of the residual tranche in the prime deal case.

Analyzing this later case, one could conclude that the HPI risk would be siz-able enough at the deal's origination. The SASC 2006-BC4 deal we analyzed in March 2011 was already severely distressed, with 48% of loans non-performing. At that point, the HPI uncertainty means less than the uncertainty of the model that predicts the future destiny of those loans. Had we computed VaR at origina-tion, the HPI factor would have turned up to be a critical one—as history proved. In addition, some of the HPI risk is attributed to the IRR because of the link between the two.

The role of the spread risk can be dominant for the senior tranches of a sub-prime deal. They are not expected to lose principal and pay floating rates.

To conclude the VaR topic, let us ask the following question: How much can we reduce the overall VaR if we perfectly hedge the IRR? Let us define a VaR reduction as

$$VaR\,Reduction = \frac{VaR_{84}\left(no\,IRR\right)}{VaR_{84}\left(total\right)} - 1$$

which is a negative number ranging from −100% (perfect risk elimination) to 0%. Figure 19.4 shows the VaR reduction levels across coupon stack, for TBAs and IOs with the horizon ranging from one day to three months. Those are the MBS types strongly affected by the IRR.

As seen, a perfect IRR hedging does not eliminate the overall risk nor does it make it negligible. Since the rates' uncertainty develops over time with a low mean reversion (Table 19.1), it resembles a Brownian motion. In contrast, the prepayment model risk is strongly mean reverting and mostly front-loaded. The relative importance of IRR elimination grows with the horizon. Even with a three-month horizon, risk reduction caused by IRR hedging can be modest, especially for an IO taken from a low-coupon pool that is much more sensitive to the housing turnover rate than to the level of interest rates.

We view these observations as important from the practical risk management standpoint. They agree with the findings of chapter 10 where we discussed the explanatory power of an OAS modeling method. These two topics are closely related because interest rates play a major role in the standard OAS systems. It is easy to show that, if we know the explanatory power of an OAS model (R^2), the VaR reduction is going to be $\sqrt{1-R^2} - 1$. For example, an 80% of weekly R^2 leads to a 55% weekly VaR reduction. A study of N. Arcidiacono et al. [2013] applied the theoretical Delta-Gamma VaR approach explained in this chapter to quan-tification of risks found in agency CMOs of various types. Generally, IOs were shown to be the most risky class, followed by POs, Inverses, Z-Accruals, PACs, Supports and Sequentials. Floaters are the least risky. The overall VaR reduction due to IRR hedging was shown to be moderate, but growing with horizon.

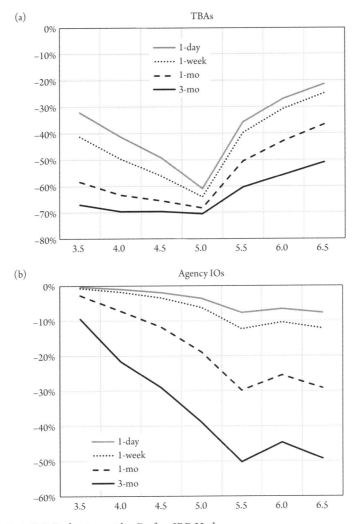

Figure 19.4 VaR Reduction with a Perfect IRR Hedge

MEASURING LONG-TERM RISK

Practitioners reading this chapter may wonder whether estimating a short-term risk is relevant to held-to-maturity assets. This section addresses the link. First, let us formulate how one can measure the long-term risk. For a held-to-maturity asset, the ultimate risk of investing can be manifested by the dispersion of future values (FV) arising from receiving random cash flows and re-investing them into random benchmark rates (plus OAS). Hence, we can write in a continuous form:

$$FV = \int_0^T CF(t)e^{\int_t^T [r(\tau)+OAS]d\tau} dt \qquad (19.3)$$

Note that unlike many valuation formulas we used throughout the book, there is no expectation operator in (19.3); the future value is computed here for a single path. For the same path, the future value of a money-market account that starts from $1 and growing at the same $r+OAS$ rate is going to be

$$FV^{MM} = e^{\int_0^T [r(\tau)+OAS]d\tau} \qquad (19.3\text{-MM})$$

Now we can compute the ratio of the two; notice that FV^{MM} does not depend on integration variable t, therefore, can be placed under the main integral in (19.3):

$$\frac{FV}{FV^{MM}} = \int_0^T CF(t)e^{-\int_0^t [r(\tau)+OAS]d\tau} dt \equiv \int_0^T CF(t)DF(t)dt \equiv PV \qquad (19.4)$$

with DF denoting the discount factor. This expression is identical to the present value for a single path; its expectation is equal to price—compare with formulas of other chapters, for example (9.1) in chapter 9. We have proven a simple, but important fact: a path-wise distribution of present value objectively characterizes long-term risk of investing. We can compute measures relevant to a particular risk definition and purpose such as absolute, relative or log-scale standard deviation[1] of PV or any percentile of the distribution. These measures can be taken in the course of Monte Carlo simulations (chapters 9 and 13) or using a deterministic scenario grid with theoretical Vasicek-like probability assignment (chapter 15). In either case, designing a new form of financial-engineering solution is not required—it is sufficient to complement the existing valuation mechanics with computing extra metrics.

How is the path-wise distribution of PV related to the short-term theoretical VaR measure described in detail in the previous section? Figure 19.5 depicts a scatter plot that combines both kinds of risk metrics for the four MBS classes we investigated: TBAs, IOs, tranches of prime and subprime securitization. In order to make the comparison fair, we limit the VaR method with economic factors (interest rates and home prices) simulated by the Monte Carlo method, and omit the model risk and the residual spread risk. This chart shows a very strong correlation between the short-term and

---

[1] The log-scale standard deviation is $\sqrt{Ln\left[1+\dfrac{std^2(PV)}{E^2(PV)}\right]}$

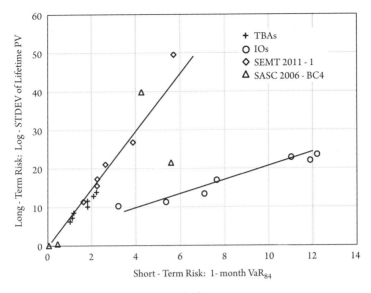

Figure 19.5 Short-Term versus Long-Term Risk

the long-term risks *within* each asset type. *Across* asset types, the relationship is more ambiguous.

EXPECTED LOSS, SHORTFALL, AND CAPITAL

The VaR approach is very suitable for measuring capital that needs to be maintained for portfolios available for sale, or trading accounts in particular. An alternative approach is to employ a simple subjective valuation model that we introduced at the end of chapter 4. That method is free from the Delta-Gamma approximation limitations and the assumption that factors belong to the normal distribution. Recall that the arguments of chapter 4 were concerned with an economic position of loan or asset insurers seeking to determine insurance premium p and required capital c given the expectation of loss μ, risk-free rate r, return on equity target R, and coverage limit l_{max}. The final formulas were expressed in the expected PV terms, see formula (4.17) for the single-period setting and (4.21) for the multi-period one.

The required capital is then determined by formula (4.18) for the single-period case, (4.20) for the multi-period continuous case.

The power of our "capital charge" approach is that it links capital and pricing, albeit from a subjective viewpoint. Let us illustrate this approach for finding the required capital together with the premium ("G-fee") for GSE guaranty. Using the multi-period formulas (4.20), (4.21) from chapter 4, we have to compute the

IOs, expected loss and shortfall entering formulas of the method. Table 19.2 lists them all, computed to maturity, with the IO multiple $IOM(r)$ calibrated to the Trust IO market as of mid-February 2013. We assumed new, owner-occupied, purchase loan having the prevailing rate of 3.6%, size of $200,000, with an unspecified US location (i.e., using the national HPI in credit modeling). We show results using risky ROE target of $\tilde{R} = 0.18$ for different combinations of critical risk parameters, FICO and LTV. The average loss and expected shortfall values are the most dependent on these parameters.

Given that the interest-rate risk is hedgeable, we excluded rate volatility from the analysis. Hence, the capital levels listed in Table 19.2 reflect those to be held against credit risk and full illiquidity, but not the interest-rate risk. With this exception, we employed the scenario-grid method introduced in chapter 15. In order to make this analysis more practical, we used $\alpha = 5\%$ in calculations of the expected shortfall.

An interesting and important measure is the P/P_0 ratio that ranges between 3.05 and 3.25; weaker loans have lower ratios. The magnitude of this ratio is an indication of risk-adjustment to the scale of subjective loss expectation that is necessary to price insurance. As a quick rule of thumb, the losses built into insurance premiums are about three times larger than expected losses. It also makes sense that the ratio dips as the loan quality deteriorates. Protection of very bad loans would not require a lot of capital as their expected losses would be closer to the worst losses, on a relative basis.

An MBS or ABS exposed to credit risk can be viewed as a long position in a credit-risk-free asset plus a short position in a Credit Default Swap (CDS) that guarantees a full compensation for loss. Hence, the capital-charge based view of the CDS writer is mirror reflective to that of the MBS or ABS investor.

Table 19.2 COMPUTATION OF GSE CAPITAL AND GUARANTY FEE

FICO	700	700	700	725	725	725	750	750	750
LTV	70	75	80	70	75	80	70	75	80
$IOM(r)$	6.24	6.23	6.20	6.25	6.24	6.22	6.25	6.25	6.24
$\tilde{R}*IOM(R)$	0.654	0.653	0.652	0.654	0.654	0.653	0.654	0.654	0.654
$L(R)$	0.226	0.357	0.555	0.142	0.231	0.370	0.086	0.144	0.238
$L(r)$	0.389	0.612	0.950	0.245	0.396	0.635	0.148	0.248	0.410
$L_{ES}(r)$	1.507	2.354	3.602	0.974	1.570	2.489	0.607	1.010	1.657
Single premium P	1.212	1.894	2.902	0.780	1.257	1.995	0.483	0.805	1.322
Capital c	0.295	0.460	0.700	0.194	0.313	0.494	0.124	0.206	0.336
P/P_0	3.114	3.093	3.054	3.187	3.173	3.142	3.256	3.250	3.227
Annual premium p	0.194	0.304	0.468	0.125	0.201	0.320	0.077	0.129	0.212

Losses, premium, and capital are in percentages.

Let us demonstrate how this method can be employed for producing various credit risk measures that enter formulas for p and c_{min}. We will use the A4 and A5 tranches of the same SASC 2006-BC4 subprime deal that has been analyzed throughout our book. On March 29, 2011, A4 was quoted at 52.09 and A5 at 25.62, by a pricing source; these quotes may or may not be needed for determining the capital.

Table 19.3 demonstrates the direct computations of capital following formula (4.20):

$$c = L_{ES}(r) - P$$

where P refers to the value of the loss term assessed as the market price discount. Fig. 19.6 depicts the loss profile across the same set of credit scenarios as those used in the previous example (introduced in chapter 15).

Interestingly enough, tranche A5 (the worse of two) requires less capital, both relative to par and even price. This is explained by the fact that tranche A5 is projected to lose its entire principal, in many scenarios including in the base case. If we projected A5 to lose its principal *in all the scenarios*, no capital would be required to hold against credit loss.[2]

Despite its convenience and simplicity, the method's assumptions may be challenged, from a practical standpoint. First, we assumed that market price is an explicit indication of credit loss: if the price is 52.09, than the loss expectation is 47.91, in present dollars. As we learned from many places of Parts 3 and 4, market values of MBS can be depressed for reasons unrelated to credit loss expectation.

Second, a traded security is more liquid than an insurance policy and holding the lifetime capital we established theoretically may be excessive. The VaR method would give us an alternative estimate of capital for a short-term holding. Taking into consideration only HPI risk and Model risk from Figure 19.3d we see that a one-month VaR_{84} should be around 8 to 9 percentage points for either bond in question; VaR_{95} would be in a 13 to 15% range.

The capital charge method could apply to measuring other capital requirements–those necessary to be held against interest-rate risk, spread risk and

Table 19.3 COMPUTATION OF CAPITAL

Tranche	Market Price	Expected Loss	84% Confidence			95% Confidence		
			Short-fall	Capital-to-Par	Capital-to-Price	Short-fall	Capital-to-Par	Capital-to-Price
A4	52.09	47.91	69.89	21.98	42.20	75.19	27.28	52.37
A5	25.62	74.38	79.59	5.21	20.33	80.72	6.34	24.73

[2] A small interest shortfall is accounted for in our analysis.

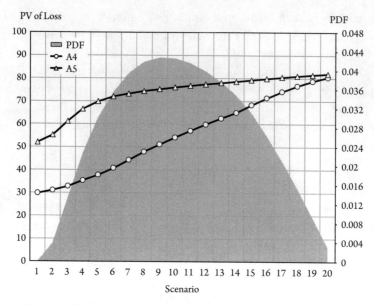

Figure 19.6 Present Values of Credit Losses on the Scenario Grid

so on–assuming no hedging. We could discount cash flows using a different rate formula, such as Coupon plus spread (used for accounting and book pricing), LIBOR plus spread (market valuation) while postulating an economically justifiable spread term. A larger spread would make all PVs lower, including expected losses and shortfall, but they would not change our results significantly.

THE USE OF DYNAMICS CREDIT RATING

We complete this chapter with a case study on using Breakpoint Ratio (BPR) as a dynamic rating measure. Recall that this metric, introduced in chapter 15, is defined as a ratio of the cumulative loss of collateral measured at a point when the tranche loses its first dollar of principal to that of the base case. BPR exceeding 1.0 means the tranche is not losing in the base case. BPR is closely associated with a distance-to-default notion; using the breakpoint grid we can assign probability to every economic scenario, including the breakpoint. The traditional credit ratings published by Moody's, S&P and Fitch use similar rationales for rating MBS.

Zheng (ADPN Oct. 2008) analyzed the 2007–2008 history of BPR for subprime bonds that are included in the four ABX indices. He established an approximate link between average BPR and ratings shown in Table 19.4.

In addition, Zheng found that, as the crisis developed, agency downgrades were in unison with the BPR slide for low-rated bonds, but lagged about half-a-year for AAAs (Figure 19.7). In essence, BPRs were sending advanced signals of deterioration. It looked as though the rating agencies viewed "AAA" as an eternal stamp of quality and went into disbelief and hesitation as economic conditions deteriorated. Such a mindset, in turn, deceived many investors, inflated their losses, and deservedly compromised the reputation of the traditional rating agencies.

Table 19.4 APPROXIMATE MAPPING OF TRADITIONAL AGENCY RATINGS TO BREAKPOINT RATIO

Moody's	S&P	Average BPR
Aaa	AAA	4.0
Aa2	AA	2.5
A2	A	1.7
Baa2	BBB	1.4
Ba2	BB	1.1
B2	B	0.9
Caa2	CCC	0.7
C/Ca	CC	0.6

Constructed using 2007–2008 data.

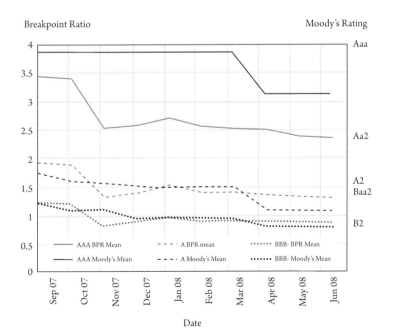

Figure 19.7 Average BPR and Moody's Rating (across all four ABX indices)

CONCLUSION

The risk measures we considered in this chapter go well beyond simple "Greeks"; they are linked to quantitative financial reasoning. Theoretical Value-at-Risk allows us to classify and combine various risk factors, such as the interest-rate risk, model risk, home-price risk, and discount spread (technical) risk, into a systematic framework. We demonstrated its use for various types of MBS and learned that the model risk plays an important role. In fact, even a perfect hedge of interest-rate risk does not make the remaining risk negligible, or even small. The VaR method can lead to a capital requirement, but so can the capital charge method we introduced in chapter 4 as a subjective valuation approach used in the absence of market benchmarks. We showed that the two methods are in a rough agreement when they are utilized to measure the credit risk of subprime MBS. Finally, we demonstrated the role of the Breakpoint Ratio as an advanced signal of credit deterioration and its relationship to the traditional rating. These methods do not exhaust all possibilities, as other methods of risk measurement do exist. However, these methods reveal the role of models and quantitative thinking in setting capital for and rating MBS and ABS deals.

20

How to Price New Loans

A healthy housing finance system should start from a prudent practice of loan origination. The period preceding the 2007–2009 financial crisis may serve as a good counterexample: a poor choice of loan products coupled with severe compromises made to the underwriting process and mispricing of credit risk inflated the housing bubble and triggered the downturn.

As most residential loans ended up in pools that back mortgage-backed securities, the information about the MBS secondary market should be considered when the originator selects and promotes loan programs and features, and sets loan rates. Models help perform these tasks along with assessing rewards or penalties for borrowers with diverging characteristics, such as credit scores, loan-to-value ratios or geographic locations. This chapter describes how a loan originator can connect secondary and primary markets and infer loan rates from a loan's quality and credit characteristics. We also demonstrate the importance of geography in pricing both new loans and loan insurance policies.

A RISK-NEUTRAL BRIDGE FROM THE SECONDARY MARKET

When an originator considers a loan application, the decision to approve its terms and conditions (including the interest rate) may be linked to the ability to place that loan in a pool and sell it to the secondary market. Understandably, loans placed in a pool will share some characteristics, but they cannot be identical. For the purpose of *loan pricing* (i.e., setting the rate), it is helpful to think of the loan as a pool of identical loans with some risk factors being common for all loans whereas others being idiosyncratic. Since idiosyncratic risks will diversify in a large pool, they may not need to be priced in.

The Credit OAS Method (chapter 13) is a theoretically sound approach to valuing both loans and securities. Our first goal is to determine the market-implied loss model and the crOAS level to use. Ideally, we would like to come up with a single model and a single crOAS that cover new loans of all types and features. When such a model exists, originators and investors cannot alter returns by mere loan selection, as every loan would be priced fairly.

We start with the SEMT 2011-1 deal as an example of a representative 2011 high-quality origination of jumbos. Table 20.1 displays this phase of the analysis.

Table 20.1 RISK-NEUTRALIZATION OF BENCHMARK'S LOSS MODEL
(SEMT 2011-1)[1]

Tranche	% of deal	Price	Physical Model			Risk-Neutralized Model		
				Loss			Loss	
			crOAS	Static	Avg	crOAS	Static	Avg
A1	92.50	100	42	0.0	0.4	37	0.0	1.7
B1	2.50	100	90	0.0	9.2	−21	0.0	23.5
B2	1.75	88.5	211	0.0	14.3	54	0.0	30.8
B3	1.25	83	248	0.0	19.2	32	0.0	40.0
B4	0.75	66.625	466	0.0	25.1	160	0.0	25.1
B5	1.25	35	830	6.6	49.0	469	56.9	75.6
A1 IO		1.5						
COLLAT	100	100	119	0.1	1.9	103	0.7	4.5

Using an unaltered physical model of home prices and loan losses, we obtain vastly differing crOAS levels as mezzanine tranches look progressively cheaper. This profile reflects both model risk and liquidity preferences. The risk-neutralized model features more conservative home-price appreciation tunings (Short-Term HPA lowered by 8%, Long-Term HPA lowered by 2.5%-relative to the HPI model we introduced in chapter 14), a more aggressive default rate scale (120% of the physical model), but a slightly more optimistic severity scale (93% of the model). This transformation enabled an increase in credit losses so that the crOAS profile flattened considerably. In fact, tranches A1 through B3 are now priced at comparable crOAS levels. Tranches B4 and B5 retain some evidence of cheapness on an crOAS basis, but, given their small relative sizes and impaired liquidity, this outcome is acceptable. At the end of this risk-neutralization process, we have the required model transformation and the single crOAS = 103 bps to use for all loans.

[1]We estimated the value of the B1-B5 bonds as they were not offered in the market.

SETTING RATES AND POINTS

We are now equipped with a powerful tool that allows us to value loans and their features. Let us start with an "average US" loan. Although loan originators will always know the exact property location, it is useful to discard this piece of information for illustrative purposes. We will then compare the average geography with any particular location to find the difference. Let us assume originating a $500,000 loan, with an original LTV of 67.5%, given to a 750 FICO, fully documented, borrower. The loan is used to purchase a one-family, owner-occupied, home. These assumptions reflect the loans that dominate the SEMT 2011-1 deal.

We now can assign the loan its rate and produce the value using Credit OAS simulations. The difference between cost of origination (assume 100) and that value are points to be paid *by* the borrower (negative points will be paid *to* the borrower). Table 20.2-US documents the points.

Table 20.2 RATES AND POINTS FOR THE AVERAGE JUMBO LOAN (MARCH 2011)

				US			
Rate	4.750	4.875	5.000	5.125	5.250	5.375	5.500
Points	1.321	0.562	−0.181	−0.907	−1.615	−2.305	−2.975

				CA			
Rate	4.750	4.875	5.000	5.125	5.250	5.375	5.500
Points	3.142	2.403	1.677	0.964	0.265	−0.420	−1.089

It is evident that the no-point rate for the US loan is just under 5.0% with the rate sensitivity around that rate being about 6.0 points per 1% rate. We can now embark on even a greater adventure. Using various loan characteristics, we can compute additional credit-linked points that originators should be charging or paying. Table 20.3-US shows the table of these points as a function of a borrower's FICO and a loan's LTV.

As one would expect, points paid by borrowers grow when risk increases (i.e., lower FICO and higher LTV dimensions). However, the relationship is not linear as it clearly contains a powerful mixed effect. When a borrower's credit is score is high, an LTV below 80% matters little. This can be used to form a possible practical hint at keeping required LTV at 80% for high-quality borrowers, while demanding a lower LTV or 1–3 points for applicants in the 700–739 FICO range.

Another interesting observation is that the additional points paid to low-LTV borrowers *do not increase* as FICO increases. This paradoxical fact can be easily explained by prepayment, rather than default, sensitivity. Low LTV borrowers are remote from a default possibility, but can refinance more efficiently thereby boosting the option cost. Hence, a low FICO acts akin to a prepayment penalty.

Table 20.3 ADDITIONAL CREDIT ADJUSTED POINTS (RATE = 5%)

US

FICO/LTV	55–60	60–65	65–70	70–75	75–79.9	80
780–799	−0.40	−0.38	−0.34	−0.25	−0.10	0.04
760–779	−0.40	−0.35	−0.23	−0.03	0.31	0.57
740–759	−0.38	−0.25	0.00	0.41	1.03	1.49
720–739	−0.39	−0.20	0.16	0.72	1.53	2.12
700–719	−0.40	−0.11	0.38	1.12	2.17	2.89

CA

FICO/LTV	55–60	60–65	65–70	70–75	75–79.9	80
780–799	−1.92	−1.66	−1.28	−0.75	−0.04	0.47
760–779	−1.75	−1.35	−0.76	0.03	1.06	1.76
740–759	−1.49	−0.87	0.00	1.13	2.54	3.46
720–739	−1.33	−0.56	0.48	1.82	3.45	4.50
700–719	−1.14	−0.20	1.05	2.61	4.48	5.64

If we reproduced Table 20.3-US for a higher loan rate (e.g. 6%), we would see that the points paid to a low LTV borrower actually increase somewhat as FICO decreases.

A similar analysis performed for a California loan reveals a higher no-point rate, a slightly lower point-per-rate sensitivity (Table 20.2-CA), but a stronger dependence on credit factors (Table 20.3-CA).

The no-point rate for CA is close to 5.3%, or 0.35% higher than for the US loan example. This serves as compensation for a higher prepayment-or-default option value, as California's real estate values are among the most volatile; our stochastic HPI model (chapter 14) is reflective of this fact. If this point is understood, it becomes clear why the credit-adjusted points in Table 20.3-CA are very sensitive to both FICO and OLTV. Further in this chapter, we provide more analysis of the importance of geographic data and geographic risk diversification.

VIRTUAL SECURITIZATION OF LOANS

So far, we assumed that the secondary market's prices can be linked to the economics of origination via constructing a risk-neutralized loss model and determining a single value for crOAS. This step is not always feasible. The risk-neutral transformation may result in an unrealistic model, or it may be impossible to reach its goals at all.

Often, credit risk and technical risk are somewhat collinear; better-protected bonds are more liquid, for example. However, there are situations when adjusting a loss model cannot explain pricing differences. Consider, for example, a case where two tranches generate similar cash flows for all economic scenarios, but have different liquidity, demand, or ability to receive financing. A more liquid, more financeable bond, in higher demand, will have a higher value, which is translated into a lower crOAS, given the same cash flows. No change in a loss model can force the cheaper bond to lose more principal than the richer bond in this example, so a risk-neutralization of that loss model cannot result in identical crOAS. In these very realistic situations, we must remain bound to several crOAS levels and find a way to price loans accordingly.

The alternative method is "virtual securitization." Let us assume that the benchmark securitization is made of just two tranches, a senior bond A and a junior bond B. Bond B protects bond A until it has principal left; once B lost its entire principal, losses are directed to bond A. Let us assume further that the benchmark deal protects bond A in 95% scenarios, using a loss model that is physical or partially risk-adjusted. The size of each tranche will depend on the quality of the loans. If loans are of high credit quality (i.e., high FICO, low OLTV, fully documented) losses are projected to be small and bond A will be large. As the loans' credit features deteriorate, the size of bond B will grow. Furthermore, let us assume that the A bond is valued at crOAS = 100 bps at the secondary market and the B bond is valued at crOAS = 400 bps, on the same model, to the observed market prices.

We now shift to loan pricing. Assume a new loan is expected to lose not more than 20% of its principal, with the same 95% confidence, on the same loss model as was used for the benchmark deal. We now can replicate the benchmark A-B structure using a large pool of loans like the one we tried to price, ignoring purely idiosyncratic data (diversified in a pool). In order to have the A-B structure replicated, we need to "slice" the loan into two virtual pieces, the 80% share and the 20% share. The former one takes no losses whereas the latter takes all losses from the loan. Hence, we have the imaginary A-B structure out of a single loan. We price that structure discounting piece A at crOAS = 100 bps and piece B at crOAS = 400 bps. The method will require a simple structuring tool that subordinates cash flows between the virtual tranches.

Let us illustrate this approach with a real non-agency deal, the same SEMT 2011-1 we analyzed earlier. As a method of analysis, we choose the scenario-based approximate probability assignment explained in chapter 15. We first select a scenario grid ranging from optimistic (scenarios 1 to 7) to base case (scenario 8) to pessimistic (scenarios 9 to 19); scenarios were defined in Table 15.6 and feature alterations of both economic factors (interest rates and home prices) and the scales of a loan loss model. Figure 20.1 depicts the bonds' loss profiles against a theoretical 3-part Vasicek cumulative distribution function (CDF) introduced in chapter 15. Since the collateral has a prominent California presence, we use a somewhat higher correlation parameter Rho = 40% in the CDF construction.

The senior A1 bond's breakpoint is "scenario 14.8" having an estimated probability of 98.9% of not reaching; Bond B1's breakpoint ("scenario 13.8") cannot be reached with 97.3% confidence, etc. Bond B5, not shown in Figure 20.1, is unprotected and absorbs collateral losses from the first dollar. For each bond, the protection confidence level is shown as a horizontal probability line that crosses the CDF curve at the breakpoint.

Once we determined protection levels in terms of breakpoint probabilities, we can value new loans. We simply determine losses at the confidence levels already established above using the same method. The process is shown in Figure 20.2 and summarized in Table 20.4 for a hypothetical average US jumbo loan with the same characteristics as those assumed in the previous sections. Since securitization of geographically diversified loans reduces the risk, we assumed Rho = 30% rather than Rho = 40%; The CDF curve in Figure 20.2 reflects this alteration.

Note that a homogenous pool of averaged, geographically diversified, US jumbo loans is less risky than the SEMT 2011-1 pool that has a large California share and is made up of *differing* loans (the worst loans produce greater losses). Hence, not surprisingly, the virtual securitization method has led us to a larger size of A1 (95.98%) than is actually observed in the benchmark deal (92.50%). Had we placed the new loan in California and assumed a full California concentration of the virtual deal, we would have to allocate only 74.86% of the loan to tranche A1, 6.58% for tranche B1, etc. In general, more risky loans would have

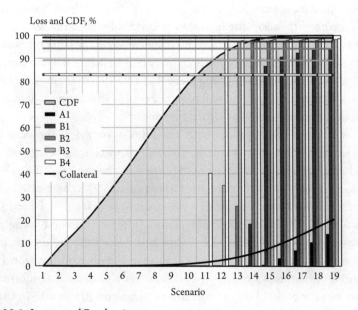

Figure 20.1 Losses and Breakpoints

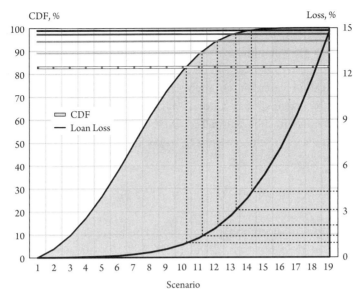

Figure 20.2 Virtual Securitization of a Loan

Table 20.4 Summary of Virtual Securitization

Tranche	Protection Confidence (%)	Loan Loss (Support) (%)	Implied Bond's Size (%)	crOAS to Use, bp
A1	98.93	4.02	95.98	42
B1	97.35	2.91	1.11	90
B2	94.26	2.01	0.90	211
B3	89.18	1.35	0.66	248
B4	82.88	0.93	0.42	466
B5			0.93	830

a lower allocation into senior tranches, hence, they would be discounted more severely. With the virtual securitization method, we can produce loan points per FICO, LTV and other features similar to those shown in Table 20.3 in the previous section.

Probability assignment that we carried out using the scenario-grid method could be performed via Monte Carlo simulations. We would be relieved from the need to make up the correlation parameter Rho, but would be confronting a requirement to account for model risk and remote events. As the A1 tranche is well protected and the largest in the deal, one would need to run many random paths to get a reliable estimate of the A1's required size. A suitably designed importance sampling method could help. As for the model risk, it could be added to Monte Carlo implementation.

The results of loan pricing using virtual securitization may or may not match those from a risk-neutralized loss model transformation. We assumed that a deal's tranches are valued using breakpoint probabilities so that tranches with the same likelihood of default will be priced at the same crOAS. This may be an over-simplification of market sentiments. MBS dealers and MBS investors should be aware of the extent of losses, bond "thickness" and other loss-distributional characteristics that must be factored-in. On the other hand, as we stated earlier, a full risk-neutralization, while preferred, may be impossible or impractical.

GEOGRAPHICAL INFORMATION AND DIVERSIFICATION

Loan originators, servicers and insurers should be aware of geographical-specific risks arising in their business. Levin (ADCP 2010) studied expected losses for three major credit shelves (Prime/Conforming, Alt-A, Subprime) and 50 states. We reproduce results in Figure 20.3 and compare them to a loan with an unknown location, the so-called "US loan" shown by punctured lines. That loan will use the national HPI index.

To exclude the effect a geographical location has on past changes in LTV, we assume a new origination (age = 0). We compute losses along the base-case line (forward rates, deterministic HPIs) as well as Monte Carlo averages (rates and HPIs are stochastic).

Comparing base-case losses (gray lines) for new conforming loans, we see that our loss estimates for "worst" geography (NV, FL) are twice as high as those for "best" geography (New England). On average, we expect only 1% of loss and a geographical average to be close to the loss of the US loan. The situation changes if we start assessing future loan losses probabilistically. Monte Carlo averages are shown by black lines and the loss ratio of worst-to-best location jumps up to 4:1. Interestingly, California is viewed as a growing/recovering state, with the base case projection better than the US national average. However, California is also the most volatile state in terms of real estate prices. Hence, the default option has a considerable time value that is manifested by the black line's peak. The averaged loss of a conforming loan originated in California is 5% with the base case loss of only 0.8%. The national HPI is much less volatile; it understates Monte Carlo losses—relative to the geographically dispersed portfolio.

We are unlikely to see loans like the Alt-A (much less subprime) origination of the housing boom soon, but the theoretical understanding of the role of the loans' credit quality remains important. As credit quality declines, the loss' estimate certainly grows, but the loss ratio of worst-to-best geography remains roughly at 2:1 for the base case. The role of volatility gradually decreases on a relative basis. The same ratio of Monte Carlo losses measured for subprime loans is only 2:1,

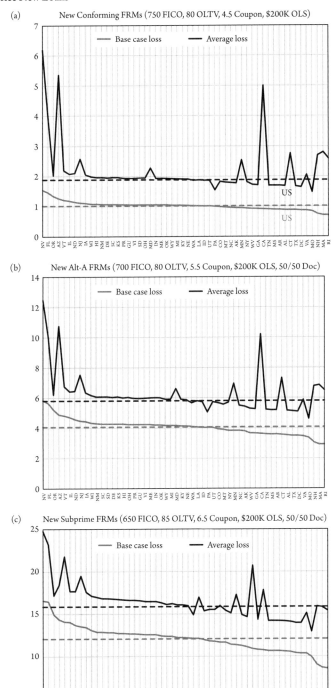

Figure 20.3 Geographical View of Loan Losses (from 2010Q2)

compared to 2.7:1 for Alt-As and the above-mentioned 4:1 for conforming loans. Good loans are unlikely to default and it would take a dramatic turn of events to inflict them. In contrast, bad loans may look grim, even in the base case.

Therefore, knowledge of geographic location has proven to be important. What if we "diversify" the HPI risk by constructing a hypothetical portfolio of loans that resembles the national home-price index? Let us choose loan weights to match the presence of each state in the US HPI. Figure 20.4 proves that the base case losses measured for the diversified portfolio and a single "US loan" are indeed very close to each other. Monte Carlo averages are not as close—the single-loan surrogate understates losses by as much as one-third (the conforming-quality case). The reason for this mismatch is that the non-linearity of option exercise: idiosyncratic home-price movements of different regions can

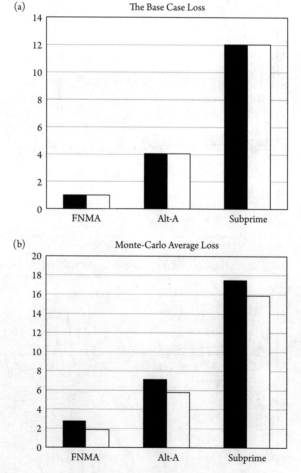

Figure 20.4 Does Geography Diversify the Home-Price Risk?
Black bars = diversified, correctly weighted, portfolio; White bars = US loan

offset each other within the national index, but the loan losses of more volatile areas (like California) cannot be offset.

This observation can be backed by the following simple mathematical proof that the average variance of home prices comprising an index exceeds the variance of that index. Let H_i be the home price of i-th home and HPI denote the home-price index for the region. For brevity of derivations and without loss of generality, assume that all houses have the same size and contribute equally to the index:

$$HPI = \frac{1}{N}\sum H_i$$

Denote mathematical expectations $\overline{HPI}$ and $\bar{H}_i$; Then, variance of H_i can be presented as

$$Var(H_i) = E(H_i - \bar{H}_i)^2 \equiv E(H_i - \overline{HPI} + \overline{HPI} - \bar{H}_i)^2$$
$$= E(H_i - \overline{HPI})^2 - (\bar{H}_i - \overline{HPI})^2$$

because $\overline{HPI} - \bar{H}_i$ is deterministic. Decomposing the first expectation term further, we get

$$E\left(H_i - \overline{HPI}\right)^2 \equiv E\left(H_i - HPI + HPI - \overline{HPI}\right)^2$$
$$= E\left(H_i - HPI\right)^2 + 2E\left[\left(H_i - HPI\right)\left(HPI - \overline{HPI}\right)\right] + Var(HPI)$$

Let us now compute the average of all $Var(H_i)$. Note that $\sum_i (H_i - HPI) \equiv 0$, hence,

$$\frac{1}{N}\sum_i Var(H_i) = Var(HPI) + \frac{1}{N}\sum_i E(H_i - HPI)^2$$
$$- \frac{1}{N}\sum_i (\bar{H}_i - \overline{HPI})^2 \geq Var(HPI)$$

because $E(x^2) \geq (Ex)^2$. The equality holds if and only if $H_i - HPI$ is deterministic for all i, or, equivalently, all H_i move in unison, by the same amount.

PRACTICAL IMPLICATIONS

The arguments made in the previous section suggest that using a home-price index in lieu of individual home prices may understate overall losses. On the other hand, adding random, idiosyncratic terms to each home's value will lead to much slower computing as well as to a less efficient Monte Carlo because the variance reduction techniques we discussed in chapter 9 (ortho-normalization, Sobol sequences) are not feasible for this high-dimensional situation.

The severity of the problem depends on two factors: (a) the extent of heterogeneity and mutual independence of home prices (and other borrowers' characteristics) and (b) the extent of nonlinearity. Home prices move more in unison within small geographical areas than within a diverse country like the US. This observation justifies a possible use of HPI at an MSA level. The use of a national HPI will likely understate losses, especially for areas of high real estate volatility (e.g. California). The use of empirically designed S-curves (see chapters 7 and 12) mitigates the problem somewhat because it views HPI as a statistical factor, among many, rather than a deterministic trigger of option exercise. The S-curves arise in modeling prepayments, defaults and loan transitions because of an imperfect correlation among the factors (including home prices) that drive borrower decisions as discussed in chapter 1.

Another good example of considering idiosyncratic risk is the option-like loss severity model introduced in chapter 12. Given an HPI point, losses depend on the actual LTV rather than the LTV determined from the index. Since we do not advocate the use of explicit simulations of each borrower's property value, we can assume certain idiosyncratic volatility around the HPI and solve for the average loss analytically (using the Black-Scholes formula). This approach has been shown to yield a smooth and realistic Severity(HPI) function.

A similar method can extend to the pay-off of loan insurance. An LTV of 95% computed *off an index* means that a particular property could be "underwater" leading to a loan loss that requires reimbursement to the investor—even if the index points to 5% equity. In general, the mortgage insurance (MI) industry should be very aware of the geographical evidence of risk shown in Figure 20.3. It is apparent that insuring loans originated in most volatile states (CA, NV, AZ, and FL) calls for a high policy premium. In our practice, we have found that MI companies do not differentiate the geographical risk pricing to its full and fair extent. Instead, they set underwriting standards that filter out risky loans.

21

The Future of Housing Finance and Mortgage-Based Securities Modeling

A central theme of this book is the uncertainty of forecasts. In light of this theme, it is with a great deal of humility that we tender the following forecasts of the future of housing finance and MBS modeling.

At the time of publication in 2014, perhaps the only clear forecast is that there will be substantial changes to the mortgage markets and mortgage modeling in the coming years. The mortgage market has not recovered from the financial crises of 2007 and 2008. About 90% of all mortgages originated in 2012 utilized the US government for securitization. Fannie Mae and Freddie Mac remain in an unstable conservatorship with no private capital supporting their guarantee obligations and the FHA insurance fund is operating well below its target reserves. Private label securitization is anemic at best. This state of the world is not stable and therefore is likely to change. It remains unclear who will originate mortgages, who will service mortgages, and who will bear the risks.

In the past few years, origination has become more concentrated with the top three originators now accounting for half of all new loans.[1] In contrast, ten years earlier, the top ten originators only accounted for one-quarter of all originations. While most of this increase is due to the increased role of Wells Fargo, we suspect that this consolidation will continue and the mortgage origination market will be concentrated in a few firms.

[1]2012 Mortgage Statistical Annual, *Inside Mortgage Finance.*

REGULATION

The substantial increase in regulatory requirements as a result of the Dodd-Frank legislation further reinforces this trend toward consolidation as few small firms have the infrastructure to meet these requirements. In contrast, regulation is currently driving servicing into smaller firms. Potentially prohibitive capital requirements from Basel III are leading many banks to reduce their servicing portfolios. New entrants are growing as servicing values reach attractive levels for investors. In the long-run however, servicing is a volume-driven cost-minimization business and we believe servicing will also be concentrated in a few firms, with possible niche players to deal with special situations.

Regulation is also playing an important role in how risks will be borne and the restart of securitization. Dodd-Frank contained many provisions prescribing new rules for securitization of mortgages while proscribing approaches that had been used in the past. While such a focus on mortgage securitization made sense in the context of reforming the financial system, the combined impact of the rules greatly reduces the economic viability of mortgage securitization. A rationalization of these rules will be necessary to move the market forward.

As a result of the financial crisis, the government has engaged in a wide range of activities that directly affect the mortgage market. These include programs for modifying loans (HAMP), programs for refinancing loans (HARP), and direct Fed investment in MBS (QE3). All of these programs have significant impact on both borrowers and investors. Changes in government rules and programs are difficult to forecast as to both their probability of being implemented and their impact if they were to be implemented. As the financial crisis eases, these interventions are likely to become less frequent, but the recent actions are likely to have effects that linger for years and possibly decades.

THE ROLE OF GOVERNMENT IN MORTGAGE-BASED SECURITIES

Our strong view is that a government guarantee of some form is necessary to maintain a stable source of funding for a large portion of the approximately $10 trillion of mortgages supporting home ownership. On the other hand, we believe that private capital can be used to bear much of the credit risk of the mortgage market. Even with a low 4% capital requirement, the market for mortgage credit risk would be about $400 billion. Perhaps one-third of that capital is currently provided by the banking sector. The credit risk on the other two-thirds of the mortgage market has been absorbed by the US government and the tax payers.

We also believe that mortgage origination and securitization function best when there is standardization, and that credit risk should be further dispersed in private hands rather than concentrated in government owned and controlled entities.

A PROPOSAL FOR THE FUTURE OF THE MORTGAGE MARKET

While the pace and direction of the transformation of the mortgage market is uncertain, here we sketch out one possible path that is consistent with these principles.

1. The Government Sponsored Enterprises, Fannie Mae and Freddie Mac, will be transformed into securitization cooperatives owned by the originators of mortgage loans.
   a. The MBS issued by the cooperatives will have a full faith and credit guarantee from the US government (like GNMA securities).
   b. The cooperative owners will be jointly responsible for violation of representations and warranties not cured by the originator.
   c. The Government guarantor will set limits on the types and amount of mortgages to be guaranteed.
   d. The cooperative will utilize risk sharing transactions such as senior subordinated structures and credit linked notes to attract private capital to bear credit risk.
   e. Approximately 30-40% of the mortgage originations will pass through these cooperatives.
2. Private Securitization will be revitalized.
   a. Rules for private securitization will be rationalized so that securitization is economic.
   b. Private securitization will provide funding for about 20-30% of all mortgage originations.
3. Direct government guarantees of mortgages will be directed to those in need.
   a. Programs such as the FHA and VA programs will be reduced to approximately 10% of all loans.
   b. Such programs will be concentrated on first time home buyers with limited income.
4. Banks will continue to be important component of the mortgage market.
   a. They will hold approximately 30%-40% of mortgages.
   b. They will continue to rely on deposit insurance and home loan bank advances to fund their investment.

The advantages of this approach are that it recognizes that given the size and scope of the US mortgage market, no one source of funding can provide the stability and liquidity of multiple sources. It provides for a government guarantee of a large segment of the mortgage-backed securities market, while providing market pricing of credit risk and protecting tax payers from loss through the use of credit-risk sharing. Cooperatives allow for standardized securitization structures and enforcement of reps and warrants while avoiding monopoly power in the hands of a single entity or excessive government involvement in the mortgage securitization process.

The government will likely to continue to play an important role in the mortgage market in other ways as well: Government involvement stems from the central role that housing plays in the US economy and its importance for social welfare. In addition to the guarantees the government provides to investors in mortgages and mortgage-backed securities, it also provides a tax incentive to borrowers through the mortgage interest deduction. Recent budget discussions have focused on eliminating or reducing this deduction, which is not a very effective tool for increasing home ownership and also encourages excess leverage in the housing finance system. Yet its elimination poses significant political obstacles. The government has also become very involved in assisting borrowers who are underwater (LTV > 100) or financially strapped (DTI > 50) as a result of the recent financial crises.

ROLE OF MODELS

Regardless of the future structure of the mortgage industry, the risks outlined and discussed throughout this book will endure. Mortgages will still need funding and will be still be subject to interest-rate risk, credit risk and model risk. A financial system that is able to measure, manage and price these risks will be more stable than one that does not recognize the inherent risks of mortgages and mortgage-backed securities.

Models can play a valuable role in the transformation of the mortgage market and housing finance from its current state. Models can help identify risks by recognizing that mortgages are subject to numerous risks and uncertainty. They can help identify appropriate capital requirements for new structures and entities and help price risks so that investors will have confidence to invest in new markets.

As models provide a framework for analyzing mortgages and mortgage-backed securities we expect to see greater role for mortgages versus ad hoc approaches: in accounting for determination of fair value and for determination of loan loss reserves; in ratings to determine the probability of default and the losses under stress scenarios; in origination for determining the pricing and hedging of new loans; and a continued and expanded role in determining value and risk for investment. We might also see a growing role of models for borrowers as they evaluate a range of product choices and become more sophisticated.

DATA

In the transformation of the mortgage and housing markets, it is likely that the amount of data available to investors and analysts will continue to increase dramatically. Mortgage analysts and investors in the 1980s primarily relied upon coupon and year of origination to produce mortgage prepayment models. By the 1990s, non-agency securitization expanded the role of additional variables such as LTV and credit score and the GSEs began making additional variables available on a pool basis. While the trend began somewhat sooner, the financial crisis of 2007 lead to in-depth loan level analysis of credit risk and the GSEs have begun to release more loan level data. The early 2010s have seen the emergence of data vendors who provide additional information about borrowers on an ongoing basis that can be linked with origination data. Throughout the economy, more and more data on consumers has become available as firms tap into the on-line search and shopping habits of consumers. This data has yet to be widely integrated into the mortgage market. The future is likely to see a further explosion of data on consumers and borrowers. Modelers will need to take this data into account to stay on the forefront.

The explosion of data creates numerous problems for modelers. First and foremost, is that it is always tempting to use more data when it is available. More data increases the chances that a model will be over fit. In sample performance can increase in accuracy while forecasts decrease in quality. The more variables considered, the more likely it is that the modeler will find spurious correlations. More data means that the modeler needs to be even more disciplined in the conceptual stages of the modeling process.

More data doesn't mean better quality data. A familiar refrain in modeling is "garbage in, garbage out." The rapid growth of the sub-prime and alt-A mortgage markets during the mid-2000s was an unfortunate example of this. Borrower credit scores, income, and home values were all manipulated to increase loan approvals and sales to the secondary market, but at the expense of true loan quality.

One of the reasons why investors are seeking more data is to verify the data that was considered unreliable. They believe that if they have more data from the origination process, then they will be able to identify quality loans themselves. This approach may not succeed. While additional data may be valuable, it is probably more important to make sure that the data that is produced is correct.

NEW MODELS

More data may also require a new way of thinking about models. The traditional approach to modeling has been to find variables that explain prepayment and default data in the past and then to find a way to transform those explanations into forecasts. The fundamental assumption behind that approach is that there are stable relationships that can be discovered in the past and applied in the future.

The history of mortgage models, however, contradicts this assumption. Modelers are continually finding new factors or altering the weighting of previously determined factors. While the basic factors remain consistent, the details are continually evolving. Perhaps a new form of modeling can be developed that incorporates new data on a more holistic and interactive basis.

We have been experimenting with a variety of methods of dealing with this issue. Adaptive or Bayesian models are one such approach. Recent actual prepayment and default data can be used to adjust forecasts. We can compare the model output to actual loan performance and adjust the model dynamically to reflect the new data. Such techniques may have the ability to reduce the amount of adjustment and "tuning" that is applied to historically determined models. The limitation of such techniques is that it is often difficult to differentiate transient changes in performance from more permanent alterations in borrower behavior. While such models will almost certainly produce better short-term forecasts, it is not clear if they will produce better long-term forecasts and produce more reliable measures of risk and value. Balancing these considerations will be an important component of building adaptive models.

COMPUTATIONAL POWER

In parallel to the increase in mortgage data is the increase in data storage and computational power that can be brought to the mortgage valuation process. In the early 1980s, mortgage analysts relied on closed form solutions to price/yield equations and books filled with tables of calculations to value and trade mortgages. Today analysts employ distributed processing to run hundreds of simulation paths on thousands of loans, using models that incorporate dozens of variables. Increases in computational power will likely make current techniques seem as quaint as a Monroe Bond Trader calculator. (Those who were not on a bond trading desk before 1990 will probably need to look that up.)

While most of our clients have preferred to own and operate their own data centers, the growth of cloud computing may see the movement of data storage and computational power to extremely large and powerful data and computation engines owned by third party vendors. In some ways, this seems like a return to the large time-sharing systems of the 1970s and 1980s. Time will tell if this is a permanent change or just another swing of the pendulum from centralized to dispersed computational power and back again.

TRADING

In the future we are likely to see a change in how risk is transferred by the market. Traditionally, mortgages have traded in an over-the-counter market, with risk transferred by one-on-one negotiations as to price. Recently more and more trading of agency MBS has moved to electronic trading through platforms such as TradeWeb. During the mid-2000s, there was also substantial use of indices such as ABX provided by Markit. Trading via these vehicles is still primarily one-on-one negotiations aided by technology. Other markets have moved largely to automated trading via exchanges. While there are numerous obstacles to such trading for mortgages, greater automation of trading and the development of new trading vehicles is all but inevitable.

In our vision for the mortgage market, the current GSEs would be transformed into a central clearing market for all types of mortgage risk: interest rate, prepayment, and credit risk. They could devise new instruments to spread these risks through the market to provide more liquidity and better risk-adjusted pricing.

The increase in computation power and data storage coupled with the growth in automated trading will likely have significant impact on the techniques used to value MBS, as there will be greater capability and need for highly computationally intensive calculations in real-time decision making. Such advances have the risk that analysts and market participants will believe that the speed and precision of such calculations is a substitute for understanding the underlying risks of the mortgage loans. More and better analysis may reduce uncertainty, but it is unlikely that any analytical approach will ever fully capture the uncertainty of a product that is so closely tied to the actions and motivations of individual borrowers.

WRAPPING UP

All of these changes, whether to the structure of the industry, the amount of data, computational power, or trading practices, mean that models of mortgage-back securities will continue to evolve. The fundamental principles outlined in this book including the uncertainty of borrower behavior, distributions of outcomes and risk-neutral pricing are likely to continue to be central themes of mortgage models even as the approaches morph into perhaps unimaginable forms. Mortgage modeling will continue to be a challenging field for years to come.

REFERENCES

Acworth P., M. Broadie and P. Glasserman (1998), A Comparison of Some Monte Carlo and Quasi Monte Carlo Methods for Option Pricing, in *Monte Carlo and Quasi Monte Carlo Methods 1996*, P. Hellekalek, G. Larcher, H. Niederreiter, and P. Zinterhof (eds), Springer-Verlag, New York, pp. 1–18.

Adelson, M. H. and D. P. Jacobs (2008), The Subprime Problem: Causes and Lessons, *The Journal of Structured Finance*, Spring, pp. 12–17.

Akesson, F. and J. Lehoczky (2000), Path generation for Quasi Monte-Carlo Methods of Mortgage-Backed Securities, *Management Science*, 45, pp. 1171–1187.

Arthur, T. and M. Kagarlis (2008), The RPX Residential Home-Price Index, in S. Perrucci (ed.), *Mortgage Real Estate Finance*, Risk Books, London, pp. 147–156.

Balduzzi, P., S. Das, S. Foresi and R. Sundaram, (1996), A Simple Approach to Three Factor Affine Term Structure of Interest Rates, *Journal of Fixed Income* Vol. 6, pp. 43–53.

Beaglehole, D., and M. Tenney, (1991), General Solution of Some Interest Rate Contingent Claim Pricing, *Journal of Fixed Income*, Vol. 1, pp. 69–83.

Belbase, E., and D. Szakallas (2002), The Yield Curve and Mortgage Current Coupon, *The Journal of Fixed Income*, March 2002, Vol. 11, No. 4, pp. 78–86.

Berkovec, J., Y. Chang and D. A. McManus (2012), Alternative Lending Channels and the Crisis in U.S. Housing Markets, upcoming in *Real Estate Economic*, Vol. 40, December, pp. S8 – S31.

Bhattacharjee, R., and L.S. Hayre (2006), The Term Structure of Mortgage Rates: Citigroup's MOATS Model, *Journal of Fixed Income*, March 2006, Vol. 15, No. 4, pp. 34–47.

Black, F., and P. Karasinski, (1991), Bond and Option Pricing When Short Rates are Lognormal, *Financial Analysts Journal* (July–August), pp. 52–59.

Blyth, S., and J. Uglum, (1999), Rates of Skew, *Risk* (July), pp. 61–63.

Caflisch, R. and W. Morokoff (1998), Quasi-Monte Carlo Simulation of Random Walks in Finance, in *Monte Carlo and Quasi Monte Carlo Methods 1996*, P. Hellekalek, G. Larcher, H. Niederreiter, and P. Zinterhof (eds), Springer-Verlag, New York, pp. 340–352.

Chan, K., G. Karolyi, F. Longstaff, and A.B. Sanders (1992), An Empirical Comparison of Alternative Models of the Short-Term Interest Rate, *Journal of Finance*, Vol. 52, pp. 1209–1227.

Cheyette, O. (1992), Term Structure Dynamics and Mortgage Valuation, *Journal of Fixed Income*, (March 1992), Vol. 1, No. 4, pp. 28–41.

Cheyette, O. (1996), Implied Prepayments, *The Journal of Portfolio Management*, Fall 1996, pp. 107–115.

Cheyette, O. (2002), Interest-Rate Models, in F. Fabozzi (ed.), *Interest Rate, Term Structure, and Valuation Modeling*, Wiley Finance.

Coase, R. (1937), The Nature of the Firm, *Economica*, Vol. 4, No. 16, pp. 386–405

Cordell, L., Y. Huang and M. Williams (2011), Collateral Damage: Sizing and Assessing the Subprime CDO Crisis, *Federal Reserve Bank of Philadelphia*, working paper No. 11–30.

Cox, J., J. Ingersoll and S. Ross (1985). A Theory of the Term Structure of Interest Rates, *Econometrica*, Vol. 53, pp. 385–407.

Dai, Q., and K. Singleton (2000), Specification Analysis of Affine Term Structure Models, *Journal of Finance* Vol. 55, No. 5, pp. 1943–1978.

Das, S. (2000), Interest-Rate modeling with Jump-Diffusion Processes, in N. Jegadeesh and B. Tuckman (eds.), *Advanced Fixed-Income Valuation Tools* (pp. 162–189), Hoboken, NJ: John Wiley & Sons.

Davidson, A. (1987), Understanding Premium Mortgage-Backed Securities: Observations & Analysis, in F. Fabozzi (ed.), *Mortgage-Backed Securities: New Strategies, Applications & Research*, Probus Publishing, Chicago, pp. 191–204.

Davidson, A., A. Sander, L.-L. Wolff and A. Ching (2003), *Securitization, Structuring and Investment Analysis*, Wiley Finance, Hoboken, NJ.

Davidson, A. and M. Herskovitz (1996), *Mortgage-Backed Securities Workbook*, Irwin, New York.

Davidson, A., M. Herskovitz, L. Van Drunen (1988), The Refinancing Threshold Model: An Economic Approach to Valuing MBS, *Journal of Real Estate Finance and Economics 1*, June 1988, pp. 117–130.

Deng, Y., J. M. Quigley, and R. van Order (2000), Mortgage Terminations, Heterogeneity and the Exercise of Mortgage Options, *Econometrica*, Vol. 68, No. 2, pp. 275–307 (March).

Deng, Y., S. Gabriel, and A. Sanders (2011), CDO Market Implosion and the Pricing of Subprime Mortgage-Backed Securities, *Journal of Housing Economics*, Vol. 20(2), pp. 68–80.

Dorigan, M., F. Fabozzi, and A. Kalotay (2001), Valuation of Floating-Rate Bonds, in F. Fabozzi (ed.), *Professional Perspectives on Fixed Income Portfolio Management*, vol. 2, Frank J. Fabozzi Associates, New Hope, PA.

Duffie, D., and Kan, R. (1996), A Yield-Factor Model of Interest Rates, *Mathematical Finance* Vol. 6, No. 4, pp. 379–406.

Duffie, D., and N. Garleanu (2001), Risk and Valuation of Collaterized Debt Obligations, *Financial Analysts Journal*, Vol. 51, No. 1, pp. 41–59.

Fabozzi, F. and G. Fong (1994), *Advanced Fixed Income Portfolio Management*, McGraw-Hill, New york.

Fitch Ratings (2008), Basel II Correlation Values, An Empirical Analysis of EL, UL and the IRB Model, May 19.

Flesaker, B., and Hughston, L. (1996), Positive Interest, *Risk*, Vol. 9, No. 1, pp. 46–49.

Fuster, A., L. Goodman, D. Lucca, L. Madar, L. Molloy and P. Willen (2012), The Rising Gap Between Primary and Secondary Mortgage Rates, presentation Dec. 3 2012, FRB New York and Boston.

Gabaix, X., A. Krishnamurthy and O. Vigneron (2007), Limits of Arbitrage: Theory and Evidence from the Mortgage-Backed Securities Market, *Journal of Finance*, Vol. 62, No. 2, pp. 557–595.

Gauthier, L. (2003), Market-Implied Losses and Non-Agency Subordinated MBS", *The Journal of Fixed Income*, Vol. 13, No. 1, pp. 49–74.

Glasserman, P. (2004), *Monte Carlo Methods in Financial Engineering*, Springer-Verlag, New York.

Goncharov, Y. (2005), An Intensity-Based Approach to Valuation of Mortgage Contracts and Computation of the Endogenous Mortgage Rate, *International Journal of Theoretical and Applied Finance*, Vol. 9, No. 6, pp. 889–914.

Gorovoy, V. and V. Linetsky (2007), Intensity-Based Valuation of Residential Mortgages: An Analytically Tractable Model, *Mathematical Finance*, Vol. 17, No. 4, pp. 541–573.

Hayre, L. (1994), A Simple Statistical Framework for Modeling Burnout and Refinancing Behavior, *The Journal of Fixed Income*, Dec. 1994, pp. 69–74.

Hayre, L. (2000), Anatomy of Prepayments, *The Journal of Fixed Income*, June 2000, pp. 19–49.

Heath, D., R. Jarrow and A. Morton (1992), Bond Pricing and the Term Structure of Interest Rates: A New Methodology for Contingent Claims Valuation, *Econometrica*, 60, pp. 77–105.

Hull, J. (2005), *Options, Futures and Other Derivatives*, 6th ed., Prentice Hall, Englewood Cliffs, NJ.

Hull, J., and White, A. (1990), Pricing Interest-Rate Derivative Securities, *The Review of Financial Studies*, Vol. 3, No. 4, pp. 573–592.

Hull, J., and White, A. (1994). Numerical Procedures for Implementing Term Structure Models II: Two Factor Models, *Journal of Derivatives* Vol. 2, No. 2, pp.37–48.

James, J. and N. Webber (2000), *Interest-Rate Modelling*, Wiley.

Jamshidian, F. (1996), Bond, Futures and Option valuation in the Quadratic Interest-Rate Models, *Applied Mathematical Finance*, Vol. 3, pp. 93–115.

Jensen, M. and W. Meckling (1976), Theory of the Firm: Managerial Behavior, Agency Costs and Ownership Structure, *Journal of Financial Economics* Vol. 3, No. 4, pp. 305–360.

Kalotay, A. and D. Yang (2002), An Implied Prepayment Model for Mortgage-Backed Securities, presentation at the Bachelier Congress, Crete, 2002.

Kalotay, A., D. Yang, and F. Fabozzi (2004), An Option-Theoretic Prepayment Model for Mortgages and Mortgage-Backed Securities, *International Journal of Theoretical and Applied Finance*, Vol. 7, No. 8, pp. 1–29.

Kaskowitz, D., A. Kipkalov, K. G. Lundstedt, and J. Mingo (2002), Best Practices in Mortgage Default Risk Measurement and Economic Capital, *The Risk Management Association Journal*, June, pp. 30–35.

Kolbe, A. and R. Zagst (2008), A Hybrid-Form Model for the Prepayment-Risk-Neutral Valuation of Mortgage-Backed Securities, *International Journal of Theoretical and Applied Finance*, Vol. 11, No. 6, pp. 635–656.

Kolbe, A., and R. Zagst (2009), Valuation of Mortgage-Backed Securities and Mortgage Derivatives: A Closed-Form Approximation, *Applied Mathematical Finance*, Vol. 16, No. 5, pp. 401–427.

Kupiec, P. and A. Kah (1999), On the Origin and Interpretation of OAS, *The Journal of Fixed Income* Vol. 9, No.3, pp. 82–92.

Leventus, A. (2008), Recent Trends in Home Prices: Differences across Mortgage and Borrower Characteristics, *OFHEO*, Aug. 2008.

Levin, A. (1998), Deriving Closed-Form Solutions for Gaussian Pricing Models: A Systematic Time-Domain Approach, *International Journal of Theoretical and Applied Finance*, Vol. 1, No. 3, pp. 349–376.

Levin, A. (2001), Active-Passive Decomposition in Burnout Modeling, *The Journal of Fixed Income*, Vol. 10, No. 4, pp. 27–40.

Levin, A. (2001), A Linearization Approach in Modeling Quasi-Affine Coupon Rate Term Structure and Related Derivatives, M. Avellaneda (ed.), *Quantitative Analysis in Financial Markets*, Vol. III, World Scientific, pp. 199–221.

Levin, A. (2002), Mortgage Pricing on Low-Dimensional Grids, chapter 18, F. Fabozzi (ed.), *Interest Rate, Term Structure, and Valuation Modeling*, Wiley Finance, pp. 469–488.

Levin, A. (2004), Interest-Rate Model Selection, *The Journal of Portfolio Management*, Winter 2004, Vol. 30, No. 2, pp. 74–86.

Levin, A. (2008), Breakpoint Grid, *The Journal of Structured Finance*, vol. 14, no. 3, pp. 37–43.

Levin, A., and A. Davidson (2005), Prepayment Risk- and Option-Adjusted Valuation of MBS, *The Journal of Portfolio Management*, Summer 2005, Vol. 31, No. 4, pp. 73–85.

Levin, A., and A. Davidson (2008), The Concept of Credit OAS in Valuation of MBS, *The Journal of Portfolio Management*, Spring 2008, Vol. 34, No. 3, pp. 41–55.

Levitin, A., and S. Wachter (2012), Explaining the Housing Bubble, *Georgetown Law Journal*, Vol. 100, No. 4, pp. 1177–1258.

Longstaff, F., and E. Schwartz (1992), Interest-Rate Volatility and the Term Structure: A Two-Factor General Equilibrium Model, *Journal of Finance* Vol. 47, No. 4, pp. 1259–1282.

Marchuk, G. (1975), *Methods of Numerical Mathematics*, Springer-Verlag, New York, Heidelberg, Berlin.

Mashayekhi, F. and J. Wang (2008), "Modeling Default Rate in a Retail Portfolio and the Estimation of Portfolio Risk," *Mortgage Risk* (March).

Mortgage Market Statistical Annual (2012), Inside Mortgage Finance, Volume I: Primary Market.

Patruno, G., N. Ilinic and E. Zhao (2006), Introducing the Unified Deutsche Bank Prepayment Model, *Deutsche Bank*, April 2006.

Pearson, N. (2002), *Risk Budgeting, Portfolio Problem Solving with Value-at-Risk*, Wiley Finance.

Pelsser, A. (1997), A Tractable Interest-Rate Model that Guarantees Positive Interest Rates, *Review of Derivatives Research*, Vol. 1, pp. 269–284.

Pennington-Cross, Anthony (2003), Credit History and the Performance of Prime and Nonprime Mortgages, *Journal of Real Estate Finance and Economics*, Vol. 27, No. 3, pp. 279–301 (November).

Press, W., S. Teukolsky, W. Vettering, and B. Flannery (1992), *Numerical Recipes in C*, 2nd edition, Cambridge University Press.

Ritchken, P. and L. Sankarasubramanian (1995), Volatility Structures of Forward Rates and the Dynamics of the Term Structure, *Mathematical Finance*, 5, pp. 55–72.

Schwartz, E. and W. Torous (1989), Prepayment and the Valuation of Mortgage-Backed Securities, *The Journal of Finance*, Vol. 44, 375–392.

Shiller, R. (2005), *Irrational Exuberance* (2nd ed.), Princeton University Press, Princeton, NJ.

Shiller, R. (2008), *The Subprime Solution*, Princeton University Press, Princeton, NJ.

Simon, D. (2006), *Optimal State Estimation: Kalman, H-infinity, and Nonlinear Approaches*, John Wiley & Sons.

Smith, L. D., S. M. Sanchez and E. Lawrence (1996), A Comprehensive Model for Managing Credit Risk on Home Mortgage Portfolios. *Decision Sciences*, Vol. 27, No. 2, 291–317.

Szakallas, D., A. Levin and A. Davidson (2006), Analyzing Specified MBS Pools using Agency Enhanced Data and Active-Passive Decomposition, in F. Fabozzi (ed.), *The Handbook of Mortgage-Backed Securities*, Chapter 27, McGraw Hill, pp.623–644.

Vasicek, O. (1977), An Equilibrium Characterization of the Term Structure, *Journal of Financial Economics*, Vol. 5, pp. 177–188.

Vasicek, O. (1987), Probability of Loss on Loan Portfolio, *KMV Corporation*.

Vasicek, O. (1991), Limiting Loss Probability Distribution, *KMV Corporation*.

Weaver K., B. Natcher, K. Reeves, and L. Lau (2007), The Outlook for U.S. Home Prices, DB's Nationwide and MSA Level Forecasts for 2007–2009, *Deutsche Bank*, June 2007.

ANDREW DAVIDSON AND CO., INC. PUBLICATIONS (AVAILABLE AT WWW.AD-CO.COM) AD&CO PIPELINE NEWSLETTER (ADPN)

Davidson, A. (Apr. 2004), Fair Value and Cost-Based Accounting, No. 21.

Davidson, A. (Aug. 2007), Six Degrees of Separation, No. 57.

Davidson, A. and E. Belbase (Sept. 2010), Origination Risk in the Mortgage Securitization Process: An Analysis of Alternate Policies, No. 89.

Levin, A. (Feb. 2005), A New Member of AD&Co: The Two-factor Gaussian Term Structure, Part 2, No. 30.

Levin, A. (Feb. 2008), How to Use Credit OAS: An ABS Valuation Case Study for the Illiquid Market, No. 64.

Levin, A. (May 2008), Full and Partial Vega, No. 67.

Levin, A. (Oct. 2008), Intrinsic Marks, No. 71.

Levin, A. (Feb. 2009), Market Prices versus Intrinsic Values, No. 75.

Levin, A. (Apr. 2009), Pricing Distressed Measured, No. 77.

Levin, A. (Jan. 2011), The Hunt for Duration…Continued, No. 93.

Levin, A. (Apr. 2011), Credit OAS: Where It Was and Where It Is. No. 96.

Searle, W. (May 2009), Credit Loss Distribution: Credit OAS vs. Vasicek - Part 3, No. 78.

Zheng, M. (Oct. 2008), A Comparison of Breakpoint Ratios and Credit Ratings, No. 71.

AD&Co QUANTITATIVE PERSPECTIVES (ADQP)

Ching, A. (2008), Loan Dynamics™: AD&Co's Approach to Modeling Credit Risk.

Belbase, E. (2012), Validation of Agency Prepay Models: Version 5.2h.

Levin, A. (2003), Divide and Conquer: Exploring New OAS Horizons, Part I: Active-Passive Decomposition.

Levin, A. (2004), Divide and Conquer: Exploring New OAS Horizons, Part II: A Prepay-Risk-and-Option-Adjusted Valuation Concept; Part III: A prOAS Valuation Model with Refinancing and Turnover Risk.

Levin, A. (2012), Recommended Term Structure Model Selection in a Low Rate Environment.

AD&Co CONFERENCE PRESENTATIONS (ADCP)

Levin, A. (2006), Universal Value-Space Refinancing Model, June 2006.

Levin, A. (2010), HPI Modeling: Forecasts, Geography, Risk & Value, June 2010.